BLACK
ENGLISH

BLACK
ENGLISH

Its History and Usage in the United States

J. L. DILLARD

Random House : New York

Library of Congress Cataloging in Publication Data

Dillard, Joey Lee, 1924–
Black English.

Bibliography: p. 313
1. Negroes—Language. I. Title.
PE3102.N4D5   427'.9'73   71–102330
ISBN 0–394–46760–4

Grateful acknowledgment is made to
the National Council of Teachers of English
for permission to reprint material from
Problems in Oral English by Walter Loban.

Manufactured in the United States of America

8   9

To

William A. Stewart

Who made possible the serious study

of Black English

IT IS ABSURD to assume, as has been the tendency, among a great many Western anthropologists and sociologists, that all traces of Africa were erased from the Negro's mind because he learned English. The very nature of the English the Negro spoke and still speaks drops the lie on that idea.

LeRoi Jones,
Blues People, p. 9

Foreword

THIS BOOK attempts to investigate the important and interesting ways in which Black English, the language of about eighty percent of Americans of African ancestry, differs from other varieties of American English. (It is, however, true—as Joan Fickett has pointed out in an excellent book which is considerably more technical than this presentation—that this language variety is in some ways even more American than other varieties of English spoken in the United States. Dr. Fickett has given the name "Merican" to this variety.) According to my thesis, differences from other English dialects are traceable to normal historical factors, specifically to language-contact phenomena associated with the West African slave trade and with European maritime expansion in general, and to survivals from West African languages.

It is my feeling, and that of many of my colleagues, that lack of adequate structural and historical information about Black English (also called Negro Non-Standard English or Merican) has been a major handicap to educational programs for Black children. Incorporation of such knowledge into future programs should be of great benefit to them. It should be emphasized, however, that this is a work on language primarily and on education almost

incidentally. Especially, it should be understood that my investigations and those of my associates did not begin as attempts to
solve ghetto educational problems. Rather, research into Afro-
American language patterns kept turning up examples of educational practices (particularly those labeling Black English a
"deficient" language!) which were absurd in the light of accurate
linguistic information.

There is very little of a technical nature in this book, but the
reader should realize that linguistics, like anthropology, is a rela-
tivistic discipline: linguists do not judge one language variety as
"better" than another, nor do they conclude that the economic
disadvantages (hopefully temporary) of any population group
are the results of "deficits" of language or of cognition.

In this respect, there may be some confusion about the use of
the term *dialect*. As used in linguistics, *dialect* means simply the
collective linguistic patterns of a sub-group of the speakers of a
language. (To put it somewhat more technically, each individual
speaker has an *idiolect*, and a collection of idiolects is a dialect.)
The popular use of *dialect* to mean "humorous speechways" or
"ridiculous language" is not relevant to this discussion. It seems
wasteful, and pointless, to coin another term, even though *dialect*
may be subject to some misunderstanding.

On the other hand, the reader should not cling to the kind of
superficial knowledge about dialectology which limits the distribution of dialects to geographic areas. For professional reasons
too complicated to go into here, I believe that the geographic
preconception about dialect distribution is, in many cases, down-
right wrong. Social dialectology is a fairly new field, not yet well
known even within the discipline of linguistics, but it will surely
have more to offer than the old-fashioned regional approach,
which has resulted from a mechanical application of the techniques of nineteenth-century European linguistics to the United
States.

Otherwise, it would be well if the reader could suspend certain beliefs about language which may have been transmitted
to him by the school system. The term *grammar* is consistently

used herein to mean not "correct use of language," but "the way a language works." In this sense, every language (and every "dialect") has a grammar; and it is irrelevant whether the grammar has been put into writing (a *grammatical description*). The usual practices of school grammar classes (such as the various parsing devices, including diagrams) are, in such a context, not so much inaccurate as unrevealing. We could diagram Black English, but we would know no more about it afterward than we did before. Terms like *noun, verb,* and *double negative* are used with approximately the same reference as in school grammars, but never with the same prescriptive intent. In this frame of reference, a statement such as "*decent* must be used as an adjective, not as an adverb" is nonsense. So are statements like "a double negative makes a positive" or "a double negative is bad English."

A few terms are likely to be completely new to many readers. Two outstanding examples are *pidgin* and *creole*, which will be used in senses unfamiliar to most readers, including some linguists. A glossary of such terms is provided.

Finally, this book attempts to extend the linguistic perspective in which Black English is to be placed. Although it operates in an environment of ordinary American English, it has structural and historical resemblances to varieties of English (and of other languages) spoken in the Caribbean, South America, West Africa, and the Pacific (especially Hawaii). There are even some historical affinities to varieties of French and Portuguese. Many of us have found the study of such languages not only interesting but fascinating. It is hoped that some of this interest may be transmitted to the intellectually curious reader who does not happen to have specialized in the study of language.

J. L. D.

Acknowledgments

THE PERSON who studies a language must be indebted first of all to the people who speak that language. In this case, these were hundreds of Black people, most of them children.

Exchange of information with William A. Stewart has been so continuous since 1965 that this book might almost be viewed as loose collaboration. (Stewart is not, however, responsible for the final form which this book has taken, and especially not for any mistakes in it.) To a lesser degree, this has been true of my relationship with former colleagues such as Marvin D. Loflin, Ulf Hannerz, and Philip A. Luelsdorff. I have also profited from the contributions of many classes of graduate students at Trinity College and Georgetown University in Washington, D.C.; the University of Southern California; the University of Puerto Rico; and Ferkauf Graduate School of Yeshiva University in New York. Stewart, Morgan E. Jones (of the State University at New Paltz, New York), Ralph B. Long (of the University of Puerto Rico), and several of my students at Ferkauf Graduate School have been kind enough to read drafts of individual chapters and to make valuable suggestions, not all of which I have been able to follow. The basic orientation of my studies would have been impossible without the writings of creolists like Douglas Taylor, Jan Voorhoeve, Stewart, and John Reinecke; nor would the tradition of such studies be what it is without the work of Melville J. Herskovits. There is a partial list of the works of those scholars in the Bibliography, but anything like an adequate account would require another book.

Most parts of this book, being historical in nature, have depended upon library research, which began in the summer of 1961 at the Openbaare Lesesaal in Willemstadt, Curaçao, and has continued on three continents and a much larger number of islands. The Institute of Caribbean Studies of the University of Puerto Rico (directed in its early years by Richard Morse and by Thomas Mathews, and now by Harmannus Hoetink) provided research and travel grants which made possible a great deal of the early investigation. Among many library experiences, I remember with special pleasure the cooperation of the librarians at the Institute of Jamaica in Kingston, and of the librarians and the learned archivist at the Arizona Pioneers' Library in Tucson. Even understocked libraries, struggling in almost complete absence of funds, like that of the Université Officielle de Bujumbura (Burundi), have yielded valuable bits of information. The major resources, however, have been the fantastic library system of New York City and the personal collection of William A. Stewart.

Contents

BLACK ENGLISH

I

Black English and the Academic Establishment

The Problem in Terms of Language History

ACCURATE and reliable information about the language of the vast majority of Black Americans is not generally available, either to the public or to educators. The educational system especially has been handicapped by the inadequacy of the language descriptions available. Current studies, however, are providing much more accurate data. These new insights come from linguists who have a wide perspective on world language situations, especially on languages used in language contact situations and often regarded as non-traditional. Regarded historically, Black English proves to be related to these languages. Understanding these relationships will help to clarify its nature and function.

American linguistics has failed to provide accurate information about Black English because of the myopic nature of most historical work on American English. Dialectologists, the researchers to whom most such investigations have been entrusted, have concerned themselves almost exclusively with patterns of migration from the British Isles and with what they think of as the spread of British regional features throughout the United States.

Although it is obvious, even visually, that many Americans are not the descendants of migrants who came directly from England, it has been assumed in our language histories and in our grammars that only the British-derived parts count. A useful perspective on the language situation in the United States has yet to be derived from a careful study of the language backgrounds of minority groups. As will be shown later (Chapters III and IV), the language of some of these groups is related to a fairly well-studied—if not popularly well-known—group of language varieties known as creoles. (See Glossary for an explanation of this term.)

Perhaps the easiest indication that the England-to-America geographic approach has important limitations is the ease with which American observers can identify sentences like

Sometime Daddy be drivin', he call people names.*

as being from a Black child, it being irrelevant whether the child is from the South or from the North.[1] For such observers there is no difficulty in identifying the socioeconomic status (poor) and ethnic group (Black) of the speakers who produced the following conversation:

> I can skate better than Louis and I be only eight. (Second child: Greg would go skatin' and the man picked up and threw him back down on the butt.) If you be goin' real fast, hold it. If it's on trios and you be goin' and you don' go in the ring, you be goin' around it. You be goin' too fast, well, you don' be in the ring. You be outside if you be goin' too fast. That man he'a clip you up. I think they call him Sonny. He real tall.†

Characteristic ghetto uses of language like "shuckin'," "jivin'," "rappin'," "coppin' a plea," and "the dozens," are now fairly familiar. Furthermore, linguistic studies by researchers like William A. Stewart and Marvin D. Loflin[2] show that Black English is very different from other dialects of American English.

Recognition of the independent nature of Black English is only part of a general recognition that American English is not

---

* A Los Angeles eight-year-old from Watts.
† Two Washington eight-year-olds from the Adams-Morgan community.

nearly so homogeneous as had once been thought. Even a cursory look shows that there are minority groups who differ from the mainstream in both language and culture. The language of some of these groups has influenced mainstream American English without becoming identical with it. (Take, for example, the many words which have been borrowed from Yiddish. It is fairly easy to tell the English of a member of the Yiddish community from that of a speaker of consensus American English who just happens to know a few phrases like *yenta, mink-shmink, schlemiel,* and *schmaltz.*) The most notable group of unabsorbed persons consists of American Blacks; it is clear that many of their folkways have remained after more than three hundred years in this country. In fact, consensus American culture has borrowed many of their ways.[3] Even after this long period of mutual influence and of a narrowing of the culture and language gaps, the language and culture of the vast majority of Blacks remain distinct from those of any large group of whites.

Because of behavior patterns retained by the Indians or brought in by immigrants (including Blacks), the culture of the United States has never been quite that of England. Our Anglophile and Anglo-worship periods are almost completely in the past, and we all know that our individuality does not constitute our inferiority. The language of the United States also is different from England's in easily observable ways, and perhaps for the same reason—influence from groups who did not migrate to America from England. The Negro has contributed, usually without public recognition, to the culture of the United States; it is not strange that he has contributed something to the language as well. But the fact that contributions have been made from one group to another—or reciprocal contributions—does not mean that they are identical. As most of us have always known, to proclaim that the English of Blacks is identical to that of whites is to allow one's theories to deny the evidence of one's senses. Unfortunately, such denials of what is universally perceived have sometimes passed for science.[4]

In some historical sense, of course, any variety of English must have roots in England. Still, for hundreds of years English has been spoken outside the British Isles, and people speaking those non-British varieties of English have come to the United States, often without touching base in England. Thus, non-British language patterns are clearly traceable in the history of American English. Some of those patterns come from African varieties of English.

Among the lesser-known varieties of non-British English (let us leave the argument over their genesis to another time) are the pidgin and creole languages which are spoken in Asia, Africa, the Pacific, the Caribbean, and elsewhere. Many of the people who now speak those languages are Africans; some indication of a specifically West African variety of English goes back to the sixteenth century.[5] Today there is a clear-cut case of a variety of American English, related to West African varieties in Gullah, which is spoken on the Sea Islands off Georgia and South Carolina. French Creole, mutually intelligible with Haitian French Creole, is spoken in Louisiana and Southeastern Texas. Both of these languages are related to the Caribbean creoles. Recent research presents evidence that the English of most American Blacks retains some features which are common to both Caribbean and West African varieties of English.

Significant research on Black English in the United States is almost entirely a product of the 1960's. In this decade a group of linguists, freed of preconceptions about the geographic provenience of American dialects, have shown that Negro Non-Standard English is different in grammar (in syntax) from the Standard American English of the mainstream white culture. They maintain that there are sources for varieties of English elsewhere than in the British regional dialects. Like the West Indian varieties, American Black English can be traced to a creolized version of English based upon a pidgin spoken by slaves; it probably came from the West Coast of Africa—almost certainly not directly from Great Britain. (The question of the ultimate origin of the English-based pidgin, interesting as it is on other grounds, is not relevant here.) Some dialects of American English, then, did not follow the route of the Mayflower.

Attempts to trace the features of Black English to British regional dialects have been carried to absurd lengths. The third person singular, present tense of the verb without *-s* (*he do* rather than *he does*) has been traced to East Anglia; the durative *be* (*he be going every day* rather than *he is going . . .*) to Anglo-Irish; and preverbal *done* (*he done go, he done gone, he done went*) to Scottish dialect. For a population group with no history of residence in the British Isles, this is a wide collection of British features. Furthermore, how did features from such diverse areas of the British Isles come into the English of American Blacks—particularly since Scottish, Irish, and East Anglian immigrants to the United States did not transmit those features to their descendants? A more important criticism of the geographers' position is that the grammar of Black English does not match the grammar of the allegedly identical features in British regional dialects. Thus even the assumption, occasionally made, that Blacks have retained archaic features (obsolete in the speech of the descendants of British ancestors) seems false. This lopsided interest in tracing American regional dialects to British regional dialects has damaged research on the speech of all American social groups, but research on the dialect of Black Americans has suffered most.

Since the days of George Philip Krapp's *The English Language in America* (1925), which at least provides a large number of significant texts for anyone with a pidgin/creole background, and before the publication of William A. Stewart's first articles in 1964, Negro dialect studies had taken a definite backward step. H. L. Mencken's successive reworkings of his very influential *The American Language* progressively eliminated references to Negro speech (primarily in terms of quotations from authors who had used the dialect in fiction). Mencken always seemed to be somewhat confused as to whether he was dealing with something real or something invented by literary men. Richard Walser, in "Negro Dialect in Eighteenth Century Drama" (*American Speech,* 1955), suggested that playwrights *created* the dialect. The 1963 *Abridgment* of Mencken's work by dialect geographer Raven I. McDavid, Jr. (the chief distinction of which is the addition of summaries of geography-oriented research in brackets throughout the text) carries research on Negro dialect to an all-time low. McDavid suggests (p. 478) that the Negro dialect (or "Negro speech") is a "veneer" contrived for the "white man boss," and that the veneer is often dropped when the white man is around the corner.

These and other writings of the early to middle twentieth century illustrate with some clarity how professional students of language can allow their powers of observation to be distorted by pet theories. Better observations were made, and better explanations offered, by non–professional observers who didn't let academic fashions get in the way of their observations. One N. S. Dodge, a contributor to *Appleton's Journal* in 1870 (Vol. III, 160–1), compared American Negro dialects to Sierra Leone Krio and Liberian Pidgin English. There were actually many such observers. Unfortunately, some of them allowed their otherwise accurate perceptions to be colored by the racist theory of influence by African anatomy ("thick lips"), the untenable notion that physiological factors determined the language differences.

Mencken, with his tremendous powers to absorb written material, could hardly have been ignorant of this kind of widespread knowledge. His acquaintance with that knowledge is illustrated in his references to a Pidgin English or "Beach-la-Mar"[6] which leaves vestiges in the speech of some of the "most ignorant" Negroes of the inland regions and perhaps in that of some of the whites. Those linguists who were not completely caught up in geographic biases said approximately the same thing.[7] The picture presented in the works of such linguists is that the earlier patterns of the (creolized, in effect) Negro speech have by now disappeared, except for Gullah. This would have remained the prevailing and convincing thesis if it had not been for the brilliant discovery by Stewart of an age-grading feature in the dialect. Relatively archaic forms are preserved in the speech of younger children, even in the inner cities of New York and Washington, D. C. Geographic factors are thus subsidiary to social factors—age-grading in this case.

Before this development the strongest indication of any historical difference between Negro dialects and other dialects had been in the work of Lorenzo D. Turner, whose *Africanisms in the Gullah Dialect* appeared in 1949. Dr. Turner's brilliant work emphasized one basic thesis—that despite the prevailing belief there were numerous African survivals in the relatively well-known Gullah dialect.[8] Although it is rather widely believed that his work shows the influence (interference) of West African languages on English as the factor which produced Gullah,[9] there is no complete working out of any historical thesis in Turner's book. Because Turner found it expedient to utilize the residents of the Sea Islands as informants in searching out Africanisms, his work was still susceptible to a geographic interpretation. It was still possible to assume that something about the ecology of isolated living influenced the development of Gullah, and the idea that geographic remoteness was only one concomitant of the more relevant cultural remoteness was hardly considered. Although there was some flirting with the thesis of an African "substratum" in American Negro English,[10] the received position toward American Negro dialects and American dialects in general remained unchanged after Turner's work had been more or less absorbed into the tradition.

Upon further examining the standard works on American English, the pidgin/creolist cannot be any happier with the general body of works than with the Mencken-McDavid book. In addition to the lack of information about Black English, there is nothing about American Indian Pidgin English, even though there is an easily available article on the subject.[11] Although there has been a large population of Chinese resident in this country for over a century, standard reference works make no mention of the readily accessible evidence for the use of Chinese Pidgin English in this country. The fragmentary sketches of the English of the Florida Keys reveal only that speech patterns there are entirely uninvestigated. And absolutely nothing which is said about English Creole of the Caribbean satisfies even the casual West Indian observer. Not the Negro alone but minority groups in general have been slighted in the prevailing white-centered attitude toward language history.

The reason for the lack of study in the area of Black English

seems to be that the theory of exclusively British origins is seriously challenged by the pidgin/creole theory. Members of the
geography-oriented Establishment must have been aware of the
possibility of a challenge from that theory for some time and
have constructed defenses against it. To trace American regional
dialects to their putative origin in British regional dialects one
must assume that the populations which speak the dialects may
be traced in something like the same way. It would fit the preconceived pattern to assume that the population of the southeastern United States consists almost entirely of immigrants from
East Anglia, but we know in fact that many of the residents of
the area—more than half of them in many places—did not arrive
there as the result of emigration from that region. In order to
maintain consistently the theory of migrating British regional
dialects, the dialect geographers have been forced into the absurd
position of asserting that all the language forms migrated from
British areas and that other migration patterns—including those
which may easily be identified by the presence of Black skins—
are linguistically non-significant. It is only a step from such an
assertion to the conclusion that those differences which Black
speakers exhibit must consist of patterns which the white speakers
once had but have now given up.[12]

Undoubtedly, the proponents of the East Anglian origins theory
and of purely geographic variation (except for the complications
of "archaism") have not realized that in their account of the
Negro as an archaizing speaker the picture which emerges is that
of a racial archaism—a Negro who just can't catch up or keep up.
This is surely the most blatantly racist position which could be
presented, if all of its implications are intentional. Since similar
linguistic forms occur in the West Indies, on some parts of the
West Coast of Africa, and even in Afrikaans, only the kind of
historical explanation which scholars like Whinnom, Thompson,
Stewart, and Valkoff give could possibly provide a basis for linguistic dignity for the Negro. The idea is so new—and terms like
pidgin are subject to such general misunderstanding—that even
Black leaders are sometimes resentful of what may seem like a

less favorable presentation of Negro language history but one which, upon close examination, turns out to be the only one consistent with Black self-respect.

Dialects do not attach themselves to skin colors, but judgments about African ancestry do. Black Americans of a certain socioeconomic group—not all Blacks—speak the dialect to be described herein. The kind of perception which the ordinary racist American has about dialect differences in Negroes of certain socioeconomic groups requires an explanation. If the older prejudice about "thick lips and thick minds" is not to give way to the newer prejudice about "deficiencies of language and concept-formation," there must be some plausible historical alternative. The vaguely conceived Selective Cultural Differentiation suggested by the dialect geographer McDavid is, insofar as it is intelligible at all, not really different from the newer prejudice. The more intelligible suggestions of the Establishment tradition remain to be examined.

Mencken himself offered, perhaps at the urging of the newly emerging *Linguistic Atlas* group, an explanation which turns out to be entirely untenable:

> The Negro dialect, as we know it today, seems to have been formulated by the song-writers for the minstrel shows; it did not appear in literature until the time of the Civil War; before that, as George Philip Krapp shows in "The English Language in America," it was a vague and artificial lingo which had little relation to the actual speech of Southern blacks.   (p. 71, Fourth Ed.)

The reader who looked to the Baltimore prose master for consistency of presentation would be as unfortunate as the one who, in Samuel Johnson's famous comment, read Richardson for the plot. That the comment about "Beach-la-Mar" and Negro dialect (p. 475) is inconsistent with this statement apparently did not occur to Mencken, who was never one for foolish consistency. In such a long work, changes of attitude are excusable and probably unavoidable, and Mencken's two conflicting opinions may perhaps be traced simply to different stages of production of the work. The quotation above undoubtedly reflects the influence of˙ Krapp, whose "The English of the Negro" appeared in Mencken's own *American Mercury* in 1924. The comparison to "Beach-la-Mar" may reflect some independent knowledge on Mencken's part.

The first clause of Mencken's dismissal of Negro dialect (that it was "formulated by the song writers for the minstrel shows") is well in accord with what has become the Establishment tradition, which has long denied that Black English is any different from the white dialect of a given area. Thus, any reports of differences by literary men would have to be the inventions of those literary men—or of a literary tradition upon which they had drawn. Paradoxically, the linguists who have held that traditional position have found it necessary to keep explaining the differences which turn up in their field work—differences which, according to their preconceptions, should not exist. E. Bagby Atwood's *A Survey of Verb Forms in the Eastern United States*, for example, lists four "characteristically Negro words and phrases" (p. 41)—*cotch, gwine, mought, what make* ('why')— without explaining what would be involved in the concept "characteristically Negro." Thus, while generally rejecting the evidence of a Negro dialect provided by the literary tradition—and also ignoring the evidence which is provided by a long line of writers of non-fiction—these dialectologists have made some statements which are fully consistent with the tradition represented in *belles lettres*.

It is difficult to judge the nature of an older stage of a language (or a language which is now "dead") from surviving literary texts, but it is the best available method—pending the invention of a time machine. Fortunately for linguists, there are certain limitations to the inventiveness even of those writers of fiction who practice the greatest degree of linguistic innovation. In one of the more amusing bits of the often deadly dull linguistic literature, Whorf shows how Walter Winchell, in his attempt to "break" the rules of English grammar and word formation, simply illustrates more clearly their nature. *Infanticipating* is possible; *mpftog* is not. This brings up a very important consideration: Can a writer of fiction actually create grammatical forms? The answer of the linguist would be an unequivocal no, even if the author happens to be James Joyce. Joyce mixed a lot of languages, and he utilized a lot of the more non-traditional resources of English; but, although he may have invented a literary style, he didn't invent a language or a dialect or anything of the sort. The deservedly anonymous authors of the minstrel shows surely were not Joyce's superiors in this kind of effort.

Yet one could develop a certain fondness for the minstrel-show origins theory, especially in light of its enormous burlesque possibilities: Suppose that a Negro saw a minstrel show, was impressed by the "invented" dialect, and carried it to his own group where it immediately caught on; that from his own group it spread to the neighboring cities, counties, states, etc.; that visiting West Indians heard the same new "invented" dialect and were so delighted that they carried it back home with them; and finally, that a few found their way back to Africa, where it formed the basis of present day Liberian Pidgin English, WesKos Pidgin of the Cameroun and Nigeria, Sierra Leone Krio, etc.! The idea is intentionally absurd, but it is not much more absurd than the original idea of a minstrel-show dialect created out of whole cloth. That minstrel-show writers may have been especially inept recorders of already existing dialects is, on the other hand, a distinct possibility.

Mencken's second clause (that the Negro dialect "did not appear in literature until the time of the Civil War") is patently wrong. In one of his own editions he quoted Negro dialect from Brackenridge's *Modern Chivalry*, which was published in 1792. Attestations (recorded literary examples) from Crèvecoeur, Cotton Mather, Benjamin Franklin, the court records of Salem, Massachusetts, and several other sources may be found before the 1790's—and all without any recourse to fictional sources. The wealth of material after that date is simply astonishing. There is, in fact, a very great deal of pre-Civil War literary Negro dialect.

The third clause (that "before that [the Civil War] it was a

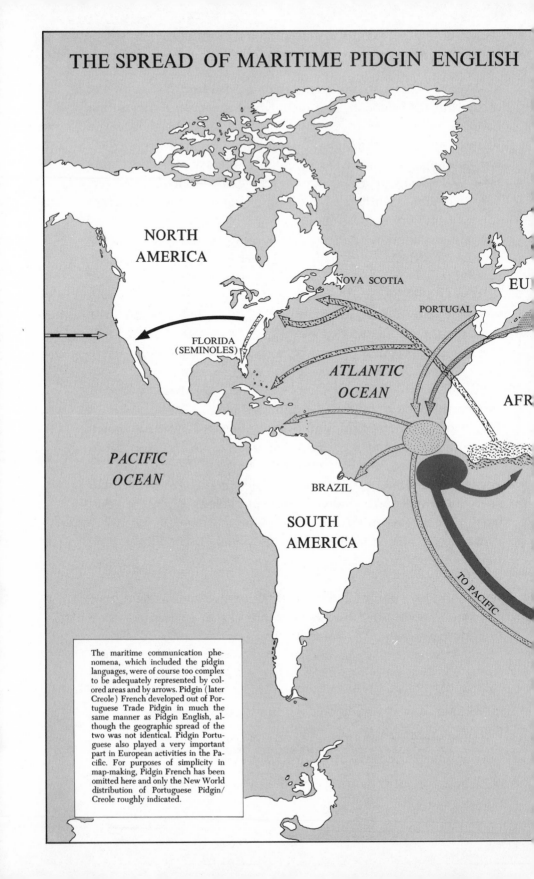

THE SPREAD OF MARITIME PIDGIN ENGLISH

NORTH
AMERICA

NOVA SCOTIA

EU

PORTUGAL

FLORIDA
(SEMINOLES)

*ATLANTIC
OCEAN*

AFR

*PACIFIC
OCEAN*

BRAZIL

SOUTH
AMERICA

TO PACIFIC

The maritime communication phenomena, which included the pidgin
languages, were of course too complex
to be adequately represented by colored areas and by arrows. Pidgin (later
Creole) French developed out of Portuguese Trade Pidgin in much the
same manner as Pidgin English, although the geographic spread of the
two was not identical. Pidgin Portuguese also played a very important
part in European activities in the Pacific. For purposes of simplicity in
map-making, Pidgin French has been
omitted here and only the New World
distribution of Portuguese Pidgin/
Creole roughly indicated.

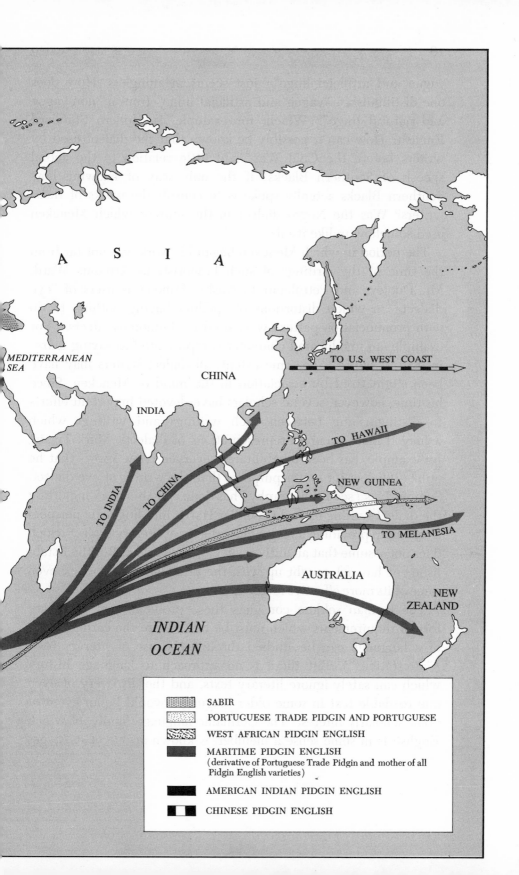

vague and artificial lingo") just seems meaningless. How does one distinguish a "vague and artificial lingo" from a "non-vague and natural lingo"? Which, for example, is Modern Standard English? How can it possibly be known that the dialect used by writers before the Civil War "had little relation to the actual speech of Southern Blacks" if the only way of knowing how Southern Blacks actually spoke is to consult the works of those writers? Was the Negro dialect in the sources which Mencken used somehow unlike itself?

The period in which Mencken began his work was not far from the time of the writings of such humorists as Artemus Ward, Mr. Dooley, and Petroleum V. Nasby, famous as users of "eye dialect," in which distortions of spelling having nothing to do with pronunciation pattern were used for humorous effects. (For example, an uneducated character is represented as saying *wurse* instead of *worse*.) To some extent, all dialect writers may have been stigmatized by association in the mind of Mencken. Since his time, however, several scholars have devoted important efforts to distinguishing between such writings and writings which achieved more accurate representations of dialects. Mark Twain, for example, has been rehabilitated; everyone now knows that he utilized dialect for better purposes than the writers of eye dialect. Sumner Ives (see Bibliography) has done valuable work in putting the dialect writing of Joel Chandler Harris into linguistic perspective, and in providing a respectable theory of literary dialect which does not assume that an author can create a dialect. But the Establishment has not caught up with the rehabilitation work of even some of its more effective members.

The layman seldom considers these problems, yet there are formal requirements which must be met before the earlier stages of a language can be studied through the use of literary texts ("attestations"). But there is no approach to language history which can safely ignore literary texts, and the discovery of even one readable text in some older languages would be an event of great scholarly interest. The Germanic language family, of which English is in some sense a member, is known at one of its stages almost entirely through Bishop Wulfila's translation of the Bible into Gothic. How do we know that Wulfila wrote down "real" Gothic, and not a "vague and artificial lingo"? The answer is, of course, that in an absolute sense we don't. But it is probable that he wrote down something more or less real rather than inventing a new "lingo," however "artificial"—especially since he presumably had other things to occupy his time. Acceptance of Wulfila's translation as representative of Conversational Gothic of the period is not uncritical. For one thing, Wulfila is believed to have translated from Greek, and he may have written a Greekified style—somewhat like the artificial style which some preachers will assume even today. But we do not assume that he "invented" something which cannot be explained in terms of real languages. If we did, we could extend the same reasoning to *Beowulf*, the *Niebelungenlied*, the *Poetic Edda* and the *Sagas*, and to all of Germanic literature. In fact, we could extend a skeptical attitude toward the reality of texts to all of language except the last sentence we uttered—or even to that. We could, in short, deny the validity of all evidence for language history and thereby deny that language has any history. Proceeding solipsistically, we could simply deny that language exists except as we (or "I" in solipsism) make it up on the spur of the moment.

Obviously, historical study cannot proceed in that way. We must utilize evidence, and for the great part of human history we must utilize mainly written records. This is especially true of language; artifacts without inscriptions say nothing of the language of the people who made them. An author who records a language may represent it inaccurately, or misrepresent it; linguists have traditionally had a way of saying that writing is an inadequate representation of speech. Even within the general area of written representations, there are levels of relative reliability. No one would take the works of Chatterton as very basic evidence for the English of the mid-eighteenth century. An author may be consciously archaic, or he may be mistaken. He may distort a language or a dialect in order to defame the speakers. All of these possibilities must be taken into account when one assesses the value of a written text for language study. There are rather few authenticated examples on record where an author has willfully distorted a language; Chatterton and Spenser utilized archaic forms which were sometimes historically inaccurate rather than doing violence to the language of their own day. People just aren't that creative where language is concerned, or culture; it is perhaps possible to change one's cultural patterns to some degree, and it is certainly possible for certain individuals to change cultures, but it is hardly possible for one person to innovate an entire culture. In those known cases where a language or dialect has been misrepresented, the sources of that misrepresentation (Middle English in the two cases mentioned above) have always been more or less traceable. Sometimes, an alleged misrepresentation is more useful than the acceptedly accurate representations: The Puerto Rican janitor who wrote

Fabol de pedil la yabe en la ofisina

(Standard Spanish: *Favor de pedir la llave en la oficina—*
"Please ask for the key at the office")

gave information about the folk Spanish which is not available from the columns of *El Mundo.*

For these reasons, it is important to consider many writers— if the linguist is fortunate enough to have many available—and to balance them against each other. But when large numbers of competent, talented, and even brilliant authors, working independently and not copying each other, represent a language or a dialect in one consistent way, then it is almost impossible that such a language or dialect should not exist and should not resemble the depiction of it by those writers in some—or in most —ways.

An important factor in the evaluation of the languages and dialects of the past is an accurate evaluation of the languages and dialects of the present. If we thought that there were no divergences in related Germanic languages today, we might find it absurd to think that Wulfila wrote in a now extinct Germanic language. Similarly, our evaluation of the representations of Negro dialect in the past rests upon a professionally accurate study of it in the present. The existence of Gullah, of West Indian varieties of English, and of other languages such as Louisiana French Creole—all spoken almost exclusively by Blacks—is undeniable. Recent work makes it clear that there exists a dialect spoken almost exclusively by Blacks in the United States today—although of course there are Blacks who do not speak that dialect.

It is easy to forget the consequences, linguistic or not, of African involvement in the New World from very early times. There seems to be a distinct possibility that the first Negro to come to the New World was Pedro Alonso Niño, with Columbus in 1492. At any rate, the same Portuguese who had opened up the slave trade in West Africa in the century preceding the American explorations had taken many West Africans to the Iberian peninsula, and the Portuguese tradition of exploration continued to be of major importance in the New World. Information on the language practices used by Europeans and West Africans to establish communication in the fifteenth and sixteenth centuries is relatively scanty, but there are many reasons why it is necessary to look at more than British dialects in order to understand the language backgrounds even of the British slave trade. Portuguese language forms turn up throughout the English traditions of Afro-America, from *pickaninny* in the American South to *kaba* in the Sranan Tongo, one of the English creoles of Surinam. The latter word, which has about the same time reference as Spanish *acabar de* (*Acabo de comer*, 'I have just eaten'), functions rather like *done* in Southern Negro (and even in Southern white) dialects. In all the English-speaking islands of the West Indies, hundreds of African vocabulary items coexist with Portuguese etymons in significant grammatical functions. The same relationship exists on such apparently French-speaking islands as Haiti, Guadaloupe, and Martinque, where a French Creole is the basic language of daily communication for most of the population.

Papiamento, of Aruba, Curaçao, and Bonaire, is popularly believed to be derived from Spanish; linguists, however, have long
seen its closer relationship to Portuguese.

Portuguese is not necessarily so distant from American English
as the reader may assume at first. Stewart, while not denying
that the English of a middle-class American could be traced
through a kind of continuum to British English, has also pointed
out that it could just as well be traced through the same kind of
unbroken continuum to a foreign language—Portuguese.[13] The
decisive consideration, in terms of linguistic relationship, is that
fewer stages are necessary in tracing the continuum to British
English. For Negro Non-Standard English, on the other hand,
some stages must be added to the progression toward British
English and some deleted from the progression toward Portuguese. The relationship, indicated below, is somewhat more complicated than has generally been realized:

Middle-class native of Detroit
Lower-class native of Nashville
Lower-class Negro of South Atlantic Coast
Gullah
Jamaican Creole
Sierra Leone Krio
Sranan Tongo (Surinam)
Saramaccan (Surinam)
Cape Verde Crioulo
Standard Portuguese

Stewart did not mean, of course, that Portuguese is closer to
American English than is British English. But he did want to
force re-examination of the facile assumption that the only source
of any importance was British English. Some words in American
English (e.g., *pickaninny*) have long been acknowledged to be
Portuguese by everybody; linguists have long known that some
(e.g., *savvy*) which are popularly traced to other sources are
from Portuguese, and there is reason, to be discussed at length
later, for the creolist to believe that a variety (pidgin) of Portu-

guese has had a very wide and basic influence on a great many
varieties of languages spread throughout the world.

For purposes of the present exposition, it is not necessary to
explore in detail the complicated relationships which lead from
Standard Portuguese through Pidgin Portuguese through the
African Portuguese creoles to Surinam Creole to varieties of
North American English. Keith Whinnom has suggested the possibility that Portuguese Pidgin, modeled upon the Mediterranean
lingua franca, Sabir, furnished the models for other pidgins
utilized during the period of European maritime expansion, including Pidgin English. The beginning in the West African
trade, including the slave trade, has not been determined with
precision; it is not really necessary to assume that the Pidgin
English developed on the West Coast of Africa, although I
happen to lean more in that direction than other linguists who
work in the same area. Suffice it to say that it is well established
that pidgin languages based upon European languages, insofar
as vocabulary is concerned at least, were definitely used in the
slave trade—and that there is abundant evidence that Pidgin
English was among them.

According to Hall, the first attestations of Pidgin English come
from American Indians in the seventeenth century. Given the
involvement of the English in the slave trade from the mid-six-
teenth century, there remains almost a century of widespread but
unattested (in writing) use of Pidgin English in the slave trade as
in other maritime ventures. By 1715, the English Pidgin was so
widely known—popularly, if not in print—that Daniel Defoe
made use of it in *Colonel Jacque, The Family Instructor* and
Robinson Crusoe without any special comment or explanation.
In the first of these novels, Defoe put approximately ten pages
of Pidgin English into the mouths of African slaves in Virginia.
His use of the West African day-naming practice for Robinson
Crusoe's man Friday, with its distortions of the original pattern,
seems to indicate that the practices had been well known for
long enough that literary improvisation on them was possible.
There are reports from West Africa and the West Indies of the

need for the use of *lingua franca* by travelers who are going there, records of what may be beginning stages of related languages like Martiniquan French Creole, and travelers' records of the speech of slaves in the British West Indies. By the mid-eighteenth century, attestations of the English of Negroes in the continental colonies which later became the United States are relatively easy to find; by the end of the eighteenth century there is a fairly well-developed Negro dialect tradition in the American drama and other literature. It seems perfectly reasonable to assume that use of the particular variety of English in the American colonies must go back into the seventeenth century; I shall assume that it goes back well into that century.

As we know, the early slave traders practiced language mixing, so that the slaves could be more easily controlled. This forced the slaves to find a *lingua franca*, or language of wider communication, which turned out to be the Portuguese Pidgin which many of them had learned in the slave "factories" on the West Coast of Africa. Apparently, pidgin versions of French (still represented in West Africa by *Petit Nègre*) and English began developing in the factories also. Slaves sent to French- or to Portuguese-speaking areas found it much easier to communicate in Pidgin French or in Pidgin Portuguese than to find an African language in common; the restricted contact of most of them with their masters precluded their learning the standard language. In the United States, slaves in the Louisiana area—and perhaps, in the early days, elsewhere—utilized French Pidgin, now represented by the French Creole ("Gombo") of Louisiana. In most of the United States, however, a variety of English came to be the language of wider communication. When new generations grew up which used only the pidgin, the pidgin became creolized—the term used here is Plantation Creole.

Pidgin and creole varieties of English—as well as of other languages—are spoken today in the Caribbean (including, for this purpose, Surinam and British Guiana on the South American continent), in West Africa, and in the continental United States (Gullah and Louisiana French Creole). These are not wildly

The New York Times (by Neal Boenzi)

The complete sign in this picture, according to *The New York Times* of August 29, 1969, reads

> To grow up decent, our children need new clothing to present themself in school in proper neat!! The sun have to shine for our childrens too. Amen.

Grammatically, this is an almost perfect example of Black English, which is thus a "written" language at least in such examples. As a plural, *themself* needs no *-ves* ending, since *them* establishes plurality (non-redundantly). *Neat* (noun) is a typical Black English derivative from *neat* (adjective); zero derivation is so common where Standard English has suffixes (*neatness*) that occurrences of derivational suffixes on Black English words can almost regularly be taken as historical influence from Standard English. In many parts of the world (and not just in those populated by Blacks), this sign would seem more natural —"grammatical"—than one involving *themselves, neatness,* and *has.*

exotic languages but languages used every day like any other languages. It happens that several varieties of these languages are spoken mainly by Afro-Americans; but they are also spoken by whites who have learned them as second or foreign languages, in many areas. Some of them are vehicles of education and literature, like Papiamento, whose speakers have profited from an enlightened Dutch attitude toward languages. But speakers of many of them are educationally disadvantaged—like speakers of French Creole on Dominica, where official recognition is given only to English.

In Jamaica, the status of the addressee may be indicated by the language in which he is addressed: the conductor on a Kingston bus says "Please step up, sir" to the affluent tourist and "Me tell unu say step up" to a group of poor Jamaicans. Speakers of the creole language are almost always disadvantaged in comparison to standard dialect speakers. Current research shows that status assignment according to language affects citizens of the United States also. The Black speaker of Non-Standard English suffers much more than the Black speaker of Standard English. What rubs salt in the wound is that the speaker of Non-Standard English is also usually much poorer.

Some Broader Aspects of the Language Problem

There is much reason to believe that structural and historical differences between Black English and the English spoken by most other Americans have practical consequences which take them out of the realm of purely academic concerns. Interpretations of such linguistic matters have, in fact, often influenced policies of basic import to the treatment of the "disadvantaged" Negro in the United States. Once it is realized that Black English is, in deep and subtle ways, much more different from other varieties of American English than has been recognized, certain other problems, particularly where education is involved, may be seen to be less forbidding than they seemed.

It has been easy to overlook the relevance of dialect difference to education; and indeed, for the best-known American dialects it poses no great problem to ignore such differences. I can learn to read the phrase *darning needle* even though I say *snake doctor* or *dragon fly* myself. And if I want to call half-sour milk *blinky*, there's no harm—I won't run into the Standard English equivalent of it in reading manuals of atomic physics or instructions issued by the public health agencies, will I?

These are the kinds of questions frequently heard. If Black English were merely the concentration of a few quaint country usages from the rural areas of England, as the Establishment dialect geographers have made it out to be, the received opinion that the matter is trivial might be acceptable. But if, on the other hand, the disadvantaged Black has a historically different variety of English from that of the mainstream-culture white, the question remains open as to whether lack of communication is part of the racial trouble in this country.

What evidence do we have as to the mutual intelligibility of the language of American Blacks and whites? While there is often an *a priori* assumption that no major linguistic barriers to understanding occur, there is enough misunderstanding between the two races to make us cautious about leaving any avenue of investigation unexplored. Serious research on the degree of intelligibility between the white man's English and Black English would be an expensive proposition, involving the presentation of carefully developed, culturally unbiased texts to adequately large informant populations speaking both language varieties and rating the ease with which they can understand and retain those texts. Ideally, for validity and reliability, not only linguists but also anthropologists, psychologists, and an information theorist should be involved.

There is some indirect evidence of an anecdotal nature. Fanny

Kemble, the nineteenth-century British actress who married a plantation owner, reports

> That 'spect, meaning *ex*pect, has sometimes a possible meaning of *su*spect, which would give the sentence in which it occurs a very humorous turn, and I always take the benefit of that interpretation.
>
> (A *Journal of Residence on a Georgia Plantation in 1838–39*, p. 118)

Mrs. Kemble, considered a great liberal in her day, probably failed to see the harm which could be done by her "humorous turns"; there may also be some doubt as to whether she always chose the interpretation which the speaker meant, once she had discounted the "humorous turn." This is clearly not a made-up characteristic; it and others like it lend credence to what Mrs. Kemble reports. Gullah, the dialect of the Sea Islands where Fanny Kemble was living at the time she records, often differs from Standard English in that the latter has an initial unstressed syllable; with our historical bias, we will probably want to say that it has been "dropped" from Gullah—and, indeed, there were English words carrying those syllables in existence before the historical processes which produced Black English began.

The characteristic extends to the other Negro dialects in the United States, which, as I hope to show, are all related historically to Gullah. Charles S. Johnson, in *The Shadow of the Plantation*, records from Negro speech throughout the post-World War I South forms like *'vorce*, where *divorce* is clearly meant. He also reports *revorce*, where the Negro speaker has tried to fancify his English in imitation of the white interlocutor and has "predicted" the wrong prefix for addition. This is very widespread: even radio comedian Andy's "Amos, ah is regusted" has this small degree of validity, apparently being a fancified form of an underlying *'gusted*.

But we understand Andy! Nevertheless, many of us, like Fanny Kemble, allow ourselves a chuckle at the form, even though our liberal consciences and whatever linguistic sophistication we have both tell us that this speech form is basically as good as any other. But misunderstanding is another and sterner matter.

In the Dallas *Morning News* for July 13, 1967, a columnist reports with not unracist glee how a Negro got himself into rather a great deal of trouble by running from some policemen who were trying to serve him with a restraining order. "They's goin' to strain me" was the explanation for his attempt to escape. Because he did not have the initial unstressed syllable in his own language system, the Black English speaker interpreted *restrain* as *strain*. A minor matter, except that *strain* means 'beat' in the language of the speaker—as it does on many islands in the English-speaking part of the Caribbean. Lucy M. Garrison, the famed post-Civil War observer on the Sea Islands, recorded the form with that meaning in the Gullah-speaking Sea Islands of South Carolina in 1861 (reprinted in Allen, Ware and Garrison, *Slave Songs of the United States*, New York, 1965).

Such usages obviously can survive even in Texas, where language problems may cause untold damage to the cause of the minority groups. On November 14, 1965, the Houston (Texas) *Chronicle* reported on seven men in death row at the state prison in Huntsville. Four of the seven were Blacks, and the statements attributed to them by the *Chronicle* reporter showed rather clearly that they were non-mainstream in language and culture. Another inmate was a Mexican-American who "didn't understand" at his trial. The other two were lower-class Texas whites who just didn't talk very much; one of them may have had a speech defect. Would the same men be in death row, even if they had committed the alleged crimes, if they had been middle-class speakers of Standard English? The question is perhaps impossible to answer; but there were no middle-class whites on death row that November, and it is doubtful that there are any now.

Death and ridicule may not be the only consequences of limited mutual intelligibility between dialects—nor even the most important, in the long run. At a small southeast Texas college I struggled to help a young Black student who had failed Freshman English twice. He was generally aware of the reason for his failures—that he was being judged by an irrelevant set of standards—and more than a little bit resentful. It finally came out that he had been a standout public speaker justly proud of his superior verbal ability in his all-Black high school. But he continued to be labeled a verbal failure in this college, even though passing marks went to white students who had no claims to verbal distinction. Other people have failed Freshman English twice and more, but I have a feeling that this boy wouldn't have— given a fair chance linguistically. As it was, he continued to fail Freshman English for a third and fourth time and finally dropped out of the college. The young white liberals of the campus, by demonstrating aggressively, had forced the administration to admit Blacks on an equal basis; but demonstrations are ineffective against subtler manifestations of Establishment policy such as received attitudes toward language.

What of the children in grade schools, some of them newly integrated, who hope someday to arrive at college? Many of them are given IQ tests which may influence the type of education (college preparatory or "general") which they are given throughout public school. Most of these tests are linguistically and culturally biased against children who speak Black English. Some intelligence testers, even those who are aware of language as a complicating factor, have suffered from lack of valid information about Black English in standard sources on American dialects. For example, Audrey Shuey's *Testing Negro Intelligence* (Second Edition, 1966) depends heavily upon a 1960 doctoral dissertation which tries to evaluate the language factor in differential scoring on intelligence tests. Although Arlynne L. Jones, the author of the dissertation, was obviously aware of the language factor, she could only conclude, using the best information about dialect variation available to her, that the Negro's "lack of facility in the use of the English language of the test was astounding" (p. 297). This "deficiency" she traced to the "common use of dialects by the Southern Negro," those dialects being "substantially *oral shorthand*" and forming "an underdeveloped language which may restrict the average Negro's perceptual discrimination and concept formulations" (*Ibid.*). Only in the writings of

William A. Stewart, beginning about 1964, would a conscientious researcher have found anything better in the literature of American dialectology.

Shuey, a serious tester, found Negro "inferiority" in such tests.* Reviewer Ralph M. Dreger ("Hard-Hitting Hereditarianism," *Contemporary Psychology*, XII, No. 2, February, 1967), while rejecting the conclusion of "innate differences," found it necessary to attribute the results to the "brutalizing effects of a system of segregation" (p. 50). Now, the implications of such a conclusion would in themselves be crushing to Negro aspirations: there is reason to doubt that a fully "brutalized" human group would be able to make a recovery. Realizing something of the same sort, anthropologist Melville J. Herskovits set about, in *The Myth of the Negro Past* (1941), to show a continuity of Black culture— and language—in the New World. As Herskovits realized, the assumption—often made in liberal and protest rhetoric—that the extreme hardships of slavery could have reduced the Black population to a sub-human level at some time in the past involves a most pessimistic forecast as to their potentialities for advancement in the future. Brutalization (if literally and not just rhetorically interpreted) would mean that the slaves lost all human behavior patterns, including the use of language and probably of thought. Yet we have historical evidence that the African slaves brought with them special skills, especially agricultural skills, which had major influence on New World economic patterns (Bruce, *Economic History of Virginia in the Seventeenth Century*, I, 331). Fortunately, it is not necessary to conclude from the results of IQ tests that such drastic events have taken place in the past. Since IQ tests are notable for cultural and linguistic bias,[14] the very retention of African cultural and linguistic pat-

---

* More recently, Arthur R. Jensen ("How Much Can We Boost IQ and Scholastic Achievement?" *Harvard Educational Review*, 1969) has attempted to resolve the obvious conflict between ghetto Negro IQ scores and the easily observable ability of the children to perform socially at a much higher level than would be expected from such scores by concluding that they are skilled at "associative" rather than "cognitive" learning. Jensen seems to be merely improvising a defense for an intelligence-testing procedure which is completely invalid because of its cultural and linguistic bias.

terns would explain why Blacks made lower scores on tests which had been standardized to white cultural patterns. It is no more a disgrace to make a low score on the other man's test than it is to lose money playing poker with the other fellow's deck of cards.

In Washington, D.C., psychologist John T. Dailey set out to devise a test free of dialect bias. He would not, his prospectus announced, discriminate between *ain't* and *aren't*—or between *had drunk* and *had drank*—both of which would be dialect-biased measures. He would only give lower scores, on his picture-elicited language facility test, to those children who made responses which were linguistically "incomplete." He would not, for example, discriminate between *He is riding a horse* and *He is ridin' a horse*—the "dropped -g" being the notion of dialect variation which he had acquired from the best information available to him. But he regarded it as self-evident that both *He riding a horse* and *He ridin' a horse* are "incomplete," and that they reveal some lack of linguistic—and probably of cognitive—ability. It happens, however, that the type of sentence which resulted in a penalty against the child who was being tested is one of the common sentence types in Black English,[15] constituting the normal way of making such a statement when no special emphasis is involved. It was, therefore, predictable that the Black children who took the test would make lower scores than competing white children.

No such results showed up in the psychologist's published conclusions. Black and white children were reported to have achieved the same scores on the test. Apparently, then, since the Negro children were unfairly penalized, they were basically superior rather than inferior.

Actually, there is a third explanation which is probably the correct one. Psychologist Dailey conducted only a one-minute picture elicitation interview with the children; but a linguistic research project on which I worked conducted much longer picture elicitations. We found that for the first minute or two the children were on their linguistic "good behavior"; they seldom if ever uttered sentences like *He ridin'* or *They walkin'* during that period of time. (This does not mean that their "real" language behavior has *He is riding* and that *He ridin'* is some kind of linguistic delinquency; speakers who have not completely mastered a foreign language, like French, will frequently suppress interference patterns from English during a short period when they know that their French is being evaluated.) Once the children relaxed somewhat, however, they produced a great many examples of that perfectly normal (in Black English) sentence type. The explanation, then, can be attributed to code-switching— a vexed topic in dialect circles but one that could be made amenable to study. Apparently, the factor of code-switching had canceled the factor of linguistic bias in this psychologist's test; he then came up with a better test of language facility than he, strictly speaking, should have.

Does the matter end there? Consider the possible use of his findings by teachers. They may learn from the results of his experiment that Negro children are equal to white children both in basic intelligence and verbal ability. So far, so good. But there is a rider on this conclusion which isn't so good. The test was based on the assumption that sentences like *He ridin' a horse* were incomplete, which is inaccurate. It also assumed that sentences of that type were not features of any dialect—which is also inaccurate, even if a kind of lucky coincidence did cause two bad features of the test to cancel each other. Now, suppose a teacher, full of this kind of knowledge, gets students into his class who use sentences of the type *He ridin' a horse*. What is the teacher likely to conclude? It is all too likely that he will conclude that he has by chance come upon a class containing some linguistically retarded children. His knowledge about the dialect situation in general will undoubtedly not be great enough to counterbalance the faulty assumptions which lead to that conclusion.

To the linguist the link between human language and human intelligence is so close that it is risking a very drastic conclusion indeed to assume that any person or group of persons is "limited" or "deprived" in language. (Here, of course, we exclude those persons with speech defects, such as cleft palates, or with patho-

logical conditions such as brain damage or severe mental retardation. We know that their language limitations come from
the same source as the inability of a totally blind person to read
ordinary print.) To a few relatively prominent non-linguists, on
the other hand, it has recently seemed quite attractive to explain
away the failures of poor Negroes in the school system by saying
that they are linguistically deprived, that their language systems
are "limited" or "incomplete."

A few have mistakenly applied the reasoning of British
sociologist Basil Bernstein, whose "restricted codes" have a great
deal of validity if it is realized that the "codes" of his writings are
not the basic structural systems of language.[16] An occasional
elementary school specialist inadvertently illustrates the function-
ing of restricted codes by showing how it is possible for Negro
dialect speakers to conduct complete conversations with the one
word *man*. (The first speaker opens with a suggestive or tentative
"Man. . . ." The second inquires as to his meaning, "Man?" The
first then makes it emphatic, "Man!" Intonational variations are of
course very important in such a "conversation.") This is an example of an arbitrary restriction *within* a language system, not an
example of a language system which is fundamentally restricted.
It is, of course, possible to perform analogous tricks with the
system of any language or dialect; but no one's language uses
such devices to any important degree. The fact that such tricks
with Black English so often come to public attention is unfortunate, since it tends to leave the impression that the dialect is
itself such a collection of tricks.

To the linguist, the explanation "He's not responsible for his
failure because he's deficient in language" is so close to meaning
"He's not responsible for his failure, he's not quite a human
being" that the linguist simply does not make statements about
deficiency in language. Particularly, he insists first upon analyzing
each language or language variety *on its own terms* before he
makes a comparison to any other language. He does not assume,
for example, that a part of *to be* has any kind of "natural" function
between a pronoun subject and a verb ending in *-in(g)*; whether

a syntactic system can so function without an auxiliary verb is part of what is to be investigated, not something that can be legislated from authoritative generalizations. In the past, English suffered in the comparisons of early grammarians (some of them extremely learned in a way) who found it lacking because it did not have the case endings of Latin. One of the early victories of linguists was to prove that Shakespeare's English was not deficient because of its lack of ablative case endings. Today probably no one feels that there's anything lacking, or that the Romans were any better off with their case endings. (Indeed, the problem is to convince students that they were not necessarily handicapped by them.) It's possible to characterize a peach as a deficient apple; in fact, it's the only conclusion you can come to if you judge the peach by the apple's standards.

There may be many reasons, most of them cultural, why a child may appear "non-verbal" in certain contexts; ambitious research projects have gone astray by failing to take such factors into account. A child's speech community prescribes for him not only the grammatical forms of his language but also the times appropriate for the use of that language. There are also certain unwritten rules as to the people whom he should address, and how often and how much he should talk to them. "Children should be seen and not heard" is a proverbial expression of at least one speech community's rules. The situations will vary: the prescriptions for speech activity contained in the second culture studied will always be a little different from those of the first. A child from the ghetto culture may be terrified at the appearance of a large number of people of a different color administering tests to him; another child, whose parents are professionals, may spend so much of his time talking to psychologists that their presence seems like a perfect backdrop for a lot of chatter. Even if two children from two subcultures are both terrified by strangers, one may be culturally conditioned to react with a lot of talk and the other to take refuge in complete silence.

Investigators who presuppose lack of verbality on the part of ghetto children have often asserted that the children do not talk to their parents. The famous (or notorious) family type with the absentee father is supposed to contribute to the child's lack of contact with adults, and lack of contact with adults is supposed to mean lack of opportunity to talk and to be taught language. But the investigations of linguists have consistently shown that, where interaction with large groups of children is possible, the peer group relationships of the child are much more important in language development than his relationship with adults. The only general exception to the principle seems to be that of certain nomadic tribes which hunt in small family groups in which the children seldom have contact with other children except for their siblings. In the ghetto culture, peer group relations govern the social activity, including language, of the child to a degree far beyond its importance among middle-class whites.

Looking at the many preconceptions and vested interests which help to distort the picture, the student of Black English should take a lesson in humility: not even creolists are perfect. Yet it seems inescapable that Black English is human language, and that if it is, it has a history as any other language has a history. Roughly speaking, a linguistic difference correlates somehow with a historical difference. We remember that after the Norman Conquest the English language was called an inferior vehicle for communication; we remember that some Romans turned to Greek because of the fancied inadequacies of Latin. Part of any saner approach we may now have to those languages is traceable to the fact that we have been able to take a careful look at the history and the structure of the languages—always, remember, on their own terms—and to develop a healthy skepticism for pre-fabricated theories about the nature of languages, no matter who made them. Black English certainly deserves the same treatment.

NOTES

[1] Carefully controlled psycholinguistic tests which have shown ability on the part of listeners to recognize the ethnic group of a speaker from tape-recorded speech cues have been conducted by Lambert and Tucker; Baratz; Baratz, Shuy, and Wolfram; and Labov (see Bibliography).

[2] William A. Stewart, now President of the Education Study Center in Washington, D. C., was idea man and chief consultant for the Urban Language Study, of which I was director in 1966–67. Stewart's writings (see Bibliography—all three sections) may be said to have opened the field of serious study of Black English in this country. It is particularly noteworthy that Stewart has been able to use his own language background to great advantage in gaining perspective on the dialect situation. Born in Hawaii, he was reared quatrilingually (English, Spanish, Portuguese and Hawaiian). While still quite young, he lived in many polyglot language communities, including the West Indies. Many of his publications have dealt with the creole languages of that area.

Marvin D. Loflin, an Indiana-trained transformational-generative grammarian, was coordinator of linguists for the Urban Language Study and is now at the University of Missouri's Center for Research in Social Behavior. The importance of Loflin's approach is that it brings mathematical rigor to the study of Black English.

[3] Reciprocal cultural influence between the Black and white communities has been demonstrated in the works of such historians of jazz music, jazz dancing, and other Afro-American cultural patterns as Alan Lomax, Marshall Stearns, Harold Courlander, and LeRoi Jones (see Bibliography). The tradition may be said to have formally begun with the work of Melville J. Herskovits, and most researchers in the area are in some way Herskovitsians. In the works produced in this tradition there is never any failure to see that influence, no matter how great and whether reciprocal or not, does not constitute identity.

[4] This is not to deny the limitations of a common-sense view of science. Linguistics, however, depends upon human perceptions in a way which is not true of the physical sciences. Language variation particularly is significant only if it is perceivable by some human speaker—or, more precisely, hearer. The naive expert informant is not, however, capable of describing that variation in any precise terms. This is why bogus explanations in terms of "thick-sounding" Negro speech have long been the grossly inaccurate

popular descriptions of the dialect difference which does exist. Strictly speaking, it is as unscientific to deny the variation itself as it is to attribute that variation to absurd causes ("laziness" or "thick lips"). In practice, however, the latter has been stigmatized, and the former called science.

To a great extent, the "scientific" approach to dialect study criticized above took the form of allegiance to the principle of origin of American English dialect forms in British regional dialects, especially as propounded in Hans Kurath's "The Origin of Dialectal Differences in Spoken American English" (*Modern Philology*, 1928), which specified East Anglia as the source area for the dialect forms of the Southeastern United States. Such allegiance has led to the further "scientific" principle that dialect variation must be primarily geographic, and only secondarily social. For withering criticism of this theoretical foundation, see Pickford's "American Linguistic Geography: A Sociological Appraisal" (see Bibliography).

[5] See Frederic G. Cassidy, "Some New Light on Old Jamaicanisms," and Ian F. Hancock, "A Provisional Comparison of the English-based Atlantic Creoles" (see Bibliography).

[6] *Beach-la-Mar* is a nearly obsolete designation for what most linguists would prefer to call Melanesian Pidgin English. The older (and non-technical) term was also somewhat less precise, and it was never perfectly clear whether "Beach-la-Mar" referred to other varieties of Pidgin English found in the Pacific area. Like *Taki Taki*, it has sometimes been used to refer to any pidgin or creole variety of English, including the Afro-American varieties.

[7] Leonard Bloomfield, *Language* (1933), p. 474; Robert A. Hall, Jr., *Pidgin and Creole Languages* (1966), passim. There is in the writings of these linguists a sophisticated anthropological awareness of cultural relativity which keeps them from designating some members of the population as "more ignorant" than others. Unfortunately, such awareness has seldom been extended to the entire study of dialect variation in the United States.

[8] Strictly speaking, Turner did not consider the problem of the origin of the Gullah dialect in historical terms, although he did point to both Africanisms and parallels to pidgin and creole languages. He did not cite texts attesting earlier stages of Gullah, and it is not certain that he was aware of such texts.

[9] *Interference* is the term for the influence of one's native language on a language acquired later. Thus, when a Puerto Rican paints the sign

MAYOR AND MINORS REPAIRS

we can be fairly sure that Spanish phonological and orthographic practices (*y* for *j*) and noun-adjective agreement (*minors repairs*) have been carried over into English. Compare such Anglo-German sentences as

Throw your father down the stairs his hat.
Toss the cow over the fence some hay.

[10] Robert A. Hall, Jr., "The African Substratum in Negro English," *American Speech* (1950); Raven I. and Virginia McDavid, "The Relationship of

the Speech of American Negroes to the Speech of Whites," *American Speech* (1951). The substratum theory, put rather simply, assumes that the interference patterns of a foreign-language-speaking community become part of the new language which that community substitutes for its former language (because of some factor like adopting the language of a foreign invader).

[11] Hall and Douglas Leechman, "American Indian Pidgin English: Attestations and Grammatical Peculiarities," *American Speech* (1955). See also Mary Rita Miller, "Attestations of American Indian Pidgin English in Fiction and Non-Fiction," *American Speech* (1967). Although Hall's works constitute the most complete treatments of pidgin and creole languages now generally available, it is disconcerting that not even his *Pidgin and Creole Languages* (1966) mentions either Seminole Pidgin English or Liberian Pidgin English.

[12] Archaism has also been asserted as an explanation for differences in other areas of culture, such as religion. It has been maintained that the emotionalism of Negro church services was paralleled in the white churches of an earlier time. The best response to this has been that emotionalism is a relatively trivial feature of Negro sermons and religious practices, and that white and Negro practices have never completely overlapped in the anthropologically more significant areas. See the work of Alan Lomax (especially *The Rainbow Sign*), Carl Carmer (*Stars Fell on Alabama*), Lyle Saxon (*Gumbo Ya-Ya*), and the older work of George Washington Cable and Lafcadio Hearn (see Bibliography).

[13] "Urban Negro Speech: Sociolinguistic Factors Affecting English Teaching," in *Social Dialects and Language Learning*, edited by Shuy (1964).

[14] For critiques of linguistic and cultural bias in the IQ tests, see Joan C. and Stephen Baratz, "Early Childhood Intervention: The Social Science Base of Institutional Racism," *Harvard Educational Review*, 1970. Other treatments of the same topic are R. B. Cattell, "Are IQ Tests Intelligent?" *Psychology Today* 1 (1968); Gilbert Voyat, "IQ: God-Given or Man-Made?" *Saturday Review*, 27 May 1969; and Lilian Zach, "The IQ Test: Does It Make Black Children Unequal?" *School Review*, February, 1970. On testing in general, see Banesh Hoffman, *The Tyranny of Testing* (1962).

[15] This structure is related to the "zero copula," examples of which are *she good* and *he hateful*. Where Standard English would have a part of *to be* as a "copula" (*She is lazy, he is hateful, they are playing*), Black English has zero (*She lazy, he hateful, he eatin', they playin'*). Many creole languages—and other languages, like Russian—have comparable structures (e.g., Haitian Creole *yo ché* 'they expensive' or 'they are expensive'). Like all these languages, Black English has "realization" of the copula in certain positions; e.g., *Yes, he is* is possible, *Yes, he is* not.

[16] British sociologist Basil Bernstein has evolved the fashionable concept of the restricted versus the elaborated "code," and has made the influential (if potentially unfortunate) suggestion that lower classes are often limited

to restricted codes. "Code" might better be labeled "strategy of discourse" in order to be consistent with linguistic terminology. According to Bernstein, all classes use restricted codes in some speech situations (e.g., cocktail party conversation). Mastery of the elaborated codes (political speech making, presentation of a paper before a professional society) requires training and may be limited to socially (and economically) favored groups, although the very favored (superordinated, or upper class) groups may feel no need of it. An obvious criticism is that Bernstein may have overlooked the fact that lower-class groups have their own types of elaborated code. For the American Black, see Chapter VI (the sections on "Fancy Talk" and "How the Ghetto Speaker Uses Language") and various treatments by Lomax and by Thomas Kochman (see Bibliography). The outstanding refutation of the notion that Black speakers have a deficient verbal repertoire is William Labov's "The Logic of Nonstandard English," in Georgetown Roundtable Proceedings 1969 (reprinted in Aarons, Gordon, and Stewart [see Bibliography], and in Language and Poverty, edited by Williams, 1970).

II

On the Structure
of Black English

T HERE have long been two directly opposed views as to the difference between Black English and other dialects of American English. Even so prominent a scholar as Charles S. Johnson could write

> Negro dialect turns out to be a repository for the seventeenth century speech of the first English colonizers. (*The Negro in American Civilization*, p. 132)

enough though the pages of his works teem with evidence to the contrary. Johnson, like other social scientists, was simply misled by the faulty language history that was available during his time. Some of the best studies of Black language and culture have been vitiated by the preconception that the Negro's customs *must* be the white man's castoffs. On the other hand, Miles Mark Fisher, a scholar who was thoroughly aware of the possibilities of African influence, could see the great differences from white culture patterns which were present below the surface of trivial resemblances. In *Negro Slave Songs of the United States*, he wrote

> They [slave owners] simply had never dreamed of the changes involved in the introduction of Negroes into the Americas. (p. 95)

In language as well as in other aspects of culture, the different system brought in by the African slaves had consequences which are only beginning to be understood.

Careful investigation reveals no archaic "gadzooks" or "forsooth" in Black English, but it does reveal underlying patterns which are very different from anything known of the language of the seventeenth-century Englishmen, as well as from such modern white dialects as the oft-compared Appalachian dialect. The deeper and more careful the analysis, the greater the differences found. In sentences like

> An' so I comin' down an' she out there blabbin' her mouth told my sister I was playin' hookey from school.

there are no words which are not in Standard English, and no word forms which white dialects do not have, although sometimes in casual or "illiterate" usage. A syntactic analysis, however, reveals a greatly different system. Syntax, the focus of more modern linguistics, is the area in which the analysis of Black English is most revealing.[1]

In the system of its verbs, Black English reveals the greatest difference from white American dialects—as from British dialects—and the closest resemblance to its pidgin and creole ancestors and relatives. At a trivial (morphological) level, one may observe that

John run

in Black English replaces

John runs

in Standard English; pidgin and creole varieties of English share this surface characteristic, as do more distantly related kinds of English. But careful analysis will show that the Black English form does not fall into the same category as the third person singular, present indicative of the Standard English form.

There are, in fact, two Black English categories which have the same surface form as *John run*. One of the clearest indications of their difference is that they may be negated in two different ways: *John don' run* and *John ain' run*. There are other syntactic functions, such as the formation of questions, in which the two versions of *John run* function differently. It is for convenience— and obviousness of presentation—that we will start the analysis from the negative patterns.

In Black English, we find *John don' run, John ain' run,* and *John dit'n run.* The three negators (*don', ain',* and *dit'n*) may or may not represent Standard English *don't, ain't,* and *did not;* the question is left open here. This complexity in the negation patterns is, incidentally, quite different from the simplicity in pidgin and creole varieties. Since the earliest documents in Black English contain the simple negation pattern, it seems reasonable to conclude that the present patterns are due to the changing nature of the language. (See Chapter III.)

The negator *dit'n* occurs in sentences like *He dit'n go yesterday,* which is of course the negative of

> He went yesterday.

Insofar as forming the negative of the past tense is concerned, the differences appear at this point to be of phonological detail (or, in the representation above, of spelling). But tense, although an obligatory category in Standard English, can be omitted in Black English sentences. The sequence

> . . . he go yesterday . . .

is perfectly grammatical, provided the surrounding clauses or sentences give the needed time cues. Action in the past may thus be represented by the base form of the verb:

> The boy carried the dog dish to the house and put some dog food in it and put some water in and bring it out and called his dog . . .
> (A Washington, D.C. informant[2])

In high-quality collections of speeches by American Blacks, like those of the outstanding folklorist B. A. Botkin, we find

> When the day begin to crack, the whole plantation break out with all kinds of noise, and you could tell what was going on by the kind of noise you hear.   (*Lay My Burden Down,* p. 60)

Any facile assumption about "historical present" is broken by the occurrence of forms like *could* in the second example and *carried* and *called* in the first. The verb forms *bring, begin, break, going,* and *hear* are consistent with occurrence in the past, insofar as the grammar of Black English is concerned. Such occurrence is *non-redundantly*[3] marked in the language. Whereas in Standard English every verb in a sequence (in a sentence or in a related series of sentences) must be marked as either present or past, in Black English only one of the verbs needs to be marked—although more than one may be so marked.

Black English does not normally use the -s in the present *he goes,* but there is an occasional borrowing of the Standard English suffix. (Hypercorrection can result in forms like *I goes* or *you loves* as well as *he goes* and *she loves.*) This is not a "present tense" in the same sense as the most similar Standard English form; Black English can, however, mark present time unmistakably, as with the use of *not* (*He not workin'*). More basically, the speaker of Black English has an option as to whether he wishes to indicate that the action of the verb went on in the past or to leave the verb in a noncommittal form.

When *he ain' go* is the negative of *he go*, the verb base marks a point-of-time category. This, again, is a creole language characteristic, and is very different from Standard English. If speakers of Standard English learn to interpret the unmarked forms as past tense, they will be (quite accidentally) right about ninety percent of the time. Most of the events which we see as points in time are in the past, and we tend to look upon current happenings as ongoing. Furthermore, there are usually co-occurrent adverbial time expressions (*yesterday, last week, a long time ago*) which remove any confusion between the two systems. Even without the time expressions, a speaker of Standard English may be right about ninety percent of the time in his interpretation of this part of the Black English structure. But a ten percent potential misunderstanding is a great detriment to human communication.

Within the particular category marked by the negator *ain'*, the speaker of Black English can say either

> He ain' go

or

> He ain' goin'

although of course they mean different things. *He ain' go* is the negative for a momentary action, whether or not in the past. *He ain' goin'* is the negative of a progressive action, whether or not in the past. In the latter, the action is progressive in almost the same sense as the Standard English "present progressive" verb form, except that it is irrelevant whether the action occurred in the present or in the past. Just as *he ain' go* almost always (approximately ninety percent of the time) refers to past actions, *he ain' goin'* almost always refers to present actions. But there are frequent sentences like

> He stood there and he thinkin'

which would be inconsistent if the assumption were that *he thinkin'* reflects the same underlying structure as Standard English *he is thinking*. We find occurrences of the *-in'* verb form with both present and past tense structures:

He got a glass of water in his hands and he drinkin' some of it.

My teacher she said I passed on the skin of my teeth. My sisters and them up there talkin' 'bout I should stayed back.

And when I come back they came back; they was outa school and so I comin' down and she out there blabbin' her mouth told my sister I was playin' hookey from school.

She real skinny, and every time you see her she eatin' Cheerios.

This verb category will be called *Aspect*. Verbs in that category are marked for the ongoing, continuous, or intermittent quality of an action rather than for the time of its occurrence. This is the only obligatory category in the Black English verb system. This is perhaps the most basic difference from Standard English, since a speaker of Standard English must mark tense but can choose to indicate or to ignore the ongoing or static quality of an action. Black English gives the speaker an option with regard to tense, but its rules demand that he commit himself as to whether the action was continuous or momentary.

Superficially similar Standard English forms are really very different in their underlying structures. The sequence *He ain't goin'* in casual or informal Standard English (or in white non-standard dialects) is not syntactically identical to the Black English sequence. Since a main verb in Standard English which ends in *-in(g)* must be preceded by a part of *to be* (*I am going, he is going*, etc.), unwary observers have been misled into assuming that the relationship between Black English *he sleepin'* and Standard English *he is sleeping* (*he's sleeping*) must be phonological—that the [z][4] of the auxiliary verb is "dropped" in the same way that the *-k* of asterisk is dropped in some speaking styles. Part of the disproof of this conclusion is that Black speakers, when trying to fancify their speech by using what they imagine to be Standard English forms, frequently insert the "wrong" form of *to be*:

> He am sleeping.

The third Black English negator, *don'*, goes with forms like

> He don' go
> He don' be goin'

but not

> *He don' goin'

(The asterisk, a convention of linguistic description, indicates ungrammaticality for the language being described.)

The sequence *don' be* (or, in the affirmative *be*) has a special function which is not marked in the Standard English verb. It indicates that the time of the action is "stretched out"—that it is reportably long for the kind of action involved in the verb being used. In the sentence

> He be waitin' for me every night when I come home

be correlates with *every night* in much the same way that *-ed* correlates with *last night* in the sentence

> He waited for me last night.

The sequence is grammatically different from

> He waitin' for me right now

the significant co-occurrence of which is *right now*. In Black English, it is ungrammatical to say either

> *He waitin' for me every night

or

> *He be waitin' for me right now.

We also find grammatical negatives

> He ain' waitin' for me right now
> He don' be waitin' for me every night
> That man be here every night; he don't want no girl

and ungrammatical negatives

> *He ain' waitin' for me every night
> *He don't be waitin' for me right now
> *That man be here every night; he ain' want no girl.

The category negated by *don'* can be called *Phase*, although *Aspect*₂ would be just as good a name.

There are, of course, certain expressive possibilities associated with these categories. If one says of a workman,

> He workin' when de boss come in

he is paying the worker no compliment; the work is coterminous with the presence of the boss, and may be for the purpose of fooling the employer. On the other hand,

> He be workin' when de boss come in

means that the work went on before and after the boss's entry and may mean that the employee is conscientious. One might also say to a scorned acquaintance's rare intelligent remark,

> You makin' sense, but you don't be makin' sense

meaning something like "You've blundered into making an intelligent statement for once," or "That's a bright remark—but it's not the usual thing for you."

In the Aspect category (the one which is negated by *ain'*) is the verb structure which differs most obviously from Standard English. We find many sentences like

> He been go
> He been eat (ate) the chicken
> He been know that.

The sentences recorded are from informants in Washington, D. C., all of them fourteen years old or younger. Botkin records from adults

> . . . when Old Missus been marry Massa John C. Bethea . . .
> (*Lay My Burden Down*, p. 148)

> I been cook for heap of these white folks.   (p. 149)

> We been bother . . .   (p. 149)

A New York City adult (born in North Carolina) recently said to me

> I been had it [an elaborate wig] a long time.

This structure is a regular one in the English-based pidgins and creoles, although it is relatively rare, at least in more nearly formal speech, in the United States from informants over fourteen or so. With older informants, however, such sentences as

> I been knowin' him a long time[5]

are quite commonplace. Detailed analysis would show that *I been know*[6] has the Point-of-time Aspect and *I been knowin'* has the Progressive Aspect. *Been* marks an action which is quite decidedly in the past; it can be called Perfective Aspect, or even Remote Perfective Aspect.

Black English resembles West African languages grammatically in this Remote Perfective form and in a contrasting Immediate Perfective Aspect, for which the preverbal form is *done*. Sentences like

> I done go
> I done gone
> I done went
> I been done gone
> I done been gone[7]

are frequent in Black English today. In some cases, the past tense forms after *done* (*went* in the third example) may be the result of influence from Standard English. We find apparently hyper-correct forms like

> . . . a li'l' cullud chu'ch what de massas an' missuses in San 'Tone done builted . . .
>
> (Brewer, *Dog Ghosts and Other Texas Negro Folk Tales*, p. 14)

There is some problem as to how it is negated, as well as to how it fits into other more complex syntactic structures. In WesKos Pidgin English of Nigeria and the Cameroons, *done* falls together with *been* (is "neutralized") when negation occurs, and something similar seems to happen in U. S. Black English.

One of the more interesting facts about *done* is its occurrence in other pidgin- and creole-related languages (e.g., WesKos Pidgin of the Cameroons, Fernando Poo, and Nigeria). Parallel forms occur in such languages even though their vocabulary base is not English but French (French Creole *fèk*, from *faire*) or Portuguese (*kaba*, from *acabar*). Sranan Tongo, of Surinam, still has *kaba*, although it is usually referred to as a form of English. It is quite probable that *kaba* came to this continent, too, although there appears to be no record of it. On the other hand, *done* has a long history in North America; and its relationship to *been* has been a complicated one. Thomas Wentworth

Higginson, who observed Black language and customs during the Civil War, wrote

> "Done" is a Virginia shibboleth, quite distinct from the "been" which replaces it in South Carolina. Yet one of their best choruses, without any fixed words, was "De bell done ringing," for which, in proper South Carolina dialect, would have been substituted, "De bell been a-ring."   (*Army Life in a Black Regiment*, pp. 191–192)

Higginson can be excused, with far more justice than later professional linguists, for an unsuccessful attempt to fix the distribution of these forms geographically and for some resultant confusion. Probably, what he observed as the "South Carolina" dialect was an unstressed *been*, which still survives in some forms of Black English as the Immediate Perfective in contrast to stressed *been* as the Remote Perfective.[8] His recording of *The bell done ringing* as a specifically Virginia form is interesting; the same line, in what is probably the same song, was recorded on St. Simon's Island in 1959 by Alan Lomax (Prestige INT 25001).

In this description, nothing has been written about auxiliary *have*; the omission is not an oversight. Although Black English speakers, including relatively young speakers, do use the *have/has* auxiliaries at times, they use and manipulate them with a lack of skill which shows that they are really borrowing them from Standard English and not using the resources of their own language. (This is one of the features of code-switching.) The forms *been* and *done* come closest to the perfective function of *have* in Standard English, but of course the correspondence is not complete. Nevertheless, it is probably this resemblance which made it possible for southern white speakers to borrow *done* in structures like *have/has done gone*.

Some of the auxiliary functions of *have* in Standard English are filled by Black English *is*:

> Three months am the total time I's spent going to school.
>   (Botkin, p. 36)

> I's hear tell of them good slave days, but I ain't never seen no good times then.   (*Ibid.*, p. 89)

> The hogs is all died.   (*Ibid.*, p. 4)

Some typical question structures are

Standard English	*Black English*
Have you seen him?	Is you see(n) him?
Have they gone there?	Is they gone there?

A typical Black English emphatic statement would be

I *is* seen him.

Another example of the complicated relationship to Standard English is that of the zero copula (*you right*), which alternates with "filler" forms (*Is he right? Yes, he is*, NOT *°Yes, he*). These fillers occur where the elliptical adjective is understood (*Is I right? Yes, you is* [right]) and in emphatic or somewhat fancified sentences (*You IS right*). There remain, however, differences in detail from Standard English. There is, for example, the use of *am* with other than first person subjects:

If my memorandum [memory] am correct.   (Botkin, p. 162)

My first child am borned two months 'fore freedom.   (*Ibid.*, p. 78)

Sam kisses his old woman who am a-crying.   (*Ibid.*, p. 256)

... with that blood they writes that he shall hang between the heavens and the earth till he am dead, dead, dead.   (*Ibid.*, p. 255)

Note especially the Standard English features like -*es* of *kisses* (verb) in the third example and the legalistic language (*shall hang*) and stylistic repetition (*dead, dead, dead*) of the fourth. It seems perfectly clear that the speakers are fancifying their language in these examples, with one—but only one—of the fancifying devices being an approximation to Standard English. Although many of these structures may have originated as imitations of Standard English, they have become so widely used that speakers are probably not aware of switching into the other dialect.

Apparently one of the most radical of the steps taken above is the description of tense as an optional category in Black English, even though it is an obligatory part of Standard English. This step turns out to be absolutely necessary. There are hints of what needs to be accounted for in published observations like those of Walter Loban, *Problems in Oral English* (NCTE, 1967), which shows that the Negro group chosen had more "difficulties" with tense than the "Low White" group, the "High White" group, or the "Random" group. It is important to note that in Loban's study the "Random" group is never notably similar to the Negro group—that is, there is strong reason to believe that the differences in language behavior of the Negro group result from something different in their own grammatical system, not from chance "mistakes" or any randomness in their language. We have overheard sentences like

That man stare at me and I ain' know him

where the phonological environment *stare at* leads us to believe that we would have heard a [d] representing the past tense if there had been one. (Incidentally, it is irrelevant whether the speaker had or did not have final [r] in *stare*.) We also have the evidence of "hyper" forms like

felled
frozed
threwed
strucked
... the drove flewed up, make such a fuss ...

(Botkin, p. 14)

These forms lead us to believe that the speaker may be acting in terms of someone else's expectations of him rather than in terms of his own characteristic linguistic behavior. (Apparently the child learns that one marker for past time makes the teacher happy, and decides that two or three would make her absolutely ecstatic.) There are also occurrences of infinitives like *to taught, to falled* which lead us to suspect that the final *-ed* had no tense significance for the speaker.

An interesting experiment revealed a more solid basis for this kind of conclusion. A linguist working on this dialect, looking especially at reading problems, gave his informants sentences like

(A) A few days ago, they walked.
(B) Every day now, they walk.

to read into a tape recorder. Listening to the sentences later, he was unable to hear anything after *walk* for either (A) or (B). Listening again a few times, he thought he detected a greater length in the vowel for the forms where Standard English would have *walked*. Another linguist listened and concluded, "Yes, there's a difference; the vowels are shorter where Standard English would have an *-ed* ending." This kind of standoff could not be permitted. To resolve the apparent contradiction, the first thought was to subject the tapes to machine analysis. But then the first linguist came up with a better suggestion: it is not the perception of the linguist or of a machine which counts, but the perception of the person who produces the language forms. If he hears a difference consistently, there's a difference; if he doesn't, there isn't any difference—no matter what a thousand machines say.

So, the first linguist gave the following test to the children, who were paid to come in on a regular informant basis and who were not likely to pay special attention to one more seemingly odd activity. They were given several sentences of type (A) and several of type (B); the sentence types differed only in having *a few days ago* with type (A) and *every day now* with type (B). The object of the investigation was to determine whether there was structurally present in the sentences of type (A) anything corresponding to the *-ed* of Standard English. Some time after the recordings were made, each child was asked to listen to a playback of his own reading of

(A) ... they walk(ed)
(B) ... they walk

and to put either *a few days ago* or *every day now* with each; the time adverbial phrases had been erased from the tapes and each child was instructed to restore them. If there really was some phonological marking for past tense in sentences of type (A), the child could be expected to put *a few days ago* with sentences of type (A) and *every day now* with sentences of type (B) a significant percentage of the time—with mistakes only for lack of attention or random error. Remember that the choice was forced: the informant was not allowed to say "neither" or "I don't know."

It happened that the informants on this test gave the "correct" answer just about fifty percent of the time. This indicates rather clearly that, if an informant did have any phonetic material associated with the -*ed* forms, it did not furnish any meaningful signal for his own linguistic system. (The fact that the reactions of the linguists who listened were at opposite poles was of course a good indication that there was no consistent phonological representation for the orthographic -*ed*.) On the basis of this kind of test, there would be justification for eliminating any *Tense* category whatsoever from the Black English grammar and treating all occurrences of -*ed* as switching toward Standard English. Considerable evidence of another type, however, supports writing it in as an optional category. Possibly, only preconceptions from Standard English lead us to refer the -*ed* ending to tense or to time categories at all.

Information of this type helps to make sense of the often topsy-turvy relationship between a white teacher and a student speaker of Black English. The teacher is all too willing to throw up his hands and to say that the student "has no grammar"—i.e., that his language behavior is random. The linguist is unwilling to admit that anyone's language behavior is random; but the imposition of language forms outside a speaker's own system may cause a great deal of variation in the forms which he produces. This explanation probably suffices for the (relatively rare) occurrences of forms like *throwned* (for Standard English *threw*) and *don't gots*.

The behavior of the grammatical categories herein called *Phase* and *Aspect* is the most obvious and immediately impressive difference between the grammar of Black English and that of Standard English. The contrast between *be* and zero as copula markers is one which Stewart (in many lectures as well as in his writings) and Loflin have made as familiar as anything in the grammatical system. The standard example is

(1) My brother sick

which indicates that the sickness is currently in effect, but of (probably) short-term duration. On the other hand

(2) My brother be sick

indicates a long-term illness; the brother may not be expected back in school for a relatively long time. Another function of this contrast is seen in these sentences:

> I say, "Mittie, looka, looka, I scared." . . . Generally, people in the country be scared of a graveyard . . .
>
> (Botkin, *Lay My Burden Down*, p. 150)

The contrast between the two categories becomes even clearer when they are made into negatives

> (3) My brother ain' sick
> (4) My brother don' be sick

and into questions

> (5) Is my brother sick?
> (6) Do my brother be sick?

It is extremely important to keep in mind that sentences such as (5) above should not be judged alone but in relationship to the other sentences in the same system with which they contrast. Thus, we may very often hear, from young Black English informants, not only (5) but

> (7) My brother's sick

and

> (8) My brother IS sick. (Emphatic, as though someone had denied it.)

Since (5), (7), and (8) are very like Standard forms, it is easy to conclude that they are really substitutes for sentences like (1). The first indication that the *'s* of (7) and the IS of (8) are really different patterns from Standard English, despite the Standard-like formation of the question in (5), is that sentences like

> (9) They sick

when turned into questions, may result in

> (10) Is they sick?

In other words, *is* functions as a question marker and as an emphasis marker, superficially as in Standard English. But when we look at its further behavior, we become aware that it is not really like Standard English at all.

The child who said

(7) My brother's sick

probably was indulging in some kind of code-switching under the influence of Standard English. Proof of this is that he also says

(11) They's sick
(12) I's sick
(13) Im is sick

on occasion. The question form of (11) is

(14) Is they sick?

and of (13) is

(15) Is Im sick?

Sometimes, under the influence of code-switching, he will produce

(16) Im am sick.
(17) Am Im sick, doctor?

or

(18) My brother be's sick [for a long time]

where (18) carried over the basically meaningless (in Black English) 's of *They's sick, He's sick,* etc.

Please note that it is not a typographical error above that *Im* (Black English) is written without an apostrophe. I would write *Im* for the Negro Non-Standard form which interchanges with *I*; *I'm* for the Standard English form which is a contraction of *I am.* That *Im* is not such a contraction is shown very clearly by the frequent occurrence of forms like *Im is ~ Im am.* A variant which seems to be evidence for the origin of this sequence in switching behavior occurs in Botkin, p. 162: *What am I's to do?*

A very serious-minded and responsible Negro woman who was a teacher of several years of experience and who happened to be my student in a special training course once reported to me, reluctantly and as though it were a great disgrace to Black people, that one of her students had asked her

Mrs. Smith, is Im failin' English?

Her shame here was double—not only was the child using "bad" English, but he was revealing excessive stupidity in not knowing that anyone who used such grammar would naturally fail English! Of course, she was really wrong on both accounts. The child was only using his own grammatical system, which is about all we can expect any child to do; and there is no *a priori* reason why we should expect him to know that the school system undervalues his system. Second, a child simply must have some rational exposition of the kind of expectations the school system has of him before he can evaluate his own performance vis-à-vis those norms, and the school system in which this child was studying did not provide such information.

Although it is possible to find forms like *I is* in British folk English dialects, it is interesting that parallel forms have developed in the Portuguese Creole languages of West Africa, as well as in the varieties intermediate between Pidgin English and Standard English there. Marius Valkhoff, in his important book *Studies in Portuguese and Creole* (1966), cites "*eu esta* (I is) for *eu estou* (1st person)" (p. 34). Since the Portuguese Creoles and West African varieties also have the dominance of Aspect over Tense which Valkhoff traces to "the verbal system of African languages" (*ibid.*, p. 104), there is reason to believe that these parallels are more significant than those with British folk English.

It may be disappointing to seekers after the exotic to discover that the differences between the grammar of Standard English and that of Negro Non-Standard are primarily of this order. We will see no picture of the Congo creeping through the grammatical system, face painted and spear in hand, but, at each point, only seemingly minor differences which become increasingly greater as we consider their systemic implications and their cumulative effect. It is because of the lack of these exotic, striking,

individual grammatical differences that teachers, laymen, and
dialect geographers—all of them inclined to treat language a word
at a time—have failed to see the great difference.

Are there no really titillating differences, no grammatical
equivalents to the sensationalism of sex-and-slavery novels like
Mandingo? No, there aren't really; no linguist is convinced that
any grammatical structure is any "stranger" or more "exotic" than
any other. The typical reaction of a pedagogical-minded linguist
would be to scold the questioner for diverting the class (oops—
the readers) from serious business by bringing up such matters.
But there is one feature of pidgin and creole languages which
often impresses speakers of European languages as being exotic:
they do not differentiate *in the pronoun system* between masculine and feminine. (*Of course* they have ways of indicating that
difference elsewhere in the total language system!) Some of this
exists among the very young speakers of Black English even
today; the speakers are five or six years old, too old to be comparable to the little middle-class toddlers who make such an
"error" when much younger. Thus, the child will say

>   He a nice little girl

or

>   I don't know her name [referring to a male linguist].

This "lack" of pronoun sex reference (which isn't a lack at all;
a pronoun system doesn't "need" sex reference any more than a
verb "needs" tense) is characteristic of Gullah and is widely found
in the Caribbean's Afro-American dialects. It may have some
influence from West African languages; Camerounians who don't
speak French too well often say things like *Il* (in this case, the
speaker's sister) *vient avec nous*. But since the feature (N.B.:
"Lack" is being considered as a feature, not as the absence of a
feature) is also present in the Pacific Ocean pidgins and creoles,
direct and exclusive West African influence is a highly debatable
matter. Those who believe that pidgins are "reduced" or "simplified" languages may say that sex reference of pronouns is a kind
of unnecessary frill anyway, easily done away with in some

putative historical scrapping of non-essentials. It is fairly easy to observe that the necessity for classifying all human (and some animal) nouns according to sex reference is as often a drag as an advantage in Standard English. Think of the embarrassment of passing routine remarks of politeness about a non-sex-identified baby to the face of a possibly militant mother who isn't going to stand for "it" as a reference for her baby.

At any rate, this feature of Plantation Creole, which involved the use of a single pronoun no matter what the sex of the antecedent, stayed around for quite a while, especially in the lower age grades.

The invariant pronoun form also occurs in the possessive. In "deeper" creole varieties, the undifferentiated first person pronoun form is *me*; *I book* would be an extremely rare form, occurring only in hypercorrection, but *me book* is commonplace. The paradigms for possessive pronouns are something like this:

creole and pidgin	*partly decreolized*
me	me *or* my
him	he
him	she *or* her

"Possession by juxtaposition" extends to the other pronouns:

On Sunday, we-uns do us washing.   (Botkin, p. 160)

The process extends to the noun system; structures like *Mary hat* have been noticed by teachers in the United States for some years now and are recorded in such works as Walter Loban's *Problems in Oral English* (1967).

The undifferentiated pronoun may also serve as a subject form, as in the pidgin and creole languages. Washington inner-city children say things like

Me help you?
Her paintin' wif a spoon.

Charles Dickens recorded in *Martin Chuzzlewit* (1844) a Negro in New York City saying

". . . him kep a seat 'side himself, sa."   (p. 164)

And there are very many such forms in Botkin:

> ... him say nothing ...   (p. 145)

> Him eat and get so full him can't hardly swallow.   (p. 6)

> Us ain't been far off from there since us first landed in this country.
>   (p. 75)

> Him try to carry on with free labor, 'bout like him did in slavery.
>   (p. 249)

Even without the geographic spread of Botkin's attestations, there would be no reason to assume that the form is confined to any particular area. Eudora Welty's *The Ponder Heart* (1953) has a speaker in Mississippi saying

> Her didn't have nothing to give me.   (p. 76)

An apparently complicating factor is that, in the very earliest texts, we find very frequent *he, we*, etc., as subject forms— especially *he*, which often occurs when the subject is biologically feminine and would require *she* by the rules of Standard English. Of course, there are frequent occurrences of *him* for a female subject. The reason for this apparent inconsistency seems obvious in view of the situation in the related pidgin and creole languages. The latter have noun classifiers attached to the verb, which look very much like the "redundant" pronoun subject which teachers have long criticized in the English of their white students. In West Camerounian Pidgin, for example, one may hear a sentence like

> Jacob i-don go?

rationalizable, and presented in works of authors like Gerald Durrell, as

> Jacob he done go?

The structure has been mistakenly called an appositive[9] in some unsophisticated studies of Black English in the United States. A form like

> Mose, he sick ...   (Botkin, *Lay My Burden Down*, p. 71)

is, on the surface, not unlike forms which teachers have long "corrected" in the writings of white schoolboys; knowledge that comparable sequences exist in white dialects probably motivated the editor to put the comma in the quoted sentence. But a deeper investigation will show the underlying difference in Black English. We not only find sentences like

>Ray sister she got a new doll baby

but also sentences like

>Ray sister go to school at Adams she got a new doll baby

and

>Ray sister seven year old go to school at Adams she got a new doll baby.

In the last sentence above, *seven year old* and *go to school at Adams* are both relative clauses, with the typical zero ("understood") relative pronoun of Black English and related varieties. The relative rule is recursive: it can, theoretically if not in observable practice, be applied an unlimited number of times (*Ray sister seven year old go to school at Adams live on S Street . . .*). In this respect Black English is like Standard English and all other languages, which must have recursive rules somewhere in their grammars. But, in the more particular matters of how the rules apply, languages differ; and Black English differs from Standard English in those particulars. *He* (or *she*) in sentences of this type can be more accurately called a Predicate Marker. It is only superficially like an appositive; in more complex sentences, it picks up the subject function, after a possibly very long sequence of intervening modifiers, and links it to the verb.

In this particular structure, Black English has retained a great deal of similarity to the ancestral Pidgin English and to still existing varieties of Pidgin English. It is interesting to note that the rules given for the Predicate Marker in pidgins, with their implications for alternation between unmarked (*him*) and marked (*he*) subjects of verbs, will apply also to Black English (Chapter IV).

Relative structures of this type are very frequent in Black English. If the relative clauses modify the object or complement of a verb rather than its subject, the Predicate Marker is not utilized. A grammatical sentence would be

You know Ray sister live on S Street go to school at Adams?

Or, to take a more adult example,

That's the chick I keep tellin' you about got all that money.

where the relative pronoun of the first modifying clause (*I keep tellin' you about*) may also be zeroed in Standard English, but where the relative pronoun of the second modifying clause (*got all that money*) must be expressed in Standard English (*who's got all that money* or *who has all that money*). I overheard the last sentence, incidentally, on Eighth Street in Greenwich Village while on my way to my office to check my files for more examples of the Black English relative structure.

Understood in relation to the relative structures of Black English, the "nominative"[10] pronouns of even the earliest attestations no longer seem to be such important exceptions to the use of the undifferentiated pronoun (*him, me, her, them*) as subject of the verb as they once did. In sentences like

He am so big an 'cause he so, he think everybody do what him say.
(Botkin, p. 161)

an underlying but deleted noun "appositive" may help to explain the occurrence of the *he* subjects along with the more basically Black English *him say*. But the speakers in this collection are obviously on their best linguistic behavior, in order to impress the collector; mixing of Black English and Standard English is apparent throughout the collection. Standard English use of the "objective" form of the pronoun where there is more than one subject (*him and me, me and you*, in casual styles) tends to mask the distinctive nature of the Black English form except in relatively infrequent instances.

Some of these factors help to explain why the authors of superficial descriptions of Black English have tended to treat it as an amalgam of non-standard features, identical to non-prestige features of white dialects. This may help to explain why people like Cleanth Brooks have conceived of Blacks as having a kind of affinity for non-standard forms, or why dialect geographers have tended to explain away Black English as being only a "high density" of otherwise widely occurring non-standard forms. (The whole thing may exemplify somewhat embarrassingly how the rather inaccurate term *non-standard* was applied to Black English.) And it is one more indication of the linguistic reason why the teacher's automatic reaction ("Find out what the student is doing and tell him to stop!") is ineffective.

Perhaps even more unfortunate is the frequent misinterpretation of Black English grammatical structures as being the result of "conceptual" difficulty. An outstanding example of a trap for the unwary is the Black English pluralization system. After a numeral or some other expression which clearly denotes plurality by itself, these varieties leave the noun unchanged:

> A whole lotta song
> so many million dollar
>
> (A Beaumont, Texas, informant)

Where other modifiers do not so clearly point out plurality, the noun forms are changed for the purpose:

> the songs
> the dollars

But the Black English speakers "conceive" plurality as well as anyone else.

Unfortunately, American students who looked at the structural situation, until very recently saw at the most half of it. Thinking in terms of Standard English, they have tended to remark the "lack" of the plural inflection, without noticing that the "absence" of such a marker is regularly distributed with reference to such modifiers as numerals. James A. Harrison in "Negro English" (*Anglia*, 1884) wrote that "the plural is often omitted" (p. 245); such a statement is, of course, correct to a certain extent but inadequate. At that, Harrison made a better showing than did

dialect geographers Raven I. and Virginia Glenn McDavid eighty
years later. In "Plurals of Nouns of Measure in the United States"
(*Studies in Language and Linguistics in Honor of Charles C.
Fries*, 1964), McDavid and McDavid attribute the use of "the
uninflected plural" to "a literary stereotype of Negro speech" and
point out that relatively few of the *Linguistic Atlas* Negro
informants outside Gullah territory attested "uninflected" plurals.
What they should have said, of course, is that *none* of the
informants manifested "uninflected" plurals—although some of
them did have *non-redundant* pluralization. Judging from the
faulty sampling procedures of the Atlas project from which their
data is drawn (as pointed by Glenna Ruth Pickford, "American
Linguistic Geography: A Sociological Appraisal," *Word*, 1956),
it is in fact rather surprising that even a little evidence as to the
structure was found. On the other hand, those who trust their
ears in preference to faulty sampling procedure have been aware
of its existence since at least the early eighteenth century.

An Atlas-oriented work like William Edward Farrison's *The
Phonology of the Illiterate Negro Dialect of Guilford County,
North Carolina* (Ohio State U. dissertation, 1936) lists such
forms, as

> forty year
> twenty bushel   (p. 202)

but as "only" syntactic and inflectional matters, not as factors of
phonology. This outmoded approach to linguistics, now followed
only by dialect geographers, was actually *designed* to miss grammatical features—or to label them as unimportant.

So far no attention has been given to such a frequently emphasized factor as the "lack" of a final -*s* on the third person singular
verb form in the "present tense." (One reason is that, as indicated
earlier, this analysis does not recognize a "present tense" in Black
English.) It seems preferable to rest the case on the statement
that the verbal categories are entirely different; it is even predictable that further research will indicate that they differ even
more greatly from the verbal categories of Standard English

than has been indicated above. That certain studies have started—and virtually ended—with a factor like the -*s* verb ending is merely an indication of the superficiality of those studies.

Much more important work still remains to be done on the clause structures of Black English. One of the things which the observer of ghetto speech soon learns is that, while the children say things on the order of

> Can he go?

they also form questions like

> Why she ain' over here?

The first question, superficially identical to Standard English, would be incorporated into a subordinate clause in quite a different fashion:

> I don't know can he go.

That sentence is a virtually exact equivalent of Standard English

$$I \text{ don't know} \begin{Bmatrix} \text{if} \\ \text{whether} \end{Bmatrix} \text{he can go}$$

and not any kind of incorporating of a kind of indirect quotation. Experiments have been performed with the purpose of testing how a child who says *I don't know can he go* fares on repetition tests when the model sentence is *I don't know if he can go*. Predictably, linguists like William Labov of the University of Pennsylvania have found that the Black English speaker becomes confused, stops and ponders the sentence, and then tends to put the repetition into his own structure.

Stewart and Baratz recently improved upon the Labov experiment. They gave a sentence like *I don't know can he go* to speakers of Standard English for repetition. Predictably, these middle-class white children hesitated, stammered, became confused, and finally said the sentence in their own language system. It is no secret that even memory of linguistic forms is subject to the grammar of the speaker being tested.

Nothing in the above two paragraphs should be construed to mean that there is no conjunction *if* in Black English; there most certainly is, and any reader who takes the trouble to listen to ghetto speakers for a while will almost certainly hear it. That brings up the reason for the perhaps pedantic inclusion of the *whether* option in (3) above: Black English "lacks" only that *if* which is so replaceable. In other words, Black English constructions like

> (I don' know) can he go

are not "adverbial" *if* clauses but "noun" subordinate clauses acting as objects of a verb. There is, however, a Black English sub-type on the order of

> A man get rich, he still pay taxes.

Standard English has the same clause type, with an initial *if* which can be deleted in casual speech; but the difference is greater than might appear from such statements. Adding an intensifier *even*, the speaker of Standard English must express the "underlying" *if*; a speaker of Black English need not do so.

> Standard English: Even if a man gets rich, he still pays taxes.
>
> Black English: Even a man get rich, he still pay taxes.

The greater differences, however, are found in those clause types where Standard English indicates the clause as object relationship by *if* or *whether* and regular statement word order; in the comparable type, Black English indicates the relational function by the *can he go* word order, without any conjunction.

Despite examples of the type given in the last paragraph, we can certainly find many of the "adverbial" clause types beginning with *if* in Black English. That they are the result of code-switching is one possibility; another is that they have a differential distribution which will not become apparent except under very careful observation. Some of the examples below (from Botkin's extremely useful collection) happen to have the conjunction form *iffen*, which is a specialized—perhaps even local—development in Black English and in other varieties of English. Otherwise, the following seem to work just like Standard English "adverbial" clauses with *if*:

> He say iffen he ever hear of him doing any more preaching or praying round mongst the niggers at graveyard or anywhere else, he gwine lash him to death. (p. 71)

> And, too, she would get the doctor iffen she think they real bad off. (*Ibid.*)

> If a slave die, Massa made the rest of us tie a rope round he feet and drag him off. (p. 76)

> If my memorandum [memory] am correct, it am about thirty year since I come to Fort Worth. (p. 162)

It seems rather obvious that the Fancy Talk—"malapropism"— characteristics of *memorandum* and *it am* are indicative of an attempt to talk in a fashion not entirely familiar to the speaker; the *if* conjunction may be due to the same factor. At any rate, any observer with open ears may amuse himself by listening to speakers of Black English and observing constructions which prestigious linguists have declared not to exist.

There are many more structural details of Black English which have not received the detailed analysis which has been given to relatively unimportant features of Standard English. Adequate attention is not likely to be given to them unless someone sets up a major research project which is not designed to prove the preconceptions of the Establishment. Differences from the structure of Standard English can be masked behind differences in the base forms for Black English, especially in the verb system. Although Black English speakers who use some Standard English can be heard using *fill, filled, filling*, etc., the basilect verb base is not *fill* but *full*; that is

> He fullin' de tank

is a grammatical sentence in Black English. In Gullah, and perhaps in other varieties, *lef* (sometimes taken as the reduced form of *left*) is the verb base; *leave* is not really in Gullah, and was not in the antecedent Plantation Creole. There are multiple opportunities for misunderstandings, as in the example cited in Botkin, where a young field hand brought into the kitchen was instructed to *heat* a dish of "hopping John." Instructions in the youth's own dialect should have been to *hot* the dish; striving to obey orders, the youth ate the food. For once, according to this anecdote (p. 50), the misunderstanding did not result in punishment of the slave. So far, there has been no opportunity to conduct the kind of exhaustive research which is needed to find out the distribution of these forms in basilect; we do have some hints from the structure of Gullah and from analogous stages of varieties like Jamaican Creole.

The derivational processes (i.e., the processes which make Standard English verb *inherit* into noun *inheritance* or verb *describe* into noun *description* and adjective *descriptive*) are very different in Black English; witness sentences like

> . . . they ain't no one to 'heritance 'em.   (Botkin, p. 154)

> A little thoughtful would have saved us all this trouble.
> > (Bedford-Stuyvesant child's response
> > to ill-designed workbook exercise)

> . . . for understandment . . .   (A Beaumont, Texas, informant)

The difference in verb derivation patterns is largely responsible for what is often taken for "disorder" in the use of verbs by Negro children in such sentences as

> I fed him [the dog] when I wanna fed him.
> > (A Washington, D. C., informant)

Similarities may be illusory; the use of "standard" vowel change preterite forms (*sang, sank*) with past time specification may not be as regular as it seems, since some of these forms may be basilect base forms. The possibilities of misinterpretation are fantastically and frighteningly high. Only some very careful, high-level research can determine the exact nature of Black English in this respect. Although the linguist usually adopts the working principle that grammar is separate from vocabulary (the lexicon), there are obvious ways in which the separation is only that of the convenient fiction according to which any scholarly discipline occasionally has to proceed. (The ultimate test is whether it becomes "inconvenient"—whether it brings more problems into the analysis than it eliminates.) A dictionary enterprise comparable in scope to that of *Webster's Third* would solve many problems for the analyst of Black English, and the importance of the dialect is certainly great enough to warrant that much attention.

As suggested already, the similarity between Black English conjunctions and those of Standard English is a deceptive one. There is no real evidence to support the oft-made contention that Black English is simpler in its relational structure because its clauses are connected by *and* rather than by more precise conjunctions. Its conjunctions are different, and the unwary observer may miss them altogether. For example, the conjunction *time* [tã·m] is often rationalized as a reduction of Standard English *by the time that*. The rough translation works in such sentences as

> Time we get there they be gone

but fails in such sentences as

> I made you a livin', gal, time I was free

sung by a prisoner to his faithless woman in a folk blues. Other examples which cannot be explained in terms of the Standard English phrase are easy to find:

> Time she said it he jumped up from the table.   (Botkin, p. 178)

There is no reason to doubt that this *time* derives etymologically from Standard English; but it got its distribution (its "meaning," which approximates Standard English *when*) elsewhere. The effect that it produces—of understandings mixed with misunderstandings in conversations between speakers of Black English and of Standard English—is typical of the entire relationship.

The correlative conjunctions have an equally subtle difference in Black English. Instead of *either X or Y*, we find *X or either Y*.

(*I can go swimming or either cut yards.*) An approximate equivalent of *neither X nor Y* is the negative (*It ain'*) *X neither Y.* These
structures, particularly the former, are less subject to age-grading
than are some other typically Black English grammatical patterns.
And of course they are not limited to specific regions.

The relative clause patterns are also a great deal different. In
Black English, we find abundant sentences like

He got a gun sound like a bee.

(A Washington, D.C., informant)

There was one woman owns some slaves . . .   (Botkin, p. 7)

I has a uncle was one of the world's heavyweight contenders.

(Farrison dissertation, p. 270, transliterated)

Constructions of this type occur in Jamaican Creole and in other
Afro-American dialects. Cassidy (*Jamaica Talk*, p. 57) compares
Jamaican Creole to the "Niger-Congo" (Greenberg's Niger-Khar-
dofanian) languages in this respect.

When Black English does introduce relative connectors, it often
uses *what* where Standard English would use *who*. In addition,
there are many occurrences of sentences like

He got a gun which it sound like a bee

where the pronoun subject of the sentence seems structurally
superfluous. It seems likely that Black speakers are here trying
to imitate Standard English and not quite succeeding in using
the unfamiliar syntactic structure; Jamaican Creole, again, does
the same thing. The example given above is contrived to show the
comparison to the first example in the preceding paragraph; it is
easy enough to find genuine examples:

Dem little bitty hat what dey wearin' 'em now.

(A Beaumont, Texas, informant)

My youngest sister, what live in Georgia, writ me about a year ago.
(Botkin, p. 77)

There was a white man named Mr. Bruce what axed . . .
(Botkin, p. 232)

What as a relative also occurs in Gullah; the following trans-literated example is quoted from Turner:

> ... we what been on the place ... (p. 267)

The prepositions of Black English are unlike those of Standard English, but in subtle ways which demand careful analysis. The inventory of prepositions is the same, but their distribution is greatly different; unwary educators may be led to believe that their Black students "lack positional concepts." We find such prepositions as *out* (for Standard English *out of*) *the house: Put the cat out the house*, as well as *The dress is made outta wool* (never *of wool*). It is not, however, accurate to say that Black English simply "reverses" the Standard English usage. Phrases like *over Granma's house* are used where Standard English would have *over at* (or *to*). *She teach Francis Pool* is the equivalent of Standard English *She teaches at Francis Pool*; in order to interpret the sentence, of course, one must know that there is such a place as Francis Pool (in Washington, D. C.), and that the girl under discussion teaches swimming there.

This slight mismatch in prepositions with Standard English is the result of historical approximation from the pidgin/creole stages of much greater differences. Pidgins tend to have a reduced inventory of prepositions, although they seem to do all right with them. There is also a tendency for a pidgin to have one universal preposition: Melanesian *blong* (possibly from the English verb *belong* or from a phrase like *belonging to*), WesKos *fo'* (possibly, although not necessarily, from English *for*). There are also many cases in which pidgin/creoles manage to indicate positional relationships without the prepositions which Standard English considers necessary.

On the borderline, perhaps, between structure and vocabulary are the expressions *here go* [hɪgo] and *dere go* [dægo], which are very like French *voici* and *voilà*, respectively. A great deal of nonsense attaches to these questions, such as the pseudo-sociology that "the culture is motion-oriented." There are also teachers who attempt to "correct" the student's *Here go a table* by saying, "The table isn't *going* anywhere." This has all the logic about it of forbidding a blind Frenchman to say *voici* or *voilà*. The twelve-year-old bidialectal boy mentioned elsewhere spontaneously translated, when given cues like "Talk like your mother" and "Talk like your playmates," between *Here go/there go* and *Here is (are)/there is (are)*.

Not all informants are so cooperative, probably because of painful experience in having their language habits labeled "inferior." A Danish dialectologist who attempted to elicit the form from Harlem boys, using his foreign accent to advantage and saying that "He thought he heard" the form *Here go a man and a lady* in response to a picture showing a definitely stationary couple, was somewhat testily informed that the phrase was *Here are a man and a lady*. The sentence was pronounced with ultra-formality: the indefinite article was [ey] (the "dictionary pronunciation" of the letter) in both cases, and *lady* was pronounced [leyt^hiy] with the aspirated *t* which is usual in English only at the beginning of words, or at the end in somewhat affected speech. Yet the Harlem boy's reaction against the "accusation" that such a form was used was only that much more proof that it is quite commonplace.

NOTES

[1] The category of Black English resulting from a composite of the features described in this chapter would be what Stewart has called *basilect* ("Urban Negro Speech: Sociolinguistic Factors Affecting English Teaching" —see Bibliography). In its "pure" form it is characteristic only of very young speakers—but speakers who are beyond language acquisition. Unfortunately, there is some tendency, even in the Black community, to label such features as "baby talk"; that is, to imply that the speakers are still learning lan-

guage. See Chapter VI for a fuller discussion of "Who Speaks Black English?"

[2] *Informant* is the technical term for the native speaker from whom the linguist elicits information. Informants are paid for their work, and such a job was a very attractive one for the children who furnished a great deal of the information contained herein. There are certain linguistic dangers inherent in such work (e.g., an informant may be over-cooperative and try to say what the linguist expects to hear), and there is a large technical literature on how to elicit accurate linguistic data. (In dealing with Non-Standard English or with creole languages the problems are compounded, since informants may try to supply the kind of language advocated by the schools rather than their natural language.) There is also an unwritten code of ethics as to what kind of information will be made public (for example, the linguist will not reveal—nor look for—anything about the personal life of the informant).

[3] *Redundancy* is a mildly technical linguistic term which has none of the opprobrium attached to it in school grammars. It is a common principle in linguistics that languages differ in the amount of redundancy they have in specific sub-systems. In English *the old men,* the information unit "plural" is conveyed once; in Spanish *los hombres viejos,* the plural signal is conveyed three times (all the final *-s's*). In this one particular English is less redundant than Spanish.

[4] Bracketed letters indicate that the symbols refer to sound units and not to graphic units. Thus, Standard English words which have graphic *-s*, like *runs, sends,* and *goes,* have [z] in pronunciation; *rats, rocks,* and *cuts* have [s].

In this particular treatment, no formal account is taken of the phonemic sound-contrastive nature of a sound, which is often signaled by enclosure in / / , and the allophonic (or non-contrastive) use, usually marked in linguistic literature by enclosure in [   ]. (An example of a pair of English phonemes would be the initial sounds of *pat* and *bat;* a substitution of one of the sounds for the other is "significant" in that it entails a change in meaning. If you have a good ear, even though you are monolingual, you can hear that the allophonic "t's" in *tot,* as naturally pronounced, are not quite identical, and that neither is identical to the medial consonant in *totter.* If you have ever heard a Spanish-speaking person say *bowels* when he obviously meant *vowels,* you may suspect [v] and [b] are not in phonemic contrast in Spanish.) The theoretical motivation for this practice is that the nature of phonological notation is changing radically under the influence of the new Chomsky-Halle phonology (*The Sound Pattern of English,* 1968). More practically, it is felt that the average reader of this book will not be concerned about such matters.

[5] In this case, Standard English *I have been knowing him a long time* is a reasonably accurate translation of the Black English sentence. It should not be concluded, however, that *have* has been merely "dropped"

from Black English. In a sentence like *You been know that*, it is impossible
to achieve a Standard English equivalent by adding *have*.

[6] *I been know* can be translated by Standard English *I knew*, except
that the Black English form is more emphatically in the past.

[7] The immediate perfective force of *done* is best approximated by
Spanish *acabo de* or French *je viens de*. There are rather minute shades
of meaning expressed in the variation between *done go, done went*, and
done gone. The first would be used in an immediately present time reference; the second as an immediate perfective in a past time; and the third
in a quasi-adjectival type of structure.

[8] See notes 6 and 7 above.

[9] *Appositive* is used here in the same sense as in school grammar, where
it means a noun (or pronoun) placed next to another noun and having
the same referent: *Mr. Smith, the teacher; Mr. Nixon, the President; my
friend he.* Schoolboy (white) Non-Standard English has a genuine apposi-
tional use of such forms as *my sister she . . .* which are superficially like
the Black English forms. The white schoolboy forms, however, do not
participate in more complex structures like

The boy sit over there got a pencil in he hand he my friend.

[10] *Nominative* is also used in the same sense as in school grammars, in
traditional grammatical works on English, and in works on Latin, French,
etc. (*Je* is nominative; *moi* "oblique"). The undifferentiated pronoun (*me,
you, him, her, us, you, them*) is often called the "accusative" or "objective"
form in school and traditional grammars. It is noteworthy that French Creole
uses the undifferentiated form *mwê* (Haiti) or *mo* (Louisiana), each of
which probably derives from French *moi*, as a subject form:

                    mwê remé ou   'I love you'

III

A Sketch of the History
of Black English

THE grammar of Black English basilect (the variety described
in Chapter II) is so similar to that of certain other Afro-
American varieties of English that the temptation to look for
historical connections has been irresistible to the small band of
linguists who have interested themselves in the problem. But the
most immediate solution which suggests itself—direct influence
from the African languages spoken by the slaves—proves to be
too simple and is made to seem unlikely by the language-mixing
practices of the slave dealers. The conventional suggestion of the
dialect geographers—that dialect forms were taken from widely
scattered areas of the British Isles to form Black English—is even
less likely in view of dialect leveling, a very well-known phenomenon in migration which means that even the white residents
of colonial America did not speak or transmit British "regional"
dialects.[1]

For the mixing of African language groups, we have the evidence of statements like that of slave ship Captain William Smith
in 1744:

> As for the languages of *Gambia*, they are so many and so different,
> that the Natives, on either Side the River, cannot understand each
> other; which, if rightly consider'd, is no small Happiness to the

> *Europeans* who go thither to trade for slaves . . . I have known some
> melancholy Instances of whole Ship Crews being surpriz'd, and cut
> off by them. But the safest Way is to trade with the different Na-
> tions, on either Side the River, and having some of every Sort on
> board, there will be no more Likelihood of their succeeding in a Plot,
> than of finishing the Tower of Babel.
>
> (*A New Voyage to Guinea*, p. 28)

Smith's statement can be matched by the statements of John
Atkins (see Bibliography) and others of the same period. It may
be noted that, among other things, they document the *lack* of
such language mixing in the early slave trade. Thus, language
mixing developed later, after some of the crews had learned the
hard way that the Africans did not welcome being enslaved.
(Smith explained this aversion by the Africans' laziness!) It
therefore seems entirely probable that some of the slave ships
contained relatively homogeneous linguistic groups. In some cases
the circumstances of slave trading brought further mixing after
the arrival of the slaves in the New World. But some slave buyers
learned to prefer Africans from specific tribes and areas, and the
language mixing practiced on the slave ships was sometimes
counteracted in the markets of the Americas. Thus, African languages survived in the New World for a time. David Dalby (see
Bibliography) has documented the widespread use of Wolof,
which seems to have a special *lingua franca* status among West
African languages, in the thirteen colonies.

Although many of the slaves may not have had to relinquish
their African languages immediately, they all found themselves
in a situation in which they had to learn an auxiliary language in
a hurry in order to establish communication in the heterogeneous
groups into which they were thrown. This mixing of speakers of
a large number of languages, with no one language predominant,
is the perfect condition for the spread of a pidgin language, which
is in a sense the ultimate in auxiliary languages. In the colonies
which became the early United States, Pidgin English served
the purpose of a *lingua franca* (see Glossary) in a very complicated language contact situation. In Louisiana, as we can tell

from historical records as well as from the current use by Black people of the French Creole sometimes called "Gombo," Pidgin French filled that function. Like Pidgin French, Pidgin English also played an important role in many other areas of European maritime expansion which are not noted for the presence of African slaves (the Hawaiian Islands, the China Sea, Melanesia, Pitcairn Island, etc.).

The term "pidgin" is not well understood, and many people feel—without cause—insulted when told that their ancestors depended upon such a language. From the point of view of the linguist, such a feeling is irrational. A pidgin language has rules (regular principles of sentence construction) like any other language. Syntactic rules of a high order of regularity can be written for any pidgin, and those rules will generate an infinite number of new sentences. On the other hand, certain sequences would not be grammatical according to the rules of the pidgin. For example,

*He go—not

is ungrammatical in some pidgins, as well as in Standard English. In short, pidgins are not formed by distortions of the syntactic patterns of the "standard" language, even if the prejudice of Europeans has usually led them to conclude that this is true.[2]

It is often maintained that a pidgin is a simple language, and this may be accurate in a way that is all to the credit of the pidgin. It is designed to be used by diverse linguistic groups. It tends to "lose" or "rid itself of" (whichever expression you prefer, since both are metaphorical) the more finicky, trivial features of language. Pidgin French doesn't have all those troublesome masculine and feminine forms for adjectives, and Pidgin English doesn't have all those irksome irregular verbs. In more important language features—like the formation of questions, commands, subordinated sentence patterns, and even in potentialities for sentence complexity—a pidgin is very like any other language. It may come to be used primarily for trade, since it is used entirely with outsiders. And nobody gets sentimental or emotional about a pidgin, or rebukes you for misusing his language. Since children do not grow up using it, it is a language primarily for adults.

When the African slaves produced children, there was no one African language which those children could use with their peer group. Even though the mothers (or fathers) spoke African languages and may in some cases have taught them to their offspring, the children would have found little use for those languages. With their playmates they would have used the common language—in some cases Pidgin English, which is classified as an English Creole as soon as it has such native speakers. (Gullah, or "Geechee," of the South Carolina-Georgia Sea Islands, survives in the creole stage today.) English Creole now acquires developmental forms, since there are young children who are learning to speak it. People can now become sentimental or emotional about it, since it is "their" language. It fills all the purposes of the normal speech community, including different styles and different modes associated with greater or lesser prestige. Vocabulary needs ("deficiencies") will be made up by borrowing from other languages, from Standard English or from the African languages of the adults, just as it's done with all other languages. The creole is now a full-fledged language like any other. It just happens to have a pidgin in its ancestry.[3]

Since statements like the above are not usually made except by specialists in pidgin and creole languages, we do not expect to find a document saying "West African Pidgin English completed the creolization process in Blacksburg, Virginia, on April 2, 1698" or anything to that effect. Drawing historical conclusions requires a certain amount of ingenuity on the part of the language historian, including, one hopes, an ability to interpret the statements of non-professionals. Perhaps the very first such statement of use to the historian of Black English is the reference to the use of English on the West Coast of Africa in a Portuguese text of 1594. In view of the general conditions of the West African slave trade, it seems reasonable to believe that Pidgin English was in use in the slave trade by the beginning of the seventeenth century, if not slightly earlier. Its chief competitor was Pidgin

Portuguese, which almost certainly antedated it by at least a few years and which had an amazing, world-wide spread during the sixteenth, seventeenth, and eighteenth centuries. The English-based pidgins have a certain amount of vocabulary (*pickaninny*, for example) from the Portuguese Trade Pidgin, and those forms of Afro-American English which have undergone least decreolization (Saramaccan, in Surinam)[4] have the greatest amount of Portuguese vocabulary.

Slaves coming to the New World by 1620 must have had some means of communicating with their masters and among themselves. A little reflection will show that the latter is probably the more important consideration. Spokesmen could be appointed who would convey the orders of the master to the great masses of slaves, and the spokesmen may have been more or less fluent in the language of the masters. But the masses of slaves still had to communicate among themselves and with the spokesmen, and a *lingua franca* or the European language of the masters constituted almost the only alternatives. Since there is an abundance of documentary evidence that they did not use the latter, it follows that they must have had some language of wider communication—the job for which a pidgin is eminently qualified. The surviving texts of the speech of slaves corroborate the hypothesis that Pidgin English was the language of the masses of slaves in what is now the continental United States. The early evidence suggests that it was as widespread in the northern states as in the South.

The Early Period

From the very early period—1620 to almost 1700—little indirect and no direct evidence of the speech of slaves survives in such manuscripts as have been printed; the search through letters, journals, etc., is only beginning, however. The period can be known, at present, only through comparison and reconstruction. There is parallel evidence from Pidgin French (called *Petit Nègre*), which came to the New World at about the same time; Goodman's *A Comparative Study of Creole French Dialects* prints Caribbean texts from 1640 to 1659. The English-based pidgin must have been spreading during that period, and it was probably very like what appears in the early documents.[5] It is also possible to draw the same conclusion through comparison to American Indian Pidgin English, attestations of which are abundant from about the third quarter of the seventeenth century.

By 1715 there clearly was an African Pidgin English known on a worldwide scale. Defoe utilized it in *The Family Instructor* (1715) and in *The Life of Colonel Jacque* (1722), in conversations like

> "Yes, yes ... me know, me know but me want speak, me tell something. O! me no let him makee de great master angry."
>
> (*Colonel Jacque*, p. 152)

as well as in the early chapters of *Robinson Crusoe* (1719). The Virginia and Maryland Negroes in *The Life of Colonel Jacque* speak the same Pidgin English which Defoe attributes to his other Africans; the white indentured servants who work beside them speak an entirely different variety of English. Attestations of the same or a related Pidgin or Creole English in Surinam date from about the same period.

In the United States (then, of course, the British Colonies) the court records of the testimony of Tituba (1692), the journal of Sarah Kemble Knight (1704–5), and a treatise on small pox by Cotton Mather (1721) provide the first known examples. These were not authors of fiction, but neither were they skilled dialect collectors; it is, therefore, necessary to separate the pidgin materials from other material recorded in the authors' own dialects. It is one of the more ludicrous facets of the situation that, following the Mencken-McDavid line of reasoning, we would have to say that the author of *Magnalia Christi Americana* was influenced by the minstrel show tradition.

In spite of the fact that it is hard to think of anyone more distant from show business, Mather was apparently being more or less light and humorous when he included pidgin forms like *grandy-many* (with the added, or enclitic, vowel), *cutty-skin* (enclitic vowel, "absence" of article—the phrase means 'cut the skin'), *by 'nd by* (probably *bimeby*, a future time adverbial of almost universal spread in Pidgin English), and *nobody have smallpox any more* (invariant verb form) in an indirect quotation. Mather begins the passage containing the quotation by saying, "I have since met with a considerable number of these Africans," the implication of "since" being apparently that the meetings had gone on over some period of time. Pidgin English as spoken by the Africans would, then, be a speech variety with which Mather had long been familiar. He knew enough about his African servants to indicate that one was of the "Guramante" (Coromantee) tribe, and in general seems thoroughly familiar with the background of the people about whom he provides information.

African Pidgin English may well have been in use in the United States long before the time of Mather's attestation. It is not, at any rate, the first. Tituba, the Barbadian slave who became famous at the Salem witch trial and who may have been part Carib Indian as well as African, must have spoken an Afro-American English variety. The "peculiar chirography" of Justice Hathorne, who recorded the testimony, contained a great deal of what is self-evidently the Justice's own language:

> With the man who hath pretty things more besides
> (Drake, *The Witchcraft Delusion in New England*, p. 278)

But he also recorded sentences like

I no hurt them at all.	(p. 271)
He tell me he God.	(p. 290)
They told me serve him.	(p. 277)

Arthur Miller, who put West Indian Creole English into the mouth of Tituba in *The Crucible*, may have been historically accurate.

Justices figure in another source earlier than Mather. In Sarah

Kemble Knight's journal (1705), a senior justice tells an Indian "It's a grandy Wicked thing to steal." The inappropriateness is pointed out immediately: "Justice Junr" objects, "Brother, you speak Negro to him." (The entire passage will be quoted in Chapter IV.) The indications are that by 1705, Negro Pidgin and American Indian Pidgin English had become differentiated enough so that some whites knew the difference and were more or less capable of speaking one or both of the pidgin varieties. "Senior Justice" speaks in English very like Mather's later example, the enclitic vowel on *grandy* being the clearest indication of the pidgin stage. *Grandy*, derived either from Portuguese or from the common Romance vocabulary of *Lingua Franca*, may have been the reason why "Justice Junr" concluded that his colleague "spoke Negro to him." Note that it also occurs (*grandy-many*) in the text from Cotton Mather. This is good counter-evidence to the notion that Englishmen "simplified" their English and taught it to the Africans and the Indians: here is a white who doesn't know the rules of Pidgin English, another who claims to know them but isn't very impressive in his performance, and an Indian who really speaks the language. Mrs. Knight says nothing about minstrel shows, and it seem rather unlikely that she ever attended one.

Black characters had apparently found their way into show business, however, by 1771. In the farcical *Trial of Atticus Before Justice Beau, for a Rape*, set in Massachusetts, Caesar, "one of our neighbour's Negroes," has two brief speeches:

> Yesa, Maser, he tell me that Atticus he went to bus 'em one day, and a shilde cry, and so he let 'em alone. (p. 22)

> Cause, Maser, I bus *him* myself. (*Ibid.*)

In these two brief passages, the pidgin/creole characteristic of non-differentiation of pronoun genders (*he, 'em,* and *him* all referring to a Mrs. Chuckle) is clearly indicated. There is also the noun classifier *he* (*Atticus he*) and some probable African language phonological interference (*shilde* for *childe*). Even the apparently inconsistent spellings *Yesa* (*Yes sir*) and *Maser*

Te joe matie kong na ienie

Joe hoso. njang ,dringie

nanga ing ,mano poeroe

joe granbere djie ing

Sranan Tongo ("Taki Taki") of Surinam—plaques for sale at Puru Pangi ("Place Where One May Pull Off the Loin Cloth") marketplace in Paramaribo. Dutch orthographic practices (*joe* for *you*) make this appear more different from Gullah—Negro Non-Standard than it is. It could be "translated" approximately:

> Time you mate (friend) come in you house, eat (nyam), drink with him, but no pull (out) you grand belly give him (i.e., "Don't tell your innermost secrets!")

(*Master*) probably reflect some care on the part of the author: *Sah* and (*Mass*)*uh* might be used by modern authors to indicate the differing pronunciations of the two final syllables. *Bus* (*buss*) 'kiss', although not unusual in the British English of the period, has survived in the Jamaican Creole and Sranan Tongo of today.

Little or nothing besides these attestations exists to guide an interpretation of the early period.[6] Whatever else may be said about the dating, however, it is transparently obvious that a language variety must come into existence at some time before it is recorded or transcribed. If we did not apply such reasoning to Old English, we might come to the conclusion that it was not spoken before about 700; but historians of Germanic languages speak confidently about much earlier stages. Pidgin languages apparently arise under different, even cataclysmic, conditions, so that exactly analogous statements probably should not be made. But it seems quite reasonable that Negro Pidgin (the name is one of convenience, and is chosen more or less in honor of "Justice Junr") should have existed, in approximately the same form attested in these early sources, in the colonies before 1650. It is not excessive to assume that it was spoken in the area for sixty-five or seventy years before a Massachusetts clergyman or a traveling diarist got around to recording examples of it. There had been Africans in the area for that long or longer, and we can be sure that they spoke *something*, even if the Puritan fathers didn't see fit to record what they spoke. They undoubtedly had cultural problems too; but the Puritans didn't record those either, except insofar as they left records of their own confusion at and misinterpretation of what were very probably the voodoo rituals practiced by Tituba.

Some of the cultural practices were certainly African, although by a special quirk of the history of scholarship the notion that African cultural patterns were completely destroyed has been most persistently argued by Negro scholars like E. Franklin Frazier (see Bibliography, Section III). Frazier is correct in his insistence that the salient social division of the slave community— the distinction between the house servants, who learned the master's culture and language, and the field hands, who didn't—was imposed upon the slaves by their owners. But there can no longer be any reasonable doubt that some African cultural patterns survived and that their influences are still to be seen in the Black communities of even large northern cities. It is very important to note that even African social stratification persisted in some cases. In 1638 John Josselyn noted, on the first of his two voyages to New England, that a Negro slave to a Mr. Maverick

... had been a Queen in her own Country, and [I] observed a very humble and dutiful garb [behavior] used towards her by another Negro who was her maid.

(*An Account of Two Voyages to New England*, p. 26)

Josselyn noted that this former queen knew little or no English of any variety; although he did not say so, it is quite possible that the maid performed the duties of interpreter ("linguist"). African tribal chieftains or kings frequently utilize the services of such "linguists."

One of the African social institutions which clearly survived was that of the *lingua franca,* a matter of as great importance in polygot West Africa as in the foreign language surroundings of the New World.[7] The fact that the *lingua franca* utilized was European-based (Pidgin English in English-speaking territory; Pidgin French in French-speaking Louisiana and certain Caribbean Islands; Pidgin Portuguese in some other parts of the Caribbean) does not make the essential social process involved any less an African one. Thus, to an extent undreamed of by those who have not lifted their eyes above East Anglia, the establishment of West African Pidgin English in the thirteen colonies and in the United States took place through African resources. Creolization was also largely independent of the white man's language influence. Decreolization, on the other hand, would almost by definition be traceable to the influence of the white man's English. The white man's contribution came late; but, with characteristic ethnocentrism, he assumed that it had been the only influence.

There have been frequent arguments to the contrary. Allen Walker Read's "The Speech of Negroes in Colonial America" (*Journal of Negro History,* 1939), quoting advertisements for runaway slaves placed in newspapers by their masters in the eighteenth century, has suggested that because many of the advertisements specify that the slave "speaks good English," the slaves must all have learned English immediately and "perfectly"—that is, of the variety spoken by their owners. This evidence has often been taken to prove that the English of the slaves of the early period was identical to that of the whites and that, therefore, such differences as those of Gullah must have developed thereafter. As Stewart has pointed out, however, it is necessary to evaluate the evidence in terms of what the owners meant by the term *good English.* It is quite possible that they meant something like 'English which can be understood' or even 'good English—for a slave.' Since the frame of reference of comparison to other slaves had already been established by the advertising medium itself, there is no chance that anyone would make the mistake of interpreting the phrase to mean that the English of the fugitive slaves was being compared to that of non-slaves.

Furthermore, there is some variability in the judgments given about the English of the runaways in those advertisements. In Read's article, in "Eighteenth Century Slaves As Advertised by Their Masters" (*Journal of Negro History*, 1916), and in Harriet Beecher Stowe's *A Key to Uncle Tom's Cabin* (1853), such advertisements have been cited. Ratings of the English of the slaves run from

very good English	(*Journal of Negro History*, 1916, p.164)
pretty good English	(p. 166)
speaks proper English	(p. 168)

to

speaks English though somewhat Negroish	(p. 175)
He speaks remarkably good English for a Negro	(p. 170)
speaks rather more proper than Negroes in general	(p. 172)

The rather clear implications of wordings like these is that some owners, at least, were familiar with the use of a somewhat different variety of English by Negroes.* It would be impossible to equate evaluations like "proper English" and "Negroish English" with such terms as *Standard English* and *Plantation Creole*, the term used in this book for the English Creole of the slaves. But we do see from both types of evidence that something was going on.

Yet, as Read pointed out in his article, the majority of these advertisements do indicate that the runaways spoke "good English"—a term which Europeans seemingly never apply to a pidgin and almost never to a creole. Although there may have

* Advertisements of another type contain wordings like "To be sold . . . Four young Negroe Men slaves and a Girl, who . . . speak very good (Black-) English" (*South Carolina Gazette*, March 30, 1734, quoted by Hennig Cohen, *American Speech* [1952], p. 282).

been an unstated modifier "for a Negro," the implication of the
term *good English* would be 'rather like the English of a white
man.'

The sociolinguistic implication here is that the runaways were
likely to be just those slaves who did attain a relative mastery of
Standard English. A runaway usually had to traverse a great deal
of territory under favorable circumstances. He might have had
to deal with a great many people who did not understand Plantation Creole. Thus, the ordinary field hand might never risk running away; or if he did, he would run away to the Indians rather
than to the North. Although to some extent the house servants
who acquired the most Standard English were culturally like
and therefore relatively loyal to their masters, the most famous
of the insurrections was led by the Standard English-speaking
house servant Nat Turner. Several of the advertisements cited
by Read specify that the runaways could read and write, useful
skills for a man seeking his freedom and sorely missed ones for a
runaway who lacked them. Reading and writing almost presuppose a certain degree of mastery of Standard English, since
nothing was written for the monodialectal speaker of Plantation
Creole. The poor field hand was not even the destined audience
for the minstrel shows. One of the owners even suggests that
the escapee may have written his own pass, an accomplishment of
obvious value but hardly accessible to the monodialectal speaker
of pidgin or Plantation Creole.

Evidence such as these advertisements seems to establish that
by the early part of the eighteenth century, at least these varieties
of English were in use by Negroes in the thirteen colonies:

> West African Pidgin English
> Plantation Creole
> Standard English

It should not be forgotten that many of the slaves may have
known and used two or more of these varieties of English; whites
who reported on their language were obviously unable to make
the complicated discriminations necessary in recognizing such

phenomena as diglossia and bidialectism. Since those slaves who escaped to the Florida Seminoles transmitted Pidgin English to the Indians but (judging from the evidence of the attestations) spoke Plantation Creole themselves, there is evidence of complicated variation in the English of the Afro-American population as of about 1750.

The advertisements specify that some of the slaves were polyglot (Dutch, French, and Spanish being other languages which some of them knew), and it is reasonable to assume that there were also some bi- or polydialectals among them. (Today, in the West Indies, polyglots are commonplace on Curaçao, polydialectals in Jamaica.) It is certain that a great deal of linguistic adaptability was demanded of the slaves in the early period; there are many records of their acting as interpreters for the linguistically less proficient whites. Quick acquisition of a utilitarian variety of English was regularly more important than the acquisition of a standard variety of English. One of Benjamin Franklin's sales notices advertised

> A likely Negro wench, about 15 years old ... [has] been in the country above a year and talks English.
>
> (Van Doren, *Franklin*, p. 129)

The differentiation of varieties of English used by Black speakers, based most probably upon social factors within the slave community, is evident by the early eighteenth century. It remains fully evident today, although all of the varieties have changed somewhat in the direction of Standard English. Any other condition, then or now, would have had to be the result of the suspension of those orderly historical processes which we know to exist—harsh as they may be when the implications of their effects upon individual human beings are considered.

The Late Eighteenth Century

By the time of the American Revolution, sufficient accounts of the speech of the slaves had been written to permit the historian who is willing to examine the documentary evidence to form a rather clear picture of the total Black language situation in the continental colonies. Some few of the slaves simply did not speak enough English to be understood by Americans or by Englishmen. British visitor J. F. D. Smyth, whose tour coincided with the beginning of the war, bought one servant who proved useless to him.

> ... for he scarcely understood a single word that I said to him, nor did I know one syllable of his language.
> (*A Tour of the United States of America*, I, p. 79)

Selling—at a profit, incidentally—this servant, whom he had purchased in Petersburg, Virginia, Smyth bought another slave named Richmond from a plantation in North Carolina. Richmond was linguistically more satisfactory, although otherwise not perfect. With some amusement Smyth recorded one of the earliest instances of "coppin' a plea":

> Kay, massa, (says he), you just leave me, me sit here, great fish jump up into de canoe, here he be, massa, fine fish, massa; me den very grad; den me sit very still, until another great fish jump into de canoe; but me fall asleep, massa, and no wake till you come; now, massa, me know me deserve flogging, cause if great fish did jump into de canoe, he see me asleep, den he jump out again, and I no catch him; so, massa, me willing now take good flogging.
> (*Ibid.*, p. 121)

Richmond's speech is full of pidgin/creole characteristics (note especially the unmarked verb forms, for which Standard English grammar would often require -*ed* forms), but it was apparently comprehensible to Smyth. Obviously, *his language* as applied to the first servant refers to an African language.

Apparently between these two would be the "great numbers, being Africans" whom Smyth characterized in these terms:

> ... many of the others also speak a mixed dialect between the Guinea and the English.   (*Ibid.*, p. 39)

In this context, "the Guinea" probably means African languages, and a "mixed dialect" between the two would probably be Pidgin English with a great deal of African vocabulary. Many West Africans still use such a "mixed dialect" in language-contact situations—that is, with speakers who would not understand their native African languages.

Other evidence that the pidgin stage is involved comes from the frequent use of *broken* in Europeans' description of the slaves' English—another pattern which can be paralleled from the West Africa of today. In 1790 John Leland wrote,

> Their language is broken, but they understand each other and the whites may gain their ideas.   (*The Virginia Chronicle*, p. 12)

Other British visitors of this period, like John Davis, provided examples of the pidgin or creole speech of the slaves:

> ... and Aunt *Patty*, the Negro cook would remark, "He good cool-mossa that; he not like old Hodgkinson and old Harris, who let the boys out before twelve. He deserve good wages."
> (*Travels of Four Years and a Half in the United States of America During 1798, 1799, 1800, 1801, and 1802*, p. 407)

Like the slaves referred to by Leland, Davis's Patty was from Virginia; but he also quotes some Virginia slaves in Standard or near-Standard English.

The British travelers agree remarkably well with the native American observers in these particulars. Charles William Janson, in the course of narrating a remarkably brutal account of the castration of a male slave who had fancied white women, quoted the emasculated slave as saying,

> Tank ye, massa doctor, you did a me much great good; white or blackee woman, I care not for.   (*Stranger in America*, p. 380)

A few years earlier (c. 1782) Benjamin Franklin, in "Information to Those Who Would Remove to America," had recorded

> Boccarorra [a form of *buckra* 'white man'] make de Black Man workee, make de Horse workee, make de Ox workee, make ebery thing workee; only de Hog. He, de Hog, no workee; he eat, he drink, he walk about, he go to sleep when he please, he libb like a gentle-man.   (*Writings*, ed. Smythe, VII, 606)

Although not with perfect consistency, both Franklin and Janson recorded the enclitic vowel (Janson, *-ee* on *blackee*; Franklin, *-ee* on *workee*).[8] The short quotation from Janson tells little about grammatical structure, but the unmarked verb forms, where Standard English would require the *-s* of the third person singular, present tense, are obvious from Franklin's report. If Janson's evidence can be taken to be reliable, the use of a past tense marker (*did*) had entered the language—perhaps non-redundantly, as in the Black English of today. Franklin's evidence, however, is perfectly consistent with the Pidgin English of a slave who had been born in West Africa or had learned his English entirely from the Black community in the New World.

In the citations by George Philip Krapp (*The English Language in America*, 1925), a great deal of documentation of Black English in this period is presented. He cites, for example, Samuel Low's *Politician Outwitted* (New York, 1789), featuring a Negro character named Cuffy who utters "short passages of Negro dialect which have the common marks of Gullah speech" (I, 256). It is one of Krapp's obvious failings that, under the influence of the dialect geographers, he mistook the part for the whole and kept giving the name "Gullah characteristics" to forms from language varieties which could have no direct relationship to the Sea Islands or to Charleston. He also cites a passage in Black English from "True African Wit," published in the *New Hampshire and Vermont Journal* at Walpole, N. H. (July 26, 1796)—an area which one would be tempted to call a long way from Gullah territory. Frequent attestations from other areas show clearly that the creole was not limited to the Gullah area.

A Black character with the significant (and only in retrospect unfortunate) name of Sambo who appears in J. Murdoch's

Triumphs of Love (1795) has been said (by Quinn, see Bibliography) to be the first American Negro to appear upon the stage. If so, he was soon joined by a host of others. Before 1850 there were many Negro characters in American (as in British) plays, none of them presented as speaking identically to any of the whites around them. Further, very few if any of the characters are from Gullah territory. In John Leacock's *The Fall of British Tyranny* (1796), escaped slaves from "Hamton" and "Nawfolk" expressed murderous feelings for their American owner, a "Cunney [Colonel] Tomsee [Thompson]," which Krapp somewhat priggishly cut from his citation. Cudjo speaks for the slaves:

> Lord Kidnapper—Can you shoot some of them rebels ashore, Major Cudjo?
>
> Cudjo   —Eas, massa, me try.
>
> Lord Kidnapper—Would you shoot your old master, the Colonel, if you could see him?
>
> Cudjo   —Eas, massa, you terra me, me shoot him dead.
>   (p. 333)

The phonology of *terra* 'tell,' along with the grammatical characteristics, marks this as Pidgin English or as very early Plantation Creole.

Incidentally, the British accept the slaves as voluntary manpower, but show them no respect—probably a projection of the author's own attitude. Kidnapper instructs the British sailors to

> Set a guard over them every night, and take their arms from them, for who knows but they may cut our throats.   (p. 333)

In the British sailors' reactions to the slaves and in Leacock's gratuitous exposition of their "disloyalty" in running away, the very early existence of racism is as well documented as the difference in language. Both the language forms used by Cudjo and his hatred of "Cunney Tomsee" are perfectly believable in historical perspective. None of Leacock's white characters speak a similar variety of English.

Around 1780, an especially significant observation was made

by Crèvecoeur in *Letters from an American Farmer,* an observation which has some implications for the interpretation of the entire corpus of attestations of the period. Observing a slave undergoing the horrible punishment of being tied in a cage so that birds may consume him (his eyes are already gone), Crèvecoeur attempts to help the poor man and actually succeeds in giving him water. The slave responds

> "Tankè you whitè man, tankè you, putè some poyson and givè me.
> Two days and me no die; the birds; ah me!"   (p. 224)

The language forms as presented by Crèvecoeur are exactly like other representations, with a couple of exceptions. *Two day* would be expected rather than *two days,* and Crèvecoeur's greater familiarity with Standard English could have distorted his memory there. But his still greater familiarity with French seems to have determined his rendering of the enclitic vowel by grave-accented *-è*.

Can it be maintained that Crèvecoeur took his practice from a literary tradition? If so, what tradition? American and British authors who used the device, and who might be suspected of having fabricated the tradition or of having borrowed it from other authors, used final *-i, -y,* or *-ee* for the enclitic vowel. Crèvecoeur's orthography, in general, is conventional; it does not reflect French practices elsewhere—probably because, as a foreigner who had learned English well, he was eager to conform to all its practices. Yet French orthographic practices show up in his rendering of Pidgin English. Why? The inescapable answer seems to be that he was not following a tradition—that he did not know other works in which Pidgin English was written—but that he was recording, with such resources as were available to him, speech which he had heard from Blacks.

In this context the authenticity of the anecdote, which has been called in question, is not important. For evidence about Black English of the period, so much the better if Crèvecoeur improvised an anecdote from a speech variety with which he had become thoroughly familiar. On the other hand, objection

to the story on the grounds of impossibly harsh treatment of
the slave is hardly convincing. Botkin's *Lay My Burden Down*
(p. 152) contains an ex-slave's account of an offense which concludes, "I knowed it was a blessing for him to die." One might
wonder how, without his eyes to perceive the coming of light
and darkness, the slave knew that he had been punished for two
days; and, since the grammatical form cited by Crèvecoeur is
without the expected grammatical device of non-redundant pluralization, it may well be that he supplied that information from
a later talk with the owner rather than remembering it verbatim
from the speech of the slave. Under the circumstances, Crèvecoeur
may be pardoned for being more concerned about social injustice
than with exact wording.

Another famous attestation is that of Hugh Henry Brackenridge in *Modern Chivalry* (1792). Cuff (probably a shortening
of Cuffee, the day name), a "Guinea Negro," presents a speech
before the Philosophical Society:

> Massa shentiman; I be cash crab in de Wye rive; found ting in de
> mud; tone, big a man's foot: hole like to he; fetch Massa: Massa
> say, it be de Indian Mocasson.—Oh! fat de call it all tone. He say,
> you be a filasafa, Cuff! I say, O no, Massa, you be de filasafa. Wel;
> two tree monts afta, Massa call me, and say, You be a filasafa, Cuff,
> fo' sartan: Getta ready, and go dis city, and make grate peech for
> shentima filasafa . . .

In this quite long speech, only part of which is reproduced
here, Cuff illustrates what must be early Plantation Creole characteristics. In only one or two cases are there enclitic vowels,
although Pidgin English pronunciation patterns are retained in
words like *tone, peech* (*stone, speech*). But his language is also
somewhat innovative in that the durative *be* seems to be developing: *I be cash* means that the catching of crabs went on
during the period of time that surrounded the action of *found*,
but the obligatory association of *-ing* with the following verb
base has not yet developed. *I be filasafa, you be filasafa* are
permanent (or at least long-term) attributes expressed with
durative *be*; the zero copula of short-term attribution occurs elsewhere in the speech. Also observable is the non-obligatory nature

of tense marking, which makes possible not only *found* but also *say* and *call* as verb forms with past time reference (incidental in the latter cases) where Standard English would use past tense forms. If we could draw such detailed conclusions from a few texts, we could say that non-redundant tense marking had developed between the time of the speech by Smyth's Richmond (1775) and that of Cuff. As it is, it would be safer to say that the feature was probably developing in the last quarter of the eighteenth century. This system of tense marking persists into Black English today, and is a source of great confusion to those whose view of grammar is simplistic.

Cuff is represented as belonging to a gentleman from Maryland, a state which "is Virginia, speaking of them at a distance" to Defoe in *Colonel Jacque* (p. 234). Nobody in the eighteenth century differentiated between Plantation Creole as used on the Sea Islands and that used in other parts of the country—and hardly between that of the United States and the varieties spoken in Africa or in Surinam. These examples, along with others like Crèvecoeur's, disprove the alleged development of Gullah from pseudo-ecological factors ("isolation") on the Sea Islands.

There is, in short, evidence that by the end of the eighteenth century slaves from Massachusetts to South Carolina used varieties of English ranging from West African Pidgin to (nearly) Standard English. To discover the evidence, one must examine some relatively obscure documents. But the documentation is available to anyone who will look for it.

The Early Nineteenth Century

By the early 1800's, representations of Black English in print were commonplace. Consequently, many are to be found in writings with which every schoolboy is presumed to be familiar.

Other sources are well known to historians of literature for reasons
other than their artistic merit, like L. Beach's *Jonathan Postfree,
or the Honest Yankee* (1807), which presents "Caesar, A Black
servant to old Ledger" in the opening speech:

> I no likee this massa Fopling—I don't know what ole missee can
> see in him to make her likee him so much:—he no half so good as
> Jemmy Seamore. . . .

There is a considerable amount of mixing here. Pidgin or Creole
English would be expected to have *for make* rather than *to make*,
and of course there is the inconsistency of *I no likee* and *I don't
know*. Beach may not have been thoroughly familiar with more
than the superficial aspects of the Black English of the period
(*likee, he no half so good*). Yet mixing of this kind of not unknown. Particularly in New York, where the play is set, Black
speakers may have been remodeling their English in imitation
of the whites.

More famous authors may have done better jobs of recording.
One of the consequences of the faulty language history associated
with Black English, however, is that those authors have been
taken to task by critics whose *ex post facto* recommendations
about dialect writing are often much inferior to the practice of
the celebrated writers. Krapp, for example, takes Edgar Allan Poe
to task because Jupiter, in "The Gold Bug," speaks Gullah-like
dialect (Krapp's opinion) when he should speak "Virginia dialect" (also Krapp's opinion). Poe put into Jupiter's mouth words
like

> Somebody bin lef' him head up de tree, and de crows done gobble
> ebery bit of de meat off.

The grammar of Black English will generate such sentences even
today; it may well be that Poe, who grew up among the people
whose speech he was representing, was a better judge of the
matter than Krapp. Nevertheless, it is a relatively rare edition of
"The Gold Bug" which does not point out this "flaw" in Poe's
writing.[9] A skeptic would say that a deaf dialectologist had led
deaf critics into a colossal interdisciplinary blunder.

Luckily, Krapp was not born early enough to intimidate Poe

or any of the many other writers of the period who made Black characters speak the same variety of English without regard to geographic locale. "The Gold Bug," set in South Carolina (Sullivan's Island), could, as a matter of fact, quite believably have a Gullah speaker as one of its characters, even if the story was written by a Virginian. On the other hand, Plantation Creole was spoken in Virginia during Poe's residence there and for many years after; writings of authors like J. W. Page (see Bibliography) reveal it clearly. Poe may, then, have represented the speech of Black slaves whom he had known in his youth—unaware of an artificial distinction which would be made over one hundred years later.

One of Poe's notable contrasts in the language of Jupiter is that between *bin lef* (quoted above) and much more immediate perfectives as

I done pass fibe big limb, massa, pon dis side.

That is, Jupiter's passing the limbs had just taken place; but the head had been left on the tree a long time ago—long enough, at least, for the crows to eat away the flesh. This is just what would be expected for Plantation Creole of that period.

One expression used by Jupiter is *sure nuff*—probably the *sho nuff* which is often regarded as a Hollywood stereotype but which is actually observable in many speech events in the Black community. (Blues singer Sam "Lightnin'" Hopkins uses it constantly as a kind of aside/refrain, and it is one of the characteristic response patterns of the storefront church congregation to the preacher.) It has a regular relationship to Gullah *sho nuff sho*, in that it drops the second part of the iterative compound; one of the notable differences between present-day basilect and Gullah is that the former does not have the iteratives.[10] Krapp hazily theorized that Jupiter's language forms "may have been derived by Poe from a not very discriminating recollection of the New England literary dialect"; if he had focused on this form, he might have concluded that Poe invented Hollywood dialect stereotypes and even the movie scenario!

Plantation Creole, the language of Jupiter, and Pidgin English were not mutually exclusive in time distribution. During most of the eighteenth century they coexisted; in the nineteenth, both of them were in some contact even with partially decreolized varieties. From 1830 Frederic Bancroft recorded, in *Slave Trading in the Old South,*

> I wishy you buy her, master, if you gwine to buy me.   (p. 303)

The enclitic *-y* of *wishy* indicates that that feature had not completely disappeared. Africans continued to arrive, if in diminishing numbers, and some of them knew Pidgin English before arrival; Hurston's "Cudjo's Own Story of the Last African Slaver" (see Bibliography) is an excellent record of that occurrence. Works like James A. Jones's *Haverhill* (1831) show an early recognition of the association of Black English forms with African cultural survivals (here religious); Coromantees, who also speak an African language "of the Gold Coast," make speeches like

> .... Accompong no need—nebber asks much pray, him berry pleased, too good pleased widout much pray. Assarki, him berry much good too.   (II, 191)

This speech, in a scene set in Jamaica but in a book by an American author, has grammatical characteristics quite similar to those attested from the United States during the period. Other Black characters in the same novel speak with even more pidgin-like grammatical structures. Olmsted and Charles Colcock Jones are cited elsewhere as evidence of pidgin-speaking Africans who came to the United States. This apparently was the case with Harry of A. B. Lindsley's play *Love and Friendship* (1809). The speech of Cudjo in *The Fall of British Tyranny,* on the other hand, is much more pidgin-like than the language of Harry or of African-born Daddy Jack in *Nights With Uncle Remus.* Slaves born on this continent picked up the language of a historically later stage than the pidgin, and "immigrants" from Africa were increasingly expected to adapt their English to that of their American-born fellow slaves. Still, the similarities remained.

Many of the recent arrivals from Africa—and therefore, perhaps, a great deal of Pidgin English—came to the Charleston area, especially after importation of slaves became illegal. The ship *Wanderer* brought 400 African slaves in 1858. For that reason, decreolization (the change of English Creole in the direction of Standard English) may have proceeded more slowly in the area around Charleston than in other parts of the United States. African words survived longer there, too; some of them may never have found their way to other parts of the country.

The main reason why scholars like Robert A. Hall have assumed that Pidgin English must have developed after the slaves' arrival in the New World is that they have assumed that the language was taught to the Blacks by English-speaking whites. But we have reports like Bolingbroke's *A Voyage to Demerary* (1813), which tells of a slave's "broken English, which he had acquired in some of the factories on the coast of Africa, and from the sailors in the course of his passage" (p. 141). The evidence, for the West Indies as for the continental United States, supports one of Cruikshank's informants in *Black Talk* (1916)

Matty a l'arn matty.[11]

Friend taught friend (gradually, little by little). This particular informant happened to be an African-born slave who learned English only after his arrival in the New World, but some of them learned some English before they left Africa. That the slaves taught other slaves is probably the meaning of the phrase "of themselves" in a statement provided by Charles Colcock Jones:

> But if I am rightly informed, many of the Negroes who are grown persons when they come over, do of themselves attain as much of our languages as enables them to understand in the things which concern the ordinary business of life.
>
> (*Religious Instruction of the Negroes,* 1842, p. 17)

In looking for historical evidence of the sequence pidgin-creole-decreolization, one should not forget that the slaves held different degrees of status, even amounting to social stratification. Those who had recently been brought from Africa had a special —and not prestigious—standing. Those from the bush (scorned as *bozales* in Puerto Rico and Cuba) ranked lowest of all, and probably spoke the least of the language of the new country. They are probably responsible for the fact that pidgin characteristics, like the *-um* (*-em*) transitivizer, occur quite late here and there. For example, song collector Y. S. Nathanson's "Negro Minstrelsy, Ancient and Modern" (1855) records

He full um fote [fort] wid cotton bale.   (Jackson, p. 48)

This kind of variation helps to explain why language historians without experience in pidgin and creole languages have often considered documentation of Black English so inconsistent as to be unreliable. For an indeterminate period—but one which lasted nearly two hundred years—there were three language groups among the slaves:

(1) Those who learned the English of their masters. Most of these were either house servants or the mechanics who were allowed to work in the towns, the wages usually being retained by the owners. The language of the freedmen and of their descendants was more or less of this type.

(2) The great mass of native-born field workers, who spoke Plantation Creole.

(3) Recent imports from Africa, some of whom brought Pidgin English with them. The others must have faced a difficult language-learning problem.

There were, from almost the very first, slaves in different parts of the social structure—if never the very highest parts. Thus different social factors governed the variety of English which they spoke. Actually, it would have been incredible had they spoken identical dialects.

Practices did vary between plantations, so that the social constraints on the dialects spoken would have been different. It is no wonder, then, that the English of the slaves had a variability which dialect fiction writers recorded rather accurately. But social variation was more important than geographic variation. Although it has often been considered that each plantation was a little world of its own, there was actually a great deal of intercourse between slaves from different plantations. The Reverend Jonathan Boucher (in a letter of 1800) and the Marquis de Chastellux (*Travels*, 1780, 1781, 1782) gave reports of the way in which a slave society existed beside but almost apart from the white community. There was no one dialect and no one life style for people with "black" skins, any more than there is today; but there was one life style and one dialect for the vast majority of them.

Interpretations of such contemporary statements as

> . . . those [the slaves] that are born here talk good English . . .
> (Rev. Hugh Jones, *The Present State of Virginia*, 1724)

have an important bearing on the matter. It is, of course, possible to interpret "good" English in such a statement as meaning "Standard" English; this has, in fact, been the conventional conclusion from such evidence. But all the evidence of actual recordings of slave conversations contradicts that conclusion. Be he a playwright, a diarist, a correspondent, or a writer on medical matters, the author who actually quoted slaves represented them as using English which can be classified with relative ease as either Negro Pidgin English or Plantation Creole English. It seems very likely that Jones meant Plantation Creole by the term *good English*; further, those not born in the Americas may well have spoken Pidgin English, which at least some of them learned in Africa and which a writer like Jones would consider "bad" English, even by comparison to Plantation Creole. Historian Charles M. Andrews accepted the theory that some of the new arrivals from Africa had learned a kind of English there:

> Many of the slaves were African Negroes who spoke no English at all or only what was called "Black English", and for that reason among others the Negro born in America always commanded a higher price in the market.   (*Colonial Folkways*, p. 150)

James Grainger's *The Sugar Cane* (1764) says about the same thing about the islands of the West Indies, where English Creole developed at about the same time as in the colonies and where it is still widely spoken—often in more or less decreolized varieties.

Black English: A Changing Language

Patterns of innovation within Black English can be observed by the end of the eighteenth century. As the researches of Stewart have shown, durative *be* came into the United States by 1830. If we take the evidence of

I be cash crabs . . . .

spoken by Cuff in *Modern Chivalry*, we can assert that the innovation had begun as early as 1792. This form seems to represent an earlier *de* (also *da* or *a*) which is still found in many creole varieties of English. The development cannot be said to be complete, since it is still going on in urban Gullah[12] today. Musicologists and folklorists have recorded the form even in interviews with Sea Islanders, who probably have been adapting their speech to Standard English as much as possible:

If I be sitting down and don't have nothing to do, I get up.
(Carawan and Carawan,
Ain't You Got a Right to the Tree of Life, p. 63)

Note the rather subtle grammatical point about this sentence. Since *be -ing* is (in the terminology of Chapter II) Phase and not Aspect, *don't have* is grammatically parallel. The sentence

*If I be sitting down and ain't got nothing . . .

would be ungrammatical within the framework of Black English innovation.

Outside the United States, the innovation seems to have been a widespread nineteenth-century phenomenon. In the *Religious Intelligencer* for 1821, accounts of repatriated slaves in Sierra

Leone (some of them written by ex-slaves whose English was not completely Standard) we find abundant evidence:

> ... you see that poor thief [at the crucifixion] you talk about—he no be good at all—he be bad, when they hang him on the cross.
>
> (April, 1821, p. 729)

The thief's badness is regarded as a long-term quality, and the marker *be* is used. In the same speech, short-term badness is indicated by zero copula:

> True, me bad—me very bad—me sin too much: But Jesus Christ can make me good.   (*Ibid.*)

Mrs. A. C. Carmichael recorded some very similar forms in her *Domestic Manners and Customs in the West Indies* (1834). Mrs. Carmichael, who claimed that she worked until she "perfectly understood the Negro dialect" (p. 221) in order to investigate the customs of the slaves, recorded contrasts like

England be very fine country. (p. 89)	England very bad country for poor servant. (p. 89)
And then it be so cold. (p. 90)	England no good country for poor servant. (p. 89)
I think we be the best off. (p. 91)	She good too much to me. (p. 90)
She be my sissy. (p. 268)	She fool too much. (p. 269)

In these examples, *be* represents long duration or "inherent" character and zero copula represents no especially long duration or a temporary state: England stops being "very bad country" when the poor servant (who objects to the cold weather rather than to British customs) leaves.

There are some reports of use of the same structure on St. Vincent today, and some indication of parallels in places like Jamaica. Most studies done in the Caribbean have concerned themselves with the "deepest" Creole forms, whereas the forms intermediate between Creole and Standard English would be more relevant for comparative purposes. Jamaicans (in admittedly very casual elicitation situations) have told me that

> He be sick

seems natural to them as an expression of futurity, but not as an expression of any kind of habituative or durative state. At the present time, there is little evidence for comparison to other West Indian and to West African varieties of English.

During the period of decreolization, another change took place which resulted in an apparently great difference between American Black English and the English creoles. From the simple negative structure of Plantation Creole and the antecedent pidgin, decreolized Black English, there developed three negators (*dit'n, don'*, and *ain'*) as well as elaborate double negative structures:

> It ain' no use me workin' so hard.
> You don' get no more from me.
> He dit'n give me no money.

Actually, the change from the pidgin/creole simplicity of negation to the decreolized complexity is a matter of surface rather than underlying change. The pidgin/creole stages had three verbal categories (Tense, Aspect, Phase, in the terminology of Chapter II), and a new negator simply attached itself to each of those categories. The older all-purpose negator *no* (*me no be fellow servant*) was dropped. The last negator, in fact, would seem very strange to a present-day speaker of Black English; to use it in the ghettos would be to invite ridicule. But, from the historical linguist's point of view, the change has been rather slight.

Thus, although Black English has changed greatly in the slightly less than three hundred years for which we have documentation for it, it retains structural similarities to the earlier stages. In this respect it is simply a normal language: languages may change rapidly in their surface features, but they are resistent to change in underlying structures. In its change patterns, as in all other respects, we can see that Black English is normal human speech.

The Civil War Period

There were enough attestations of the English of Black slaves in the pre-Civil War period to permit rather detailed tracing of innovations like that of durative *be*. It was in the period of abolitionist agitation just before the war, however, that the language of the slaves became familiar to almost every serious reader in the United States. Crusading abolitionists like Harriet Beecher Stowe, whose *Uncle Tom's Cabin* was only one of many writings which indicate her awareness of Black English, published book after book which contained—only incidentally from their point of view, of course—testimony of their perceptions of the differences between the language of *most* of the slaves and that of the whites. During this period, also, the writings of local-color fiction writers like Thomas Chandler Halliburton ("Sam Slick") attested the existence of Black English all the way from the American South, by way of Boston and Connecticut, to Halifax, Nova Scotia.

The abolitionist papers alone contain enough evidence of Plantation Creole to prove the wide spread of the language before the middle of the nineteenth century. Writers less well known than Mrs. Stowe produced many examples.

> You [the mistress of the slaves, who are under the influence of a "forceful" preacher] no holy. We be holy. You in no state o' salvation.
>
> (Harriet Martineau,
> *Views of Slavery and Emancipation*, New York, 1837, p. 37)

This report of a conversation heard during a visit to the South contains the grammatical patterns of Black English: *You no holy*

and *you in no state o' salvation* contain the zero copula of temporary state (i.e., conversion is not permanently withheld) and
we be holy reflects the permanent state of grace of the true con-
vert. On this evidence, the grammar of Plantation Creole would
seem to be quite adequate for the expression of Pauline theology.

None of these sources presents *all* of the Blacks using Black
English; certain members of the Black population are consistently
pictured as speaking quite Standard English. Lewis and Milton
Clark, half-white house servants of a Kentucky master, would on
the evidence of the narratives of their *Sufferings* (see Bibliography) be assumed to have spoken nothing but Standard English.
But Lewis Clark's *Narrative* also quotes field workers:

Massa sick?   (p. 51)

Yes, yes; he sure to go, this time; he never whip the slave no more.
(p. 113)

Farewell, massa! pleasant journey; you soon be dere, massa—*all the
way down hill!**

Works of the apologists for slavery (like Nathaniel Beverly
Tucker, whose *The Partisan Leader*, 1836, is a remarkable prediction of the Civil War) also contain vast amounts of dialogue
attributed to slaves. The language forms in these dialogues match
those of the writings of the pro-abolition writers to an amazing
degree; but the taint of pro-slavery writing may have been what
turned many American academic liberals against the use of documentary evidence from the Civil War period for the history of
Black English. Fortunately, there are balancing accounts like
those of Clark, Martin Delaney (a Black whose *Blake: or, The
Huts of America* surveyed the slave states), and by Frederic Law
Olmsted, a Northern scholar whose aversion to slavery was subordinated to his professional concern for exact description (see
Chapter V).

During the Civil War itself, Yankee liberal and literateur
Thomas Wentworth Higginson, a colonel in the Union army
during the war, commanded a Negro regiment whose language

---

* It is hoped that no one will miss the point of this jest: "massa" is dead!

and customs he observed carefully. In 1870, he published *Army Life in a Black Regiment*, with copious materials on the language and customs of his soldiers. As a highly literate person who was conscious of the problems of recording dialect, he is as close to the reliability of a professional linguist representing the period as we could hope to come. He is quite explicit about his recording procedures:

> The words will be here given, as nearly as possible, in the original dialect; and if the spelling seems inconsistent, or the misspelling insufficient, it is because I could get no nearer. I wished to avoid what seems to me the only error in Lowell's "Biglow Papers" in respect to dialect,—the occasional use of an extreme misspelling, which merely confuses the eye, without taking us any closer to the peculiarity of the sound. (p. 188)

Higginson was, in short, a conscious craftsman in his dialect recording practices. He further tells us, concerning the songs which he wrote down:

> Writing down in the darkness, as I best could,—perhaps with my hand in the safe covert of my pocket,—the words of the song, I have afterwards carried it to my tent, like some captured bird or insect, and then, after examination, put it by. Or, summoning one of the men at some period of leisure,—Corporal Robert Sutton, for instance, whose iron memory held all the details of a song as if it were a ford or a forest,—I have completed the new specimen by supplying the absent parts. (p. 188)

It is true that much of Higginson's book is set in Gullah territory, and that the regiment was for some time actually stationed at Port Royal; nevertheless, there are specific materials concerning the dialect outside Gullah territory:

> "Done" is a Virginia shibboleth, quite distinct from the "been" which replaces it in South Carolina. Yet one of their best choruses, without any fixed words, was, "De bell done ringing," for which in proper South Carolina dialect, would have been substituted "De bell been a-ring." (pp. 191–2)

Although there was a more complicated situation than Higginson's geographic statement indicates, it is apparently true that there have been two systems all along, one which uses stressed *been* for remote past and unstressed *been* for recent past and another which uses *been* for remote past and *done* for recent past. The latter—which Higginson and probably his informants considered "Virginian"—is the one which had most widespread influence in the United States. This is hardly strange, since the English language system uses stress to indicate additional information on the same grammatical form rather than two different grammatical forms. Compare *I will stóp beating my wife* with *I wíll stop beating my wife*.

In one way or another, Higginson documents most of the grammatical features of pidgin/creole grammar (see Chapter II). He documents non-redundant pluralization for nouns:

de seben dollar   (p. 238)
Gib tousand tank ebry day   (p. 169)
Ten dollar a month   (p. 238)
We hab some valiant soldier here   (p. 194)
How much wife (p. 241. The context makes it clear that this is
          not a functional shift into the mass noun category although
          admittedly such phrases as *how much wife* and *too much wife*
          are not inconceivable in Standard English!)

The pronoun forms illustrate very clearly the principle of non-differentiation according to sex:

I lub he (p. 243. "He" was "a most unattractive woman" who "hab
          seben chil'en")
Ole woman one single frock he hab on.   (p. 168)

The subject-object forms are not distributed according to Standard English, or even according to "Schoolboy Non-Standard":

Him brought it on heself   (p. 63)
Best ting for do de driver,
     O, gwine away!
Knock he down and spoil he labor   (p. 210)
dat only jess enough for stretch we.   (p. 39)

The first example, *Him brought it on heself*, is an interesting exception to the rough general principle that decreolization proceeds in the direction of Standard English. It does, roughly; but an attempt to substitute subject form *he* for invariant form *him* (in Plantation Creole) can result in a form like *heself*, where "uncorrected" *himself* would have done quite well.

Higginson recorded many clause and question forms which are much as they still are in Black English basilect today:

And I ax her, How you do, my mudder?	(p. 201)
faid for truss ['afraid to trust']	(p. 168)
Run to the wood for hide	(p. 168)
Didn't I care for see 'em blaze	(p. 188)

Some of these subordinate clause patterns are rather similar to those of white non-standard dialects; others are uniquely Black English features.

Finally, there is the subject which has to be approached most carefully—apparent malapropism. (The term *apparent* should be insisted upon because, from a purely structural point of view, each language variety establishes its own "correctness" and it is the other dialects which produce malapropisms.) Higginson gives us forms like

percept [except]	(p. 103)
condemned [condensed] milk	(p. 147)
expeditious [expedition]	(p. 147)
amulet, epaulet, or omelet [ambulance]	(p. 148)

Striving to operate in a system essentially foreign to them, the Black soldiers made occasional mistakes. Especially, they slipped into what the linguist calls hypercorrection: the speaker who said 'sep' (except) in his own dialect knew that his prestigious officers said something else, with an extra syllable on the front, and in trying to do it himself he added too much (and the wrong thing) and came up with *percept*. All but the most talented adult language learners do this when operating in a new system; Higginson shows that he knows this by adding a malapropism from a Dutchman—*blockheads* for *blockades* (p. 117).

The early records show clearly that all the varieties of Black English were spoken in the North. Cotton Mather and several local Massachusetts historians attest its presence in Massachusetts, Benjamin Franklin and Anthony Benezet in Philadelphia, Harriet Beecher Stowe and James Fenimore Cooper (among others) in New York, and Thomas Chandler Halliburton ("Sam Slick") for all points between South Carolina and Halifax, Nova Scotia. There is little doubt, however, that Plantation Creole was more slowly decreolized in the areas of the plantations, where large groups of slaves lived largely autonomous lives and affected the behavior patterns of their masters as much as they were affected. By the time of the Civil War, what is generally regarded as "Negro dialect" had come to be associated with the southern states.

The Post-Emancipation Period

To the extent that, after Emancipation, the field slave simply became the agricultural worker and sharecropper, the social conditions under which Plantation Creole was maintained did not change much. Works like Johnson's *The Shadow of the Plantation* (1934) document the lack of change in social conditions even seventy years after Emancipation. They also document a language which is quite similar to Plantation Creole. The informants, however, are adult; and it seems quite evident that younger informants would have given evidence of greater similarity. The various Federal Writers' Projects of the 1930's, resulting in such works as B. A. Botkin's *Lay My Burden Down*, reveal the same dialect throughout the southern states. It was fairly easy for academic observers, by the early years of the twentieth century, to formulate the opinion that Black English (known to them only through the formal usage of adults) was virtually identical to southern white English. The opinion of all laymen, that southern dialect was the result of influence of Negro dialect on the speech of whites (which turns out to be accurate—see Chapter V) was rejected as "unscientific" by the new discipline of dialect geography. Gullah, a clear survival of the Plantation Creole stage, was ignored until the time of Turner's *Africanisms in the Gullah Dialect* (1949); it was then conveniently (and inaccurately) explained away in terms of "isolation." Between white southern dialects and the Black English of the southern states there were similarities, of course; but the differences were obvious to residents of the region who had no axe to grind. Paradoxically, there was a period during which those residents of the South who had not studied dialectology had more exact knowledge of the dialect situation than those who had.

The series of quasi-legal southern reactions to the Fourteenth Amendment did much to confuse the history of southern dialects. Lumping descendants of house servants and of freedmen with the descendants of field hands, they made linguistically and culturally variant groups legally—and, to some degree, even sociologically—identical. Thus, both children whose dialect differed greatly from that of the white children of the region and those whose dialect was almost identical to that of the whites were barred from the schools which the master caste attended. There was literally no Negro dialect in the sense that there was no one dialect spoken by everyone branded "Negro" by the Jim Crow laws. But the Black English–speaking majority, descendants of the numerically greater population of field hands, exceeded the minority who spoke Standard English or the regional dialects of the area by a factor of perhaps ten to one. White southerners— and linguists—were, on the other hand, likely to know only the descendants of the house servants.

Some of the emancipated slaves escaped this process by returning to Africa, especially to Liberia. It is mathematically almost certain that the field hands prevailed numerically in this group. In Africa, they joined other uprooted Africans whom British Navy ships had dumped there after taking them from the slave ships which HMN had declared illegal. Actually, the "repatriation" had begun as early as 1820, and there were about 4,500 "civilized people of American origin in the country" in 1847 (Brawley, A Social History of the American Negro, p. 20). By 1867 the American Colonization Society and its auxiliaries had been directly responsible for sending more than 12,000 persons to Africa. In the nineteenth century as a whole, at least 15,000 were sent.

Actually, the Liberian repatriation was nothing new, but rather a stage in a long series of such repatriations going back at least to the late eighteenth century. In the 1790's, some of the Maroons (escaped slaves) of Jamaica were forcibly removed to Nova Scotia (where a few of them seem to have remained) and then to Sierra Leone. Surviving documents show that those Maroons spoke Pidgin English, as did probably most of the Africans who had fallen victim to the British part of the Atlantic slave trade. Since Francis Grose's Classical Dictionary of the Vulgar Tongue (1785) cites many phrases like

> no catchy, no havy

as "the Negroe language," it seems likely that it was known throughout the English-speaking world that Pidgin English was used by most of the slaves. Repatriated slaves—some of whom, of course, were not sent back to their original part of Africa—had some influence on Liberian Pidgin English and Sierra Leone Krio, both of which are widely used today. It is not certain, however, how important that influence has been. Since there was Pidgin English in West Africa by the early years of the slave trade (see Chapter IV), it seems likely that the slaves who were returned to Africa encountered varieties of English very similar to those which they had learned in the New World. To an extent which has only begun to be realized, Black English has been an important language of Afro-America for nearly four hundred years.

Today, Pidgin English is widely used in West Africa. Even in officially French-speaking East Cameroun, it is widely used between members of different tribal groups; the Yaoundé bartender who spoke only French to me shouted "Fo' outside" to some children who were trying to sell peanuts to his customers. The first person who spoke to me on Fernando Poo was a teenage girl who shouted "Kotch'm, massa, kotch'm; he no wear clothes!" of the two- or three-year-old boy who was apparently her little brother and who was indeed unclothed. More formal use of Pidgin English is made by authors like Cyprian Ekwensi and Amos Tutuola, who have made the language rather widely known in world literature. In Ekwensi's *Jagua Nana* (1961), Nana and Freddie converse in Pidgin English, although they both speak Ibo, in order to avoid "too many embarrassing reminders of clan and custom" (p. 1), which might disrupt their life in Lagos. Some of the charm of Tutuola's *Palm Wine Drinkard* and *My Life in the Bush of Ghosts* is in the slight exoticism of the language; but the talk of a great deal of West Africa shares that quality. The late British author Joyce Cary caught pidgin-influenced West African English remarkably well in *Mister Johnson*.

In Liberia, a somewhat defensive position is apparent in a kind of official silence about the use of Pidgin English. There is a great deal more openness in Sierra Leone, where the creolized English (called, appropriately enough, Krio) receives some official recognition. Although Liberian "Pidgin" is undoubtedly creolized—at least for some speakers—defensive imaginations in that country work overtime on the discovery of other influences for Liberian English. Brawley, for example, wrote

> Literature has been mainly in the diction of Shakespeare and Milton; but Shakespeare and Milton, though not of the twentieth century, are still good models, and because the officials have had to compose many state documents and deliver many formal addresses, there has developed in the country a tradition of good English speech. (*A Short History of the Negro*, p. 209)

This sounds suspiciously like statements which could be made about West African Standard English anywhere (cf. the prose of Chinua Achebe). In many cases, the West African Standard has just a few traces of pidgin/creole influence, which its defenders prefer to believe are relics of seventeenth- and eighteenth-century British English.

Some of the defensiveness on the part of West Africans is undoubtedly due to the lack of valid information on the role which these varieties of English have played in African and Afro-American culture. Everywhere the history of Black English has been done half-heartedly if at all; scholarly treatments are only beginning to appear. A compendium like Hall's *Pidgin and Creole Languages* (1966) leaves out some of the varieties (Liberian, Seminole) altogether and glosses over the extent of Black English in the United States. Even a more specialized study like Gilbert D. Schneider's *West African Pidgin English, An Historical Overview* (1967) does not consider the possibility of influence from the English of repatriated American ex-slaves. John Reinecke, in some respects the most remarkable Pidginist of them all, pointed out in 1937 (*Marginal Languages*, p. 613) that there were different varieties of Pidgin English along the West Coast of Africa and that there was also Liberian English, "similar to the Southern dialect of the United States." E. S. Sayer (*Pidgin English*, 1939 and 1941, privately printed) points out the similarities between the English of the Negro in the southern United States and that of Africans who do not speak a "perfect" pidgin. Yet better-known historians of the language have not followed these suggestions. Probably the outstanding insights into the history of Black English in the United States will come from the study of "repatriated" varieties. But, for the Establishment historian of American English, the West Coast of Africa might as well be on Pluto.

In the years after World War II, desegregation, Negro rioting, and Black Power agitation forcibly brought Black English, along with other Black cultural patterns, to the attention of whites. When children speaking basilect (itself very like Plantation Creole) have entered formerly all-white schools, they have brought the dialect dramatically to the attention of educators. Huge research projects have been spawned to study the matter; lacking information about Plantation Creole and decreolization processes, they have often assumed that the Black children are actually deprived of language. Noting the few obvious features shared with southern regional dialects, they have too often assumed that Black English has *all* the features of southern white dialects. Authoritative-sounding treatments have been written to educate teachers' organizations like the National Council of Teachers of English to this state of affairs, and the writers have been well paid for their misinformation. The miswritten history of Black English and of American English in general has cost the United States government and private foundations millions of dollars in misspent research funds.

The Future

What of the future of Black English? Scholarly writers before and after Harrison in 1888 have urged that it be described in haste before schoolteachers drive it into oblivion. Even Langston Hughes, in *The Book of Negro Humor* (1966), characterized it as "a language that will not be with us much longer" (p. 47). Pedagogues, Black and white, have urged its extinction. But outside the United States, in West Africa and the Caribbean, related varieties are thriving. Pidgin or Creole English varieties can still spread at the expense of Standard English, as happened in the Bamenda area of the West Cameroon in the early 1960's, the immediate cause being not isolation but the increased communication brought about by a new road. Brought into contact with large numbers of people who knew only pidgin or had to learn even that (there are so many African languages in the area that an auxiliary language is an absolute necessity), residents of the area, according to educators working there in 1964, tended to give up Standard English and take up pidgin. It is, therefore, not only chauvinistic but outright wrong to assume that non-standard varieties of English maintain their existence only when their speakers are isolated from the "advantages" of Standard English. Reports of the death of a pidgin or creole can be exaggerated.

A dialect or language variety is maintained by social pressures within its own group of speakers, although the speakers are seldom fully aware that they are maintaining it—language having a high threshold of awareness. In many cases, subconscious pressures maintain the dialect while the speaker's every conscious effort is to change to another. Group identity is perhaps the strongest of such pressures.

There is no real evidence that exposure to another language system through electronic media (TV and radio) has any especially great influence. Thus, the ubiquity of such media in the United States will not necessarily mean a change in the language of the Black community. In certain parts of the nation, like Vermont, it seems unlikely that the density of the Black population is enough to permit retention of Black English. In New York City, on the other hand, it is not only being retained but is even being transmitted to the Puerto Rican community in some sections. Black English thrives in Nova Scotia, as it has since about 1760, perhaps because of the aloofness of the white population from the Black.

By the end of the 1960's there were indications that Black artists and intellectuals were picking up Black English and making it a symbol of Black unity. Today an impressive school of Black poets is producing poetry in Black English and expressing pride in the expressive power of the language. LeRoi Jones has defended the language and written in it for several years now. Gwendolyn Brooks, who has been aware of Black culture for many years, has lent her support to the movement. Don L. Lee is a poet of power and artistry who utilizes a form of the language. June Jordan, Ted Joans, Margaret Walker, Nikki Giovanni, Gil Scott, Mae Jackson, David Henderson, Michael Harper, Pauli Murray, Zora Neale Hurston, Langston Hughes, and others have used Black English effectively in artistic prose and poetry. A few features of Black English, such as the durative *be*, occur with increasing frequency on the "Soul" program on educational television. So far, however, Black writers have not utilized the most extreme form of Black English, basilect.

It is not completely impossible that the United States will become a bidialectal nation in the near future. This would involve giving a certain amount of official recognition to Black English: grammars, dictionaries, translations even of some official and governmental documents into the language, use in some school systems, etc. Again, the variety could no longer be referred to as "Non-Standard"; the process just described is essentially what the sociolinguist means by the term *standardization*. And many whites would undoubtedly learn Black English, as they did in the Old South before the Civil War (see Chapter V).

How Much of It Is African?

Although slaves in the New World did not use African languages exclusively, it was not necessary to abandon them completely. Especially in the early days of slavery in the Americas, many of the transported Africans would have been able to find other speakers who understood their native languages. There was special utility in certain African languages which were used for *lingua franca* purposes, like Wolof. Even after the slavers had learned to mix the language groups, slaves would occasionally find speakers with whom they could converse in their native languages.

In some ways, even the use of Pidgin English promoted the retention of a certain amount of African vocabulary. The situation must have been something like that of the West Cameroon today, where a vocabulary item like *poto poto* 'mud' is of practically universal use in Pidgin English. (It is even used in the French of the East Cameroun—*Il y a trop de poto poto* 'There is too much mud'.) Descriptions given by American and British visitors to West Africa today are often very similar to that given by Ingraham in 1860:

> She is African born, and still retains many words of her native dialect, with a strange gibberish of broken English.
>
> (The Sunny South, pp. 115–116)

The use of *dialect* instead of *language* is typical of colonialist (and even of African) usage: French and English are classified as "languages" and Bulu and Bamoun as "dialects." If conditions in the period of early slavery were in fact comparable, there would have been more opportunities than have usually been acknowledged for the survival of African vocabulary.

Denials of the influence of African languages on American English have historically taken the form of rejecting influence from languages spoken by the slaves. No one seriously doubts that some words in English—British as well as American—have African-language etymologies. Words like *banana, chimpanzee,* and *safari* would not be traced to Proto-Germanic or Latin by anyone. Further, no one has thought to claim that they cannot be of African-language origin because they are widely spoken in areas not populated by Africans. The prejudice, as usual, has been against the American Negro rather than against the African; reluctance has been limited to acknowledging any contributions by the slaves to the American English vocabulary, perhaps because such acknowledgment would constitute an opening for re-examination of the whole matter of Negro dialect. Until the time of Turner's *Africanisms in the Gullah Dialect* (1949) the line was sternly maintained at the border of the United States; Turner (pp. 5–11) quotes some of the many categorical denials that any appreciable number of Gullah words came from African languages. After Turner's overwhelming demonstration that this position was erroneous, the lines of defense were redrawn. It was simply held that only in Gullah, now pictured as an isolated language phenomenon limited to the Sea Islands and discoverable only by intrepid feats of field work, was there any appreciable number of African words.

It is a strange characteristic of the reception of Turner's work that it has never been allowed to stand as Turner characterized it. Turner quite openly states, even in his title, that his book is mainly about Africanisms in the Gullah dialect. He does not lay claim to having discovered this dialect, which would be absurd; his abundant references to previous treatments show clearly that the dialect was well known. It is only in the past few years that the absurd concept of Gullah's developing in isolation through some mystic process called "selective cultural differentiation" has developed. It is taking nothing from Turner's remarkable feat of field work to say that his achievement, beyond showing the need for Negro researchers and others sensitive enough to gain and deserve the confidence of the Gullah people, was not that he discovered the existence of the dialect but that he discovered the large amount of West African vocabulary in it. Turner is supposed to have said, "You know, there's a dialect called Gullah spoken out in the depths of the Sea Islands which is a lot different from Standard English." What he actually said was, "You know that Gullah dialect that's all around Charleston and that everybody knows about? Well, there are a lot of Africanisms in it."

The use of Charleston as a port for the direct importation of Africans even into the middle nineteenth century probably accounts for the late survival of African vocabulary in that area. But as the limited evidence we have shows, there were once African vocabulary items in Plantation Creole in all parts of the United States. These came quite early. Benjamin Franklin (see p. 89) attests *buckra* for Philadelphia, and Julian Mason (*American Speech*, 1960) shows that it eventually migrated even as far as Oregon. There is hardly any reason to assume that any of the Africanisms listed by Turner were limited to the Gullah area in the eighteenth and nineteenth centuries. The abundant evidence of the day names (see below, pp. 123–130) tends to indicate a wide distribution, at least in the East and South.

Still, there is no special reason to assume that very many of them occur far out of Gullah territory today. In estimating the amount of African vocabulary in American English which was transmitted by the slaves, we will probably conclude that the number of words is small. Even at that, it is larger than has ordinarily been allowed. There is no real doubt about the following words:

goober	cooter	okra
jazz	pinder	juke
hoodoo/voodoo	juba	bozo
tote	banjo	doney
gumbo	chigger/jigger	
buckra/buckaroo	*nyam/yam 'eat'	

Turner, in his review of Mathew's *Some Sources of Southernisms* (*Language*, 1950), suggested the addition of

gunger 'ginger'
tabby 'a kind of cement with which oyster shells and pieces of
    brick are mixed'

McDavid, in his review of Turner's *Africanisms in the Gullah Dialect* (*Language*, 1950), suggested the further addition of

joggling board
jinky board/janky board
sweet mouth
bad mouth
yard ax 'untrained preacher'
shout [as a religious expression]

Some of the last two lists must be loan translations, not direct borrowings from the African languages. It has also been suggested that expressions like *big eye* 'greed' belong in the same group. Although *big* and *eye* are obviously not African, their combination in that meaning may be. Since compounds and phrases

---

* According to Krapp, *The English Language in America*, I, 125, "present infantile *yum-yum*" may be related to this word.

are much more difficult to trace etymologically than individual words, it will be difficult if not impossible to determine the exact extent of such influence.

More recently, a group of West Africanists like Dalby and Hancock (see Bibliography) have been suggesting West African origins for many other Americanisms. Notable among these are *cat* 'person, man' and *hepcat* (Wolof *hipicat* 'man who is aware or has his eyes open'). It is, of course, a commonplace of the jazz language that *hep* is a white man's distortion of the more characteristically Negro *hip*; there are anecdotes about how one famous jazzman or another has put down a white who was proclaiming "I'm hep!" with "I'm hip you're hep." Although most of the Africanisms in the West Indies and in the United States tend to be Pan-West Africanisms rather than borrowings from any specific language, Wolof may have acted as a *lingua franca* for Africans in the slave trade, thereby paralleling some of the American Indian pidgins which seem to have been used before and along with American Indian Pidgin English. If that is the case historically, it is quite believable that Wolof contributed some vocabulary items.

The list of words is not large, and some of them are not in wide distribution. On the other hand, it is not much smaller than the number of widely functional American Indian words in American English—place names excepted. When it is considered that American Indians survived as essentially monolingual tribal groups while Africans in the New World did not, the "contribution" to American English by Africans begins to seem impressively large.

There has been some quibbling about all of the African etymologies, with the possible exception of *buckra*. *Tote*, for example, has not been so accepted by the pundits of dialect geography. McDavid (Mencken-McDavid, p. 133) refuses to believe that the first part of such compounds as *tote road*, *tote sled*, etc., used in "the lumbering country of Maine, the Adirondacks, and Lake Superior" could possibly be of Negro transmission. This is in accordance with the principle that Africanisms transmitted *by the descendants of slaves* cannot exist outside areas where Negroes are the majority in the population.

The trouble with words is that they don't know their own etymologies and that, once adopted into a language, they will refuse to stay around either the people or the place of their origin. McDavid's absurd requirement of tracing words of African origins only to areas populated predominantly by Negroes would never have arisen but for the necessity of protecting the East Anglian origins theory. Try applying the same line of reasoning to non-African words. By this line of reasoning, very little of the United States should know *cole slaw*, since few of our regions have a preponderance of Dutchmen. Practically all of us know *kayak* and *igloo*, even though we do not live in areas populated predominantly by Eskimos and may indeed never have seen an Eskimo outside the movies. (We know about *husky*, and *malemute*, and *mush!*, even with the same restrictions on our social life and experience.) The Louisiana term *lagniappe* has an accepted etymology from Quechua; are we to believe that the areas of Louisiana and Texas where the word is primarily used are populated primarily by Andean Indians?

Turner, p. 203, shows a clear possibility of African origin. M. M. Mathews, who in his *Dictionary of Americanisms* traces the term *tote* in English to Virginia as far back as 1677 (thus in the very early times of Negro Pidgin or of Plantation Creole in the United States), makes probably the only sane comment on the word, which is present in any of the standard reference works:

> The earliest available evidence for the word is southern, but, as the quotes below show, it has spread widely in colloquial use.

(p. 1751)

It is only necessary to get the word into American English through African influence, i.e., that of the slaves; it is not necessary to account for its spread through African or slave influence. We can spread a term like *blitzkreig* all over the country, even during a period when no German would have dared show his face and when even German shepherd dogs may have suffered anti-Nazi wrath on occasion. We can order *sake* without being able to tell a Japanese from a Filipino. Texans can eat *chile con carne*, and order it more or less by that name, while pitying the poor Mexicans for their lack of a real language. If it is really necessary to have the word *tote* carried to the north woods by an ethnic group, I nominate the Indians—who picked up their English, in the first place, mainly from the Negro slaves (see Chapter IV).

Within the Negro community, the use of Africanisms has been demonstrably larger in the past; allowing for relexification, we can still see a great deal of indirect influence. *Buckra* may be gone from the vocabulary of many who replace it by *white folks* (singular); in effect, *white folks* continues the work of the African etymon and is thus indirectly an Africanism.

In Black English a few Africanisms turn up which are masked well enough not to be expected by the casual observer. There is, for example, *say* in *He tell me say*, which turns out not to be the same in origin as the second word in *They say that* . . . . Used in English varieties on the West Coast of Africa and in the Caribbean, the word in this function comes from Akan or Twi *se* 'that' or from some other West African form; in Jamaica, according to Cassidy's *Jamaica Talk* (p. 63), it has come to be identified with the English word *say*, just as it has in the United States. In Gullah and in the Caribbean and West African varieties, it occurs in any kind of indirect quotation situation:

> I hear say . . . .
> He think say . . . .
> We know say . . . . .
> etc.

In the United States, outside Gullah territory, it is now almost entirely restricted to *He tell me say* . . . , and is probably behind the frequent repetition of *He tell me, he say.* Joel Chandler Harris' frequent *Brer Rabbit says, sezee* reflects the same syntactic function if not the same etymon. It is apparently one of the few Plantation Creole forms which is not age-graded; in Washington, D.C., at least, it is used mainly by old people. It is interesting that one of the few bits of information about Negro dialect in the linguistic geography tradition comes from the quoting of a passage which contains this form:

> Some ob 'em [preachers] git to preachin' say you cullud folks pray, you got a soul to be saved.   (Farrison, *The Phonology of the Illiterate Negro Dialect of Guilford County, North Carolina*, p. 245)

There is a small number of words from Portuguese (the Trade Pidgin, that is) which were most likely transmitted by Negro Pidgin and Plantation Creole. Notable is *pickaninny*, which could not have been transmitted by any other language variety; *savvy* may have been transmitted by Negro Pidgin, or by American Indian Pidgin English, or by Chinese Pidgin English, or by all three, with undoubtedly some Southwestern influence from Spanish *sabe*. *Pone*, as in *corn pone*, has an Algonquian etymology, but the fact that Sierra Leone Krio has *pon* also makes it more than a little suspicious that Portuguese *pão* (with nasalized vowel readable by an English speaker with an [on]) may have had some influence. The Portuguese Trade Pidgin was in West Africa so early and so completely that languages like Temne still have traces of its vocabulary; some of its influence on Pidgin English may have come through the African languages rather than directly. *Cabá*, the Portuguese Trade Pidgin form for the recent perfective in the verb system, does not seem to be attested on the North American continent; it is, however, in Sranan Tongo (*kaba*), the English Creole of Surinam. *Done*, of both Negro and white Southern dialect, is its relexification (see Glossary. Haitian *fèk* (French Creole), Hawaiian Pidgin English *pau* (relexified with a Hawaiian word), Melanesian Pidgin English *finish* constitute other relexifications of *cabá*.

Although one could for sentimental reasons wish it otherwise, the conventional verdict that relatively few words come *directly* from African languages is probably sound. Syntactic influence is a subtler and more complicated matter. In a Black English sentence like

    He look the road see something

not only the "verb stacking" of *look . . . see* but the "absence" of a preposition after *look* may reflect African language habits. It is, however, quite characteristic of English pidgins to have a reduced inventory of prepositions, and such structures could be traceable to that source. As in so many other cases, reinforcements and multiple etymologies are distinct possibilities. It seems very likely that, once the resistance of the academic Establishment to this kind of research were overcome, many such examples could be turned up. But seekers after exoticism might just as well conclude that no pocket of Niger-Khardofanian languages is going to be found in the United States.

The problem of the African contribution to Maritime Pidgin English (see Chapter IV) is an extremely complicated one. It is altogether possible that the structure of West African languages had a great deal to do with it. But, even if they did not, there is no reason to conclude that African linguistic and cultural continuity is not represented in the language and culture of the slaves in the United States. A language "belongs" to the group which speaks it, and African Pidgin English is in a real sense as African as ivory carvings.

West African Naming Practices Outside Gullah Territory

Although their complete historical and geographic spread has been glossed over in conventional treatments, there were West African naming practices in the Black communities of the New World—including the United States—from as early as the seventeenth century. In some forms and in certain isolated areas, they survive to the present time. Turner's *Africanisms in the Gullah Dialect* pointed up the abundance of such names in the Sea Islands in the 1940's, and West Indianists (see Cassidy and DeCamp in Bibliography) have treated them in some detail for those islands, especially for Jamaica. N. N. Puckett's article on slave naming (see Bibliography) establishes the historical spread of those names in the United States; a great deal can be added, in terms of geographic spread, to his excellent treatment.

The most obviously West African of the names involved are the day names, names given to children according to the days of the week on which they are born. There are fourteen such names, with many variants—some of which are only spelling variants. The best-known forms are listed below:

	MALE	FEMALE
Sunday	Quashee	Quasheba
Monday	Cudjo	Juba
Tuesday	Cubbenah	Beneba
Wednesday	Quaco, Kwaco	Cuba
Thursday	Quao	Abba
Friday	Cuffee, Cuffy	Pheba, Phibbi
Saturday	Quame, Kwame	Mimba

These names, which continue to be used in Africa as in the famous case of Kwame Nkrumah, were in use at one time in all parts of the New World into which African slaves in great numbers were brought. Translation of the names (Friday for Cuffee) was very common in the United States, and has been practiced in West Africa and in the West Indies.

Cassidy and DeCamp have shown in detail how the names came to change their function in Jamaican English, becoming common nouns and undergoing semantic pejoration. There is perhaps no more instructive example in Afro-American sociolinguistics than how Quasheba came to mean 'the colored mistress of a white man' or even 'a prostitute'. In Jamaica, Quao came to mean 'an ugly stupid man,' and the other names suffered equivalent pejoration. In other parts of the New World there are parallel developments: Collymore, in *A Glossary of Barbadian Dialect*, reports "Cuffie. Contemptuous name for a Negro" (p. 29). In the United States there are traces of such pejoration, but the names themselves apparently became rather rare in most areas of this country in the second half of the nineteenth century.

Cuffee seems to have been the most widely known of the day names; its translation, Friday, is on the whole even better known. The translation is and has been practiced in West Africa; P. Grade's "Das Neger-Englisch in der Westküste von Afrika," (*Anglia,* 1892) illustrated the use of Pidgin English by "Ein Kruneger, Friday" (p. 393). It seems very probable that Defoe, who knew his African pidgin traditions, utilized the day name for the character in *Robinson Crusoe*—although of course Friday is not an African. Caroline Gilman's *Recollections of a Southern Matron,* set in Charleston, South Carolina, illustrates the use of both the day name and its translation, without any indication that Mrs. Gilman realized that they were related in Negro practice. A family slave is known as Friday; a bogus "French" cook named Cuffee is hired by a somewhat naive householder. It seems plausible that the "foreign" cook might have used the less familiar African version in order to add to his name an exotic flavor which did not exist in his cookery. If he did, the other slaves of the household must have been in on the joke. Lucy M. Garrison, in her famous observations on the Sea Islands in the 1860's, recorded both Monday and Cudjo as names—on the same page (*Slave Songs of the United States,* p. xxx). Thaddeus Norris, in "Negro Superstitions" (*Lippincott's Magazine,* 1870, reprinted in Jackson), related an anecdote about "an old servant by the name of Friday" who worked for "a gentleman in Alexandria, Virginia" (p. 139). Examples are everywhere.

The name is not limited in its geographic scope, any more than Plantation Creole and the entire complex of African culture were so limited. In 1741, a "Cuffee, Gomez's" was involved with a Quaco in a slave plot to burn New York City. Cuffee and Cudjo were perhaps the most influential of the Jamaican Maroons; very possibly the African associations of the day names meant something to those slaves who were inclined to revolt. In several instances, the translated names (Friday for Cuffee) belonged to individuals who were not noted for leadership or for any other outstanding qualities. Before the semantic pejoration which reflects the dominance of values of the whites, men with the untranslated day names were men of confidence, ability, and achievement; "King Cudjoe" among the Florida Seminoles (K. W. Porter, *Journal of Negro History,* 1950) was apparently such an individual.

The New York City plotter was apparently not the first Cuffee to be known in the colonies; Mencken records the name from 1713. This would mean that records of the day names are roughly coterminous with attestations of Negro Pidgin. Cuff, the Negro in Brackenridge's *Modern Chivalry* (1792), whose Plantation Creole has been discussed at some length, quite obviously represents the same tradition. There is nothing to prevent an owner's calling his slave after the end of a shirt sleeve, but it seems unlikely and is unparalleled elsewhere in slave-naming practices. In the records of the slave plot to burn New York City in 1741, one slave is called both Cuffee and Cuff. Only the most ardent and uncritical adherent of British origins could today connect the name with British *cove,* although Bartlett did so in 1859.

Although rather mild when compared to what happened to the name in Jamaica, the fate of *cuffee*—a common noun derived from the proper name—in the United States is good enough as an indicator of slave standing. Bartlett defined *cuffy* or *cuffey* as "a generic name for a Negro, akin to 'Sambo,' 'Quashie,' etc." (p. 186), thus documenting, although he did not know it, the common semantic development range of the West African names. In Tucker's *Partisan Leader* (1836), not only does the Yankee soldier speak of the putatively stupid Negro as "a cuffee," but the stage directions by Tucker (who is, of course, in on the gag) read "cuffee advanced in silence"—with a small *c,* note. Samuel Northrup (*Twelve Years a Slave,* 1854) used Cuffee and Sambo (see below) as generalized slave names. To some extent they served as Rastus came to later—perhaps not always as insulting names, but never as flattering ones. In Jamaica, Cuffee means 'a stupid Negro'—and worse. Perhaps the most prevalent meaning for Cuba is 'an effeminate man.'

Like many other features of African survival, these day names serve to illustrate how absurd is the theory of Gullah's being the only repository of African practices because of its "isolation."

Jonathan Dickinson was bringing a young slave boy named "Cajo" to Philadelphia—where Benjamin Franklin nearly a century later attested to a pidgin-speaking slave who used the Africanism *buckra*—when the misfortunes described in his *God's Protecting Providence . . .* (see Bibliography), occurred in 1696. *The Plantation; or Thirteen Years in the South*, by "A Northern Man" (1853) mentions Daddy Cudjo "in the far off South" (p. 99). William Hayne Simmons' *Notices of East Florida* (1822) mentions a "Cudjoe, one of the principal characters of the place" (p. 41) and a Friday (p. 7) among the Seminoles. With typical white perspicacity, Simmons traced the translated name to the influence of Robinson Crusoe's Friday in Defoe's novel. Zora Neale Hurston's "Cudjo's Own Story of the Last African Slaver" (*Journal of Negro History*, 1927) presented a Cudjo who still spoke very pidgin-like English in his old age. According to Porter's "Negro Guides and Interpreters in the Early Stages of the Seminole War" (*Journal of Negro History*, 1950) "Cudjo is a common name to this day among the Negroes in Seminole County, Oklahoma" (p. 178). Cudjo Key, in Florida, is disproof of the cliché that there are no African place names in the United States.

A writer does not have to be very perceptive to provide evidence about day names. The sentimentalizing of slavery in Orlando Kay Armstrong's *Old Massa's People* (1931) makes virtually any general conclusion which he might draw suspect; however, when he provides information about a custom, like the day names, which fits the pattern perfectly, there is no reason to doubt that even a sloppy thinker may report the facts accurately at times. When he writes

> Names for the days of the week were not common, but there's old Uncle Monday sitting beneath his vine and fig tree in Middle Georgia. (p. 61)

we may reasonably conclude that "Uncle Monday" is accurate but that the generalization about the rareness of "names for days of the week" reflects the author's lack of competence in observation. (*Uncle*, as a designation of limited respect for an elderly Negro, is the kind of term which an observer at Armstrong's level of ability is capable of discovering.) Armstrong further reports how a slave described his own naming:

> When my Pappy bawn, his Pappy look in de cabin do', an' say: 'Whut day is dis? Friday? Do tell! Name him Friday!   (pp. 60–61)

It is probable than many Southern observers, no better qualified than Armstrong, were able to get barely a hint of the Negro naming practices which surrounded them. Since the names were sporadically reported from many areas, it seems probable that they were simply all over the place.

Northern observers like Lucy M. Garrison, although more liberal and inclined to treat the slaves as human beings, were equally naive in the face of West African cultural survivals. Garrison interpreted Cudjo as "Co' Joe" or "Cousin Joe" when she encountered it on the Sea Islands shortly after the Civil War, and the same garbled etymology has been applied elsewhere. The newly freed Blacks, like the slaves before them, were accustomed to masking their cultural systems from the whites. Probably, they did not see fit to reveal such matters to Northern benefactors, who were, after all, white. Or perhaps in some cases the Blacks themselves had forgotten the meaning of the day names.

Quaco 'male born on Wednesday' was one of the earliest day names to be attested in the United States. A Kuaco who participated in the "Maiden Lane Incident" in New York City in 1712 is reported by Otterly and Weatherby, *The Negro in New York* (p. 23); the variation in spelling, for names which were not represented in any orthographic tradition, does not provide any difficulty in determining the origin. There are many other examples after that time. For some reason, however, the translated name (Wednesday) was much rarer than Friday or Monday.

Some of the other day names do not appear in historical sources as frequently as Cuffee, Cudjo, and Quaco. An apparent common-noun development of Quamin 'Saturday' must be responsible for references like "one of the little quaminos" in Hall's *Travels*, Vol. I, p. 20 (see Bibliography); such common-noun reference was so widespread by that time (1827) that Hall may have brought it with him from England rather than having heard it in the United States. He was not especially observant, and provides no real information about the slaves, whom he discusses in the most general terms. There are scattered occurrences of the other day names, like the Quash (Quashee 'Sunday') who was among the slaves returned from the prize ship Victoria at Castle Island, Massachusetts, on October 12, 1779, according to Moore's *Notes on the History of Slavery in Massachusetts* (p. 168).

The female day names are comparatively rare in available sources. The most frequent may be Cuba 'Wednesday,' possibly because the owners thought it represented the island. The popularity of Phoebe as a slave name is probably to be traced to its resemblance to Phibbi; indeed, the "two" names are virtually homophonous. Given the obvious condition that both Southern Negroes and Southern whites early learned to accommodate to the different phonological systems of the other, the slave girl was probably quite unaware that her master thought her name referred to a classical name for the moon—or on the part of the owner that the slave herself considered her name to be Friday. In 1742, the will of Colonel William Randal in Virginia left "unto my Daughter Mary Five Negroes" one of whom is named "Phibby" (*Virginia Historical Magazine*, 1896, p. 264); in 1782, the estate of Captain Samuel Flournoy, in Virginia again, had an inventory including "38 Negroes to wit . . ." with the name "Phebe" among them. It seems unlikely that the spelling marks historical change; it is rather differential awareness of the slaves' actual naming practices by owners of slight perceptiveness. Benah, from Cubena, was frequently misanalyzed as Venus. Garrison also recorded "Ahvy," which she took for a pronunciation of Abby, but which was probably Abba 'Thursday.' In some cases, the slaves themselves may have misunderstood the relationship. More frequently, perhaps, they simply choose to keep their own practices to themselves. West African naming practices have long given considerable latitude for giving the same person different names under different circumstances.

Ironically enough, even the name Sambo—for all that it may be hated as a symbol of the stereotypes in the Black community —has a respectable derivation from West African naming practices. Turner gives three separate West African etymologies for the name:

Hausa	sam_3bo_1	'name given the second son in a family'; 'name given to anyone called *Muhammadu*; 'name of a spirit'
Mende	sambo	'to disgrace'; 'to be shameful'
Vai	sam_3bo_1	'to disgrace'

David Dalby has added a fourth, from Wolof. The varied possibilities for derivation of so seemingly simple a name exemplify something about the unsuspected complexity of the West African importations, a complexity which the Southern owners, with their gullible belief in the simplicity of their slaves, obviously almost never suspected. (The subscript numbers in the Hausa and Vai names refer to lexical tones—higher numbers indicating higher pitches. The question of West African tone language influence on slave pronunciation of English is a vexed one; there will probably never be any reliable evidence as to whether the slaves themselves differentiated between the Vai-Hausa forms and the Mende form in pronunciation, although it seems almost certain that the whites did not.)

Both of the practices indicated here—the giving of names according to order of birth in the family, and (more especially) the adding of extra names (like English nicknames, in the etymological sense) because of some family event—are still well-known practices in West Africa, the Congo, and other parts of Africa. One of the possibilities is that the event will be a misfortune to the family or will bring disgrace upon it, and such an eventuality is often reflected in the naming of the children. A native of Burundi—which is outside the area from which slaves were drawn for the New World but which has Bantu peoples and therefore possible cultural affinities—explained to me that his name meant 'We have been persecuted.' He said that it was known in Burundi that his family had once enjoyed great prominence; the rather unfavorable name, applied to him, did not imply a loss of face. Applied indiscriminately to a member of another family, it would have been a terrible insult. Probably there was in the beginning something of the same pattern with regard to Sambo; whether or not it is insulting to call a person "Disgrace" depends upon the exact circumstances of the disgrace or misfortune for which he is named.

The evidence is, however, that the slaveowners and their white associates did not bother to adapt their usage to the realities of whatever African survivals there were in the naming practices of the slaves. The name Sambo is and has been widely misunderstood; to some users, it came to represent a kind of pejorative of Samuel (Samuel, Sam, Sammy, Sambo representing a kind of descending order of respect for the person being named). But there are seventeenth-century references to the name Sambo in West Africa (see *Recueil de Divers Voyages* . . . in Bibliography) and even some hints that the stereotyped use of the name to refer to any African began in West Africa. The application to "all colored persons," comparable to the use of George or the even more insulting Rastus, is probably the most objectionable part of the use of the name by whites insofar as the Black community is concerned. The same has been true in the West Indies. Around 1850 Charles William Day, having referred in his usual condescending manner to a West Indian as "Sambo himself," explained in a footnote

"Sambo" a generic term for Negroes.   (II, 76)

Again, this is obviously the pattern for other genuine survivals in naming practices. Stanley M. Elkins, in *Slavery, A Problem In American Institutional and Intellectual Life*, treated the "Sambo stereotype" as typical of the objectionable features of that practice. The general presentation is an intelligent one, but, when he undertook reasoning from language distribution (p. 84),

Elkins fell into a familiar academic trap—he did not even consult
Turner's *Africanisms*, although he did refer to certain rather
irrelevant works on slavery in South America. It may be historical
accident that we have had no *Little Black Cuffee* to teach white
children racism while they learn reading.

The name has all the evidences of a very widespread use in
the United States. Besides being in use, according to Turner,
in the Sea Islands, it has appeared frequently in literature and in
historical accounts. The first Negro in American drama, according to Quinn's *History of the American Drama* (pp. 332–3), was
Sambo in J. Murdoch's *Triumphs of Love* (first presented on
May 22, 1795). But this is not the earliest occurrence of the
name; N. N. Puckett traces it to Maryland in 1692 ("Names of
American Negro Slaves," 1937). Hitchcock, *A Traveller in Indian
Territory*, pp. 157–164, reported a guide named Sambo among
the Seminoles in the mid-nineteenth century. Mrs. Anne Royall's
The Tennessean: A Novel, Founded on Facts (1827) has a promi-
nent character named Sambo.

In Jamaica, although linguists have chosen to ignore the existence of Sambo as a proper name, it is attested in important
sources like Russell's *The Etymology of Jamaican Grammar*
(1868) and Charles Rampini's *Letters from Jamaica* (1873).
There is a word *sambo*, meaning 'the offspring of a black person
and a mulatto,' which seems to be accidentally homophonous. It
has been almost equally widespread, and was confused with the
proper name by Elkins.

By the time that Lorenzo Turner was doing his field work in
the 1940's, gaining information on the use of such names was
somewhat difficult, possibly because the Negroes of the Sea
Island area (and elsewhere) had tired of white misunderstanding
and ridicule of their naming traditions. It is rather easy to
imagine a large number of situations which would result in
embarrassment—the name was applied in earnest by the white
and was taken by the Black to be given in ridicule; the name was
applied in ridicule by the white and was either understood correctly or misunderstood by the Negro, etc., etc., etc. It thus took

an outstanding act of sympathetic and discreet inquiry by a Black researcher, Turner, to come up with the fact that thousands of naming patterns traceable to West African practices were still in effect among the Gullah speakers. It is highly unlikely that in the 1940's there remained any other area with such a heavy concentration of survivals as in the Sea Islands. Since no one with Turner's talent investigated any area in the nineteenth century—or in the eighteenth—it will perhaps never be known with certainty whether there were equal or greater concentrations elsewhere in earlier times. Undoubtedly, the fact that African imports to Charleston went on well up to the middle of the nineteenth century has something to do with the explanation of why the day names, like other West African survivals, are found in greater abundance there.

There are undoubtedly such survivals, rather thinly distributed, in most parts of the United States where there are Black communities. In most cases, they are subject to what Herskovits termed *masking*. According to Stewart, Cuffee survives in Washington, D.C. and in Chicago, but is rationalized as Coffee—referring to the color of the skin. This masking process may in the beginning have been a way of keeping the whites in the dark about Black culture; to some extent, it actually became the pattern.

For the person who is naming human beings and not worrying over anthropology or etymology, it does not matter whether Phoebe originates in a classical name for the moon or in an African name for one born on Friday. To the girl and to her friends, neither is of any real significance. The name cannot be said to be a real survival unless it is given more or less as a matter of policy to girls born on Friday, although of course it can be a quite lively survival and not be given to all girls born on that day. For purposes of comparison, the Greek tradition seems even more removed: What American parent ever has the moon in mind when he names a girl Phoebe? The day-naming practices may well be moribund, or even stone cold dead, for practical reasons today. Yet they survived long enough to provide clear

evidence that West African language and culture did not magi-
cally disappear when slaves reached the United States.

The West African Pidgin English work names—given now to
a man who leaves his home village for some special purpose, as
to get a job—may have developed early enough to be transmitted
to the New World. (It is not necessary to assume that the names
were work names during the earliest period—or even that they
were in Pidgin English.) Julia M. Peterkin, an excellent writer
of Gullah dialect, gives one of her characters the name Tramsee—
short for Try 'em and See (*Black April*, p. 293), a name which
I recorded in the slightly less basic pidgin form Try and See in
Santa Isabel, Fernando Poo, in 1965. Other such names, as I Go
Try, are widely used in the West Cameroon.

These are essentially gift names of a West African type acquired by a person later in life. They describe a developed (or
wished for) characteristic. Fauset's *Sojourner Truth* (see Bibliography) describes the acquisition of such a name by the slave
girl who had been known only as Isabella. Names for Father
Divine and his disciples like

> Faithful Mary
> Beautiful Love
> Quiet Devotion
> Glorious Illumination
> Crystal Star
> Job Patience
> Celestial Virgin
> Fineness Fidelity
> Flying Angel
> Rolling Stone
> Quiet Love
> Wonderful Devotion
> Blessed Life
> Happy Star
>
> (see Sherif and Cantrill, 147–167)

seem to belong to the same tradition. Iceberg Slim (the nick-
name given to Robert Beck, see Bibliography) is not dissimilar,

although it admittedly would not be especially strange in an American white nicknaming tradition. In some cases, the two traditions obviously overlapped.

There are possibilities, however, of a much more lively influence from West African naming traditions than has been acknowledged. Turner makes a great deal of translation of typically African names, which may have had influence on the whole of American naming practices. This process gave names to the Sea Islanders like Blossom, Wind, Morning, Cotton, Easter. Such names are far from unknown in the white community. The subject has not yet been investigated, but it seems possible that the West African influence on Southern onomastics has been very great indeed.

NOTES

[1] For a summary of dialect leveling in the English-speaking American colonies, see Allen Walker Read, "British Recognition of American Speech in the Eighteenth Century" (see Bibliography).

[2] Theoretically, any language can be pidginized, although historically not all have been. The fact that Portuguese, for example, developed a pidgin in the fifteenth century or even earlier is traceable to the priority of the Portuguese in world trade, not to anything about the structure of Portuguese. The reason why Spanish did not develop such a pidgin in the maritime expansion of the western European nations seems to be that Spanish traders and explorers found it easier to utilize the already developed Portuguese Trade Pidgin—with the addition of a great deal of Spanish vocabulary. This is well attested in the history of Papiamento, the language of Aruba, Bonaire, Curaçao, and a few sections of other Caribbean islands.

[3] The dividing line between "language" and "dialect" is not an absolute one, as linguists have long known. Creoles present a special challenge to the defining power of general linguistics, which has not met the challenge especially well. It is customary to speak of an "English-based" or "French-based" or "Portuguese-based" creole language. Laymen—often including the native speakers of a creole—tend to call it a "dialect" or even "bad" English, French, etc. One important consideration in classifying a creole as a "language" rather than a "dialect" is that there is slight mutual intelligibility

between a creole language and the "standard" language. Monolingual speakers of Indian Ocean French Creole, Louisiana French Creole, and Haitian Creole understand each other quite well; monolingual Frenchmen do not understand any of the three very well.

[4] Saramaccan is one of the English Creoles of Surinam (formerly Dutch Guiana). Others are Sranan Tongo ("Taki Taki") and Djouka. Saramaccan and Djouka are "bush" languages, whereas Sranan Tongo is spoken in Paramaribo and environs.

[5] It is much easier to document the spread of a pidgin language in time and space than it is to explain "how" it spread. Accounts of the process, necessarily kept by laymen, are fragmentary and unreliable at best. Although alleged explanations are abundant, they differ among themselves and all are to some degree improbable. It is clear that pidgins are useful in polyglot language situations, as in places like present-day Nigeria and the Cameroons. Where only two languages are in contact, bilingualism is a more likely eventuality. In my interpretation, pidgins do not "develop" in mixed language situations but are brought in from elsewhere. (See Chapter IV on how Africans and Chinese brought Pidgin English to the United States, and how the former transmitted it to the American Indians.) Ultimate explanation of the origin of a pidgin is almost as vexed a problem as the origin of language—about which there is no respectable theory.

[6] Pioneering work on the earlier U. S. history of Black English was done by Stewart in two seminal articles, "Sociolinguistic Factors in the History of American Negro Dialects" and "Continuity and Change in American Negro Dialects" (see Bibliography). Some effort is made, in this chapter, to avoid duplicating attestations cited by Stewart. After about 1790, however, there are such superabundant documents for the history of the speech of slaves that many such books could not exhaust them.

[7] Early records (see John Barbot, John Atkins, and William Smith in Bibliography) document the use of the Mediterannean Lingua Franca (sometimes called Sabir) on the West Coast of Africa during the early period of the slave trade. The origin of Sabir itself is no more known than is that of pidgin languages. Pidgin Portuguese, French, and English were apparently modeled upon Sabir—but the problem of the chicken and the egg should make one cautious here. The Lingua Franca was used by sailors, traders, and soldiers in about the same way that Latin was used by scholars in the late Middle Ages. Surviving records (see Schuchardt in Bibliography) show that Lingua Franca could be made predominantly Portuguese, French, Italian, etc., in vocabulary. This vocabulary replacement process may be called relexification (see Taylor, Whinnom, Thompson, and Stewart in Bibliography, Section III). One theory of the origin of Pidgin English holds that it is a result of the replacement of other vocabulary in Lingua Franca with English vocabulary.

[8] See Glossary for an explanation of the term *enclitic*. It happens that there is a reasonably good indication of the historical development of the enclitic vowel. Writing of the inhabitants of Dominica specifically—but by

implication of great numbers of speakers of other languages—the Earl of Cumberland reported in 1596:

> . . . saving that to all words ending in a consonant they always set the second vowel, as for Chinne, they say Chin-ne, so making most of the monasillables, dissillables.   (Samuel Purchas, *Hakulytus Posthumus or Purchas His Pilgrimes,* Vol. XVI, p. 56)

[9] An outstanding exception is the edition by Hervey Allen and Thomas Ollive Mabbott (see Bibliography), in which the editors point out the striking recall exhibited by Poe for physical details of Sullivan's Island, South Carolina, the setting for *The Gold Bug.*

[10] Because of the popular belief that French Creole is "bad" French or English Creole "bad" English, native speakers of the creole languages often strive to change their language in the direction of the standard language. Frequently, mixed forms are produced in this process. In Jamaican Creole, for example, the plural of *car* is *car-dem.* A speaker of creole, attempting to use Standard English, will often form plurals like *cars-dem.*

[11] The entire text follows. The author represents himself as having asked "an old African" whether he knew any English when he came to Demarara:

"Engreesh! Whi'side me go l'arn um?"

"You know no English at all when you come to Bakra Country?"

"'T all 't all!"

"Who teach you when you come?"

"Who l'arn me? Eh-eh! No me matty?"

"How he learn you? Gi'e you book and so?"

"Book! Youse'f too! A-we nation got book? Fo' a-we book *yah*!"

He touched his chest, where the Negro "mind" is supposed to reside; his memory was his book.

"What fashion you learn?"

"Da Uncle me a lib wit' he se'f l'arn me. Uncle a say, 'Bwoy, tekky this crabash (calabash)—de crabash dey a he hand—go dip watah. *Watah— watah* da ting inside da barrel O' So Uncle do, sotay me a ketch wan-wan Engreesh."

"So all of you catch Bakra talk, little by little?"

"Ah! Same thing! Matty a l'arn matty, matty a l'arn matty. You no see da fashion pickny a l'arn fo' talk—when he papa a talk he a watch he papa mout'?"

Translation:

"English! Where would I learn it?"

"You didn't know any English at all when you came to the white man's country?"

"None at all!"

"Who taught you when you came?"

"Who taught me? Eh-eh! Who else but my friend?"

"How did he teach you? Did he give you a book and so on?"

"Book! You gotta be kiddin'! Does our people have books? Our books are *here!*" . . . .

"In what manner did you learn?"

"It was Uncle whom I lived with who taught me himself. Uncle would say 'Boy, take this calabash—the calabash would be in his hand—and go dip water. Water—water, the thing inside the barrel.' So Uncle did, until I picked up English little by little."

"So you all picked up white man's talk, little by little?"

"Yes, that's it. A friend would teach a friend, that friend would be teaching another friend. Haven't you ever seen how a child learns to talk—when his father is talking he'll be watching his father's mouth?"

[12] There is a kind of continuum from Sea Island Gullah to slightly decreolized forms of Gullah to Negro Non-Standard dialect (Black English, in the form known to most Americans). Mason Crum's *Gullah* (1940), in spite of a generally amateurish orientation toward language, discusses this continuum in a relatively intelligent way (p. 103). In Charleston, a mildly risqué joke has a Negro workman reporting to a friend

    I be layin' linoleum.

In Sea Island Gullah, the "deepest" variety, this would be

    Me de lay linoleum.

Mixed forms of Gullah are found in the writings of authors like Julia Peterkin, whose first language it was (see Isadora Bennett, in Bibliography):

Las night I been know somebody gwine dead! Yes, Lawd! Somebody gwine dead! A sign sesso. De hoot-owl ain' talk! De wind ain' whine.

(*Black April,* p. 37)

IV

Pidgin English in the United States— Black, Red, and Yellow

ANY thorough investigation of the historical records will show conclusively that there have been three varieties of Pidgin English spoken in the United States—by Africans, by American Indians, and by Chinese. (There have undoubtedly been Hawaiians who spoke the Pidgin English of their islands, too; but they apparently have not come in such numbers as to leave the overwhelming influence on the record which the other three groups have left.) These are large population groups, and most of them have been with us for centuries, yet the official histories—like the school systems, the legislative processes, and such economic planning activities as we have had—have taken little or no account of them. The languages and the cultures of these people must have contributed greatly to the nature of the United States today, as have the languages and cultures of other minority groups. But the historiography of the black, red, and yellow groups in the United States is a story of whitewashing.

The information that these groups spoke Pidgin English is potentially misleading information—it is necessary to reaffirm most strongly once again that Pidgin English is not impoverished language. The three groups have been economically exploited, but it would be a tragic oversimplification to assume—as has been assumed in prominent studies—that the "imposition" of a non-standard variety of English is part of that exploitation. In the beginning at least (and, in the case of the Chinese and the Indians, up to the present) most of the speakers of Pidgin English retained their native languages. Many of each group learned Standard English instead of—or in addition to—Pidgin or Creole English. Pidgin has been tied in historically with a lot of re-grettable racial and economic policies, but it would be very bad ecology to assume that such policies were the *cause* of the Pidgin.

The maritime expansion of the Western European powers was the ultimate mechanism of transmission of Pidgin English to the three groups. Developing out of the Mediterannean and West African *lingua franca* traditions, Pidgin English was ready for world-wide circulation by the seventeenth century.[1] It spread east to China and the Pacific, west to the Americas. The eastward expansion is still to be felt not only in Chinese Pidgin English but also in Australian Pidgin English, Melanesian Pidgin English, and in other varieties like Pitcairn Island dialect (the legacy in some sense of Mr. Christian and his *Bounty* mutineers). In the West, especially, Pidgin English became associated with the slave trade. Remaining on the West Coast of Africa in various forms today (Sierra Leone Krio, Liberian Pidgin English, "Wes-Kos" of the Cameroons and Nigeria), Pidgin English also left its traces in the West Indian islands, on coastal South America (British Guiana, Surinam) and in what is now the continental United States. Pidgin French accompanied Pidgin English east (Indian Ocean French Creole of La Réunion, Seychelles, Mauritius and Madagascar, Pidgin French of Vietnam) and west (French Guiana, Haiti, Martinique, Guadaloupe, Dominica, Louisiana). Portuguese Trade Pidgin preceded and then accompanied both, and left Portuguese creole languages in West Africa (Annobon, São Thomé, Cape Verde and Guinea), India (Goa), Malacca, China, the Philippines and in the West Indies (Papiamento). The wake of the Lingua Franca-Portuguese Trade

FIRST PART

The Things whe we must believe

1.

TRUE THINGS WHE EVERY MAN HE MUST SAVI FOR GO FOR HAEVEN

1. *Who he ben make heaven and ground ?*
God he ben make heaven and ground.

2. *Who he be God ?*
God he be big King for all things. He dash the good men, and he punish the bad men.

3. *For wath God he ben make we ?*
God he ben make we to savi him, to like him, to work for him for this ground, and to be glad with him for heaven, for all times.

4. *Wath i be heaven ?*
Heaven i be place for glad, where Angels and Holy People them look God, and them get glad too much whe i pass all glad, for all times.

5. *After die, bad men them go for who's side ?*
After die, bad men them go for hell.

6. *Wath i be hell ?*
Hell i be some place for trouble, where bad angels and bad people them no look God, and them get trouble too much, for all times.

East Camerounian Pidgin English. Note the Portuguese lexical items (*savi, dash*), the use of *ben* to mark past actions, the use of the pronominal noun classifier (*God he, bad people them*), and lexical differences from Standard English (*ground* means 'earth' or 'world'). Actually, though, this text reflects many influences from Standard English.

Pidgin-Pidgin English/French tradition is that of European colonialism.

Pidgin English may well have started in Africa, since the best historical accounts available show that there was a Pidgin English in West Africa during the sixteen century.[2] Indirect evidence goes back to 1594.[3] When John Barbot traveled through West Africa and the West Indies in 1678–82, he reported the use of "a little English" here and there by Africans, although his most important reports concern the widespread use of Lingua Franca or "Broken Portuguese."[4] In 1735, John Atkins, Gent., published *A Voyage to Guinea, Brasil, and the West Indies*, which attributed phrases like *grandee shippee* to the Africans and which contained one long section of reported discourse in Pidgin:

> ... they [the Cape Corso Africans] would reply that after Death the honest goodee man go to Godee, livee very well, have a goodee wife, goodee victuals, &c but if a *Rogue* and *Cheatee*, he must be tossed here and there, never still.

This passage is very like the one which Cotton Mather, in 1721, attributed to "these Africans"; Mather, Atkins, and Mrs. Knight (1704–5) attributed the form *grandee* to the West African Pidgin.[5] William Smith's *A New Voyage to Guinea* (1744), an important source for the practices of slavers, quotes an African as saying:

> No, this [a monkey of an unusual species and color] no my wife, this fit wife for you.   (p. 53)

Thus, it appears that the West African Pidgin English extended by this time from West Africa to the New World (the continental colonies and the West Indies).

Records of this Pidgin English in the speech of Africans are scanty, but fortunately some idea of its structure may be gained from an investigation of the other two varieties of Pidgin English which have been widely used in this country—American Indian Pidgin English and Chinese Pidgin English. Early records are far more abundant for the speech of the Indians, possibly because the Puritan consciences of the founding fathers did not trouble them as much about the dispossessed Indians as they did about the enslaved Africans.

Transmission to the Indians

There is little direct evidence for the transmission of Pidgin English—the whites who kept the records being little concerned with the speech of Blacks and Indians—but there is great circumstantial evidence. The first known slaves in the continental colonies arrived in Virginia in 1619. There were 20 of them, and it is not known how they communicated with the new British immigrants; but they were given names like William Tucker, and must have communicated in some kind of English. This was the century after the development of African Pidgin English, and there may have been one or two in the group who had acquired the language before coming to Virginia.

In Maryland the first slaves arrived around 1634.[6] They were treated as indentured servants, and given their freedom after seven years of labor. One of the first Maryland group, who somehow acquired the name of Mathias DeSousa, became a prosperous trader with the Indians after his servitude was over. In Massachusetts the first slaves seem to have arrived around 1638. In all three places, Indians had preceded the Africans as slaves and continued to be their fellow slaves for some time. In all three places, the first attestations of American Indian Pidgin English came ten years or so after the arrival of the Africans.[7]

The time table for the spread of Pidgin English from African slaves to Indians is a workable one. By all evidence, moreover, African-Indian cooperation and resistance to the English took place at a very early period. It is known that even in Connecticut Negroes and Indians had by 1658 conspired to destroy several houses of their masters in a move for freedom. Because of the scarcity of documents, and because of the overwhelming focus of interest of historians on the Civil War period, even a work like Herbert Aptheker's *American Negro Slave Revolts* (1939) is thin on the early years. But what evidence there is indicates that the period of African cooperation with Indian fellow slaves and African runaways to receptive Indian tribes coincides exactly with the spread of Pidgin English in the colonies. This would be a part of the largely unwritten history of the cultural relationship between the two groups, the importance of which Herskovits pointed up some time ago.[8]

In 1649, Colonel Henry Norwood, the Cavalier traveler in Virginia, reported that an Indian named Jack who served as an interpreter for his exploring group had a "sprinkling of English" learned "at our plantations."[9] Since there were at least 300 African slaves in Virginia at that time,[10] and since they often worked beside the Indian slaves whom they eventually replaced, it seems highly probable that "Jack" learned his English from them. The reference is a passing one, with no elaboration, but it fits well into the total picture.

In Massachusetts, what is usually considered to be the first attestation of American Indian Pidgin English is dated 1641, a few scant years after the arrival of the African slaves but not too short a time for the transmission of Pidgin English. It is a rather inconclusive attestation:

They say, Englishman much folle,—Lazie squaes![11]

It may, in fact, be the kind of stumbling around with English which Pidgin English is often inaccurately represented as being. There are actually several other attestations of "broken" English —which may or may not be Pidgin—by Indians at about the same time and from the same area. Roger Williams's Indian friend Wequash "confessed"

Me so big naughty heart, me heart all one stone.
(Winslow, *John Eliot*, p. 104)

It should be remembered that Indians, since the time when Sebastian Cabot presented three of them at court in 1502, had

had some limited opportunity to come into contact with English. It is quite probable that some of them developed the foreign-accented English which we hear often from immigrants to the United States who have had no contact with Pidgin English. That kind of English was probably what was used by Samoset, who during the Pilgrims' first year (1621)

> ... came boldly down the street and greatly to the surprise of the Pilgrims welcomed them in broken English.
> *(Commonwealth History of Massachusetts, p. 73)*

There is, as always, a problem—perhaps unresolvable in absolute terms—of the meaning of *broken English*. We know that it can mean either 'a foreigner's accented English' or 'Pidgin English.'

Less reliable than any of these textually, but in the authentic tradition, are the warrant and commentary on justice in the "praying villages" of the newly converted Indians which are sometimes attributed to the historical Waban:

> You, you big constable, quick you catch um Jeremiah Offscoe, strong you hold um, safe you bring um afore me, Waban, Justice Peace.

> Tie um all up,—and whip um plaintiff and whip um 'fendant, and whip um witness.

Probably the most noteworthy grammatical feature of this text—which is not recorded in any of the earlier texts—is the transitive verb marker *um*, which almost certainly spread historically from one place to another in the Maritime Pidgin English tradition. There have been arguments that it derived "spontaneously" from English *him* or *them* (or both—it would have to be both in the Waban text) at a variety of times and places, but such identical developments seem highly improbable.[12] It is a feature which is present today in West African Pidgin English and in Chinese Pidgin English, but which was never in the English of the white "colonizers." By far the most simple explanation is that it was present in West African Pidgin English in the sixteenth and seventeenth centuries and in the (perhaps antecedent) Maritime Pidgin English.

Pidgin English would have been very useful to the Indians in the transition period between their pagan state and more or less complete Christianization, but it may have been even more useful in their relationships with the Africans. Negroes were being brought into the area at about this time, the first having arrived around 1638. John Eliot taught mixed classes of Negro and Indian children to read in his last days, say between 1685 and 1690. If Waban learned Pidgin English sometime between 1652 (the date of his "confession," which was translated from Algonquian into English for the records) and 1673, his case would provide interesting evidence of the state of things at about the midpoint between 1638 and 1690. Kittredge (see Bibliography), who exposed the philological unreliability of the warrant texts, felt that the language itself was authentic.

It is a characteristic of pidgin languages that some vocabulary items and idiomatic expressions from indigenous languages, varying a great deal with individual practices and circumstances, are occasionally brought in. Thus, there is good evidence that the Pidgin English in Massachusetts in the second half of the seventeenth century had some Algonquian vocabulary. There is no direct evidence, but it may well have had some West African words and turns of phrase, particularly as it was used by African slaves. Pidgin English on the West Coast of Africa today has its own varieties—or "dialects"—with variable amounts of vocabulary from the tribal languages. There is evidence that the American Indian Pidgin English of the early years of the eighteenth century had its own dialects, depending upon which ethnic group used it.

In 1704, according to Sarah Kemble Knight's Journal, a "Senior Justice," attempting to interrogate a Connecticut Indian who was on trial for receiving stolen goods (from a Negro slave:), addressed him in the following words:

> You Indian why did you steal from this man? You shouldn't do so—
> it's a Grandy wicked thing to steal. Hol't Hol't cryes Justice Junr,
> Brother You speak Negro to him I'le ask him. You, sirrah, why did
> you steal this man's Hoggshead? Hoggshead (replys the Indian)

me no stomany. No? says his Worship; and pulling off his hatt,
Patted his own head with his hand, sais, Tatapa—you, Tatapa you;
all one this Hoggshead. Hoggshead all one this. Ha! says Netop [a
conventional name for an Indian], now me stomany that.

Among the "Indian" (as apparently distinct from "Negro")
Pidgin forms which had to be used in establishing communication
were *stomany* 'understand' and *all one* 'just like, identical to.'
Wequash also used the latter phrase, and it turns up elsewhere
in American Indian Pidgin English; it is virtually identical to
allee samee, which is attested in Chinese Pidgin English. In its
more specifically Indian form, however, it may have been altered
to agree semantically with Algonquian. Mrs. Knight thought that
Tatapa must have been an approximation of *Tatta pitch* 'I cannot
tell.'

It is hard to see how whites so inept at Pidgin English as these
justices—who would hardly prevail, linguistically, if it were not
for the power of their office—could have taught it to the Indians.
The pupils would in some mysterious way have become better
than their teachers. It is, on the other hand, easy to understand
how the escaped Africans, or fellow slaves of the Indians, could
have done the teaching. The Negro slave from whom "Netop"
received the hogshead must have communicated with the Indian
in some way, and Pidgin English is a very credible hypothesis.

Transmission to the Whites

There was involved, therefore, the seemingly paradoxical process
of a variety of English being taught to some Englishmen by non-
Europeans. In West Africa today, this would not seem a paradox.
If one wants to learn "WesKos" Pidgin English of the Cameroons
and Nigeria, he had better learn it from Africans if he wants to

learn it well. But language historians, who have thought only in terms of the transmission of English from England and who have never considered the West African situation, have been puzzled by such a possibility. It would be more accurate, in fact, to say that they have never considered it at all.

The most noteworthy attempt to account for American Indian Pidgin English in terms of transmission from the whites to the Indians was made by Douglas Leechman and Robert A. Hall, Jr., whose place in the history of pidgin studies is secure because of the pioneering nature of their efforts.[13] In an attempt to document what they conceived of as the process of transmission by historical accounts, they chose a passage from Richard Irving Dodge's *Our Wild Indians*, published in 1889—decidedly late for the purpose!

> When the white trader invaded the solitudes of the Indian, he took with him, or soon picked up, a small stock of words which, by his constant use among the tribes, have become, as it were, common property; thus 'squaw', the Narragansett word for woman, the Algonquian 'papoose' for child, and many other words, have become universal among all the North American Indians east of the Rocky Mountains, when speaking to a white man, or Indian not of their tribe.   (p. 47)

What this passage really seems to say—contrary to the Hall-Leechman interpretation—is not that the whites *taught* something *to* the Indians but that they *learned* something *from* the Indians. Predictably, Dodge treated only vocabulary, and—not being a linguist—paid no attention to the structural system within which the words were used; but even today there are those who insist that, for the Plains Indians, *squaw* is "a white man's word."[14]

Actually somewhat nearer chronologically to the formation of the pidgin is a statement by James Fenimore Cooper, who wrote in *Redskins* (1846):

> The colonists caught a great many words from the Indians they first knew, and used them to all other Indians, though not belonging to their language; and these other tribes used them as English, a sort of *lingua franca* has grown up in the country that everybody understands . . .   (p. 148)

This is not only as explicit a statement about pidginization ("used them as English," "everybody understands") as is ever likely to come from a layman, but it is accurate with regard to the Indian language "they first knew."[15] The specific Indian language was Algonquian, and it is historically true that the Algonquian words spread to the other Indian languages. The mechanism whereby they spread has never been investigated, but a pidgin ("lingua franca") is a possible medium by which *Sago* (a salutation), *moccasin, squaw, papoose, tomahawk, yankees*[16] were transmitted to other Indian languages and, most probably, to Standard American English. We shall see later that it was almost undoubtedly through Pidgin English that some of this same vocabulary went to the Florida Seminoles.[17]

The novels of Cooper are, as a matter of fact, remarkably consistent in indicating this relationship. In *The Redskins; or, Indian and Injin,* the "Injins" are whites who impersonate Indians and who, in doing so, speak Pidgin English. All of Cooper's *Satansoe* series (of which *The Redskins* is the concluding novel) represent the Negro Jaap (or Yop) and the Indian Suquesus, whose relationship is enduring if not quite cordial, as speaking varieties of English which are almost but not quite identical. Both use the zero copula; Yop is represented as saying

> . . . she nutten but gal . . . Young masser Mordaunt take fancy to her, and make her he wife. (p. 131)

Susquesus uses the same structure:

> What tribe "dem Injin?" (p. 134)

Both use the pluralizer *dem*:

> Susquesus: "dem Injin" (p. 134)
> Yop:　　　"What dem feller want?" (p. 228)

One of Cooper's white "Injins," "speaking in his natural voice, though affecting an Indian pronunciation" (which may well mean something like 'using the grammar of Pidgin English') speaks rather less believable Pidgin English:

> "How do, how do?—where come from, eh?—where go, eh? What you say, too—up rent or down rent, eh?" (p. 209)

Although it is dangerous to overestimate Cooper's knowledge of the linguistic situation of some seventy years earlier, his materials parallel rather strikingly those of Mrs. Knight.

Transmission to the Seminoles

If some possible doubt about the direction of borrowing of Pidgin English remains in the other cases discussed above, there is clear African-to-Indian transmission in the case of the Seminoles. Around 1730, refugee slaves from the British colonies had come among the Florida Seminoles in large numbers; occasional fugitives had been added for about a century. We find Pidgin and Creole English spoken by the Seminoles and the African slaves who escaped to them, respectively; and the likelihood that the Indians transmitted the Pidgin to the escaped slaves rather than vice versa is approximately as great as that the Gauls taught Latin to the Romans.

There are few early records about the Seminoles and the Negroes who joined them, since neither group was eager to attract the attention of the whites. But when travelers began to take notice of them, in the early nineteenth century, they found the Blacks well established among the Indians. John W. Griffin observed, around 1818:

> Some, however, possess extensive herds of cattle; and Negroes, to whom the culture of rice, Indian corn, and potatoes is confined.[18]

William Haynes Simmons reported in 1822:

> ... the cometas ... had recently carried off a body of Negroes ... .[19]

The standard white point of view was that the Blacks served as slaves to the Seminoles, but this may have been a projection of the white attitude. Simmons also reported

> ... the Negro settlement of the Big Swamp ... .[20]

. . . at the house of Cudjoe, one of the principal men of the place.[21]

As many of these Negroes were refugee slaves . . .[22]

The total picture which emerges is rather that of cooperation between the Seminoles and the refugees from slavery. There are indications of intermarriage, including Simmons's observation of "an Indian Negro."[23] In general, the Blacks were anything but inferiors:

> The Negro slaves are in fact, the masters of their owners, who seem fully conscious of their own mental inferiority. If a Seminole wishes to convey a high idea of his own cunning, he will say, "Ah, you no cheat me. I got real nigger wit."[24]

The Africans transmitted a great many patterns to the Seminoles, in areas like agriculture[25] and music.[26] They seem to have made an especial contribution in language. Many of them were interpreters:

> Ben Bruno, the interpreter, advisor, confidant, and special favorite of King Billy, is a fine, intelligent-looking Negro.[27]

Abram[28] and Gopher John[29] are other Black interpreters whose work for the Seminoles is recorded. So was Cudjo, whose African day name seems especially significant. The latter's variety of English can be identified with some certainty:

> He [Cudjo] was a runaway, and consequently gave his answers in the common Negro jargon of the plantations.[30]

The speech of such an interpreter in 1836, as recorded by Ethan Allen Hitchcock (later General Hitchcock), bears out this description:

> Well, massa, he say he live dis country berry well and no wants leabum.

> Well, massa, I tell um. He say he like dis country where fader live and mudder. Don' want no new country.

> Pretty much same t'ing he say 'fore, massa—Bress God, dis berry fine country. Fader, mudder live here, an' chil'n—he no wanto [sic] go nowhere 'tall. (p. 110)

Writers of the mid-nineteenth century were generally aware of the nature of the English spoken by the Blacks among the

Seminoles. Novelist T. Mayne Reid, who elsewhere displayed a virtuosic knowledge of Afro-American language patterns,[31] represented the historic Abram in his *Osceola The Seminole* (1858); the interpreter defies the white army

> Abram was the spokesman on the part of the Indians, and delivered himself in his broken English, "Da tarms we gib you are dese: you lay down arm, an' stop de war; your sogas go back, an' stay in der forts; *we Indyen* cross ober da Ouitalochee; an' from dis time forth, for ebber affer, we make the grand ribber da line o' boundary atween de two. We promise libe in peace an' good tarms wi' all white neighbor. Dat's all got say."   (p. 342)

Parts of the above speech are undoubtedly standardized, since Reid probably knew that a speaker in such a situation would elegantize his English to some degree, with inconsistent success. In another speech, when the tables have turned and emotion disturbs Abram's linguistic control, his speech is much less like the English of the white man

> An' what for we submit . . . we not conquered! We conquer you ebbery fight—we whip you people one, two, tree time—we whip you; dam! we kill you well too. What for we submit? We come here gib condition, not ask um.   (p. 343)

Under emotional stress, Abram uses the Pidgin transitivizer *um*; elsewhere, he is represented as using the pre-verbal durative particle *a* (*Your a gwine*, p. 41).

Because Andrew Jackson's "heroic" efforts made life in Florida impossible for most of the Seminoles—especially those with one degree or another of African ancestry—large parts of the tribe migrated to Bracketville, Texas. Some of them went on to Mexico in 1849, and some of the last group later returned to Texas in 1870. Language records are scanty, since the Seminoles were understandably eager to avoid whites who could, among other things, record their speech. But the speech of the famous Seminole Indian Scouts of Fort Clark (Bracketville), Texas, has been referred to as

> . . . a broken plantation English, sometimes with a Gullah twang.[32]

And there are enough records to indicate that they carried along a fair number of African customs with them.[33]

In 1935 anthropology graduate student Lawrence Foster published, among materials which he had gathered during his field work among the Texas Seminoles, a speech by Mrs. Becky Simmons, an old woman who had been a member of the first party to cross the Rio Grande:

> John Horse he told dem when we wus ready to tell de Mexicans dat we wus dare. Later Wild Cat took sick with de pox and he die. We all wus crying fur we done lost him. He was so good. John Horse or Juan Cavallas, our next head man, but the Injuns most of dem been gone back to the territory.[34]

Although Mrs. Simmons must have been super-conscious of the white graduate student who was transcribing her speech and may have standardized her English quite a bit, the results are still very much like the Black dialects of other groups with different recent histories.[35] Non-redundant tense marking is clear in *Wild Cat took sick with de pox and he die*; zero copula fades in and out (*John Horse our next head man*); the *been* remote perfective marker is perhaps the most extreme "slip" of all.

In recent years there have been a few indications of the type of language spoken by the Texas Seminoles. A newspaper article reported in 1924

> . . . Renty Grayson, a Seminole Negro . . . speaks a mixed language of English, Seminole, and Spanish.[36]

Terms like *mixed language* in a newspaper article may mean almost anything, but it seems quite likely that something like the process of relexification is documented in such a report. For example, if Grayson had said *Me savvy Indyen ojus*, the reporter could have observed (correctly) that Seminole and English words were involved—and his classification of *savvy* as Spanish would be in good popular tradition. Seminole *ojus* relexified American Indian Pidgin English *heap*. Like most such observers, the reporter would have been indifferent to the fact that the sentence is in fact Pidgin English with some relexification by Seminole.

Behind them, in the swamps of Florida, the Black Seminoles left Pidgin English with the (largely Indian) Seminoles who chose to hide out from the whites rather than to run. Gifford reported

Their Negro slaves helped them corrupt English words.   (p. 36)

Corrupt is, of course, as close to *pidginize* as such an observer could be expected to come.

As late as 1910, the Indian Seminoles who remained behind in the Florida swamps spoke what was clearly a Pidgin version of English. A restricted number of them spoke it, for purpose of trade with the whites and for other practical reasons, as is often the case with a pidgin language. Minnie Moore-Willson's *The Seminoles of Florida* (1910) contains many quotations from the Seminoles which are clearly in Pidgin:

Me don't know.   (p. 59. Said to be a typical Indian response
                                                    to inquisitive strangers.)

Indian no fight. Indian no kill. Indian go.   (p. 78)

Ugh! White man's squaw heap purty!   (p. 116)

Tallahasse blind *ojus* (heap).   (p. 83)

White man fraid *ojus* (heap).   (p. 142)

Heap pickaninnies, pickaninnies *ojus* (plenty).   (p. 85)

He poor man, give 'em him. Indian no want 'em.   (p. 63)

Whiskey, me no take 'em, lemonade, me take, cowboys wy-o-mee
[whiskey] take.   (p. 149)

Billy Bowlegs lock-a-dox *ojus* (lie too much)   (p. 158)

Through the time of Billy Bowlegs, second only to Osceola in Seminole fame, Pidgin English remained at least reasonably well known to the Florida Seminoles. There seems to be no doubt that it was an unbroken tradition up to the time that the Willsons found it just prior to 1910. Today? It is rather shocking to discover that no one knows enough about the Seminoles of Florida to know how they speak English. Shocking, perhaps, but not surprising. Academic ignorance of the language of minority groups in the United States is so all-pervasive that it would be astonishing to find any area of knowledge.[37]

Some of the most important linguistic information about Seminole Pidgin English is provided inadvertently by Willson, whose glossary of Seminole is appended to his wife's book. Among the vocabulary items which he gives is *squaw* 'woman,' which we know—although Willson apparently did not—to be from Algonquian. It is, in fact, one of the *lingua franca* items specified by James Fenimore Cooper, who seems to be vindicated to a degree by the occurrence of the word in far-away Florida and another Indian language. Another of the words which Cooper indicated to be in the frontier *lingua franca* was *papoose*, which Mrs. Willson amusingly assumed to be an attempt to produce English *baby*. At that, her instincts were basically right—the word probably did come into Seminole through a variety (pidginized) of English. Willson's glossary lists

pic-a-nin-ny 'child'

apparently unaware that it is Portuguese—or Portuguese Trade Pidgin—and thus spared the labor of theorizing about its transmission. In default of professional linguists, complete innocents like the Willsons (who could not possibly have been trying to prove a theory) are the best sources. R. B. Braden Moore, who wrote an introduction to the book, testified to Willson's devotion to gathering Seminole vocabulary in the course of "ten or fifteen years of daily intercourse with members of the tribe." Without the conscious knowledge of Willson, Mrs. Moore-Willson, or Moore, the three corroborated the theory of a Pidgin English *lingua franca* advanced by Cooper (and scorned by allegedly sophisticated critics) and documented the spread of that Pidgin into the swamps of Florida.

Indian Pidgin Evidence for the Nature of
West African Pidgin English

Unfortunately, only a few brief attestations of the unmistakably pidgin stage of Black English survive. Given, however, the very probable historical relationship with American Indian Pidgin English, we can speculate about the nature of some of the details of the pidgin which the Black slaves used.[38]

The characteristics of American Indian Pidgin English are familiar ones everywhere, in spite of the different transcriptional practices in the sources which must be used. It should be remembered that the records were kept by whites, most of whom did not know Pidgin English well, and that Pidgin did not have its own writing tradition. Although, for example, we may wish to discount statements about "reduction" of verb forms as being linguistically biased, we can recognize verb forms without -s and -ed of Standard English in all varieties of the Pidgin. There is frequent attestation of a tendency to "leave out" the copula verb; we can easily recognize this as being zero copula:

Him no good for me.   (Cremony, *Life Among the Apaches*, p. 173)

That him.   (Calkins, *Tales of the West*, I, 85)

I sure.   (White, *Blazed Trail*, p. 455)

Him nice boy.   (*Ibid.*, p. 180)

The copula is realized under certain circumstances, the most likely of which is imitation of Standard English—a constant possibility in the attestations from both Indians and Blacks.

Contrast of zero copula with durative *be*, a distinguishing feature of the more completely decreolized stages of Black English, may well be a characteristic of at least some stages (perhaps of a creole stage only) of American Indian Pidgin English, although I have been unable to find anything as clear-cut as the Black English examples. The text *Poor Sarah* from *The Religious Intelligencer* of 1812 has *be* forms and zero copula forms, but it is not perfectly clear that the former indicate any kind of longer duration. In John O'Keeffe's *The Basket Maker* (1790), we find

    and I be your fellow servant   (p. 345)

which apparently indicates a lifetime or at least long-term relationship, as against

    Me no fellow servant   (p. 363)

which apparently marks a short-term relationship. If American Indian Pidgin English acts like Negro Non-Standard, we should expect a negation of the long-term relationship

    Me no be fellow servant.

This would not preclude the speaker's being a "fellow servant" on a short-term basis, and it would be hypothetically possible to say

    Me your fellow servant, but me no be your fellow servant.

Verbs generally have a single uninflected form, although occasionally that base form may be drawn from the Standard English preterite (e.g., *lef* not *leave*) and may give an illusion of marking past time.

    Me lose um last spling clossin' liver.   (Calkins, II, 70)

    Dey go up river, dey look for somethin'.   (White, p. 194)

    One man no have cork boat.   (White, p. 454)

Here, the marking of past time is essentially taken from the co-occurrent adverbial expressions (*last spling* 'last spring'), as happens very frequently in pidgin and creole languages. In some sentences, it is not considered very important—from the viewpoint of the pidgin speakers—whether the action was in the past or not.

When the action was significantly in the past, pidgins and

creoles, including basilect, use *been* (*bin*) as the preverbal marker with striking frequency. It may be added either to verb base forms or to "zero copula"; in the latter case it is sometimes regarded by superficial observers as a "reduction" from *have/has been*:

I been hate all palefaces.
       (Baker, *The Red Brother and Other Indian Stories*, p. 136)

Me been sick.   (Thoreau, *The Maine Woods*, p. 105)

Been seems somewhat less frequent in American Indian Pidgin English than in the Afro-American creoles—it is certainly less frequent in the fictional attestations of the former than in comparable accounts of Gullah—and its presence may be a more striking proof of borrowing from the Negroes than in those varieties which appear to be without it. *Done* as a preverbal marker of less remote completion (*He done go* as a more recent action than *He been go*), which appears in many Afro-American varieties, does not seem to be attested in American Indian Pidgin English. It is possible that neither of these features was in the seventeenth-century Pidgin English which was transmitted to the Indians, but came in with later speakers of African Pidgin. Both were certainly in Plantation Creole; *been Verb* and *done Verb* are in both Gullah and basilect, and the latter has been transmitted to Southern whites.

Another positive feature is the transitivizer (spelled by different writers as *'um, 'em, am,* or *'m*), used widely in English pidgins and seemingly impossible to trace to interference from indigenous languages. It has sometimes been assumed that this is simply the result of the throwing around of *him* by an English speaker who is using baby talk to the foreigner, but an examination of the forms listed should establish the point that not all of these could have come from *English him* or *'im* (the unstressed form). Forms like the initial example from Thoreau, below, or the Hawaiian advertising slogan for a Honolulu used car dealer *Geev 'em low low prices* could, of course, be explained in terms of the baby talker's using *'em* as a reduced form of *them*; it depends upon how many *ad hoc* explanations for one structure are acceptable. Where the following object is first person (*He shootum me*, in Dressler, *California Chinese Chatter*, p. 501), the derivation from *him* (or *them*) seems wildly absurd. The theory is helped, admittedly, by the Pidgin English use of *him* for feminine singular subjects and objects, as in the second example below, from the Reverend Peter Jones's *History of the Ojibway Indians* (1861):

Sometimes I lookum locks.   (Thoreau, *The Maine Woods*, p. 23)

White people have law forbidding throwing away wife, be he ever so cross!—must keep him always.   (Jones, p. 80)

Dey go camp gettum boss.   (White, p. 195)

You get'm out quick.   (Edmonds, p. 531)

Me thank him Great Spirit we [Indian and white man] no nearer brothers.   (*The American Pioneer I* [1842], 263)

Squaw make um bed; heap sleep.   (Calkins, I, 118)

Um no hallar like um Yanktonais.   (*Ibid.*, p. 85)

John come,—digum hole,—findum money heap.
                    (Forbes, *Nevada Indians Speak*, p. 69)

You trade 'em gun for pony?   Hayes, *Apache Vengeance*, p. 29)

While *he, I, we,* and *they* occur in the sources among other forms which serve as subject pronouns, they very probably represent mixing with Standard English, especially when the Indian is talking to a paleface. The undifferentiated form, corresponding more or less to the "objective" form or "accusative case" in Standard English is the regular subject form:

Me policeman, many other policemans here. Next time no wait, all policemans shoot you on sight. (Wissler, *Indian Cavalcade*, p. 122)

Me burst all to smash!   (Forbes, p. 36)

Me not understand spectoolation.   (Forbes, p. 36)

No, him eat plenty labbit.   (Calkins, II, 71)

Him white man, him hunt too.   (White, p. 171)

As in other English-based pidgins and creoles, the undifferentiated pronoun, juxtaposed to the possessed noun, often serves as possessive:

White man put him hand over money.   (Forbes, p. 69)

He got mad at speyets and have bayed um in um cave.
                                                      (Calkins, III, 7)

She purty soon got all me money.   (Forbes, p. 36)

The use of *he* and *she* as subject pronouns, as in the second and third examples above, occurs as a feature of mixing with Standard English. It is all too facile, however, to assume that the pidgin has become identical with Standard English; the same forms then become possessive and even objective forms:

When he no find bear and deer, he hunt he friend.
                                                      (Coppinger, p. 80)

As frequently happens in pidgins and creoles, pluralization is nonredundant; no plural marker is needed on the noun if there is a plural numerical modifier in front of the noun. Adaptation in the direction of Standard English makes this an inconsistent characteristic; there is probably also the factor that the transcribers, who heard with their own language system, transcribed plural suffixes where the informants did not use them.

Two Injin run after him.   (Forbes, p. 59)

Four Indian grab him.   (*Ibid.*)

Catch um three beaver last week.   (White, p. 325)

Boss he gone on river trail two, three hour.   (*Ibid.*, p. 195)

Twenty shirt no good; me never see woman have twenty shirt—
heap too *mucho!*   (Dan DeQuille [pseudonym of
                            William Wright], *Washoe Rambles*, p. 96)

. . . give 'um Pah-Utes heap Goddam.   (Forbes, p. 69)

When the numerical plural modifier is not present, the pluralizing suffix used is not always identical to that of Standard English:

Him heap 'fraid white mans.   (Calkins, II, p. 70)

One more structural feature of American Indian Pidgin English will be represented by several examples, it being impossible to describe all of them outside of a complete grammar. Chosen because it is typical of English pidgins and because it is a positive factor of "addition" rather than of "simplification" (although the prejudiced can always say that it is "unnecessary"), this structure will be called (after Hall, *Pidgin and Creole Languages*, p. 83) a *Predicate Marker*. Miscalled an "appositive" in studies of Negro dialect by dialect geographers who are naive with regard to pidgins and creoles, it is better described by Hall as "a feature of morphologically distinct pronouns that recapitulate subjects and introduce predicates."

Some examples are

Wawatam, he very much hate to go by himself.   (Baker, p. 18)

That mounting, that mounting, he come 'way up this way since two yea' now.   (Calkins, III, 7)

Boss he gone on river trail two t'ree hour.   (White, p. 196)

Buckland he heap bad.   (Forbes, p. 58)

Then one, he run for river.   (Forbes, p. 58)

Bull Shield he get better.   (Wissler, *Indian Cavalcade*, p. 345—
                                    the citation being from a letter
                                    written by an Indian to Wissler.)

Hall, somewhat uncharacteristically overwilling to see the influence of Standard English, traces this structure to the "substandard" English habit of recapitulating a subject by means of a pronoun (p. 83). In the case of Melanesian Pidgin, however, he also recognizes the influence of a similar structure in Marshallese. Such influence seems highly unlikely in any of the American pidgins. On the other hand, some of the West African languages have a similar feature; we may be allowed to wonder why influences which are operative in the case of Marshallese could not also be active in the case of the West African languages. There is the even more serious problem of whether "substandard" English in the United States even had the feature at a period before it was itself subject to the influence of Pidgin and Plantation Creole.

Both Plantation Creole/Black English Basilect and American Indian Pidgin English sources often have a considerable degree of apparently free variation, in the same conversation or text, between *him* and *he* as subject forms. It seems likely that an underlying and historical structure like

> *Noun i-Verb*

(which is the structure in Melanesian Pidgin and in WesKos) alternates with the pronominal substitute

> **Him** *Verb*

with the former being metanalyzed,* under the influence of conditions which always result in Standard English being considered "correct," to

> *Noun*-he *Verb*

Since *Noun* is deletable under certain conditions in pidgins and creoles, sequences like *He Verb* and *Him Verb* will both occur. A simplified underlying formula for all the varieties up to and including basilect would be

> (1) (*Noun*) he *Verb*
> (2) Him *Verb*

This will account for sequences of sentences like American Indian Pidgin English

> Bull Shield he get better. Him say tell you maybe now you have believe medicine things powerful.   (Wissler, p. 345)

and Black English

> Him am so big and 'cause he so, he think everybody do what him say.   (Botkin, *Lay My Burden Down*, p. 161)

> Us still a-setting in this tree, ain't we? We ain't never wanting to see no more hanging, is we, Zack?   (*Ibid.*, p. 52)

---

* *Metanalysis* describes the analysis of words or groups of words into new elements. An example in English would be *apron*, which originally came into the language with an initial *n*: *a napron* was metanalyzed to *an apron*.

One of the best-known pidgin structures, but one which is now completely missing from Black English, is the simple negative syntax *Subject no Verb* found regularly in American Indian Pidgin English:

Pah-Ute man no kill 'um whites.   (Forbes, 69)

Winnemucka no sabe!   (*Ibid.*)

It is also found in the very early attestations of Black English, including the transcript of the trial of Tituba, the part-Indian Barbadian woman whose probable belief in voodoo complicated the 1692 Salem witch trials:

I no hurt them at all.   (Drake, *Witchcraft Delusion in New England*, p. 271)

But he no let me blood with it as yet.   (*Ibid.*, p. 271)

No, he no let me see.   (*Ibid.*, p. 297)

The Frontier *Lingua Franca?*

There were, as even the writers of Western movies knew, Chinese in the West—particularly around the time of the Gold Rush. These Chinese were demonstrably users of Pidgin English, in which respect they obviously resembled the Indians. Even the highly flexible phonology of Pidgin English favors such use, since it accommodates the tendency of either Chinese or some Indian languages not to differentiate *l* and *r* (*spling* for *spring*, *liver* for *river*). It is not even possible to attribute such cases with certainty to either Chinese or Indian language influence. While this is some handicap for the language historian, it is none for the Pidgin language. The structure—particularly the phonology —of the latter has developed to accommodate diverse linguistic groups.

What happened when a speaker of American Indian Pidgin English came into contact with a speaker of Chinese Pidgin English? Or what happened when the two came into contact with a speaker of creolized or partially decreolized Black English? Since the records are kept by whites, who weren't particularly interested in people of other colors, evidence can only be gleaned in small bits from scattered sources. But the numbers of Black, Red, and Yellow residents of the United States—particularly in the West—in the nineteenth century was not small; it is, at any rate, a fairly safe bet that they did not speak French, Swahili, or Marshallese.

As a part of the general whitewashing of American history which does not deny the existence of such groups but which banishes the Negroes to the cotton patch, the Chinese to the laundry business or to an occasional exotic restaurant, and the Indians to war parties (painted, whooping savages, riding around the settlers' wagons and shooting arrows), the Pidgin English which was demonstrably at least part of their linguistic performance has not been allowed to darken the picture of American "white" English. Mencken allowed "Beach-la-Mar" to be out in the Pacific; even McDavid permitted the apparently unrecognized danger of speculating upon the relationship of Gullah to pidgin languages to remain in his "abridgement"; but, beyond a quotation of the old "No tickee, no washee" joke—which is in something at least a little bit like Chinese Pidgin English—the poor Chinaman wasn't given a chance.

We know they were in the West, but we wouldn't know that they talked at all if an occasional, unlikely work like Jess G. Hayes's *Apache Vengeance* (University of New Mexico Press, 1954) didn't have a Chinese speaking Pidgin English. The one in question is Onion Jack, who is camp cook—an occupation known to have been delegated to Chinese as unworthy of white cowboys. He says

> Velly good chow fo' unhappy mens . . . Beef, glavy, potat', coffee, blead, and velly fine apple pie.   (p. 66)

That isn't necessarily pidgin, but it is certainly Chinese English! The same may be said of the "Belly cold" uttered by a Chinese in a story related by Lee,[39] who specifies that the Chinese spoke "in his pidgin English." More conclusive evidence can be rather easily found, it turns out. Many sources, like DeQuille's *The Big Bonanza*, have genuine Chinese Pidgin English:

> Me no can sleep; me one leg he crook up, me belly (very) sore.
>
> (p. 294)

To find abundant evidence that Chinese Pidgin English was used in the West, one need only move away from the writings of those professors whose professional responsibility is to describe the language situation in the United States. A few of the abundant attestations are referred to herein, but there are so many—in so many varied types of sources—that even a causal collection would fill a book much longer than this. And these pidgin-speaking Chinese associated a great deal with pidgin-speaking Indians:

> Indians also frequently associated with Chinese, especially along the Humboldt and, in the early 1900's at Wadsworth and Hawthorne. Some intermarriage took place, and many Indians took up opium-smoking. The Chinese-operated opium and liquor dens proved all too attractive for many natives, especially for those on the Walker River Reserve.   (Forbes, *Nevada Indians Speak*, p. 13)

The outrage to Western morality may, of course, be one reason why the Chinese are censored out of the more popular treatments of the West; but they were there, they associated with the Indians, and that association should presumably be part of a historian's responsibility, and the language it was conducted in should be a part of the language historian's responsibility.

What did they speak to each other, so that a language historian could have some idea of the area of his own responsibility? Since the written sources which survive come mainly from whites, we have little direct evidence; but there is considerable evidence that both Chinese and Indians often spoke Pidgin English to those whites. In DeQuille's *The Big Bonanza*, Nevada Indians

and Chinese are quoted in Pidgin English. We do have Indians
speaking *about* Chinese:

> Irishman comes—Dutchman come—American man come—China-
> John come,—digum hole,—findum money heap . . .
>
> (Forbes, p. 69)

Clearly, an Indian could speak Pidgin English *about* the Chinese;
his practice did not differ, in all particulars, from that of the
white: *China-John* in the above quotation is very like *John
Chinaman,* a favorite nineteenth-century designation in the West.
When Indians and Chinese married, it seems reasonable to suppose that they conversed in Pidgin English rather than in Chinese
or in an Indian language. In many cases, their children must
have grown up speaking Pidgin—which means, technically, creolization on the Western frontier. Anthropologist and U. S. Indian
expert Clark Wissler, in *Indian Cavalcade, or Life on the Oldtime Indian Reservations* (1938), wrote a chapter on "The
Enigma of the Squaw Man" (non-Indian married to an Indian
woman) and told of the opprobrium attached to a white who
did so. Squaw men were not always white, but if a man of color
married an Indian woman, no one seemed shocked (p. 223).
"Men of color" obviously includes Chinese, since Pidgin-speaking
Ping Shoo ("wantee eat and sleepee? Good, takie chair, suppy
quick"—p. 224) is immediately presented as an example. Unfortunately, the wives are not quoted.

Since neither pidginization nor creolization is a genetic or
ethnic characteristic, there were undoubtedly always some of
those speakers—Chinese, Indians, and mixtures of the two—who
learned to speak Standard English. It is well known that many
Chinese "progressed" linguistically beyond the Pidgin. The title
character "Young Mr. Yan," an upward-mobile young Chinese
in Wallace Irwin's *Chinatown Ballads* (1906), is pictured as
making that step in common with his elegantly dressed girl
friend:

> They spoke good English an' grammar, too. Most as proper as me
> an' you.   (p. 15)

"Yan's old man," who was, in Irwin's racist terminology, a "Canton chink," was unable to share or sympathize with those ambitions:

> So he didn't take stock in the mission school. An' spoke of 'is son as a "hip big fool." (p. 14)

Among Chinese, apparently, as we know it to have happened among Negroes and as we may be virtually sure it must have happened among Indians, "upward" change in language has not been without its element of family tragedy. The trend in generational snobbery has, of course, occasionally been reversed: Americans over forty may remember the linguistic elegance of the movies' Charlie Chan and his distaste for the slang affected by his offspring.

It is, *a priori*, reasonable to assume that Chinese bidialectals developed; literary attestations so indicate, although of course we have nothing from professional historians of American English. John Steinbeck, in *East of Eden*, presents the Chinese servant Lee, who speaks Chinese Pidgin but who eventually reveals that he knows Standard English, even though he feels forced to use Pidgin:

> "It's more than a convenience," he said. "It's even more than self-protection. Mostly we have to use it to be understood at all . . . Pidgin they expect, and pidgin they'll listen to. But English from me they don't listen to, and they don't understand it." (p. 142)

Despite its being the product of a writer's imagination, this has the ring of sociolinguistic truth about it. The late Professor Hans Wolff, in an article entitled "Intelligibility and Inter-Ethnic Attitudes," established the principle that extra-linguistic expectations have a great deal to do with making oneself understood.

The Steinbeck scene looks like a good fictional example of what McDavid, supposedly describing the actualities of American dialects, called the "dialect veneer," and there is no real doubt that such use of non-standard varieties of English is sometimes socially reinforced. Authors of fiction are often more accurate than academic investigators who are bound to untenable theories. Steinbeck, at least, does not indulge in any such ridiculous suggestion as that Chinese Pidgin *originated* as a "veneer." There is, of course, the same kind of counter-evidence for such an origin in the case of Chinese Pidgin as there is in the case of Negro Pidgin.

More usual than complete bidialectism in such cases is dialect mixing, and we have better than fictional evidence for that. The first section of Albert Dressler's *California Chinese Chatter* is devoted to telegrams sent by Chinese in Downieville, Sierra County, California, in 1874. These are clearly the work of Pidgin English speakers who are trying to write Standard English— with varying degrees of success. There are abundant examples like

> If no win me send no money.   (p. 12)

in which the Pidgin characteristics come through clearly even in competition with telegraphic style. The comment of Milton J. Ferguson, of the California State Library, Sacramento, in a letter to Dressler, is rather typical:

> And who would imagine so many Chinamen in such a telegraphic
> hurry!   (p. viii)

It is a typically American attitude to ignore the possibility that members of minority groups may communicate a great deal by all media, and that they may use their own variety of English in doing so. The impossibility of Western Union's transmitting a message in Chinese may be a partial explanation of the need to use English in such a situation; but Pidgin English as a *lingua franca* for speakers of very different varieties of Chinese is at least as likely. With the Indians, Chinese Pidgin speakers would have found the Pidgin necessary, since it was linguistically similar to American Indian Pidgin English and there was no other *lingua franca*. Linguistic pretension may have caused each group to use as nearly Standard English as it could; but convenience would have favored the pidgins, which are remarkably similar. Both, for example, have the transitivizer. It is well known in Chinese

Pidgin, but for the sake of form an attestation is offered from Chinese Pidgin in the United States:

I fetchem—you sabe me! (Irwin, p. 42)

The citation also documents the use of *savvy*, frequently spelled *sabe* in illustration of the prevalent belief that it came from Spanish *saber*. (A more reasonable ultimate source is, of course, Portuguese—specifically Portguese Trade Pidgin, which must be the same kind of relexification source for Chinese Pidgin as it is for Negro Pidgin and American Indian Pidgin.) Both used the word *heap* both as a noun quantifier and as an adverbial modifier of verbs—the former a reasonable expectation as a development of British English, the latter not. The different distribution of *l* and *r*, which is so well known a characteristic of Chinese, is also true of some Indian languages, so that a form like *velly* 'very' from an Indian does not necessarily mean Chinese influence. On the other hand, the usual circumstances of language contact would apply; there is no reason to doubt that an occasional Indian learned his Pidgin from a Chinaman or at least had it changed somewhat by Chinese influence. And, since there is no proof that all the Chinese who came to the United States knew Pidgin already, some of them may well have learned it from the Indians. It is illogical to suppose that compartmented "Chinese Pidgin" and "Indian Pidgin" maintained their separate existence in those parts of the West where there was a great need for some common medium of communication.

The really fascinating question seems lamentably unanswerable, except through the imagination: How did the Negro resident of the West, usually relegated to the same tasks and therefore very probably to the company of the Chinese and Indians, communicate with these speakers of Pidgin? We can document the close association of Negroes and Indians:

> Living with every Indian tribe are numbers of men, Americans, Frenchmen, Germans, Mexicans, Negroes, who, having purchased wives, are regarded as belonging to the tribe.[40]

At an earlier time, 1765, and in less happy circumstances, there
were other relationships between Negro and Indian:

> They [the Illinois Indians] have a great many Negroes, who are
> obliged to labor very hard to support their masters in their extrav-
> agant debauchery.[41]

Little is known about the language situation in these cases, but
we can analogize from the Seminole situation: most of the Negroes must have learned the Indian language, and many of them
may have given up any variety of English entirely; some may
have been valued as interpreters to the white man; and a few
Indians may have learned Pidgin (Plantation Creole) from the
Negroes in their midst.[42]

In a Negro folk tale related by folklorist J. Mason Brewer,
"How Uncle Steve Interpreted Spanish" (*Negro Folklore*, p.
106), a Negro boasts of his linguistic ability and is given an
opportunity to act as translator for his white boss, whose Mexican
interpreter is not available. Faced with the problem of using his
non-existent Spanish, Steve reverts to something very like Pidgin
English:

> Oh, hombre, fo' how muchee you sellee the hossy?

Brewer has another such story in *American Negro Folklore*, in
which a Negro "interpreter" interrogates a Mexican:

> Who, hombre, who ownee de lanee?

It is quite possible that these tales represent genuine traditions,
although of course the distortion for humorous effect is obvious.

The jazz community has long known of the Chinese use of
Pidgin English. Witness the Porter Grainger lyrics for a song
which Bessie Smith made famous:

> I'm gonna tell him like the Chinaman
> If you don't bring 'um check
> You don't get 'um laundee, if you break 'um damn neck.

There is some evidence of the speaking of Plantation Creole
in the West. (Julian Mason, in "The Etymology of Buckaroo,"

American Speech, 1960, assumed that it had to be Gullah.) There
are literary attestations like that of Dan Rose's "Billy Brazelton,
Highwayman," which presents Negro soldiers who say things
like "Who am you?" and "I believe you am." These can be either
stereotypes of Negro dialect from literary sources or the results
of actual observation of switching behavior between Black English and Standard English. At any rate, it seems certain that
Black English was used in the same area and at the same time
as Chinese Pidgin English and the Western varieties of American
Indian Pidgin English.

In many features, the structures even of Negro Non-Standard
English and American Indian Pidgin English would be similar
in a deep sense, the differences being more superficial. Negro
speakers in the West must have found it fairly easy to learn to
communicate in the Indians' variety of English (Pidgin in some
cases), without "reverting" in any mystic sense. Awareness of
Chinese Pidgin was quite widespread by 1870. *Appleton's Journal
of Popular Literature, Science, and Art* for Sept. 24, 1870 (Article
on "Chinese Theatres") refers to

> ". . . one numba one sing-song Pidgin"—as Pigeon English jargon
> has it.   (p. 393)

The same journal ("Varieties," Sept. 10, 1870) reports that

> The number of Chinese in the country at the end of 1869 was esti-
> mated as ninety thousand.

Apparently, everyone knew of them except the academics.

Two not inconsiderable groups in the Old West spoke Pidgin
English, another respectably large group probably spoke Plantation Creole or an incompletely decreolized derivative from it.
How many other groups learned one or the other variety? If
Julian Mason's theory is correct, those Westerners who came to
use *buckaroo* must have had intimate contact with Plantation
Creole (Gullah). Such people as railroad foremen who directed
large gangs of Chinese must have had to learn Pidgin (or Chinese,
which is highly unlikely). There is, in fact, some reason to believe
that the average resident of the West in the times around Gold

Rush days found Pidgin either very useful or absolutely necessary. What, for example, of the police and the courts, who would have had to deal with the exotic Chinese crimes and vices of which the stereotypes make so much? Wright (pseudonym Dan DeQuille), in *The Big Bonanza*, p. 295, shows a white man entering an opium den as a sightseer, and greeting the proprietor "in pigeon English." (The term *pigeon* or *Pidgin* itself, varying with *broken English*, seems to have been applied almost exclusively to the speech of Chinese.)

Dressler's *California Chinese Chatter*, which was intended mainly to illustrate the use of English by Chinese, provides an example of a Standard English speaker adapting himself in the direction of Pidgin. As the transcription by the court reporter shows, "Court" begins in formal legal language, but winds up asking "You no take out your pistol try to shoot him?" (p. 57) of Ah Jake, who is defending himself both directly in Pidgin and through an interpreter who speaks Chinese to Ah Jake and Pidgin to "Court." The accommodation does not result in complete pidginization in "Court's" talk; more interestingly, it results in a special kind of speech style. For example, "Court" does not use the transitivizer as does Ah Jake. Yet in this instance, the white speaker of Standard English is clearly learning from the oriental speaker of Pidgin.

It could hardly be that a language so widely used in the United States as Chinese Pidgin English would completely escape the notice of American students of language. The honor here seems to belong to Mamie Meredith, whose "Longfellow's Excelsior Done Into Pidgin English" (*American Speech*, 1929) is a more perceptive article than what is suggested by the linguistically trivial topic indicated by the title. Meredith was aware that Pidgin English was the medium of business between Americans and Chinese, some of whom were bankers, merchants, and importers. She even compared Chinese Pidgin English to "the *lingua franca* of the Mediterannean Sea" (p. 150). Somehow, no reference to this article by Meredith got into Mencken-McDavid, although references to her other articles are plentiful.

Less professional observers have seen the influence of the contact language. Discussing the language of the cowboy, Philip
Ashton Rollins wrote,

> Pidgin English contributed its quota of words and phrases. Its
> "long time no see" conveniently set forth the status of a searcher
> for some lost object, while its "no can do" definitely expressed per-
> sonal impotence.   (*The Cowboy*, 1936, p. 78)

Rollins also quoted the Pidgin English of "a Sacramento Chinaman" (p. 80), speculated on why "the average cowboy was a bit
ruthless in his treatment of grammar" (p. 81), and documented
a cowboy cultural debt to the Southern Negro (p. 107).

There was a great deal of Pidgin English spoken in the Old
West; in many contact situations, it was the *lingua franca*. The
Chinese, besides being laborers, participated in the business activities of the West. Wright (pseudonym DeQuille) shows how
they were active even in stock trading; he also reports (p. 436)
how the at least temporarily proverbial expression "washum one
pan, catchum one color" was traceable to Chinese miners. Insofar
as is now known (and there is an incredible lack of information
on the subject), the pidgins are not at present spoken in those
areas where they were so commonplace during the years after
the Gold Rush. The descendants of the Pidgin-speakers (according to the best contemporary estimates, there are well over
1,000 Chinese in Arizona today) presumably speak a variety of
American English—perhaps a relatively non-standard variety.

Did Pidgin (and Creole) English leave a mark on the English
of the West? It hardly seems reasonable to assume that it disappeared without a trace. Probably, a great deal of the peculiarity
of Western American English is somehow the result of mixing
with Pidgin/Creole, although there have been other influences.

The easiest way to demonstrate such influence is to discuss
vocabulary acquisitions. Mason's case that Gullah (Plantation
Creole) is the source of *buckaroo* (from *buckra*, the earliest attestation being spelled *bukhara*) rather than Spanish *vaquero*,
seems convincing. It is also probably symptomatic: the influence
of pidgin/creole forms will often be hidden behind apparent

origins in other sources. *Chow*, from Chinese Pidgin English, is a clear-cut case, having been recorded as a Chinese usage in a Sacramento, California, newspaper in 1856. *Chow chow* must have come in at the same time; Meredith reported that it meant 'food' in 1929, and was "accepted American slang," but it has meant a special dish notable for pepper content for some time now in many parts of the United States.

According to Hall (*Pidgin and Creole Languages*, p. 100), *savvy* came into English from various sources. There is no reason to assume that the borrowing into American English was a once-and-for-all matter, either; since the word was in Plantation Creole, American Indian Pidgin English, and Chinese Pidgin English, there is a high probability that it was borrowed from each of the three at different times and places. Despite its absence from Establishment dictionaries, the verb use came to Jamaica at least as early as 1828 (*Marly; or A Planter's Life in Jamaica*). Absent from Turner's work on Gullah, it co-occurs with *know* in Gullah texts of an earlier date:

> Buh Rabbit, him no care so eh sabe isself. Him bin know say . . .
> (Charles Colcock Jones, Jr., *Negro Myths from the Georgia Coast*, 1888, p. 105)

Day's *Five Years Residence in the West Indies* reports from St. Kitts around 1850:

> Me no sabby why dat officer make noise wid dat ting.   (II, 218)

Spanish *sabe* undoubtedly had some reinforcing influence—particularly in the Southwest—and knowledge of the related French forms probably did something to facilitate the borrowing of the word in other areas. Not even the most British-minded of etymologists has ever questioned that the word was borrowed in the United States from one or more of these languages. Any occurrences in East Anglia take place relatively late and as a result, presumably, of having crossed the Atlantic from west to east.

Of course, as the works of Defoe show clearly, pidgin was known to some Englishmen from other than American sources. The *Oxford English Dictionary's* first attestation of British use

(Grose's *A Classical Dictionary of the Vulgar Tongue*, 1785), calls it "negroe language" and quotes it in the phrase 'massa, me no scavey.'

There is not really much doubt that *joss* (British *joss-man*, *joss-pidgin-man* 'a man who knows about religion,' 'a minister of religion,' *Oxford English Dictionary;* American *joss house* 'temple, church') comes through Pidgin English, ultimately from Portuguese (Trade Pidgin) *deos* 'god.' *Josh* 'to indulge in banter or ridicule' ('satirically to treat one as though he were a god'?) seems more likely to come from this source than from *Joshua*, its accepted etymology in the *Dictionary of Americanisms.* The *Dictionary of Jargon, Slang, and Cant* by Barrère and Leland listed the spelling *josh*, with a suggestion of such a relationship, in 1889.

Equal possibilities of borrowing from one or more pidgins, although primarily in the West, are involved in the use of *heap* 'very, very much,' particularly in its adverbial function. The use of *a heap of* X to mean 'very much X' or 'very many X's' can be traced to the British English of about 1661 (*Oxford English Dictionary*); this is somewhat early for pidgin influence on British English, although not so early as to make it completely out of the question. The adverbial usage, on the other hand, cannot be traced to British English; the earliest recorded uses are in the area of pidgin/creole influence. Let it be noted that an explanation of this extension of usage as a "natural development" is begging the question: the job of the historian of language is to explain those "natural developments" and to make clear why they are "natural" with respect to the language involved, not to hide behind them. The ultimate etymology of the word is Germanic, as is Dutch *hoop*, the presumed source of Papiamento *hopi*, which functions in the same way as the Pidgin English word. This is essentially what is behind the Stewart-Taylor concept of relexification: the vocabulary items themselves come from the European languages, but the different grammatical functions derive from another source. Pidgin English *heap*, like Papiamento *hopi*, is a relexification, with Germanic material, of something in the original Pidgin or Sabir; a still further relexification takes place in Seminole Pidgin, where *heap X* becomes *ojus X* or *X ojus,* the latter word order presumably reflecting Seminole structure. The ultimate absurdity would be to derive *ojus* from something in the East Anglian dialect.

Some writers, like Mencken, have been embarrassed by the very currency of the knowledge that American Indian Pidgin English contained phrases like "Ugh!" and "Heap big chief" and have concluded that such well-known facts must be wrong.[43] It is, of course, possible to distort the picture by having the Indians say nothing else; we know that no sentence, or even phrase, has any great frequency in language performance. But we have seen from Irwin that a Chinese speaker of Pidgin could say *heap* (*hip*) *big fool,* and Richardson (*Beyond the Mississippi,* p. 390) tells how a Chinese called him "Big man—heap big man!" For most syntactic purposes, *chief* comes in the same categories as *fool* and *man.* A grammar of American Indian Pidgin English should have the capacity to generate "Ugh! Heap big chief," even though it may be true that no Indian ever uttered the phrase. (Incidentally, a great many Indian languages do have an interjection [ux], which early observers tried to represent by the spelling *ugh.* The *gh* was an attempt to represent a velar fricative which is not in the phonemic inventory of English. The word is not, of course, [əg] like the first syllable in *ugly.*)

From Mencken, we can derive the information that *heap* "was commoner in the United States than in England" (Supplement I, 1945, p. 45). As a piece of apparently unrelated information, he also shows that it is not an East Coast word. In the *Virginia Literary Museum,* quoted by Mencken, it is described as "Southern and Western." Such Western currency is obviously traceable to something non-British, particularly given the additional grammatical function. The pidgins are a good candidate for the job. As Mencken points out, Adiel Sherwood listed the word in his *Gazeteer of the State of Georgia* (1827). The same influence from Plantation Creole which spread the word to the Seminoles must have been operative in the Georgia area.

Humbug, in the sense in which Scrooge used the word, is

derived from "Beach-la-Mar" or Pidgin English in the Pacific. The West African Pidgin English sense of 'a disturbance, an argument, a swindle' occurs in Black English. In the Afro-American varieties, *humbug* can also be used as a verb (*Him wife de humbug him too much* 'His wife is always giving him trouble.') It is attested from New Orleans in Ann Fairbairn's *Five Smooth Stones*. In the Chicago ghetto, *humbuggin'* means 'fighting'![44] And a Los Angeles Negro informant complained that he had been sent to prison "on a humbug." The entire semantic range of these examples is paralleled in West African Pidgin English.

American English phrases like *look-see* ("I'll take a look-see") and *no see 'um* (a very tiny gnat) are very much in the grammatical structure of Pidgin English; the latter even has the transitivizer. The former is an instance of what Herskovits called "verb stacking," a feature which some West African languages share with pidgins and creoles. Phrases cited by Rollins and others, like *long time no see* and *no can do*, have obviously the same kind of structure; Richardson (p. 390) reports the use of the former by Chinese Pidgin English speakers in the West. Meredith reported *look-see man* 'tourist' or 'sightseer', which seems to have disappeared since 1929. If anything like the time and resources which have been expended in unproductive attempts to link American to British isoglosses were devoted to a search for pidgin influence, many more such examples could undoubtedly be found.

The varieties of English, pidgin or otherwise, which were used by Black, Red and Yellow speakers, do not depend for their importance upon their having made contributions to the English of whites. It is hoped that this brief suggestion of influence will not be taken as a pandering to that notion. Had they remained totally without influence, they would still be worthy of investigation. Nevertheless, research in terms of the contribution of these varieties to the more publicized forms of American English would seem to be justified also in terms of what it can reveal about linguistic Americanisms. The population of the British colonies and of the United States in the early days was astonishingly polyglot, and the widespread use of a *lingua franca* was almost obligatory. There is more evidence than can be given here of the pre-eminence of Pidgin English in the contest with Spanish and other languages for that function.[45] Serious investigation of the implications of such factors cannot be said even to have begun, but gaps in the historical treatment of American English exposed by the study of Black English and its antecedent Pidgin may have far-reaching implications for the study of the English language on this continent.

NOTES

[1] Robert A. Hall, Jr., *Pidgin and Creole Languages* (Cornell University Press, 1966), which differs from this account in many particulars, agrees substantially on this dating (see pp. 6–7).

[2] This is approximately the viewpoint of Frederic G. Cassidy, "Some New Light on Old Jamaicanisms," *American Speech*, 1967, pp. 190–201; *Symposium on Multilingualism* (Brazzaville, 1962).

[3] Ian Hancock, "A Provisional Comparison of the English-based Atlantic Creoles," in Hymes (ed.), *Pidginization and Creolization of Languages* (see Bibliography).

[4] Barbot, *A Description of the Coasts of North and South Guinea; and of Ethiopia Inferior, vulgarly Angola* (1732). Some of the most valuable information provided by Barbot in his apparently contradictory

> either *Portuguese*, or *Lingua Franca* (p. 103)
> *Lingua Franca*, or broken *Portuguese* (p. 129)
> a little *Portuguese*, or *Lingua Franca* (p. 136)
> a sort of *Lingua Franca*, or broken *Portuguese* and French
>   (p. 249)

(all spoken by Africans). This apparent contradiction can be resolved by the information that Lingua Franca, more or less relexified (see Glossary) with Portuguese words, could appear at one time to be non-Portuguese, at another time to be "broken" (Pidgin) Portuguese, and at still another time to be intermediate between the two stages. Hugo Schuchardt (see Bibliography) has shown that this was the normal condition for Lingua Franca.

P. Alonso de Sandoval, S. J., *De Instauranda Aethiopum Salute* (1627), cited evidence of the same kind of apparent inconsistency in the variation between "broken" Portuguese and Spanish on São Thomé.

[5] Schuchardt (*op. cit.*) cites Lingua Franca forms

cucinero grande	'great cook'
scrivano grande	'great writer'
patrono grande	'great patron' or 'big boss'

In the English Pidgin, *Noun grandee* becomes *grandee Noun* in accordance with the normal word order of English. Dow's *Slave Ships and Slaving* (see Bibliography), quotes a letter from "Grandy King George" of Old Calabar, 1773, which uses phrases like *grandy man*. This syntactic reordering is paralleled in Seminole Pidgin English (below, this chapter), where *heap Noun* of American Indian Pidgin English became *ojus Noun* and then *Noun ojus* in accordance with Seminole word order. This is an excellent case of relexification (see footnote 4 above and Glossary); some of the sources cite *heap* in parentheses for *ojus*.

[6] Philip T. Drotning, *Black Heroes in Our Nation's History* (New York, 1969), p. 7.

[7] Douglas Leechman and Robert A. Hall, Jr., "American Indian Pidgin English: Attestations and Grammatical Peculiarities," *American Speech* 30 (1955), pp. 163–171. Leechman and Hall are somewhat careless about the authenticity of their texts, as in the glaring example of Waban's warrants (see Kittredge, in Bibliography). Students are warned to check individual sources cited by Leechman and Hall. American Indian Pidgin English was first directly related to the English Creole tradition in Mary Rita Miller, "Attestations of American Indian Pidgin English in Fiction and Non-Fiction," *American Speech*, May, 1967, pp. 142–147.

[8] In "Next Steps in the Study of Negro Folklore," *Journal of American Folklore* LVI, No. 219 (1943), pp. 1–7, reprinted in *The New World Negro*, ed. by Frances S. Herskovits (see Bibliography). In *The American Negro* (1928), Herskovits pointed out that Negroes "have mingled with the American Indians on a scale hitherto unrealized" (p. 16).

[9] *Force's Collection of Historical Tracts*, Vol. III, No. 10, p. 43.

[10] This information is taken from Philip A. Bruce's *Economic History of Virginia in the Seventeenth Century*, a very conservative work slanted in the direction of the whites and emphasizing their activities. It is probable that a strong case for the presence of a larger number of Africans could be made by a Black-oriented history of the colony.

[11] The book by Hall (see footnote 1) and the article by Leechman and Hall (see footnote 7) cite this attestation without commentary or explanation except for calling it the first attestation of Pidgin English. Note that *squaes* (*squaws*) is an Alonquian borrowing which is almost universal in American Indian Pidgin English, even among the Seminoles (see references to James Fenimore Cooper in this chapter and the end of the section entitled "Transmission to the Seminoles.")

[12] One such argument would make this transitivizer (transitive verb marker) a "linguistic universal." Whereas it is rather likely that transitivity is a linguistic universal, it is inconceivable that the form (morpheme) *um* (*am*, *'m*, etc.) is universal. In fact, it is contrary to all linguistic theory to assume that any form (word or "morpheme") is universal. Further, if *um* is "universal" even in English, why does it not occur in those dialects which have no relationship to Pidgin English? None of these objections need be altered in deference to the historical truism that *'em* "reductions" of *them* are traceable to Old English *hem*, or that there are *um, em*, etc., forms in British "regional" dialects.

[13] See footnotes 1 and 7 above, and Hall in Bibliography.

[14] Richard Lancaster, *Piegan* (1966).

[15] Cooper's statement was given cavalier treatment by Krapp, *The English Language in America*, who asserted "If this *lingua franca* existed, of which Cooper speaks, certainly Cooper made little effort to use it" (II, 266). Yet this very denial is in the midst of Krapp's citations of Cooper's use of Indian "dialect." Thus Krapp, while questioning Cooper's use of any *lingua franca*, himself provides all the documentation that is needed for Cooper's practice. Krapp consistently underestimated Cooper's powers of language observation, as did Mark Twain in his celebrated "Fenimore Cooper's Literary Offenses":

> They [the "rules governing literary art in the domain of romantic fiction"] require that when a personage talks like an illustrated, gilt-edged, tree-calf, hand-tooled, seven-dollar Friendship's Offering in the beginning of a paragraph, he shall not talk like a Negro minstrel in the end of it.

Besides inadvertently pointing up (as does Krapp) the historical relationship between Negro dialect and American Indian Pidgin English, Twain clearly illustrates the lack of understanding of diglossia (see Glossary) which has characterized too many historical studies of American English. Thus, when Twain further asserts

> He even fails to notice that the man who talks corrupt English six days in the week must and will talk it on the seventh, and can't help himself.

he only illustrates with great clarity how Twain had not observed the kind of diglossia which goes on in complex language communities. On the island of Antigua, for example, speakers who use a still largely creolized English for everyday affairs have a highly standardized "reading the Bible" style for Sunday. Such alteration between "corrupt" and "educated" or standard language, on the part of one speaker, is, in fact, commonplace on a world-wide scale.

[16] If Cooper was correct, the accepted etymology of *Yankee* (which has been greatly debated) must be changed. Mencken-McDavid (p. 122) accepts the origin in Dutch Jan Kees, a kind of 'John Doe'. Of course, Dutch origin would not preclude Pidgin transmission.

[17] *Papoose* (*plantain*) and *pone*, another Algonquian word, were some-

how transmitted to Jamaica (Cassidy, *Jamaica Talk*). The existence of Temne *kɛ - pɔn* in West Africa seems to indicate that there may have been some influence from Portuguese (Trade Pidgin) *pão*. Other words of undoubtedly Indian etymology may have been transmitted either by Pidgin English or by Plantation Creole. Such a word is *hominy* (Algonquian *rockahominy*). Wilson, *Travels* (1807), reported

> The chief food of the Negroes was Indian corn, which they bruised in mortars they had for the purpose and then boiling it in water, make a sort of hasty pudding. They ate their *hominy*, as they called it, sometimes with salt, sometimes without. (p. 52)

Loss of initial (presumably unstressed) syllables (*rocka-*) would fit well into the African pidgin/creole pattern, although there may well be other explanations.

[18] Reprinted as "Some Comments on the Seminole in 1818," *The Florida Anthropologist* Vol. X, No. 3–4 (November, 1957), p. 42.

[19] *Notices of Florida*, 1822, p. 41.

[20] Ibid.

[21] Ibid.

[22] Ibid., p. 44.

[23] Simmons, op. cit., p. 48.

[24] Gifford, *Billy Bowlegs*, p. 19.

[25] Edwin C. McReynolds, *The Seminoles* (see Bibliography), p. 48, makes the point of African superiority in agriculture. It seems likely that this talent was a major factor in the demand for West African slaves; see Craven, *The Southern Colonies in the Seventeenth Century*, p. 25.

[26] Frances Densmore, *Seminole Music* (see Bibliography).

[27] John C. Gifford, *Billy Bowlegs and the Seminole War* (1858), p. 19.

[28] Kenneth W. Porter, "Negro Guides and Interpreters in the Early Stages of the Seminole War, December 28, 1835–March 6, 1837," *Journal of Negro History* XXV, No. 2 (April, 1950), pp. 174–183. Note that boys' novelist T. Mayne Reid also wrote of Abram (see footnote 31 and text below).

[29] Ibid; also McReynolds, *The Seminoles*, p. 234.

[30] John Benrose, "Reminiscences of the Seminole War," quoted in Kenneth W. Porter, op. cit., p. 175. For the day name Cudjo 'male born on Monday' see Chapter III, Section 3, "West African Naming Practices Outside Gullah Territory."

[31] Reid, an Irishman who came to the United States as a young man and by his own account worked as a slave driver—among other things—before beginning to write, wrote in many dialects, including American Negro and West Indian dialects. In his *Osceola the Seminole*, he differentiated rather well between the Indian Seminoles and the Negro Seminoles. He put still another dialect into the mouths of the plantation servants. In *Ran Away to Sea*, he wrote of "bastard Portuguese, (the best-known language in these parts)" (p. 207) and had thirsty slaves calling "in that language best known along the African coast—the Portuguese—'Agoa—agoa!'" (p. 258)

[32] Kenneth Wiggins Porter, "Seminole Negro-Indian Scouts, 1870–1881," *The Southwestern Historical Quarterly*, January 1952, p. 358.

[33] In the article "Black Watch of Texas," San Antonio *Express*, November 16, 1924, it is reported

> In the matter of religion, the Seminole Negroes are distinct from any particular sect or denomination. Their rites and ceremonies are a blend of those peculiar to the Roman Catholic and the old-fashioned Hardshell Baptists. They call themselves "Mt. Zion Baptists" and practice baptism by immersion, yet they keep Lent . . .   (p. 24)

Since the article goes on to say that the Texas Seminoles banned pork from the diets of believers, it is to be doubted that the interpretation of the origin of their religious beliefs found in the newspaper article can be taken as literally true. See treatments like Lomax, *The Rainbow Sign* (see Bibliography) for the African-Christian syncretism in such belief patterns.

[34] *Negro-Indian Relationships in the Southeast*, Thesis in Anthropology, University of Pennsylvania, 1935, p. 42. A long passage of the same dialect, quoted from a 95-year-old former Florida plantation slave named Martha Jane, is included in Moore-Willson, *The Seminoles of Florida*, pp. 42–52. (See below in text and footnote 37.)

[35] My own all-too-brief exposure to the Black community in Bracketville, Texas (where the old Fort Clark is now a tourist motel), and Eagle Pass, Texas, tended to confirm the notion that the dialect of the Black adults is essentially that of Black English everywhere in the United States. Unfortunately, I was unable to work with children. There are some traditions of the Indian-Negro relationships in the town, but the Blacks seem reluctant to talk of them. Whites have by now adopted the racist (and inaccurate) view that Seminole townswomen degraded themselves in intermarriage with the Black scouts (whereas in fact they belonged to the same community from the beginning). The poor graveyard in "honor" of the Seminole scouts is a flimsy excuse for segregation even in burial, but names like BOWLEGS and WARRIOR (with the apparent variant WORRIO) are still to be read in crude lettering on the rough wooden crosses.

[36] San Antonio *Express*, op. cit.

[37] According to Mrs. Moore-Willson (see above and Bibliography), "only a few of that tribe speak broken English [in 1910]. The chiefs disapprove of it on general principles for fear they will talk too much." (p. 113) The chiefs also show a great deal of intuitive sociolinguistic wisdom, since bilingualism characteristically brings the threat of divided loyalties.

[38] There is interesting fictional evidence for the relationship between Plantation Creole and the English of nineteenth-century Indians in the writings of William Gilmore Simms, whose dialect writing has long been praised. In the collection *The Wigwam and the Cabin*, Simms presents Indian and Negro characters who speak varieties of English which are quite similar but not identical. In "Oaktibbe, or the Choctaw Sampson," an

Indian is described as speaking in "broken English" (p. 197) and makes speeches like

> Me drunk, me fight—me kill Loblolly Jack! Look ya! Dis blood pon my hands. 'Tis Loblolly Jack blood! Me dead! I stick him with de knife!

The speech of Mingo, the Negro driver in "Caloya; or the Loves of the Driver," shows the same general tendencies. The driver taunts the Indian:

> Nebber man is freeman, ef he own arm can't fill he stomach. Nebber man is freeman if he own work can't put clothes 'pon he back . . . I reckon you wife can make he pots, as ef we bin stan' look 'pon 'em.   (p. 387)

Pidgin/creole forms like possession by juxtaposition (both speakers), zero copula (the Indian), use of base form of verb for both present and past tense (the Indian), use of masculine pronoun for feminine referent (the Negro), and *bin* as past marker (the Negro) are in these passages. Notice that both use *'pon* (modern Gullah *pontop*) as a preposition. Elsewhere, Mingo is represented as saying *yer* and Oaktibbe *ya* for 'here'. Although the Negro's adverb is probably not meant to contain [r], he is obviously somewhat closer to white speech than the Indian. This is not an unexpected development, since the Indian would have used his native Indian language as part of his verbal repertoire.

Association of the two varieties was apparently widespread in the nineteenth century, misleading even Thomas Wentworth Higginson, whose *Army Life in a Black Regiment* is such a good source of historical information (see Chapter III):

> "I would do anything for Oonah,"—this being a kind of Indian formation of the second person plural, which they sometimes use.   (p. 234)

Since *oonah* (*unu*) is an undoubted Africanism, Higginson's statement cannot be historically correct. If, however, he had heard it from Indians before assuming command of his Black regiment, he would naturally have assumed that it was a borrowing from the Indians by the Blacks rather than *vice versa*.

[39] Rose Hum Lee, *The Chinese in the United States of America*, 1960, p. 74. Among the many works which attest to the use of Chinese Pidgin English in the American West is Asbury, *The Barbary Coast* (see Bibliography).

[40] Col. Richard Irving Dodge, *Our Wild Indians: Thirty-three Years Personal Experience* (1890), p. 600.

[41] Lieutenant Alexander Fraser, quoted in Francis Parkman, *The Conspiracy of Pontiac*, Vol. II, p. 253, footnote 1.

[42] Amusingly, the same scholar, Allen Walker Read, who (in "The Speech of Negroes in Colonial America," *Journal of Negro History*, 1939) interpreted statements in advertisements for runaway slaves to mean that the Blacks of the eighteenth century spoke English which was identical

to that of the whites, has written another article ("The English of the Indians," *American Speech*, 1941) in which he concludes

> The American Indian appears to have had a linguistic aptitude that served him well in his adjustment to the coming of English-speaking settlers.
>   (pp. 73–74)

No one doubts that the Indian, like other human beings, had a linguistic aptitude (perhaps "aptitude" could be spelled *p-i-d-g-i-n*—see J. Dyneley Prince, in Bibliography); but all the situations of Indian English which we have from the period are pidgin-like. Probably, where Read interprets the phrase *good English* to mean 'Standard English', it should rather be interpreted as 'effective and appropriate for its purpose' or even 'good, considering that the speaker is an Indian'. In other words, Read's article on Indian English is subject to the same reinterpretation as that made of his article on the English of the fugitive slaves by Stewart ("Sociolinguistic Factors," see Bibliography). It seems instructive that the parallels between American Indian Pidgin English and Black English have been inadvertently pointed up by scholars whose intention was anything but to do so.

[43] A small amount of evidence that something like Pidgin English is still spoken by some Indian tribes in a Standard English-influenced ("depidginized"!) form is available from literary texts like Dan Cushman's *Stay Away, Joe* (1956). In that novel, Grandpère, when excited, speaks pidgin-like English:

> Very old. Me, chief Two Smokes, hundred and five years old. Longtime been around. Long time see things go to hell. When I was young, shoot buffalo. With musket, sharps rifle, shoot buffalo. All buffalo long time gone. See steamboat come, railroad firewagon come, skunkwagon, devilbox come.   (pp. 191–192)

> White man don't live long in cave . . . No more factory for make penicillin, pretty soon white man die. No more big town like Havre to buy wheat, buy beef. No factory for build skunkwagon. No skunkwagon, no use for roads. No factory build barbwire. Boom! Big bombs blow 'em up. Horses come back buffalo come back, good country again . . . Me, Chief Two Smokes, live long time, see plenty, see things come, see things go.   (p. 218)

Especially noteworthy is the use of *long time* in affirmative constructions. Borrowed into general American English, it seems to exist only in the negative (*long time no see*).

[44] Thomas Kochman, "Rapping in the Black Ghetto," *Trans-Action*, 1969.

[45] Gail Rottweiler, "Sociolinguistic Contact and Communication: The California Gold Rush" (unpublished), points up a report (*Overland Monthly*, February, 1893) in which a Digger Indian says

> La misma oso. Me no quiero zapato.

in which the first sentence makes sense only as a relexification (see Glossary) of Pidgin English *allee samee bear* (i.e., his foot was just like a bear's and thus he did not want a shoe). This is not to assert that the direction of influence was everywhere so direct and simple. There are many areas which should be explored; e.g., the role of *savvy* in cowboy movie and small-boy Spanish (*Vamoose, hombre, savvy?*). Ian F. Hancock of the London School of Oriental and African Studies has pointed out to me that *galoot* (Sierra Leone Krio *galut*) and *caboodle* (Krio *kabudu*, with typical Black English vocalization of final [l]) are also worthy of such study. Speculations about the etymology of these words have been erratic. Barrère and Leland would derive *galoot* from Italian *galeotto* 'a galley slave' and *caboodle* "a New England expression originally used by coasting sailors" from Spanish *cabildo*. Although not to be taken with literal seriousness, these etymologies look no worse than later efforts (e.g., the *Dictionary of Americanisms*). And "Spanish" and "Italian" might be interpreted as one way of expressing relationship to the general Romance nature of Lingua Franca vocabulary.

V

The Negro Dialect and Southern Dialect

On the basis of the evidence presented above, Pidgin English seems to have been a highly innovative factor in American English. It remains to be seen whether Plantation Creole was equally influential. The sources are abundant enough; but, not surprisingly when one considers the emotion which surrounds the topic, they have not been put together and evaluated for the sake of determining their collective import.

Without evidence, but loyal to a commitment to the British origins theory, dialect geographers have assumed that the Negro got his dialect from the Southern white—that the influence has been almost exclusively unidirectional. Because it is impossible to explain in this way, for example, the dialect of a Northern Negro like Cooper's Jaap,[1] the evidence of such a literary attestation has simply been disallowed. In spite of the fact that there is no attestation of any similar dialect among the poor white population, it has been assumed that some unattested stage of white Southern dialect corresponded to present Negro dialect, which is thus "archaic." Such "archaism" can be "explained" on the basis of lack of mobility in the Negro population, although it is hard to see how the same explanation could be used for the supermobile Negro population in the post-World War II period, or how the "archaic" features, explainable in terms of geographic isolation, have moved North to the nation's largest cities.

The explanation on the basis of archaism is patently bogus, made up to support the untenable, preconceived notion of the East Anglian origin theory. Since Blacks obviously did not migrate to the United States from East Anglia, the East Anglian theory can only suppose that the Blacks got their language forms entirely from whites. The theory will not allow for the spread of Negro dialect features to the white Southern population, except in very restricted areas adjacent to Gullah territory. Orthodox works like Cleanth Brooks's *The Relation of the Alabama-Georgia Dialect to the Provincial Dialects of Great Britain* (1935) have been specifically aimed at dispelling the heretical notion of Negro influence on white speech which was propounded in L. W. Payne's article "A Word List from East Alabama."[2] As the very title of his article shows, Payne had rather modestly suggested some Negro influence:

> For my own part, after a somewhat careful study of East Alabama dialect, I am convinced that the speech of the white people, the dialect I have spoken all my life and the one I have tried to record here, is more largely colored by the language of the Negroes than by any other single influence. (p. 279)

Payne, let it be pointed out, suggests several areas of influence which were not dealt with by Brooks, who limited himself to a highly unsystematic approach to pronunciation matters.

Brooks also aimed at James A. Harrison,[3] who makes a rather believable case in some particulars but whose viewpoint—that Negro influence constitutes some kind of disgrace—is regrettable. Harrison reports

> It must be confessed, to the shame of the white population of the South, that they perpetuate many of these pronunciations in common with their Negro dependents; and that, in many places, if one happened to be talking to a native with one's eyes shut, it would be impossible to say whether a Negro or a white person were responding. (p. 232)

We may blush for Harrison and his *to the shame of the South*;
but we blush more for G. P. Krapp, who, trying to exorcise the
spectre of Negro dialect as a genuine language variety, cites the
above quotation only from the word *if*, making it appear that
Harrison has said that Negro speech and white speech are never
distinguishable in the South, and suggesting that Harrison's
article is evidence for the identity of Negro dialect and white
Southern dialect.[4] It is, in fact, a statement that the two dialects
are generally distinguishable but that some Southern white dialects have been strongly influenced by Negro dialect.

The proponents of the exclusively white influence theory would
undoubtedly be as glad to get rid of some of their supporters as
of some of their opponents. In the "Who needs enemies with
friends like you?" category is H. P. Johnson, whose "Who lost
the Southern R?",[5] a weak exposition of a position which can be
argued either way, indulges in racist claims of this calibre:

> As those who have long resided in the South know, the Negroes
> are the imitative part of the population.   (p. 383)

Johnson, in perhaps the all-time champion etymological howler,
summarizes,

> . . . but apparently the Negroes have made only one contribution
> to the language of the English speaking world. They have given it
> the word, *buckra*, which means *white man.*

Hopefully, it is not even necessary to refer to the word list in
Chapter III to show how absurd Johnson's statement is.

More talented and more intelligent observers have seen different relationships. Sir Charles Lyell, a clear observer if not (on
this evidence) a liberal in language matters, reports on a family
in which Negro children were learning to read along with white
children, and further observes

> Unfortunately, the whites, in return, often learn from the Negroes
> to speak broken English, and in spite of losing much time in
> unlearning ungrammatical phrases, well-educated persons retain
> some of them all their lives.
>   (*A Second Visit to the United States
>   of North America*, 1849, II, 20)

Other whites, either more sophisticated in language matters or luckier, wasted no time in "unlearning" the English of their Negro playmates, but utilized it in memorable literary productions. These whites—Joel Chandler Harris, Ambrose Gonzales, Charles Colcock Jones, Jr., William Gilmore Simms, George Washington Cable, Lafcadio Hearn, and others—already have secured literary fame, and their reputations seem likely to grow rather than to diminish. At any rate, we may easily observe that both those who wished to unlearn "ungrammatical phrases," and those who became comfortably bidialectal, were rather commonplace in Southern white society. They were, if Johnson will pardon the use of his phrase, "the imitative part" of Southern society. The Negroes seem, on the other hand, to have been the relatively creative and innovative group where language is concerned.

In the West Indies there are abundant reports that the same thing happened among the more or less permanently resident whites who grew up in a population which was predominantly Black and which spoke a language historically related to Plantation Creole. Charles William Day, the thoroughly prejudiced Englishman who wrote *Five Years Residence in the West Indies* (1852), reported several such cases. There was, for example,

> Our captain, a white man from Anguilla, [who] called himself an Englishman and hated everything French. Yet he had never been out of the West Indies and spoke a very singular dialect, all but Negro. (II, 259)

Elsewhere, Day reports

> Once heard, the Creole drawl is never forgotten. They positively speak broken English. (I, 15)

To interpret this second quotation, it is necessary to remember that to Day, *Creole* meant a white who had grown up in the West Indies—a use of the term quite different from that of linguists who write of *"creole languages"*—and that *broken English* is as near to a technical linguistic term for a pidgin or creole language as any available to an Englishman of the period. Day's frequently racist comments about the "indolence" and "inferiority" of West Indian Negroes (who seemed to have two basic failings in Day's opinion: [1] they were improvident; [2] they saved their money and bought property!) should not hide the fact that he gives about the same evidence of the relationship of the dialects of Black and white as was given by other English visitors to the United States. All of them noted the influence of the Black on the white.

Marly; or, A Planter's Life in Jamaica (1828) contains an amusing incident wherein a Miss M'Fathom, a "Creole" girl in this sense, responds to a question when off guard: "Him no savey, Massa." This *lapsus linguae* is said to reveal her "island education" (p. 210). *Lady Nugent's Journal* (Jamaican) of 1802 reports:

> The Creole language is not confined to the Negroes. Many of the [white] ladies, who have not been educated in England, speak a sort of broken English . . . I stood next to a lady one night, near a window, and, by way of saying something, remarked that the air was much cooler than usual; to which she answered, "Yes, ma-am, *him rail-ly too fra-ish.*"   (p. 98)

That theory which will not allow for innovations on the part of the Negroes themselves, and which of course will not allow for the spread of Negro dialect features to the whites, is in effect (although probably unintentionally) the most racist theory of all—that of racial "archaism."* Even the "thick lips" theory is kinder to the Negro: A man might suffer from a physical handicap like thick lips or a cleft palate and be as bright as the next man, although handicapped; but the man who, being physiologically normal, simply remains a hundred years or so behind the times must be mentally deficient.

If we take the brief quotation from Crèvecoeur's *Letters from an American Farmer* (c. 1780) or from Brackenridge's *Modern Chivalry* (1792) as evidence, we can easily see that Negro dialect is, in its basic structure, unlike anything in the white dialects of the time. Although Crèvecoeur says little or nothing about other

---

* Of the slight amount of evidence which exists for retention of some archaic features in Negro dialect, one of the more convincing cases is *ax* [æks] 'ask,' which resembles the postulated Old English source (through metathesis) of Modern English *ask*. Before *ax* is concluded to be an archaic British retention, in U. S. Negro dialects or in the West Indies, it would be well to remember that the Surinam form is *hakisi*. Many Jamaicans vary between *haks* and *aks*.

dialects, Brackenridge was interested enough to represent other varieties of English; none of them is in the least like Cuff's speech.

If the Negro dialect is, then, "archaic"—if the relevant white dialect should be sought not in 1780 and 1792 but in 1680 and 1592—must we regularly expect to find Negro dialect 100 years behind the times? If we had attestations of Negro dialect in 1692, would they be like some white dialect of 1492? How far could we carry the process? If there had been Negro slaves at the legendary crossing of the Angles, Saxons and Jutes in 449, would they have spoken the language(s) of 349? To the philologist, it is almost a pity that there were none, since there is no *direct* evidence of the language of the Germanic invaders of England while they were on the continent!

The whole proposition is patently absurd, even without the counter-theory of pidgin and creole origins. The theory of East Anglian dominance among American dialects is so weak that it could be disposed of even without the problem of Southern and Negro dialects; in forty years, it has produced nothing more than a few dots painted on maps in accordance with faulty sampling theory.

Turned around the other way, the relationship between Negro and Southern white dialects begins to make sense: the Negro dialect, a new force on the "Anglo-Saxon" population, was innovative rather than archaic. It is much more likely to have produced *some*—not all—of the differences between Southern white dialect and Northern white dialect than to have been originally identical with a white Southern dialect. Overt statements of this type are not hard to find: Thomas L. Nichols asserted in his *Forty Years of American Life* (1864) that

> Southern speech is clipped, softened, and broadened by the Negro admixture. The child learns its language from its Negro nurse, servants, and playmates, and this not unpleasant patois is never quite eradicated.
>
> (Quoted in Mamie Meredith, " 'Tall Talk' in America
> Sixty Years Ago," *American Speech* IV, No. 3
> [February, 1929] p. 291)

G. L. Campbell in *The London Magazine* for July, 1746, reported much the same thing from his travels in the American colonies. Mrs. Anne Royall wrote,

> But the children of both classes are good specimens of dialect, as the better sort, in this country, particularly, consign their children to the care of Negroes . . . Those who have black nurses . . . are at much pains and cost for teachers to unlearn them what they need never have learned, had they kept illiterate people from them at first. This is not the case with the poorer class of people, as the children are nursed by themselves, and speak *their* language.
>
> (Quoted in Mathews, p. 94)

That Mrs. Royall's observation is in company with a harsh value judgment need concern us not at all; it is necessary to sift fact from prejudice in judging all such attestations. It happens that she is joined by no less than the great Dickens, in a letter of April 15, 1842, to Forster: ". . . all the women who have been bred in slave states speak more or less like Negroes, from having been constantly in their childhood with black nurses . . ."

Fanny Kemble also reported that her daughter showed such influence, thus giving some corroboration to Dickens's suggestion that it was the Southern women's speech which was most affected. Kemble has several overt statements of that type:

> . . . The children of the owners, brought up among them (the slaves) acquire their Negro mode of talking—slavish speech surely it is—and it is distinctly perceptible in the utterances of all Southerners, particularly of the women, whose avocations, taking them less from home, are less favorable to their throwing off this ignoble trick of pronunciation than the varied occupation and the more extended and promiscuous business relations of men. The Yankee twang of the regular down Easter is not more easily detected by any ear, nice in enunciation and accent, than the thick Negro speech of the Southerners . . .   (pp. 210–211)

In spite of her relative intolerance in the area of language (not really bad when compared to the norm for day), Kemble apparently gives evidence for a diglossic (see Glossary) situation among the Southern men, but not among the women. This would explain why Dickens got his impression only of the Southern women: the men, confronted with a distinguished Britisher,

would use the dialect of wider communication; the women, unable to do so, would have to use the Negro-influenced home
dialect, pieced out with such formalities and literary influences
as they could draw upon. Men's dialects and languages as well
as women's dialects and languages are well known to the sociolinguist; seldom can there have been more explicit evidence for
the manner in which sex-associated differences have developed.

According to Caroline Gilman, not all women were so limited;
but then Mrs. Gilman was not a limited woman:

> . . . although, at the time of which I speak, I preferred to talk to
> the Negroes in their dialect I never used it to the whites.   (p. 41)

Thus, some of the women of the time were apparently both
bidialectal and diglossic.

Statements of this type are legion during the period just before
the Civil War. Before Emancipation, the children of the slave-
owning class had plenty of opportunity to acquire Black English;
individual families obviously differed as to whether the acquisition was welcomed or resisted. The knowledge of Negro dialect
displayed by outstanding white dialect writers like Joel Chandler
Harris, Ambrose E. Gonzales, and Charles Colcock Jones, Jr.,
must have been acquired in this way. John Bennett, in "Gullah:
A Negro Patois" (*Atlantic*, 1908), reported that the younger
children of the "best families" in Charleston spoke Gullah even
during times much later than the Civil War. Commercial recordings by Charleston whites like Dick Reeves (see Bibliography)
reveal that bidialectal ability in that group is not a thing of the
past. White bidialectism obviously did not cease immediately
after the Civil War: there are occasional writers of Negro dialect
like John B. Sale, author of *The Tree Named John* (1929), who
continued to attribute his facility to association with his Negro
"playmate of long ago" (p. IX).

Social class and sex may have been two major factors in the
social determinism of bidialectism during this period. Bidialectal
switchers seen to have been primarily upper-class males. Negro
dialect or Negro-influenced dialect is not, of course, a sex-linked
characteristic in any physical sense, any more than the ethnic

component is physiological; but social conditions at a given time
may favor the performance of a certain kind of linguistic activity
by one sex or the other. In the mid-twentieth century, it is a
commonplace that Negro females find it easier to acquire Standard English than do the men—usually not becoming diglossic
but leaving Negro Non-Standard English behind.

Neither sex nor absolute class status may have been the determining factor in Fanny Kemble's rather unsophisticated—even
for her time—horror at her daughter's being influenced by the
speech of the slaves:

> I am amused, but by no means pleased, at an entirely new mode
> of pronouncing which S [Sally, her daughter of about four years]
> has adopted. Apparently the Negro jargon has commended itself as
> euphonious to her infantile ears, and she is now treating me to the
> most ludicrous and accurate imitations of it every time she opens
> her mouth. Of course I shall not allow this to become a habit. This
> is the way the Southern ladies acquire the thick and inelegant
> pronunciation which distinguishes their utterances from the North-
> ern snuffle, and I have no desire that S_____ should adorn her
> mother tongue with either peculiarity.   (pp. 238–9)

In Kemble's case, it is probably not so much insecurity in social
status as her avowed and troublesome liberalism which makes her
unwilling to share the linguistic attitudes of her Southern matron
acquaintances, just as she was unwilling to share their racial and
political views. In spite of her distressing purism—which might
have been one reason why her child mixed the two dialects instead of being bidialectal—and in spite of her use of terms like
"thick" and "inelegant," Fanny may have been close to a basic
truth about language learning. Although it is hardly necessary
that a language variety "commend itself as euphonious" to a
four-year-old in order for that child to learn it, it is quite believable that a four-year-old with Negro nurses, servants and
playmates should learn to produce an accurate imitation of the
dialect—or, more accurately, should learn it. As everyone except
H. P. Johnson has always known, "the imitative part of the
population," linguistically speaking, is the youngest part, irre-
spective of ethnic composition.

Caroline Gilman documents a healthier attitude toward her children's use of Negro dialect:

> I have never felt any more apprehension with Negroes, lest their dialect should be permanently injured, than I should have at listening to the broken English of a foreigner. (p. 41)

Although Mrs. Gilman includes her children ("they" in the above quotation) among the whites to whom she never spoke the Negro dialect, she is intuitively aware of diglossia, although of course not in command of the terminology for it. In considering —and discarding—the possibility that her children's English might "be permanently injured," she is being neither more or less inaccurate about language matters than most educated people of the time.

The existence of the bidialectal Southern white child, chiefly among the landed and wealthy class in the period before the Civil War, is so well documented as to be beyond any real doubt. The rather facile, and somewhat sentimental, explanation is usually that the child learned the dialect from the Negro "mammy" who suckled him. Several ex-slaves tell of the relationship in B. A. Botkin's collection *Lay My Burden Down*. The Hillsborough (North Carolina) *Recorder* protested, in 1825, against the custom of

> delivering a child over into the hands of a nurse . . . where it may first learn to lisp vulgarity and obscenity, and from whom it inevitably acquires a pronunciation and accent, such as may never be fully corrected.
>
> (quoted in Guion G. Johnson,
Ante-Bellum North Carolina, p. 252)

Louis H. Blair, a Southerner but an objective observer and no apologist for the ante-bellum aristocracy, testifies to the relationship:

> Most of us above thirty years of age had our mammy . . . Up to the age of ten we saw as much, perhaps more, of the mammy than of the mother . . . The mammy first taught us to lisp and to walk . . .
>
> (*The Prosperity of the South Dependent Upon the
Elevation of the Negro* [1889], p. 105)

Even Thomas Nelson Page's *Social Life in Old Virginia*, saccharine
as it is in its idealization of Southern society, can be trusted as a
source for this relationship because of its agreement with so many
others.

Of course, these observers are essentially wrong in one particular: one learns a dialect, or a language, better on the playground than at the breast. Blair's phrase "taught us to lisp" is a
strong claim about the influence of the mammy on the Southern
boys' speech—too strong in terms of what we know about language-learning processes. Another of his statements probably has
more relevance to the process of language (or dialect) learning:

> And when we became youths and played with Negro boys, went
> fishing and hunting with them, gathered berries and nuts together,
> climbed the same trees . . .   (*Ibid.*)

"Mammy's" real linguistic influence was less direct, but not a bit
less important: she provided the children with whom the white
Massa played. Many sources testify, as does Orlando Kay Armstrong's *Old Massa's People*, that

> Every plantation had its "play children," little black boys and girls
> who spent most of their waking hours with the master and mistress.
>   (p. 73)

Armstrong forgot—or perhaps he never noticed—that it was often
"back to the fields" for such "play children" when they fell out
of favor. The ex-slaves in Botkin's collection did not, however,
overlook that detail.

There was obviousy abundant opportunity for the white child
of a slave-owning family to learn the Negro dialect during the
pre-Civil War period. Occasionally, a master or his employees in
charge of field hands would find such knowledge useful or even
indispensable. Olmsted, in *The Cotton Kingdom,* tells of a
woman field slave who

> . . . was a native African, having been brought when a girl from
> the Guinea coast. She spoke almost unintelligibly; but after some
> other conversation, in which I had not been able to understand a
> word, she said, he jokingly proposed to send her back to Africa . . .

"Why? . . . I lubs 'ou, Mass'r, oh, I lubs 'ou. I don't want go 'way
from 'ou."   (p. 191)

The fact that the woman's protestation sounds like something
put into a slave's mouth by the "hireling and the slave" tradition
should not prejudice the evidence of a reliable historian like
Olmsted. Although Olmsted does not quote the white man's
words, he makes it clear that the "Mass'r" understands the African
variety of English and apparently speaks something rather like it.

The use of Negro dialect by at least partially bidialectal Northern whites is so contrary to the usual theories that one is tempted
to reject evidence that it sometimes happened. Nevertheless, such
evidence is not lacking; considering the attestations of Northern
Negro speech in such sources as Cooper's novels, it is not really
unlikely that the dialect was familiar, although in more completely decreolized form to some Northerners.

Thomas Ashe's *Travels* (1808) reported an encounter, in Kentucky, with a German immigrant

. . . who had lived long enough in Virginia to pick up some Negro-
English.   (p. 79)

Tucker's *The Partisan Leader* presents Northern soldiers who,
having invaded Virginia, are familiar enough with Negro culture
patterns to know the day names, or their common noun derivatives, and to be misled by an assumed dialect into classifying a
loyal household servant as a (potentially disloyal) field slave.

Thomas Wentworth Higginson, in *Army Life in a Black Regiment*, was perfectly aware of

That semi-Ethiopian dialect into which we [the Northern white
officers in his Civil War regiment] sometimes slid.   (p. 241)

Higginson, who reports in some detail his practices in copying
down the Black soldiers' songs and checking them with individual
soldiers, frequently reproduces sentences in a respectable version
of Plantation Creole. He reports no difficulty in understanding
it. Like many others of his time, he used "Ethiopian" in a rough
sense much as we would use "African."

The impressions of many observers were that dialects of whites

in other parts of the United States were influenced by Plantation
Creole or by the later, decreolized stages. Thus, John H. Beadle,
in *Western Wilds and the Men Who Redeem Them* (1878),
reported a "Hoosier language" which

> . . . is the result of union between the rude translations of 'Penn-
> sylvania Dutch,' the Negroisms of Kentucky and Virginia, and
> certain phrases native to the Ohio Valley.   (p. 19)

Although observations like these are slim evidence, it should not
be forgotten that the counter-claim—that the Negro has had no
influence on American English—is a pure assertion not supported
by even this much evidence. The grammatical sketch of the "language" given by Beadle seems to indicate what was indeed a
dialect influenced by Plantation Creole:

> *Perfect Tense*:—I gone done it, you gone done it, he gone done it.
> *Plural*:—We 'uns gone done it, you 'uns gone done it, they 'uns gone
>   done it.
> *Pluperfect*:—I bin gone done it, you bin gone done it, etc.
> *First Future*:—I gwine to do it, you gwine to do it, etc.   (p. 18)

It is rather puzzling what Beadle meant by "perfect tense," which
quite obviously doesn't fit the Plantation Creole use of *go* or of
one of its derivatives as a future marker. Forms like *we 'uns*,
you 'uns, etc., have so many different possibilities of origin that
an argument on either side would be largely wasted. But the use
of *bin* in the "pluperfect" (that is, quite markedly in the past)
looks very much like Plantation Creole.

But of course it was the Southerner, and almost exclusively the
Southern child, who really learned the Negro's variety of English.
Few adults of the time can have been as linguistically sensitive
as Higginson, a noted member of the literati. The relationships
which made such learning possible for quite undistinguished
Southerners were so commonplace that they have been per-
petuated even in the stereotype. Literature for white Southern
children, only incidentally and perhaps unintentionally racistic in
nature, frequently utilizes such scenes. Of course, few of the
writers had Mark Twain's ability to show the thorns of reality

among the roses of the Old South. Margaret Devereux's *Plantation Sketches* (1906), reminiscences of the Civil War period which are no worse and not much better than the average, presents a situation in which the master's children, in charge of a "mammy," speak Negro dialect to the mammy and to her assistant. Among many fictional sources which record this relationship is Louise Clarke Pyrnelle's *Diddie, Dumps, and Tot*, for a long time and perhaps even up to the present a favorite children's book among Southern middle-class families. The white children in this book, incidentally, speak a dialect which is similar to, but not exactly identical to, that of their Negro playmates.

Like Fanny Kemble, other Southern parents apparently often had a finicky, purist objection to their children's faculty for picking up the slaves' dialect. This attitude has lasted, even among non-bidialectals. Sale's *The Tree Named John* presents a child who had been reared mainly by his "mammy" but whose pronunciation had been so "improved" by school and parental precept that he "spoke fairly good English until he was excited, and then he forgot" (p. 144). Young John's language habits reflect a not uncommon type of disglossia in which one variety (*basilect* is Stewart's term) comes to be thought of as appropriate to children; that such incidences are not entirely fictions is illustrated in *North Carolina Folklore*, where *goobies* 'peanuts' (from *goobers*, perhaps the most certain African etymology) is listed as a "child's word" (I, p. 546) with apparently no recognition of its African origin. When John later attempted to share his "improvement" with his "mammy," he precipitated a tirade from her. After deciding that domestic relationships are more important than "correctness" in speech, he attempts to propitiate her with a present and the rather non-standard language, "Look here, Ai' Betsey, whut I got you" (p. 146).

There are other opinions about the language relationship between "mammy" and her charges. Anne Weston Whitney expressed the opinion that

> She [the mammy] knew perfectly well what was correct in both dialects. Her own dialect might consist largely of words and ex-

pressions once proper for the master, but now given up by him;
she would recognize the difference, and any signs of falling into
the dialect form of speech would be met with

"Dat no way for white child talk."

("Negro American Dialects," *The Independent*,
Vol. LIII, August 22, 1901, p. 1980)

Of course, there is no special reason why both Sale and Whitney
cannot be partly right: individual "mammies" undoubtedly varied
that much.

Evidence exists that, before the time in which their activities
were available for direct observation by dialectologists, there was
abundant opportunity for Southern white children to learn the
dialect of their Negro playmates. Olmsted reported

> I am struck with the close co-habitation and association of black
> and white—Negro women are carrying black and white babies
> together in their arms; black and white children are playing together
> (not going to school together); black and white faces constantly
> thrust together out of doors to see the train go by.
>
> (*A Journey in the Seaboard Slave States*, 1865, p. 17)

The indications are that, although the relationship favored the
development of diglossia on the part of white children, it did no
such thing for the Negro children. For them, there was no home
language and school language dichotomy; but it seems to have
been their dialect which prevailed in play situations, perhaps
because they were greater in numbers and possibly because any
adult who intervened in the play situation was likely to be a
Negro adult. The non-fictional evidence supplied by Olmsted
parallels, at any rate, such fictional evidence as the pump scene
in *Huckleberry Finn*, which has some literary quality added by
a novelist who knew what he was about in terms of describing
race relationships.

On the subject of slave bidialectism there is considerably less
evidence, and it is perhaps to be concluded that there was simply
less Negro bidialectism at this stage. One reason may be that
even writers like Fanny Kemble were likely to know the slave
owners better than they knew the slaves, and therefore to be

able to report on the former's diglossia; but the more important reason may be that the sociolinguistic conditions simply did not favor the use of a second dialect by the slaves. There are even occasional representations of polyglot slaves, coming perhaps from the West Indies, who speak only the Negro dialect of English.

A famous theory of distribution of the slaves separates them into house servants and field servants, and of course the house servants would have had much more opportunity to learn the owners' English. There is evidence, however, that the dichotomy was not quite complete; there are many literary representations of house servants who speak quite palpable Negro dialect. Although the house servants usually considered themselves an elite and were often much better treated than the field workers, there are indications that field slaves were sometimes promoted to the house and house servants banished to the field.

Also, in many cases the house servants returned to the slave quarters at night and associated with the field servants. What may be more important than all this is that, like the Chinese servant Lee in Steinbeck's *East of Eden*, some slaves were expected by their masters to speak like Negroes, while others who worked in the household were expected by different masters to speak like whites. The rules of conduct are all-important in dialect variation, and the evidence is that the rules varied.

Thus, a critic like Nathaniel Beverly Tucker, who in his strangely prophetic novel *The Partisan Leader* (1836) complained of the dialect representation of house servants, might have been giving valid evidence of his own experience without disproving other evidence furnished by someone else's experience:

> I crave the forbearance of all critics, who have taken their idea of a Virginia house-servant from Caesar Thompson, or any such caricatures, for giving Tom's own words and his pronunciation of them. It is not my fault there is but little peculiarity in his phraseology. His language was never elegant, and frequently ungrammatical, but he spoke better than the peasantry of most countries, though he said things that a white man would not say; perhaps, because

he had some feelings to which the white man is a stranger. A white man, for example, would have said he was *glad* to see Douglas, whether he were or not. Old Tom said he was *proud* to see him, because he *was* proud to recognize his former pet in the handsome and graceful youth before him.   (p. 100)

This statement in itself does not, of course, say that Negroes had a dialect different from the whites, but only that the English of the house servants with whom the author was familiar differed little in dialect from their owners. Elsewhere in the same work there is ample indication that the author is thoroughly familiar with another Negro dialect, apparently that of field hands. Since there is room for a great deal of variation in a diglossic situation such as that on many of the plantations, there is no reason to doubt that both the representation of Caesar Thompson and that of Tucker's Tom are as accurate as literary conventions made possible.

In some cases, it seems that house servants considered themselves far above field hands. Sales's Aunty Betsey, long after the days of slavery, "considered field hands a lower order of being and always treated them with condescension and frequently with disdain" (*The Tree Named John*, p. 4).[6] Nevertheless, Betsey does not speak the English of her employers.

In other cases, a house servant might be punished by being sent to work on the field. Margaret Devereux, in *Plantation Sketches* (1906), recalling the period just before and during the Civil War, reports the demotion of a slave named "Shoe Joe" or "Gentlemen Joe" from house work to field work; "in consequence of this, he always bore his young master a grudge" (p. 31).

Lewis H. Blair (*The Prosperity of the South Dependent upon the Elevation of the Negro*, 1889, p. 37) makes field slaves superior to "their relatives in Africa" and house servants "greatly superior in appearance and every other respect" to field hands. In the excellent Negro novelist Charles W. Chesnutt's "Hot Foot Hannibal" in *The Conjure Woman*, a field servant replaces a house servant, disgracing the latter and permanently damaging his courtship of a female house servant.[7] A more successful house servant rubbed it in, but not in standard English:

> "I doan see w'at 'casion any common fiel'-han' has got ter mix wid de 'fairs er folks w'at libs in de big house."   (p. 214)

In such cases, the class or caste lines would remain fluid and no great deal of dialect differentiation could be expected.

Elsewhere, it was well recognized that employment as a house servant made a great deal of difference compared to work as a field slave. Olmsted reports a conversation that occurred when he commented to a group of Southern whites that a nearly white slave girl could "pass" for white if her personal history were not known. A Southerner replied:

> "Oh, yes, you might not know her if she got to the North, but any of us would know her."
> "How?"
> "By her language and manners."
> "But if she had been brought up as a house servant?"
> "Perhaps not in that case."   (*The Cotton Kingdom*, Vol. II, p. 210)

Olmsted's reports, here and in many other places, document the Southern tendency to overstereotype the Negro; but there is no real reason to doubt that Southerners, thoroughly familiar with the Negro dialect as well as with their own, would recognize the former and differentiate it from the latter better than would Northerners, who might react to the common unfamiliarity of the two dialects as though they had a kind of identity. And, since *manners* here may just as well mean 'mannerisms' as 'features of etiquette', it is quite believable (as Herskovits has pointed out) that gestural and kinesic cues might "give away" a member of the Negro subculture to people who knew that culture. Since neither culture nor language is genetic but varies according to membership in cultural groups, there is nothing surprising in the statement that membership in the field slave group had consequences in language and demeanor. The evidence of the attestations is that the lines (probably caste lines in this case) were sometimes drawn between house servant and field hand, sometimes between black and white. At any rate, behavorial distinctions—including language distinctions—followed the social divisions.

The group which could escape from the field slave caste was not always limited to household servants as such. A classical statement is that of E. Franklin Frazier:

> These skilled mechanics, who constituted a large section of the artisans in the South, formed with the house servants a sort of privileged class in the slave community. The greater the integration of the slaves into the activities and family life of their white masters, the more nearly their behavior and ideals approximated those of the whites.   (*Black Bourgeoisie*, p. 13)

Behavior, obviously, would include linguistic behavior.

To return to Tucker: his powers of dialect description are probably not so good as he claims them to be (few, if any, linguists would claim to be able to "give his pronunciation," as does Tucker, the relationship between pronunciation and any kind of transcription being such a tenuous one), but his practice exceeds his theory. He apparently recognized the existence of a Negro dialect quite different from Tom's, which was associated in the minds of his characters with a lower status than that of the house servant; and he perhaps even recognizes bidialectal ability among the slaves. In a later chapter of the novel, which was written years before the Civil War, Northern soldiers are pictured as being captured by a ruse perpetrated (although—alas for Tucker's understanding of racial abilities—not planned) by a Negro slave who fools the invaders by speaking the dialect of the field slaves. Clearly, even the Yankees realize that those slaves having white dialect patterns would also have ideals "approximating those of their masters." The dialect is pretty close to what is meant herein by Plantation Creole:

> "Who, I, Massa? My name Jack, sir. What I love him for? Hard work and little bread, and no meat? No, Massa, I love soldier 'cause I hear 'em say soldier come after a while, set poor niggur free."
>   (Vol. II, 22)

When the ruse has worked and the Yankee soldiers are in the trap,

> A voice not unlike that of their friend Jack, which informed them, in good English . . .   (Vol. II, 24)

gives the duped soldiers to know, as much by being Standard English as by anything else, that they have been dealing with a slave who is close to and therefore loyal to his master. Whatever may be thought of Tucker's racial and political preconceptions, the picture which he presents is consistent. The dialect which his household servant uses to play the field hand is like that which all other evidence would assign to field hands, and the whole picture rings true in terms of what we know of the situation from many authorities, observers, and students. (The most questionable note is, of course, that of the simple-minded Northern soldiers; but some such license is expected in a rabidly Southern novel.)

Perhaps more usual than bidialectal slaves, but still rather rare—according to the records—are Negroes with no trace of the dialect. (It should always be kept in mind that the speaker of "perfectly" Standard English might have been a bidialectal who kept one side of his language behavior from white observers.) Quite characteristically, all observers point up these occasional cases and comment upon them as something unusual. James, the Englishman who set *The Old Dominion* (1836) in the Virginia which he had visited, had one of his characters comment on a talented Negro:

> "The most extraordinary thing of all," she answered, "is that he has not the slightest touch of the Negro pronunciation'."   (p. 46)

James—or rather his character—goes on to comment quite naively about the "inability" of most Negroes to "speak English properly." But an inability to interpret what he has heard in linguistically relevant terms is certainly no indication that a writer hasn't heard anything. Another character in the same novel, based upon the historical Nat Turner, is also specifically pointed out as not speaking "the Negro's jargon" (p. 101).

If, in looking at printed representations of the speech of historical Black figures in the nineteenth century, one looks only at the speech of Frederick Douglass, one comes away with the impression that the Negro must have spoken like a well-educated white. On the other hand, if the public utterances are those of Sojourner Truth, the reader sees something which is not usually called educated Standard English, and which does not resemble the speech of illiterate or lower-class whites in any special way.[8] Both conclusions are true: a Negro of the nineteenth century spoke or did not speak the non-standard dialect—or Plantation Creole—according to his social position and background. But the experience of the vast majority of whites who had contact with Negroes was, according to all records, with those who spoke one or another variety of Negro dialect—even though they were likely to have had more contact with those Negroes whose English was relatively like the white man's. In establishing the causes, the observers chose to indulge in inane speculations rather than taking the obvious step—asking a Negro. Douglass, when questioned directly, gave what is probably the best answer from the nineteenth century:

> I have been often asked during the earlier part of my free life at the North, how I happened to have so little of the slave accent in my speech. The mystery is in some measure explained by my association with Daniel Lloyd, the youngest son of Col. Edward Lloyd.
> (Quoted in Wish, *Slavery in The South*, p. 65)

Note that Douglass's questioners spoke of a "mystery"—evidently expecting some kind of exotic explanation, perhaps having to do with physical characteristics—and received a social explanation. Professional linguists have done worse than Douglass.

Literary records also show Negroes who use only Standard English; in some cases they clearly do so even in talking with other Negroes. Stewart ("Sociolinguistic Factors") gives the example of such a conversation in *Blake: or the Huts of America*, by Negro novelist Martin R. Delaney. It seems significant that such Negro authors as Delaney and Charles W. Chesnutt (especially in *The Marrow of Tradition*) describe a linguistic differential among their Negro characters. The ones who have had access to the white man's culture (especially to his schools) always speak the variety which is closest to Standard English.

Yet those who have had intimate knowledge of the South, white or black, have always expressed the feeling that the Negro whose dialect is not different from that of the whites is somehow unusual. The scene from *Diddie, Dumps, and Tot* where a Negro queries Ann, a Standard English-speaking slave who is the mother of a nearly white boy, seems typical:

> "Wy, yer talkin' same ez wite folks," said Uncle Bob. "What yer git all dem fine talkin's from? Ain't you er nigger same as me?"
>
> (p. 100)

In other words, rules of conduct based upon social status should determine speech patterns; and Ann, although she has been close enough to whites for such obvious activities as mating (the author somewhat Puritanically has her married to the father of her child before falling victim to such misfortunes as being sold on the block), is recognized as a Negro and should be subject to the Negro rules. This pull of the rules of conduct was undoubtedly the greatest deterrent to Negro bidialectism, which otherwise would be a great asset.

What we can call code-switching was noticed very early among Negroes in the United States. Sidney Lanier, a noted dialect writer and critic of the dialect writing of others commented

> . . . the commonest mistake in reproducing the Negro's dialect is to make it too consistent.[9]

and he also explained how this "inconsistency" arose:

> . . . and you need not think, therefore, that in allowing the same speaker to say (for example) sometimes "*dat*" and sometimes "*that*,"—as I arranged the dialect here and there—there is any lapsus. The Negro, especially since the war, tries hard for the *th* instead of *d* in such words as *the, that*, etc., and thus the same speaker often uses both forms. That remark applies to many other peculiarities.[10]

Lanier would, of course, be reporting from his own experience, in which he heard the speaker of Negro dialect trying to talk Lanier's own dialect—which is the classic situation for linguistic interference—and would have no special reason to know how even Negroes well known to him talked among themselves. In very many places today—including islands of the Caribbean and very possibly the cities of the United States—Negroes speaking dialects historically related to the one Lanier is writing about attempt to speak the English of outsiders, with varying degrees of success because of different degrees of proficiency in overcoming interference. Many of these speakers are diffident about speaking their home dialect among outsiders, and they will frequently deny that they have any acquaintance with a language variety which they in fact speak quite well. There is more than a little reason to believe that Negroes in the United States also switch automatically to more standard English in more public situations. Antiguans call their own speech variety "Bad Talk" or "the bad way"; and the ethnocentric white world chooses to call its variety "Good English."

Lanier's comment about this kind of switching taking place "especially since the war" seems significant also. Emancipation, even if it did not result in anything like equal opportunity, must have given the ex-slave some kind of status vis-à-vis the white man. Sociologists find that such newly acquired status almost always finds some kind of linguistic expression, with the speaker (usually an adult whose linguistic habits are relatively fixed) often unable to complete the linguistic transition as effectively as he would like to. The would-be speaker of the more prestigious dialect often suffers the ridicule of those who perceive his unsuccessful attempts. It is typically only those who have that status assured—who are, so to speak, born with it and grow up with it—who are able to begin the linguistic transition in their youth and to make it more or less perfectly.

Today? A young Washington informant of mine, twelve years old and the son of one of my Georgetown graduate students, once

walked into my office at a time when it happened that the elicited
sentence, in standard spelling,

> Here go a man and a lady

was on the blackboard. Asked to read the sentence aloud and to
interpret it, he waved me aside, "First you have to tell me who
said it." Cued that it had been spoken by one of his playmates,
a disadvantaged Negro child, he read it "Higo . . . " and interpreted it to mean 'A man and a lady are here.' Then, prompted
that the same sentence might have been uttered by his mother,
a white woman who taught part-time at the University, he read
the sentence with Standard English pronunciation and interpreted
it to mean 'A man and a lady are walking here.' Clearly, this
young boy was quasi-bidialectal; he was able, to some degree,
to subject his use of the two speech varieties to conscious control.

The son of a white professor of English as a second language
and a Negro professor of English Literature, this young boy did
not learn one dialect from each parent; the father's English is as
standard as the mother's. But the high-rise apartment building in
which they live is surrounded by poorer apartments, most of them
occupied by the Negro disadvantaged. The young boy played
with these children, and learned their dialect under the best
possible circumstances. His mother discovered his other linguistic
skill only by accidental overhearing; being a graduate student
in linguistics, she was sophisticated enough to record the children
and make a study of their dialect rather than trying to "correct"
it.

Other Negroes are clearly bidialectal, but the reasons are not
always so easy to find. A professor of economics who lives in
Chicago relates the history of his daughter, who grew up in
Persia while the father was employed there. Returning to the
United States, she was perfectly bilingual, at the age of about
twelve, in Persian and English—but she knew no Negro dialect.
Finding herself uncomfortable among members of her own race
in their new residence, she consulted her father, who proceeded

to teach her to speak Negro dialect. There are few people in the United States so intelligent and sophisticated, yet this particular professor is a living example that sensible attitudes can prevail.

Of course there is, in the United States today, a fairly large Negro middle class which manipulates Standard English with the ease and confidence of the native speaker. Many of these do not speak "Negro" Non-Standard at all; others may utilize it only in relaxed, casual situations. Disclaimers voiced in articles like Earl Conrad's "The Philology of Negro Dialect,"[11] when closely examined, object primarily to failure on the part of white dialect writers to treat that "vast host" of Negroes who speak "no special dialect at all, no idiom apart from general, white American idiom" (pp. 154-155). Conrad's point is, of course, well taken; it should also be pointed out that some, if not a "vast host," of the slaves, from almost the earliest times, belong to this group. Conrad also documents code-switching behavior: "They can often 'shift languages' when they want to" (p. 154). Our particular social and sociolinguistic system makes overt recognition of such activity unfortunately rare.

But back to Southern white dialects. If they are to be left alone while Negro dialects are dissected historically, then the Negroes referred to above are justified in their complaints. Bidialectism may be predominantly a Negro problem today, but evidence has already been presented that it was not so in the nineteenth century. What happened to the generations after Caroline Gilman and Fanny Kemble? Did they all take a trip to East Anglia to restore their English, or did they bring in teachers who taught them British dialect—dull but pure? Or would it be possible to determine from the speech of Southern whites alone that there had been a pidgin and a creole around?

It is well known that the aftermath of Emancipation brought a different social relationship between Southern whites and Negroes; unfortunately, the end of slavery was not the only consequence. When freedom took the Negro—not immediately, as we know from a great many accounts—away from the aristocrat or near-aristocrat, and brought him for the first time into close contact with the Southern poor white, the conditions for bidialectism diminished greatly. To the cracker, the Negro was not a piece of property—sometimes even a beloved piece of property—but a competitor. Lacking the security of the aristocrat, the poor white, especially the one with some pretensions to upward mobility, would be more likely to avoid the Negro when possible. In extreme cases, he migrated to bleak and isolated environments (like my birthplace, Grand Saline in Van Zandt County, Texas) and improvised his own laws that Negroes were not to be allowed in that territory. (In Grand Saline, the owner of the salt mine—the only industry in town—had a Negro maid whom the towns-folk managed to overlook. But any *other* Negro in town after dark was in physical danger. The folk tales related how the local heroes had strung up a poor fellow who had been found cowering in a ditch and thus had been caught red-handed—or rather black-handed—in the terrible crime of being a Negro in Grand Saline after sundown.)

To such people, the tracing of one of their language or behavior patterns to Negro influence was the bitterest of insults. Yet the typical migration pattern to Texas had been from Mississippi, where there were many Negroes. Practically any farmer who came to the local "First Monday," at which worthless possessions were traded for other worthless possessions and at which an occasional tourist is swindled today, could give his interpretation and imitation of Negro behavior—although never sympathetically, one may be sure. But I well remember that *goober*, one of the most certain of the African etymologies of all words in American English, was an every-day term in "downtown" Grand Saline—in the meaning 'penis' as well as 'peanut'.

For such people, any foreign influence on their English posed much greater problems than it did for the aristocrats, since the poor white was concerned with "getting it right" in a grim struggle almost for his very existence, rather than as a matter of switching between two codes for the purpose of achieving the optimal effect in a given communication situation. To become bidialectal meant to become quickly declassé, and only a few

risked it. Aversion for the Negro played a part, but there were
many other factors. A few, like Lyle Britten in James Baldwin's
very perceptive play *The Blues for Mr. Charlie,* dealt with and
exploited the Negro community. From my own memory of later
boyhood in Terrell, Texas, I can identify a storekeeper who was
amazingly like Britten, who got rich by selling shoddy merchan-
dise to Negroes at exorbitant prices, and who was unable to enjoy
his wealth because white society rejected him. In an especially
clever touch, Baldwin makes Britten use Negro dialect forms like
the zero copula.

It might be expected that Negro dialect would have little
influence on white dialect and vice versa, under the new conditions in which segregation replaced slavery. Not dealing directly
with language, Dowd reasoned that

> Under slavery the races knew each other through their intimate
> personal contacts. The domestic slaves, especially, not only had
> opportunity to know the white people, but grew like them in taste,
> manners, disposition, and often in habits and morals. Following the
> slave relationship, the Negroes who worked for the white people
> continued to live in cottages on their former masters' premises.
> The home life of the Negroes was still under the observation of the
> white people, who continued their oversight of the Negro families,
> lending their personal services in case of sickness or other misfor-
> tune. Later, the Negro servants ceased to live on the premises of
> the white people, and came to reside in segregated quarters which
> entirely removed them from any intimate observations or familiarity
> with the whites . . . Gradually . . . all paternal oversight of the
> Negroes has been abandoned and the relationship of the races has
> become entirely commercial and impersonal.
>
> > (*The Negro in American Life,* pp. 548-9)

The Jim Crow laws threw house servants and field hands together
as Negroes, to the famous distress of groups like the New Orleans
gens de couleur. From his reluctant new associates among the
"poor buckras" or "white trash," the Negro's occasional use of
Standard English drew not the earlier admiration accorded to
Douglass and others, but resentment and accusations of being
an "uppity nigger." Any assertion of status on the part of the

Negro was resented; small boys in my home town of Terrell threw rocks at any car driven through by Negroes, especially if it was a relatively expensive car. And they had very definite ideas about how Negroes could, should, and did act. We knew, for example, of the Afro-American fondness, documented in many other sources, for bright-colored clothes; but, of course, we attributed it to lack of taste rather than to a different taste.

Under such circumstances it might be hard to find a function for Negro dialect forms—much less bidialectism—in the language behavior of lower-class or lower-middle-class whites. It might therefore be assumed that all borrowing from the Negro dialect to the white dialect ceased abruptly. But there were probably real-life situations like the fictional one in E. P. O'Donnell's short story "Canker" (*Yale Review*, 1936), set in the Louisiana Delta, in which a seven-year-old white boy is pictured as speaking the Negro dialect of his playmates while his poor farmer parents speak Standard English.

Recognition of the influence of Black English (by whatever name it has been called) on white speech has never been lacking. John U. Lloyd wrote, in "The Language of the Kentucky Negro" (*Dialect Notes*, 1901):

> . . . the talk of the old slave, as well as the language of ignorant whites raised among the Negroes, in my opinion, was largely *patois*.
> (p. 180)

There are the usual value judgments and loaded words (*ignorant, patois*) in such statements. The creolist, however, can remember with something like amusement that creole languages, like Haitian, are regularly called *patois* by amateur observers.

My small-boy group in Terrell in the 1930's knew how we thought Negroes talked; and we talked that way under certain circumstances. If a rise in status is a social desideratum, a fall is an occasional harsh necessity; and it is often expressed in language forms: *dramatic low status assertion* is the term which West Indian anthropologist Reisman uses. Insofar as my memory serves, we talked like "niggers" in time of defeat, to accept humiliation with as comic a grace as possible. Such talk was a regular part of our vocal repertory (how accurate it was is an entirely different matter), and we must not have been alone among Southern white boys.

Inez Lopez Cohen[12] gave me quite a start, what might be called the "shock of recognition," when she reproduced in her book *Our Darktown Press* a quotation from a Negro newspaper about how a white policeman "adjusted his mouth to talk like a Negro"; on my reading the passage, my facial muscles involuntarily "set" themselves in just the way that the policeman's must have. The description is, of course, not a very good one in terms of articulatory physiology; but it is close enough to a description of an action which had been in my childhood verbal repertory to cause a feeling of uncanniness near to that of shock. Obviously, the Negro community is more sensitive to this kind of activity on the part of whites than the whites themselves. The activity is, of course, racist, based on linguistic naiveté, and generally reprehensible; but it is something that has been present, probably for a long time, in Southern white verbal activity—and it represents imitation, even if poor imitation, of Negro speech patterns by whites.

Such considerations bring up the unfortunate but unavoidable subject of caricature, a subject which many a liberal white and many a middle-class Black would like to have banned. Caricature of the Negro's mannerisms, in speech and otherwise, has long pervaded white society in the South; it takes no explanation that the speaker is a Negro when a joke has someone passing through a graveyard ask, "Who dat say who dat say who dat?" The linguistic forms, like the names and attitudes, are all stereotyped; but a caricature is a distortion of something that exists somewhere. The zero copula and the kind of relative structure represented are both features of Negro Non-Standard (see Chapter II). Needless to say, it is irrelevant that no one ever heard a Negro utter that particular sentence. Some of the stereotyped names for Negroes had a basis in African naming practices (see material on *Sambo*, section on "West African Naming Practices

Outside Gullah Territory," Chapter III). Ridicule and unauthorized caricature are, of course, potentially harmful things; but what makes caricature damaging is that its distortions are based upon real features. Even the Southern white's parodying of Negro dialect shows pretty clearly that the Negro dialect is always with him, that it is the single most important fact of his linguistic environment.

But, in spite of mutual influences, Southern white and Southern Black dialects are far from identical.[13] No large groups of whites anywhere now speaks according to the grammar described in Chapter II. The cultural patterns of the great mass of Southern Negroes, including the constraints on the use of language, remained different. When, for example, Southern Negroes during Reconstruction found themselves unexpectedly and unprecedentedly in public offices, they predictably lacked some of the language habits which go with such office. They seem to have responded by using their Fancy Talk tradition (see the relevant section of Chapter II), a logical enough step, but one calculated to draw maximal misunderstanding from whites. One reason is, of course, that Fancy Talk is not basically a pattern of the childhood use of language where Black and Southern white had shared linguistic systems. A somewhat racist chronicler of Reconstruction like Claude G. Bowers[14] could predictably—if inaccurately—comment "Even their vocabulary has expanded in the light of freedom" (p. 50) and report, probably with complete accuracy, of an ex-slave

> " 'Perusin' my way to Columbia' he replied," for peruse had a royal sound.   (*Ibid.*)

Whether in bidialectism, in misunderstanding or in caricature, the Negro dialect has long been with the whites of the South in their everyday life. They may have reacted to it either like Fanny Kemble or like Caroline Gilman. Even an enormously sympathetic evangelist like Charles Colcock Jones can adomish his preachers that their language in preaching be "not accommodated at all to their *broken* English."[15] Jones, whose writing of "Negroes

who are grown persons when they come over" seems to attest
to the widespread speaking of Negro Pidgin English at the time
(1842), undoubtedly missed a grand opportunity for some really
progressive evangelism; but his desire to have the preacher retain
his linguistic "dignity" at the cost of communication is not necessarily evidence of bigotry. People who ought to know better
often develop silly prejudices against important languages: an
African professor at the Université Officielle de Bujumbura went
to great lengths to keep his children from learning Swahili, the
most important language in the city, even if it does not enjoy
the sentimental protection which is accorded Kirundi. He failed.
Fortunately, it seems that Jones did too: his son was Charles
Colcock Jones, Jr., the apparently bidialectal Southern author of
Negro Myths of the Georgia Coast. Jones's documentation of
Southern white familiarity with Negro speech patterns is valuable
enough to cause us to excuse his failure in the areas of communication, education, and evangelism.

If contact with the Negro dialect is, then, the prime fact about
Southern white dialect, what indication is there that the oldest
belief of all about Southern dialect is after all the right one? What
chance is there that the ever-present Negro had more influence
on the speech of the Southern white than the far-away East
Anglian—or the occasional Scotsman or Irishman? In my opinion,
the chances are that the tradition had it more or less right.

Such intuitions as have been expressed about Negro influence
on Southern speech have centered upon the more informal styles,
and the intuitions may be correct. On the other hand, one can see
quite readily why Negroes like Conrad and Juanita Williamson
might object to the implication that formal language is somehow
above Negro influence, since there is no doubt a possibility for
ridicule based upon that opinion. It should, however, be understood that any such conclusion as that Negro-white speech interaction took place on the comparatively casual stylistic level does
not preclude the development of formal styles within the Negro
speech community. Today, in the big city ghettos, we see evidences of formal styles of Negro Non-Standard in the speech of

the storefront preachers and others; in most of these cases, it is true, the formal style is used where whites are essentially excluded. The Negro does have his own formal style patterns; such patterns probably existed even in Plantation Creole, although of course they were not widely recognized.

Recognizing that any speech community develops its formal stylistic devices is not incompatible with the observation that the white speech community may have interacted with the Negro Non-Standard-speaking community primarily through the use of its relatively informal speech styles, and that the influence of the Negro may be primarily on those speaking styles. The formal speaking styles, although they occur even in non-literary societies, are in most of American culture tied up with the schools; Olmsted's report that the white and black children played together but did not go to school together is rather significant in this respect. Something like an effect on informal speech styles is apparently what Conrad is claiming when he writes, rather defensively, of the contributions of "the contractions," "the blurrings," and "the melodic ripplings which Negro voice contributes to language" (p. 150). More formal linguists than Dr. Conrad, who would be more hesitant to use words like "blurrings," have suggested that Negroes may have carried over from African languages certain affective tonal devices. Yet the professional linguists cannot claim any progress beyond Conrad in serious investigation of possible influence.

It has long been recognized that certain forms of Southern white speech have been influenced by the Negro. As long as it was assumed that the only significant variety of Black English in the United States was Gullah, considered to be confined to the Sea Islands, such influence could be considered to be confined to a small area close to the Charleston-Sea Island area. With the new perspective, which shows no geographic limitations on Plantation Creole, we can see that it is not strange that all of the Southern white dialects should have been so influenced. In fact, it is what one would normally expect.

Serious investigation of specific areas of Negro dialect influence has so far been almost entirely prevented by the pundits of dialect geography, who have jumped with both feet on the most modest attempts at investigation. When Elizabeth Udell attempted to trace the "grunt of negation" to African sources (*American Speech*, 1964), McDavid pontificated that Africanisms in American English must "show concentrations in the Charleston area and (to a lesser extent) in eastern Virginia, with less frequent occurrences in other regions" (*American Speech*, February, 1955); in other words, McDavid asserted that Africanisms migrate only a short distance from Gullah territory.

No such restrictions can be accurately placed. As Mason has shown, the undoubtedly African *buckra* occurred as far away from the Sea Islands as Oregon.[16] The equally certain Africanism *goober* occurs in many Southern white communities other than those in which "the community contains a large Negro group."[17] To require that such a word be spoken only in a predominantly Negro area in order to be considered an Africanism, and that some other etymology be found for it if it is spoken where the majority of the inhabitants are white, is to indulge in the very worst kind of circularity. Linguistically, it is the Hindu rope trick with a difference—after you get to the top, they give you permission to acquire a rope. Without committing oneself one way or another on Miss Udell's theory about the "grunt of negation," one can see that unreasonable conditions have been placed upon her and upon other investigators who have wanted seriously to evaluate the African (or Negro) contribution to American English.

The Southernism *tote* 'carry' is of almost certain African origin. The English-based Krio of Sierra Leone uses *tot* in an identical meaning. Canadian Creolist Ian F. Hancock[18] offers evidence that the similarity is traceable to the origin of Gullah Africanisms in the Sierra Leone area. M. M. Mathews, in the *Dictionary of Americanisms*, lists the form, from the *Virginia Magazine*, as early as 1677, which would mean, in the terms of this book, a quite early borrowing from Plantation Creole. He further specifies that "The earliest available evidence for this word is Southern, but, as the quotations below show, it has spread widely in colloquial use" (p. 1751). There is no reason whatsoever to insist that the word, or any other word, once into the everyday English of white Southerners, could not also spread to white Northerners. Along with other citations, Mencken (Supplement I, 1960) quotes Dunglison as early as 1829, who said the word was then "common in Massachusetts" as well as in the Southern states. The *Dictionary of Americanisms* shows it in New England by 1769—a quite believable spread in 92 years, by any except the artificial conditions imposed upon vocabulary items which happen to be brought in by the slaves. Elsewhere, I have argued that the Northern use of the same word in compounds like *tote road* and *tote sled* need not be referred to another origin simply because the majority of the residents in the areas where it is used were not Negro.

The use of *carry* to mean 'conduct someone' (as in "Carry Me Back to Ole Virginny") is grimly asserted in the works of the Establishment to be "archaic" British, even though the same meaning occurs in Jamaica (Cassidy, *Jamaica Talk*, p. 398) and even though it might be thought something of a coincidence that the "archaic" use was preserved only in areas subject to creole influence. At any rate, the distribution of *carry* in this sense in a complementary relation to *tote* ("I'll carry you, but I ain't gonna tote you!") depends upon the existence of the Africanism in the Southern vocabulary. Again, distributions of this kind are considered by the linguist to be more basic than the bits and pieces which are themselves arranged in the patterns.

The familiar Southern use of *evening* to refer to any time of day after 12 noon is just as aggressively traced to British regional dialects. It is, however, commonplace in Afro-American English, and even in West African French (substituting *soir* for *evening*, of course).

Despite many disavowals, the Southern use of *done* (both Negro and white dialect) as a recent perfective no doubt traces to the pidgin creole source. It is a natural kind of relexification of Pidgin Portuguese *cabá*, which remains in Sranan Tongo although that language is usually considered to be an English-based creole. In the Pacific, *finish* (with some slightly differing word order rules in which the word is postposed to the verb) and Hawaiian *pau* serve the same relexification purpose. Postposed *done* in something like the same function occurs in Jamaican, although Cassidy (*ibid.*, p. 65, and in the *Dictionary of Jamaican English*) is at great pains to trace it to

> *Verb (and be) done*

in spite of the fact that the allegedly underlying words never occur in such a phrase. Cassidy may be subject here, as elsewhere, to pressure to keep alive the Establishment explanation in terms of British origin and archaism. A preverbal *done* can be found as far back as Dunbar,[19] but in a causative meaning which the creole/pidgin and the Southern dialect usage does not have. The recent perfective function which the American and African varieties have is not at all like the older British usage, and makes sense only in the pidgin/creole tradition. Southern dialect (my own variety, at least) has only

> I done gone
> I done went

whereas Negro Non-Standard basilect has both these and

> I done go.

White Southern dialect also has

> I've done gone
> I've done went

which, when they occur in Negro dialect, should probably be considered as borrowings from other varieties of English.

Mathews, who says that *done* in this sense is "used colloquially or ignorantly" in such meanings as "already" (*Dictionary of Americanisms*, p. 505), lists it first from Adiel Sherwood's *Gazeteer of the State of Georgia* (1827). Actually, it is easy to find earlier attestations. A. B. Lindsley's *Love and Friendship* (1809) presents the Charleston slave Phillis saying

> Missy, Mr. Seldreer done come, he dere at de door, I shall—

a usage which represents clearly its recent perfective force. Still earlier examples can probably be found (unless, of course, the intention is to exclude Gullah or Negro Non-Standard usage from "Americanisms"). The only historical problem would be to determine when *done* replaced *kaba*. It is rather unlikely that the *done Verb* structure, in this meaning, goes back to the earliest slaves who brought African Pidgin English to the United States.

Many more examples could be cited, and it would be most instructive to make a really thorough examination of the claims of Negro influence which Payne made in 1903—whether, for example, white speakers really used *I'm am*. It is obviously not adequate to dismiss those claims after applying irrelevant tests to a few and neglecting to examine the majority of them in any way, as did Brooks in 1935.

Let us consider, as a final touch, one of the most interesting of all: *Dixie*, the name of the Confederacy and the title of the song most closely identified with it. Although there has been a pathetic struggle to find some other etymology, it is pretty clear that the word does come from a Plantation Creole pronunciation of the second surname in the *Mason-Dixie Line*, which was laid out in 1763–7, well within the Plantation Creole and even the Negro Pidgin period. Mathews, who records *Dixie* first from 1859, records *Mason and Dixie's Line* almost as early—1861. (He does not record it along with the evidence for the etymology of *Dixie*, but if one looks under the other subheadings in Establishment reference works one can find out a great deal that wasn't meant to be pointed out.) Besides being a natural development from *Dixon* according to the phonological structure of pidgin/creole (which utilizes a consonant-vowel canonic syllable pattern), *Dixie* is found as a pronunciation of the surname among the Negro Seminole Scouts—with the spelling *Dixey*.[20]

The Confederate national anthem? It was composed by Daniel Decatur Emmett, in 1859, as a "walk-around" for a minstrel show. Everyone who knows the words knows that they contain at least the minstrel show imitation of Negro dialect. This has not always been pleasing to professional Southerners. On August 26, 1904, the Daughters of the Confederacy met in Opelika, Alabama, as a Joint Committee Appointed to Consider and Report on a Selection of New Words for "Dixie."[21] It seems rather fitting that the music which is more or less the theme song of Southern rejection of the Negro should be set to words and given a title which demonstrate clearly the overwhelming influence of the Negro on Southern whites.

NOTES

[1] Jaap (the name is also spelled *Yop* in the novels of Cooper) says

I'm York nigger born, and nebber see no Africa . . . (*Satansoe*, p. 149)

Cooper's language practices have been somewhat hesitantly defended by Louise Pound ("Cooper's Notes on Language," *American Speech* IV, No. 3 [February, 1929] pp. 294–300) and by Tremaine McDowell ("Negro Dialect in the American Novel to 1821," *American Speech* V, No. 4 [April, 1930] pp. 291–296), who tells us

Black slaves had waited on Jamie Cooper in his boyhood and youth; their purchase and sale had directly concerned Squire Cooper in his maturity.
(p. 293)

But the strongest argument in favor of Cooper's recording of dialect is that his practices accord with the most convincing historical interpretations made on other grounds. (See the defense of his recording of "Indian dialect"— American Indian Pidgin English—in Chapter IV.)

Although there have been many authoritative pronouncements in the last few years that Black English came to the Northern cities only after World War II, it is noteworthy that there were slaves in New York (then New Amsterdam) by about 1626 (see Ottley and Weatherby, *The Negro in New York*). Amusing indications of a kind of academic compulsion to find a Southern origin for Black English are found in such works as Grier and Cobbs, *Black Rage*. They write of a Black psychiatric patient that he "had been born in a large Northern city" but that "His speech was the patois of the rural uneducated Negro of seventy-five years ago." Even if such statements were geographically accurate, they could hardly be other than nonsense historically.

[2] *Dialect Notes* III (1903), pp. 279–328, 343–391.

[3] Negro English, *Anglia* VIII (1884), pp. 233–279.

[4] *The English Language in America*, I, p. 250.

[5] American Speech III, No. 4 (April 1928), pp. 377–383.

[6] Bertram Wilbur Doyle, *The Etiquette of Race Relations in the South* (1937, 1968) cites, in Chapter VI, footnote 27, several historical accounts of the scorn of house servants and freedmen for field hands. Many of the other points made in this book are thoroughly documented in the Doyle study.

[7] Chesnutt's novels, although not militant enough to please LeRoi Jones (see "The Myth of a Negro Literature," Bibliography), are invaluable in showing perception of dialect differences by a Black writer. (There are, of course, many others, of whom James Weldon Johnson is probably the most celebrated.) In Chesnutt's *The Marrow of Tradition* there is a Dr. Miller, a Negro educated in the North, who has returned to the South because his dedication to his own people calls him to do so. Dr. Miller speaks elegant Standard English. Chesnutt has a subtle touch in his depiction of race conflict in the town in that he shows white speakers of a non-standard dialect which would place them much lower on the social scale than Dr. Miller, if it were not for the overriding power of the race-caste system. A key scene of this novel depends upon the dialect difference. In the dark, specifically because of his speech, Dr. Miller is taken for a white man, by armed whites who are out to crush the rebelling Negroes. In spite of his failure to impress modern militants, Chesnutt was no Uncle Tom. *The Marrow of Tradition* is a protest novel, and a good one, written many years before protest novels by Black novelists became fashionable. Chesnutt's *The Conjure Woman* deals very effectively with the folklore of rural Blacks who are closer to Africa in their behavorial patterns than those who are featured in most modern Black literature. One of the better things that can be said about Chesnutt is that he was aware of variation—including language variation—in the behavorial patterns of both Blacks and whites.

[8] It has been reported (see Hughes and Meltzner, Bibliography) that Sojourner Truth "spoke [English] with a Dutch accent," having worked for Dutch masters. Fauset's biography (see Bibliography) says that she learned English at the age of twenty, when she also changed her name from Isabella. At any rate, there is little suggestion of Dutch influence in recorded utterances like

I ain't goin' to die honey—I's goin' home like a shootin' star.

(Hughes and Meltzner, p. 339)

Dey talks 'bout dis ting in de head—what dis dey call it? . . . now dey is askin' to do, de man better let 'em.

(Bancroft, *Slave Trading in the Old South*, p. 169)

(These sources, like most writings on Sojourner Truth, seem to have drawn heavily upon Harriet Beecher Stowe's *Atlantic Monthly* interview. See Bibliography.)

The use of Dutch Creole in New York (as in the Virgin Islands) seems probable, although there are no studies of the matter. The nature of this Creole, however, is highly problematic. As a matter of fact, it seems highly likely that the Dutch (and Danish) creoles were based on Pidgin English, with a great deal of added Dutch (and Danish) vocabulary. The confusion between Dutch Creole and English Creole has persisted, particularly in the case of Sranan Tongo, and there have been amusing cases (cited by Schuchardt, *Die Sprache der Saramakka neger in Surinam*, Bibliography) where laymen have taken the English creoles for dialects of Dutch. At one time the situation in New York State may have been analogous to that of Louisiana today, where French Creole interference complicates and reinforces the Black English patterns and actually impedes the decreolization process.

[9] *Works*, ed. Garland Greevey, p. xxviii.

[10] Letter to *Scribner's Monthly*, Nov. 23, 1879 (*Works*, X, p. 156).

[11] *Journal of Negro Education*, 1944. It seems that Conrad was motivated by a perfectly accurate feeling that Negro dialect must have a history and a legitimate structure just like any other dialect or language.

[12] Mrs. Cohen's husband was Octavus Roy Cohen, an even more famous (or notorious) writer of Negro dialect. Conrad (see footnote 11) and Nelson, *The Negro Character in American Literature*, attacked Cohen and accused him of writing at the minstrel show level. This is not an entirely justified accusation, as Kaplan ("A Master of the Negro Dialect," *The Jewish Tribune*, 1927) pointed out. Some of Cohen's dialect is very good, and his observations of Negro behavioral patterns were far from inaccurate. (For example, he had a great deal of accurate information about the lore of the numbers game.) Even in portraying his stock character, Florian Slappey, as a sharp-dressing, fast-talking wheeler-dealer, Cohen was not inventing a type which cannot be found—insofar as the surface features of the personality are concerned—in almost any large Black community. (See the works of Robert Beck, "Iceberg Slim," Bibliography.) The trouble was that Cohen failed completely to depict the serious side of Negro life—indeed, he left the impression that there was no such serious side. For his *Saturday Evening Post* readers, the eternal plot of Florian attempting to hoodwink an amorous but unattractive rich lady in order to have enough money to marry a beautiful young girl—he never married, any more than the Lone Ranger—was adequate. Deeper probing would have seemed out of order. It is easy to understand the impatience of the Black community with the exclusive concentration on such themes by white authors who wrote fiction about Black characters. Yet Cohen was, in his way, a student of Black culture.

[13] Eager to avoid the Charybdis of physiological explanation of Negro dialect differences, certain "scientific" dialectologists have offered themselves—apparently without even looking for another way out—to the Scylla of assertion that there is no difference at all. This has involved them in a large number of absurdities, although not so many as those generated by

the "thick lips" theory. For those who asserted that Negro dialect was the same as Southern white dialect, the use of [d] and [t] for spelled *th*-initially (*them, think*) in the speech of uneducated Southern (and Northern) Negroes posed great problems. While the individual "substitutions" may be paralleled in "regional" white dialects, the total distribution cannot, especially since the *th* is frequently [v] and [f] in Black English when occurring in medial position (*mother, nothing*) or in final position (*breathe, both*). Further, even in the case of [d] and [t] for initial *th*-, Negroes frequently have those pronunciations in regions where the whites do not. It is note-worthy that most Southern (and Northern) Negroes pronounce *aunt* or *aunty* with the [a] of the "New England" or "Bostonian" pronunciation, whereas Southern whites of the same area use [æ]—the vowel of *ant*. Thus, the geographic approach has come dangerously close to the absurdity of calling Black English "Northern-Southern" or "Southern-Northern" dialect.

This unwarranted geographic wandering infects even the work of the outstanding sociolinguist William Labov in his recent *Study of the Non-Standard English of Negro and Puerto Rican Speakers in New York City* (see Bibliography). Thus Labov cites the dialect of Charleston, S. C. (pp. 220, 349), "Southern Mountain" dialect (p. 304), and even Mississippi dialect for his comparison of New York City Negro dialect to "Southern casual styles." It is never explained how all these "regional" dialects might have combined into Harlem dialect. Nor is it explained why "Southern casual" styles are so important for structures which are also used in formal styles in Black English. The explanation given, less formally, by Conrad (see Bibliography) as to the influence of Negro dialect on the home language (and therefore casual styles) of Southern whites would seem to fill the gap left by Labov in this area.

When confronted with their own inconsistencies, dialect geographers have often wandered even further, pointing out that some of these same "sub-stitutions" are found in British English. This is true, but irrelevant. In the case of [f] and [v] for *th*, Cockney (!) pronunciations have been cited—although it would seem impossible to conceive of a less relevant dialect. Anyway, Cockney has some of the [f] and [v] substitutions for *th* in initial position—which Black English in the United States does not have. This kind of guessing on the part of dialect geographers seems to be motivated by the tenet that dialects in a former colony *must* derive in some direct fashion from dialects in the mother country, that dialects of specific regions survive migration. This preconception does not seem to be borne out historically (see articles by Bernard and by Leopold, in Bibliography).

The very complexity of the geographic explanation seems to defeat its purpose. The distribution of Black English is social; the internal contradic-tions of the geographic approach point up that fact almost as well as does the primary data from Black English itself. Perhaps the most interesting factor in all this is the clear indication of how emotional—rather than intellectual—considerations move American dialectologists to support "regional" explanations for dialect variation. The Caribbeanist William A. Stewart, not subject to the emotional constraints of the dialect geographers, has stated flatly, "I know of no community in even the deepest South in which the nonstandard speech of monodialectal Negroes is identical to that of monodialectal whites" (in Baratz and Shuy, *Teaching Black Children to Read*, footnote 24; see also Stewart in all three sections of Bibliography).

Although Stewart, Loflin, and others have taken syntactic as well as phonological factors into account in formulating their conclusions, even those linguists who have limited their investigations to phonology (pronunciation) have begun to perceive patterns of Black-white difference. A representative statement from this group of linguists would be

> It is of course inaccurate to state that Black English is equivalent to general southern English.
>
> > (Susan Houston, "A Sociolinguistic Consideration of the Black English of Children in Northern Florida," see Bibliography)

Without regard to whether differences perceived are phonological or not, an experiment by Tucker and Lambert (see Bibliography) and others by Baratz (see article in *Child Development*, Bibliography) and by Baratz, Shuy and Wolfram (see Bibliography) show that respondents are able to identify speakers as Negro or white about eighty percent of the time from auditory cues (listening to tape-recorded speech) only.

[14] *The Tragic Era* (1929).

[15] Charles Colcock Jones, *The Religious Instruction of the Negroes* (1832). An even more revealing comment by Jones is his "From childhood we have been accustomed . . . to their broken English . . . " (p. 103).

[16] Julian Mason, "The Etymology of 'Buckaroo'," *American Speech*, Vol. XXXV (1960), pp. 51-55. Mason recapitulates some evidence of the Negro cowboy's presence in the Northwest (see Graham, in Bibliography) and shows some awareness that Plantation Creole (not the term he uses) was used outside the Sea Islands ("there is evidence that Negroes in other areas used the word too"). See also Beryl Loftman, "A Note on 'Buckra'," *American Speech* XXVII (1952), p. 143.

[17] The dialect geographer Raven I. McDavid, Jr., with Virginia Glenn McDavid, attempted (in "Relationship of the Speech of American Negroes to the Speech of Whites," *American Speech* XXVI [February 1951], pp. 3–16) to limit African influence to such areas. McDavid and McDavid establish Black English influence on Southern white speech, but conclude (erroneously, in my opinion) that such influence is limited to a few geographic areas covering a very small portion of the South. See footnote 21 below.

[18] "A Provisional Comparison of the English-Based Atlantic Creoles," in *Pidginization and Creolization of Languages*, ed. Hymes (see Bibliography).

Hancock suggests that certain American English words like *tic tac toe* (the children's game which is known as "noughts and crosses" in England) may be related to African forms (Sierra Leone Krio *titato*). David Dalby, "Americanisms That May Once Have Been Africanisms" (see Bibliography) suggests much more far-reaching African language influence (in many cases, specifically Wolof influence) in the American English vocabulary.

[19] In the works of Dunbar and of other Scottish writers of the sixteenth century, there are frequent occurrences of *have/has done Verb* (with the verb usually, but not always, in the past participle form). Some of these are cited by Curme, *Syntax* (6Ad[1], p. 23), who then cites occurrences of "the same" structure in Southern American English—his earliest examples actually coming from the Uncle Remus stories. Grammatically, however, not one of the Scottish forms is unambiguously a recent perfective; in fact, all appear to be more nearly causatives. Some forms are listed below; all but the first were cited by Curme:

The lork has done the mirry day proclame
(Dunbar, "The Thrissil and the Rois," 1, 24)

How that my yowth I done forloir
(Dunbar, cited by Curme as from "XXII, 2")

As I afore have done discus
(Lauder, *Tractate*, 340)

Thay are Wolfis and Toddis, quha [who] have villently done brokin in the dyr of the sheipfald　　　　　　　　　　　(Beme, *Disput*, 78, V)

It is noteworthy that, of all these citations, only the second lacks auxiliary *have*; modern editors often add it, in brackets. The third example from Lauder, is marked by the time adverbial *afore* as not a recent perfective.

There is the further historical objection to assuming that the Scottish forms are somehow the source of the Black English forms ("Southernisms") in the three-century gap between Curme's sixteenth-century citations and his nineteenth-century citations. No one has, to my knowledge, provided any attestations from the intervening centuries.

There is a marginal possibility that the Scottish forms somehow contributed to Maritime Pidgin English (see Chapter IV), or that language contact forms related to the English Pidgin were utilized by Englishmen in the originally foreign-language situation in Scotland. These conjectures are remote from the present subject matter, and will not be considered further here.

A few writers on American English (including Mathews, *Beginnings of American English*, 1931, 1963) have asserted that these forms come from Ireland (Mathews: "probably obtained from Ireland," p. 105). Since no evidence whatever is offered in support of this conjecture—not even proof that *done Verb* forms do exist in Irish English—it seems obviously just another manifestation of the tendency to derive American English forms from the British Isles at all costs.

[20] Kenneth Wiggins Porter, "The Seminole Negro-Indian Scouts," *The Quarterly of the Texas State Historical Association*, January 1952, p. 360. The phonological process is the same one which produced "cunney [colonel] Tomsee [Thompson]" in John Leacock's *The Fall of British Tyranny* (see Chapter III). Ian F. Hancock reports (personal communication) that a similar phonological development is common in Krio of Sierra Leone.

[21] Hans Nathan, *Dan Emmett and the Rise of Negro Minstrelsy* (University of Oklahoma Press, 1962), p. 274, fn. 58. Nathan's study contains valuable texts of "Dixie" (which is clearly in a minstrel show version of Negro dialect). Chapter I, "Negro Impersonations and Songs in Late Eighteenth Century England," shows that more or less accurate knowledge of the nature of Plantation Creole (or "the negroe language," in the terminology of Francis Grose's *Classical Dictionary of the Vulgar Tongue*, 1785) extended to England in that century and that playwrights knew that American Blacks and West Indian Blacks spoke more or less alike.

VI

Who Speaks Black English?

IF Black English is not identical to Southern white dialects—although it has influenced the latter over a period of two centuries or more—there remains the problem of who speaks it. The best evidence we have at the present time—and it is admittedly incomplete—indicates that approximately eighty percent of the Black population of the United States speaks Black English.[1] (*Black population*, in this case, would mean all those who consider themselves to be members of the "Black" or "Negro" community.)[2] There are others who speak the same dialect; for example, many members of the Puerto Rican community in New York City have learned Black English in addition to Puerto Rican Spanish.[3] In the past, there were—as has been indicated above—many white speakers of the Black variety of English, especially among the Southern plantation-owning class.[4] At an earlier period, the pidgin stage of Black English spread to the Seminoles and to other Indian tribes.[5] But, in the twentieth century, this particular dialect has come to be identified almost exclusively with the Black community. The historical affiliations with other Afro-American varieties, such as the creole languages of the West

Indies, are clear to the language historian; but American Blacks are quick to perceive pronunciation differences on the part of West Indians who migrate to cities like New York and are somewhat slow to accept them into the in-group.

The greatest risk in dealing with ethnic behavior patterns—including speech patterns—is that someone will conclude that those patterns are genetic in nature. To write of Black English, or Negro Non-Standard English, or of Negro dialect is to risk having someone conclude that the dialect differences are caused by physical traits—the infamous "thick lips" theory. It also invites, from a professional point of view, irrelevant "disproof." A demonstration on the order of "X is a Negro, and he speaks just like any other college professor" is to easy to perform. This is why it should be emphasized that social factors are more important than racial—or geographic—factors in determining dialect patterns.

This social distribution of Black English vis-à-vis Standard English is no new development. Considerable pains have been taken to point out that there were Black speakers of West African Pidgin English, Plantation Creole, and Standard English at fairly early times in the history of the American colonies.[6] Even today, there are Black speakers of Creole (Gullah), Negro Non-Standard, and Standard English. Further, there are now—and were in the past—Black bidialectal speakers of more than one of those varieties. And there have always been at least a few whites who spoke each of these dialects. Yet the preponderance of speakers of all except Standard English (and, of course, of the non-standard dialects not under discussion here) have always been Black.

One of the harsher sociolinguistic facts which must be dealt with is that the history of the Afro-American languages and dialects correlates with the existence of a caste system. It is as clearly demarcated in the United States as in India.[7] John Dollard has sociologically shown the existence of the caste system, although the great Black sociologist E. Franklin Frazier was (perhaps emotionally) unwilling to recognize it. George Washington Cable expressed the sociolinguistic situation for Louisiana French

Creole in the days of slavery in one of those fantastic blazes of perception which that inconsistent observer often had:

> It chimed well with the fierce notions of caste to have one language for the master and another for the slave . . .[8]

It hardly matters that the remainder of the sentence expresses a completely untenable theory of the origin of French Creole.

The sociolinguistic situation in the English-speaking areas was closely comparable to that of French-speaking Louisiana. In New Orleans, the mulatto-quadroon-octaroon group was aloof from and even scornful of the "Negroes" until the Jim Crow laws lumped them all together. The elite *gens de couleur* group also tended to use Louisiana Standard French rather than "Gombo" French Creole. In other states, the freedman and the house slave complicated the picture of a color-based caste system; but they varied between Black English and Standard English in much the same way that their social status varied. In 1870, Elizabeth Kilham quoted a "highly educated colored woman" who disliked to go to Negro churches because she was "disgusted" with "bad grammar and worse pronunciation." Appropriately, the "uneducated" adherents to the Africanized Protestant services rejected her, too, putting her "away off in a dark corner, out of reach of everybody." Miss Kilham was a considerably less skilled observer than Cable, but the realities of the social situation appear through her naive reporting, which regards the type of religious service still found in the storefront churches of even Northern cities as a complete breakdown of religion.

The passage of a century has effected some change, with the overall pattern being assimilation of Black language and culture to white patterns. But the process is far from complete, and it has not been unidirectional. Although it would be ethnocentric to regard those groups which are least like the whites as cultural failures—or those who are most perfectly assimilated as successes—it is true that the economically disadvantaged Blacks of today are primarily members of the unassimilated group. (The explanation of their financial limitations is not difficult to find: the field hands who were their ancestors faced Emancipation, in a capitalist society, without even the forty acres and a mule which some overoptimistic whites had promised them.) It is the members of this undervalued culture who are the basic population for a study of Black English.

Two populations formed the groups studied for most of the conclusions drawn within this study, although examples have been taken from most parts of the United States. (Essentially the same grammatical forms have been found in all the geographic areas studied.) The first was a block-long community in an area inhabited almost exclusively by Blacks, where a white person must either be a social worker or someone up to no good. There were sixty households on this block, which was also the locale of a small grocery store and of a storefront church. Children under fourteen accounted for more than half of the population of two hundred. About half of the households fell below the S. S. A. poverty line of $3,300 annual income for the time of the study (1966–67); furthermore, chronic unemployment for male heads of household (when they were present) was so great a problem that even the mothers of pre-school children were often employed as part-time domestic workers. In New York City, it appears that children in foster homes are most often speakers of the basilect form of Black English.

Yet the children on the block which was studied were not altogether objects of misery—certainly not by the standards of Africa, of South America, or of rural Mississippi. On the block, the sidewalk teemed with children and each had to defend his (often small) amount of space, physically at times; but there was abundant companionship. There was a playground nearby, a shopping and entertainment complex (small bars, movies, stores around the corner), and many of the children were capable of traveling a few miles, on their own, to the city park and zoo. (They die in great numbers in tenement fires and suffer great physical damage from lead poisoning when they eat the paint from the walls of antiquated apartments, but they can take care of themselves remarkably well in the face of dangers which they can confront more fairly, like the traffic of Times Square.) A white visitor to the area can remember spontaneous greetings from friendly children under six; it was the older ones who had grown suspicious and resentful—guarded in their reactions even after long acquaintance. It was a low-rent area, and piles of garbage collected behind the houses. But there was one minor advantage to the children: they were approximate equals, and economic· snobbery seemed a very minor part of their troubles. Being stigmatized as a "Bama" (recent migrant from the South) was worse than not being able to keep up appearances with a new bicycle.

The other population, studied primarily through two nearly bidialectal boys but also through recordings of nearly a dozen youngsters, was very different. Spot-zoning exceptions had turned a formerly one-family residential street, once lined with American elms and white oaks, into an area of decidedly mixed social and economic nature in which areas of the ground were completely bare. No family on the block had a total income of under $5,000; at least one had $25,000. There were no welfare cases and, therefore, no social workers; but whites as well as Blacks came and went regularly. There was one interracial marriage, in the higher income and education group. Four residents had doctoral degrees; some of the other adults had not finished high school. From the point of view of the twenty-five children on the block, the $5,000–$25,000 spread in family income resulted in a keen awareness of the prestige value of more expensive toys, bicycles, and athletic equipment.

The two who served as informants—ten- and twelve-year-old boys—were able to attend major league baseball games on a fairly regular basis and to go to non-charity summer camps. These two, it turned out, were keenly aware of language differences. There was a way of talking that they used with their friends and a way they spoke around their parents (Black English and Standard English, approximately), and they had kept them apart without devoting any special effort to doing so. When their attention was directed to the differences, the twelve-year-old, especially, was able to project himself into alternate roles and to identify the language forms used in each. Neither, however, was perfectly aware of the exact point of separation. Unfortunately, the interview situation (working as linguistic informants) seemed to confuse them as to the relationship between the two varieties.

In this second area, there was a continuum from reasonably "deep" Black English to Standard English; a fourteen-year-old girl of a family with a $15,000 income had virtually no Non-Standard forms in the sample of her conversation which was recorded for analysis. A ten-year-old boy from a $5,000 income family, on the other hand, had a Non-Standard speech almost like that of the first, all-Negro block. In all cases, however, there was a difference; the continuum on the mixed block went further into Standard English and not quite so far into Black English as the other.

Age-grading,[9] a major sociolinguistic discovery for the Black English community made by Stewart, was a feature of both populations—as was language variation in terms of sex and of economic and educational status of the parents.[10] Each population of children had its stereotypes of language behavior, and each was able to assign an age range to certain grammatical forms with relative consistency.

Age-grading was probably the most important sociolinguistic factor in the dialect of the children from the poorer block. Differentiation by sex takes place only after the children become relatively older—say eight years old or a little more. Both boys and girls in the five-to-six range have purposive futures like *Im put* (*the doll-baby there*). As they grow on toward seven and older, they acquire *Ima put* . . . and then *Imõ put* . . . when a year or two older. This form may remain for the entire lifetime of a low-status individual, or it may be in the most casual style of even a social climber. Most of the children are saying *Imonna* . . . and even *I'm gonna* . . . by the time they are fourteen or so. At some stage in the age-grading process, they actually do begin using what are contractions of *going to*; the *a* of *Ima* is much more likely to be a historical survival related to a continuative

NUMBER OF 1A DEVIATIONS PER 1,000 WORDS OF SPOKEN VOLUME
High Caucasian, Low Caucasian, Negro, and Random Groups
Grades Kindergarten through Nine

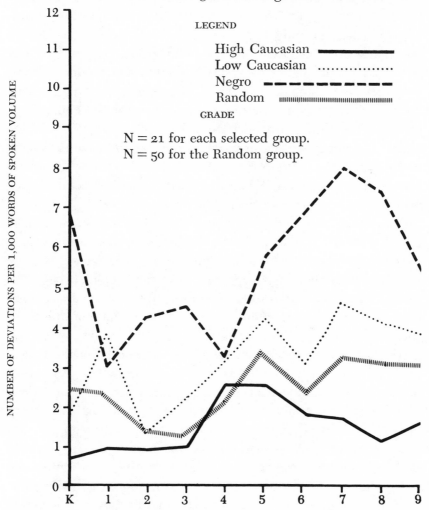

A graph which illustrates age-grading, from Loban *Problems in Oral English*, NCTE, 1966. Reprinted with the permission of the National Council of Teachers of English and Walter Loban. Since more than one grammatical factor may be responsible for the "lack of agreement" involved, this graph may actually exaggerate the age-grading feature to some extent.

particle *a* (a variant of *de* and *da*) which turns up in many of the English creoles.

This comparatively archaic character of the speech of the younger children—always those who are beyond the stage of language acquisition, of "learning to talk"—is sociolinguistically perhaps the most exciting factor in Black English. It is no mystic process, at any rate; the older the child grows, the more he has to adjust his language to something like mainstream culture. Linguists have long known that the popular metaphor about "mother tongue" is almost meaningless; beyond the earliest beginnings, the child learns most from his peer group. As a matter of fact, current studies of language acquistion minimize the factor of imitating the parents in the case of any young language learner. Parents may not like it, but they really have little influence on the behavior of their children.

Children in every culture learn a fascinating amount from their peers, often things which the parents either never knew or have completely forgotten. Consider such children's games as hopscotch, which their aging parents probably couldn't begin to teach them. Opie and Opie, in *The Language and Lore of School Children,* show how this holds true for British children; the West Indian folklore studies of Elsie Clews Parsons document the persistence of Africanisms in the games of children in the Caribbean. It is probably true of child culture everywhere. Age-grading is also probably a near-universal in language. Hattori found division of the Ainu into an under-thirty and an over-thirty group.[11] Everyone knows that American teen-agers go through a phase of using slang; parents and teachers often worry about it, but linguists know perfectly well that they will "grow"—or age-grade—out of it. The affirmative use of *any more* (*We go to that place any more*) is characteristic of the speech of younger Americans, and is not limited to any specific region. In Standard English, vocabulary seems to be the main factor which is affected by age-grading.

The ghetto community proves to be a notably age-graded community, even in terms of the relatively superficial factor of gang structures. The middle-class white who reads Warren Miller's *The Cool World* is astounded by the things attributed to boys in the fourteen-year-old range; the twenty-year-old former leader is, you may remember, a has-been. But the picture seems to be an accurate one: a vast amount is expected of the ghetto young-ster, and he performs just about what his social system expects of him. Among other things, a high degree of responsibility is delegated to Black community children. Quite early, they be-come the caretakers and disciplinarians of their younger siblings; they impose the rules of conduct upon them, including the rules of language conduct. (Of course, such rules are not overtly stated; they are of the more effective type of rules, those which are out of awareness.) It is not known whether the age-grading in the Black community is in any way a survival of African social patterns, which tend to feature up to seven clearly marked and named age grades. At any rate, the age grades are very im-portant in Afro-American culture.

Linguistically, there are certain features which mark age-grading rather clearly and others which are more or less immune to it. Not all archaic forms are characteristic of the young age group, since there are no mystic factors involved. The *say* of *He tell me say* . . . seems to be largely characteristic of the older group. Forms like the Creole identity of pronoun gender reference (*He a nice little girl*) disappear by the age of five or six in most cases. The use of the undifferentiated pronoun as subject (*Me help you?*) goes almost as soon. The *He Noun* possessive (pos-session by juxtaposition) lasts a bit longer; it is still prominent in the speech of many children around the age of fourteen. The use of *been* in structures like *I been wash the car* seems to go out (or, at least, to be eliminated from conversations with out-siders) at around the age of fourteen; *I been knowing him a long time* and *I been sick*, which can be "masked" as Standard English in a casual style, probably last all the speaker's lifetime, even in formal and public utterances. The *be*-durative tends to become less frequent, in the affirmative, with age; in the negative, which is a more complex structure, it figures even in formal written sentences. Robert H. deCoy's *The Nigger Bible*, which is in relatively Standard grammatical structure in spite of its conscious identification with lower-class Negro culture, contains

Then, you know that I don't be lying none.   (p. 289)

In the United States—and in the West Indies where English Creole comes in contact with Standard English—age-grading tends in the direction of Standard English most of the time, but not in every case.[12]

Age-grading is somewhat complicated by other factors, such as status-grading. An upwardly mobile child may quickly acquire English which is more Standard than that of at least one of his parents. One Washington, D.C., boy of twelve, whose mother was a teacher, had a much more Standard brand of English than did his father, who worked as a day laborer. But more typical ghetto boys may be hesitant to use Standard English forms because of the danger of being rejected by the peer group. Those who master most perfectly the norms of the school may be stigmatized as "lames" or even as "sissies" on the block.

A combination of age-grading, status-grading, and peer group influence causes a special feature to operate among young males at about the age of puberty. At that time, their graph of standardness will actually swing "downward" a bit. It just isn't being a regular guy to speak Whitey's language too much. (See the graphs from Loban's *Problems in Oral English*.) On the other hand, the young teenager would scorn to take up the little boy forms again. The historical relationships between basilect and acrolect are known only to the historical linguist, and of course they do not figure directly in the linguistic expression of loyalty to the ghetto community.

Since it is commonplace that Negro women in general find it easier to affiliate with the middle class than do Negro men, sex-grading and status-grading are often closely associated. In the case of the oldest profession, the low status of the women may, however, override both age- and sex-grading. There is abundant opportunity to practice with speakers of Standard English, but only in limited contexts. Like their counterparts on the Maagden-straat ('Virgin Street'!) in Paramaribo, Surinam, the girls at Seventy-third and Amsterdam manage Standard English for the short periods of conversation necessary in most cases. But many white men (middle-class or not) may hear Non-Standard English primarily in those situations. All of these factors complicate the picture and may confuse an investigator.

There is a complex interaction of these sociological factors. There are also probably some personality factors which make for a kind of individual variation. But we can be sure that an upward mobile female Negro past the age of about fourteen will speak something relatively close to Standard English; on the other hand, a six-year-old ghetto resident (male or female) will usually speak something which is amazingly different from Standard English, especially when full syntactic distribution is taken into account. Sex and upward mobility factors do not usually come into effect until some time later—a still undetermined age or range of ages, since the research has so far not been done. Because of sex-grading, "problems" (in the school sense) persist longer for males than for females.

For the relatively upward-mobile Negro who somehow survives the cultural and linguistic mismatches of his schooling—especially of reading instruction—and finally gets through high school and into college with a nearly Standard brand of English under his control, there remains the important necessity of continuing to identify linguistically with his own group. Most of these people rely heavily on ethnic slang; it is the recourse of the Black who is not phonologically nor grammatically like his ethnic group but who wishes to retain some linguistic similarity. Listen to Adam Clayton Powell's *Keep the Faith, Baby* for an excellent illustration. The speaker of basilect has some familiarity with the slang—even that part of it which the Yippies learn—but he is usually not so familiar with it as is the Black college student. Slang is that part of non-standard language which is most nearly *above* the threshold of awareness; a legion of popular writers have noticed it and have mistaken it for "the ghetto language."

It receives more attention than it deserves, but it would be a distortion to leave it out altogether.

Vocabulary and Ethnic Slang

When the language of the Black community has caught the national attention, in Sunday supplements and in national magazines, it has been the slang of the group which has been called attention to. There is a certain exoticism, even cuteness, about ethnic slang. It is no surprise that this has been the feature—essentially the only feature—picked up by such imitative groups as the Beats, the Hippies, and the Yippies. There has been endless treatment of this subject, and any recapitulation here would add little to it. We all know of *soul* and *soul food* and *soul brother* or *sister*; of *chick* 'girl,' *vines* 'clothes,' *Hog* 'Cadillac,' and *bread* 'money.' We ought also to know enough to avoid making generalizations about the personalities of large groups of people on the basis of evidence like this. Ethnic slang, as such, tells us little or nothing about either the "creativity" or the "adjustment" of the Black community. Still, it has its special interest and its influence on the slang of other groups, as when *Oreo* 'a Black who is "white" on the inside' influences the Chinese community to produce *banana* in the sense of one who is "yellow" (Oriental) in skin color but not in culture.

Paradoxically, investigation of the "exotic" nature of ethnic slang has been one of the factors which has contributed most to the notion that Black English is archaic British English from a variety of "regional" dialects. *Bread* 'money' apparently does come from Cockney rhyming slang (*bread and honey*); *cat* 'female sex organ,' widely used in Iceberg Slim's *Pimp* (see Bibliography, under Robert Beck) and elsewhere, proves to have been of long currency in England. To make such an observation is, however, to achieve no more significance than to say that prostitution—and pimping—are not Afro-American innovations. In spite of the sensational nature of some of the slang vocabulary, it is of no more special interest to the linguist than prostitution is to the anthropologist. It is perhaps in these typically European cultural activities that we find the most certain evidence of British English "archaism" in the Black community.

The lengthiest treatment of ethnic slang known to me is a dissertation at Columbia University Teachers College by Herbert Foster, who was steered onto the subject as a study of the "cant" of "emotionally disturbed" youngsters and discovered that it was not cant and that the youngsters were culturally different rather than emotionally disturbed. In recent months, there have appeared in magazines and newspapers several "turnabout" tests—some of them very cleverly designed—which show how a member of mainstream culture can be culturally "disadvantaged" when the norm is that of the ghetto and how he can become "non-verbal" when the vocabulary is changed. In the same way that Jim Crow can become Crow Jim (attaching excessive value to incidental features of the Black culture), statements about the richness of the vocabulary can become as embarrassing as the more prevalent mistakes about "deprivation"; the most extreme example of the former known to me is by Mezz Mezzrow, who in *Really the Blues* praises the "cleanliness" of the phrase *to get one's ashes hauled* 'to have sexual intercourse.'[13]

The attitude of the linguist toward popular treatments of any kind of slang has been one of polite but bored amusement. Linguists have often tried to persuade English teachers to reconsider their horror of teenage slang, which is a natural age-grading feature that children everywhere are likely to go through in one form or another, and which does not "threaten the language," "impede the child's intellectual development," or anything of the like. Looking at the ethnic slang of the Black community, Stewart has frequently pointed out that it is not the same as Black English; that in a sense it tends to be used by those Blacks whose English is most Standard (as a means of retaining some feature of ethnic solidarity); and that, being under the conscious control of the user rather than out of awareness like grammatical structure, it poses no special teaching problem.

As a strategy of presentation, it has been useful to consider that Black English and Standard English share the same vocabulary, except for such relatively superficial features as slang. This is, as a matter of fact, not entirely true. The study of the lexicon (vocabulary) has to be a part of the total study of the distributional patterns which make up any grammar. The lexical structure of Black English is also somewhat different. The most recent Labov-Cohen-Robins-Lewis report (see Bibliography) points up how Black English *You throw a rock in the water and it say "Splash"* differs from white (including non-standard dialects and Southern dialect) *You throw a rock in the water and it go(es) "Splash."* There are many other such differences. Black English, like any language, deserves a dictionary of its own.

In the superficial way in which regional vocabulary differences have been treated by dialect geography, Black English does not indeed differ much from other dialects. Both white and Black paper boys *serve* the newspaper in inner-city Washington, D.C.— although by now the relatively well-to-do white children are not likely to have to indulge in such labor. In Dallas, Texas, where not all white neighborhoods would permit Black delivery boys, they *deliver* the paper. If they talk of such insects at all, both white and Black residents of a given area probably use *snake doctor*, or *mosquito hawk*, or *dragon fly*. In the inner city, *frying pan* is much more usual than either *skillet* or *spider*, although the former may have been brought in from the South. The names used by standard brands and in national advertising have become the predominant ones. Just recently, the very conservative dialect geographers have taken the forward step—a very radical one for them—of asking for names of parts of the automobile instead of such horse-and-buggy terms as *whiffletree* and *singletree*. Like the city-bound whites, Black children in the city react slowly to the questionnaire of the Dialect Atlas, with its extreme rural emphasis.

In less-examined areas, there are more significant patterns and greater differences. A Washington, D.C., inner-city teenage magazine reported "a delema between the officers and Melvin Jones," in what Standard English would undoubtedly call a dispute or even a battle. A militant teenage gang was named RAVE, for Resembling All Violence Equally; Standard English would have used *Reciprocate* rather than *Resemble*. The Howard University student who submitted the report wrote that an officer of the gang

> . . . informed them [prospective members] to give the names of everyone present.

Standard English would have used *instructed* instead of *informed*, but Black English has its own rules even for this type of usage. In at least some forms of Black English, *borrow* is a reciprocal verb (it covers the Standard English meaning 'lend' as well as 'borrow'); the reciprocal use of *learn* ('teach' as well as 'learn') is shared with certain white non-standard dialects.

Some of these differences may persist even after most of the more basic structural differences from Standard English have disappeared or have been assigned to more casual speech styles. The student paper quoted above is notably Standard in other respects. In Jamaica, where the Rastafarians write letters to the editors of the Kingston newspapers or expositions to foreign professors, it is easy to find passages like

> Ever since Man has found himself the master of planet Earth, from primitive man till this time he has always sectionally upheld some deification to a higher concept . . .[14]

This different use of vocabulary is close to Fancy Talk (see next section). And it can tell a great deal about semantic structure. One may wonder what meaning certain words had for speakers like my favorite Fancy Talker, Jelly Roll Morton, who "invented" just about everything musical and who began his autobiography with the creation of the world (Alan Lomax, *Mr. Jelly Roll*). All around him, he saw musicians of varying talent (mostly white) taking over traditional tunes and calling them their own "compositions." In such an environment, where *compose* was roughly synonymous with *appropriate for one's own*, it would be fairly easy to develop a new sense for *invent*.

Serious research on vocabulary differences in the Black community has been done in a few cases. A Swedish former quiz kid (on an *honest* television program) named Ulf Hannerz has produced "The Rhetoric of Soul,"[15] which demonstrates the relationship between the use of the word *soul* in various combinations and the social factors which produce an attachment for certain features of ghetto life style. Many collections of "hip talk" or "jive talk" have appeared in popular newspapers in the past few years. One of the most interesting, John M. Brewer's "Ghetto Children Know What They're Talking About,"[16] shows that the ten-to-twelve age group is highly innovative in slang. In Washington, children thirteen or slightly under seem to be innovators in such matters as dance steps—or, at least, the most dedicated and successful in keeping up with the latest trends—and there may be a cultural generalization about age groups which can be made from such data. In Foster's material, it often appears that the junior high school group is more innovative than the high school group in ethnic slang.

Ethnic slang did not begin just a few years ago, when the newspapers and magazines discovered it; nor did its influence on the white population begin then. Some expressions appear to have originated in the Black community and to have spread to the white. *The gravy train* seems to be one of these; the first citation in the *Dictionary of Americanisms* is from Botkin's *Lay My Burden Down* (1945), but Botkin himself, in *A Treasury of Mississippi River Folklore* (1955), traces it—still from Negro informants—to Lee's *Beale Street* (1934).

The influence of Black and white in slang and special vocabularies has been mutual and reciprocal. It is well known that Black influence has been especially great in areas like that of popular music. Herskovits has pointed out that *hot*, as applied to a type of jazz, is an Africanism and that the same metaphor is used in French Creole.[17] Other metaphorical uses of *hot* have long been in English, and some of them have passed from white dialects to Black English. It is an amusing sidelight on Establishment scholarship, however, that the *Dictionary of Americanisms* does not include the application to music among several figurative and slang uses of *hot*. Not so widely known outside musical circles but a definite part of jazz language is *cut* 'defeat in a musical contest,' which parallels Sranan Tongo *kotsingi* 'strife by songs, abusive songs.'

Fancy Talk and Elegant Behavior

In one of his many perceptive and wholly sympathetic portrayals of Negro customs in the United States, Mark Twain wrote

> Our Negroes in American have several ways of entertaining themselves which are not found among the whites anywhere. Among these inventions of theirs is one which is particularly popular with them. It [the cakewalk] is a competition in elegant deportment . . . All that the competitor knows of fine airs and graces he throws into his countenance. He may use all the helps he can devise: watch-chain to twirl with his fingers, cane to do graceful things with, snowy handkerchief to flourish and get artful effects out of, shiny new stovepipe hat to assist his courtly bows . . .
>
> ("In Defense of Harriet Shelley,"
> Author's National Edition, XXII, p. 2)

There is also such elegantizing behavior in language in the U. S. Negro community; after Stewart, I call it Fancy Talk.[18]

In many ways it is unfortunate that there has been some resentment of white recognition of these traits on the part of the Negro community and of course some ridicule of them on the part of the whites. Why should elegance, either in speech or in behavior, be something to ridicule or to be ashamed of? On the contrary, it seems like something for the Negro community to be proud of and for the white community to admire. The fact that for long periods of time, the attire of the elegant slave or freedman had to be the castoff splendor of the white man is undoubtedly part of it. In language, there has been the constant snobbery of "good" English—for which the speech of educated whites scant suffices and which has been considered to be virtually out of the reach of uneducated Negroes. Elegant language behavior which does not happen to correspond to an arbitrary norm can be called malapropism—among other things—and the rhetorical flowers of the Negro community have been mostly thorns in interracial relationships.

Nothing, however, could be clearer than that Fancy Talk is not merely the result of poor imitation of white language behavior. Other parts of Afro-America had the same tradition; on Barbados, for example, it has been more overtly recognized:

> Entertainment at these functions usually took the form of vocal items from the ladies and flights of oratory from the men.

> The theme of the men's speeches might be historical, e.g., 'The Battle of Bacaclava' declaimed with mime, gesture, and much lurid detail, or scriptural . . . There was, however, always something educational or edifying about it in intent . . . [It] had as its worthy objective the training in public speaking of those who orated . . . Often the restless speaker, afraid to wait any longer on his unreliable memory, would plunge headlong into a sea of dog-Latin . . . And so the speaker would lead his impressed and admiring hearers through the labyrinthine maze of classical eloquence, always ending with 'And now, ladies and gentlemen, I will redound to my sanctum sanctorum.'   (Louis Lynch, *The Barbados Book*, pp. 241–243)

Although Lynch does not say so, this kind of activity is called a Tea Meeting in both Barbados and Jamaica. Here are documented the actual training in the elegantizing tradition—informal training, perhaps, but quite palpably training nevertheless—and the elements of conscious elegantizing: use of intentionally glittering and sesquepedelian words and phrases, and the type of disregard for dictionary precision of meaning which can be documented from many Afro-American sources. (What it loses in schoolteacher precision it more than makes up, at its best, in creativity.) Further, this free-wheeling approach to eloquence results in the one factor which has led, because of misunderstanding of the medium involved, to ridicule by narrow-minded and racist whites—near or outright malapropism.

Lynch gives one excellent example of this type of talk:

Ek-keehomo, behold the man.
Ek-kee homo, here I stand:
    I will now rise from my esteemed seat
and I will say Bon Swar or Good Evening to the
ladies and gentlemen of this nocturnal congregation.   (p. 239)

He remarks that "amusing malapropisms abound" (p. 143), and we are almost willing to include *esteemed seat* among them. Lynch reports that "the use of polysyllables was expected" and then supplies the excellent example of "phantasmagorical valetudinarianism" (p. 251); it might almost be added that "malapropisms" were also an expected feature of the style. Certainly, Fancy Talkers have never been bound by schoolmarmish injunctions to use the plain word where it will do, to avoid words with which one is not entirely familiar, etc.; schoolmarms are notoriously incapable of elegance of any kind. The important thing, as Lynch also notes, is that there be "a sensible feeling for word music," in comparison to which a pedagoguish subservience to "accuracy" seems stiff and unproductive indeed.

The process can be duplicated in the United States, down to the spontaneous, though not classically exact, use of Latin. In Henry W. Ravenal's reminiscences of a South Carolina plantation (reprinted in the *Yale Review* for 1936), a Negro selling on the streets of the city livened up his calls with bits of Latin and with consciously bogus literary allusions like "manufactured by Shakespeare."

The elegant activity noted in the United States by Twain and the fancy speech documented by Lynch are combined in J. H. Ingraham's observations of Natchez in about 1935, recorded in *The Southwest by a Yankee*:

> The [slave] males prefer collecting [on Sunday] in little knots in the streets, where, imitating the manners, bearing, and language of their masters, they converse with grave faces and in pompous language, selecting hard, high-sounding words, which are almost universally misapplied, and distorted, from their original sound as well as sense to a most ridiculous degree—astounding their groping auditors 'ob de field nigger class,' who cannot boast of such enviable accomplishments.   (Vol. II, 56)

Ingraham's account is obviously less sympathetic—and less accurate—than that of Lynch, because Ingraham was looking from the outside at an institution unfamiliar to him. There does not appear to be any real reason to assume that they were "imitating . . . their masters," except perhaps insofar as their clothing had to be the cast-off clothing of their masters. It should be noted, however, that Ingraham specifically attributes this behavior to an elite group and does not make it part of any mythical "Negro nature." A hyperbolic use of language, called by many observers exhuberance, has been remarked by many writers on the West Indies, and there is no special reason to assume that it came as an imitation of the whites. And Lynch's wording is certainly better than Ingraham's "misapplied" and "distorted." Nevertheless, for all his inability to place Fancy Talk in its cultural context, Ingraham could see that it was there; and his description checks with other partial descriptions which we have.

We can find descriptions of such linguistic activity in many places and from many times. Robert A. Hall, Jr., in his book on Haitian Creole, describes even the educated Haitian's French as "grandiose, flowery, imitiated from eighteenth-century models, over-literary"; he further finds it "inexact in comparison with metropolitan French usage." Hall is an experienced field worker in linguistics, and not one to describe something that is not there. It seems strange, then, that he contributes, even so slightly, to the myth of the Negro's predilection for the eighteenth century.

In this respect, he is strangely like a very different linguist with his own particular claim to acuteness of observation, Thomas Jefferson writing of Negro author Ignatius Sancho

> his style is easy and familiar, except when he affects a Shandean fabrication of words.
>
> (Quoted in Wish, *Slavery in the South*, p. 227)

But at least Jefferson was not indulging in archaizing fancy when he alluded to Lawrence Sterne's most famous creation; it still *was* the eighteenth century! Sumner Ives seems to be much nearer to accuracy than either of the two when he writes of "richness of imagery" as a "peculiarity of Negro speech" ("Dialect Differentiation in the Stories of Joel Chandler Harris," *American Literature*, 1955). Of course, Ives should probably have added "from the viewpoint of the middle-class listener" or some such phrase; nevertheless, Ives's statement is not in any sense patronizing, and he is perhaps entitled to "let himself go" in such a way from time to time. Cultural relativism is a rare and valuable attitude, but carrying it around all the time can become something of a burden.

There are perhaps two basic characteristics of Fancy Talk, both of them hinted at by the observers quoted above: (1) flashy vocabulary, often beyond appropriateness to the subject under discussion from the point of view of the speaker of Standard English; (2) "poetic" diction, or "highly seasoned" talk. The latter may be somewhat condescendingly treated, by outsiders, as an admirable characteristic—as when Negroes are complimented on their "natural" rhythm. Certain side effects, which are somewhat more easily characterized in conventional linguistic terminology, include dropping of weakly stressed syllables (e.g., the somewhat racist joke involving a confusion between *mo' 'lasses* and *molasses*); derivational morphology considered deviant from the Standard English viewpoint (*remorial* for *memorial*, *revorce* for *divorce*); and, trickiest of all because it may be a masked example of any of the above, malapropism. The feeling that these side effects are similar to Fancy Talk is undoubtedly due to the difficulty of escaping completely from the linguocentrism of Standard English, of perceiving these side effects as merely functions of the co-occurrence distributions (including derivational distributions) of Negro Non-Standard.

Flashy vocabulary certainly may be observed in many parts of Afro-America. A West Cameroonian hotel worker who wanted a job as my steward explained that he was leaving the hotel job because it "didn't suit his policy." The rather racist writer Octavus Roy Cohen—whose dialect, however, is quite good, and who knew a great deal about Negro folklore—makes flashy vocabulary a primary characteristic of his fictional Florian Slappey; and his wife, Inez Lopez Cohen, collected many real examples from the Negro press which she published in *Our Darktown Press*. There are abundant items like

> He was charged with contributing to her moral delinquency by giving her money—viz: twenty-five cents.   (p. 7)

and

> Palpitating hearts, half-closed eyes, filled with exoticism, feet shuffling as if subtly struck by an epidemic of St. Vitus dance, beautifully gowned women and immaculately dressed males, marked the gargantuan chapter of entertainment proffered at the casino.
>
>   (p. 2)

Although apparently hated by the Negro community, Cohen was not without his liberal side. In his foreword to his wife's book, Cohen represents himself as remonstrating against his wife's chuckles over the Negro press, by saying, "Most Negro newspapers are exceedingly well written and edited." And he agrees with his wife's qualifier, "But they do express things in an amusing way" (p. vii). More closely examined, these two statements may not be at all contradictory.

The historical and geographic range of this institution of elegant speech is strikingly great. In Lynch's materials on Barbados, in Crane's "The Monster," in the Kingfish-Sapphire sequences of *Amos and Andy*, and in many other examples, it is the male who indulges in the "flights of oratory." Crane's representation of fancy courtship talk is rather like that called Courtship Questions in

"Folklore and Ethnology," by the editors of *The Southern Work-man* (1895; reprinted in Jackson, *The Negro and His Folklore in Nineteenth-Century Periodicals*, pp. 280–1). The girl's speech is extraordinarily fancy in this dialogue (as in Crane), but her talk is plain compared to that of her suitor. No documentation of the "training in public speaking" in the continental United States has come to my attention; yet there is every reason to believe that occasions providing for such practice, or "training," were indeed a part of Black culture from the earliest days.

Oratorical splendor, at least, seems to have a good chance of being African in origin. Richard Austin Freeman reported in 1898 that

> The art of oratory is in West Africa carried to a remarkable pitch of perfection. At the public palavers each linguist stands up in turn and pours forth a flood of speech, the readiness and exuberance of which strikes the stranger with amazement . . . These oratorical displays appear to afford great enjoyment to the audience, for every African native is a born orator and connoisseur of oratory.
>
> (*Travels and Life in Ashanti and Jamaica*, p. 61)

and Newbell N. Puckett observed some years later

> Both in Africa and in America the Negro seems to find decided pleasure in altiloquent speech.
>
> (*Folk Beliefs of the Southern Negro*, 1928, p. 28)

In Jamaica, this kind of verbal splendor is referred to as *cutting English*, and it often has as one of its side results the mixing of dialects. In 1868, Thomas Russell pointed out the widespread nature of the practice and recorded some typical sentences:

> Me good sista, me tell she, but him tink fe her own way better than fe we. You see she pass we gate yer.
>
> A was been told you of it.
>
> (*The Etymology of Jamaican Grammar*, p. 13)

The *me* and *him* subject forms, for example, are "deep" creole—much like Plantation Creole—and the *she* and *we* oblique forms are the result of imperfect switching to Standard English. Fanciness is partially correlated with standardness, but not perfectly.

The female is likely to be more standard in English, just as
the male is likely to be more fancy. A children's biography which
is rather good on dialect matters, Jeannette Eaton's *Trumpeter's
Tale*, has Lil Armstrong say to her famous husband Louis,
"Honestly, Satchmo, when are you going to give up that Perdido
Street dialect? You can talk just as good English as anyone else
if you feel like it. Why do you talk as if you were in a minstrel
show?" To which Louis answers, "Why, for fun!" (p. 168) It is
not known just how Miss Eaton arrived at this conversation, but
it seems less suspect than it might otherwise be since it fits so
well into an established pattern: Louis is both more non-standard
and fancier than Lil. It may or may not be significant that, in his
musical production, Louis was both more unconventional and
more talented than his second wife, who was quite insistent upon
her classical background in music.

Upon review, the evidence seems to be overwhelming that
Fancy Talk effects must be the result of an institutionalized
tradition. To attribute them to individual differences, whether
personal or "racial," seems contradictory to common sense. Yet
especially those people who have been most eager to support the
Negro may have been inclined to explain those effects away in
terms of individual talent or of inclination. The proof of the
pudding, in this case, seems to be in the imitation; those who
seek to achieve the same effects apart from the tradition achieve
only a watered-down usage of ethnic slang. An analogy from
dancing suggests itself: to achieve the dances mastered by the
Negro community, one needs much more than simply "freedom
of expression." A recent newspaper article illustrates how the
hippies, imitators of Negroes without knowledge of or training
in Negro traditions, rely upon such instructions as the following:

> ". . . find the moving rhythmic spot inside yourself, and then find
> another, and another and let them come together until they bring
> you up off the floor expressing yourself with your bodies."
>
> (Nicholas Van Hoffman, "The Acid Affair,"
> *The Washington Post*, October 26, 1967, pp. E1–2)

The unfortunate hippies tried to "express themselves," with the following results:

> . . . they knew no dance steps and could only stamp and flutter their arms. (*Ibid.*)

A Negro girl watching exclaimed

> My God, my God, what are those people doing? . . . They can't dance. They can't keep time; what *are* they doing . . . ? (*Ibid.*)

Training in the traditions, whether formal or informal, obviously has something to offer for which "self expression" can never substitute.

The factor of "poetic" diction or "highly seasoned" language is, of course, not easily distinguishable from that of flashy vocabulary—or even from the side effects mentioned. Yet many observers who know their Afro-American dialects have remarked upon some such characteristic. Cassidy compares Jamaica Talk to pepperpot, a spicy type of Jamaican soup (*Jamaica Talk,* p. 3). The culinary metaphor is recurrent, as in Lafcadio Hearn's title *Gombo Zhèbes* 'A Gumbo of Herbs'—a collection of proverbs from which came the only words of creole which were appearing in Port-au-Prince newspapers when I was there in 1962. The ability to use flowery diction in a manner that is not highly suspect even in the midst of the white man's highbrow institutions is apparently a feature of the appeal of Adam Clayton Powell, yet even he slips into an occasional near-malapropism (hypercorrection) like "the Israeli-ites" (*Keep the Faith, Baby*).

Powell's appeal obviously depends also on a use of certain ethnic-identification factors in the midst of well-tailored suavity; among these is ethnic slang. Slang, the most easily picked up feature of the Negro culture, is also the trademark of the hippie; and the use of slang without the carefully cultured grace that goes with Fancy Talk is perhaps one of the many reasons for the frequently observed failure of the hippies to win over the ghetto community. Again, the cry of the Negro girl watching the hippies try to dance comes to mind: "They're so ugly!" The Negro tradition definitely includes elements of linguistic beauty—the elements, whether "exotic" or not, forming part of a harmonious interrelationship—and the mere appropriation of a few of the simpler elements ("Like . . . ," "Baby") does not constitute an acceptable imitation. The esthetic tradition concerned constitutes the least-observed, although the most important, feature of the Afro-American institution.

Fancy Talk characteristics impinge upon features of Black English. Given the well-known factor of "loss" of an unstressed prefix, familiar in Gullah as in other American Negro dialects, it is easy to understand how forms like 'vorce 'divorce' came about. The form revorce must be explained with some caution; it may be a kind of inaccurate attempt to produce Standard English, or it may be Fancy Talk—or it may be both, since to some extent Fancy Talk does tend in the direction of Standard (or even hyper-Standard) English. Cassidy, who has a great deal to say of fanciness in Jamaica Talk, writes

> Malapropisms are represented by strive for thrive (although over-correction may be at work here) and ignorant for indignant.
>
> (Jamaica Talk, pp. 5–6)

"Malapropisms" of this sort may be either morphological (like the above-cited revorce, or like empire 'umpire,' remorial 'memorial') or phonological (like the Washington Negro Non-Standard homophony of fairy and furry), producing forms which might be interpreted by a speaker of Standard English as Cinderella's furry godmother. In the case of a delema [sic] between the officers and Melvin Brown, from a Washington teen-age Negro newspaper, one may suspect simple searching for the impressive word at the expense of exact diction—something which is not unusual among teenagers. The generally inflated vocabulary of sports reporting would render the Grambling College publicity release describing the blinding gait of a football player almost unnoticeable for many readers. Clearly, ethnic rhetorical characteristics may cross with professional jargon, and perhaps only a predisposition can make one believe that he is able to sort them out. The drunken prospective employee in Washington who excused his unsteady gait to me by "I have to bob and weave in order to mitigate" [navigate—itself a stale metaphor coming ultimately, perhaps, from armed forces slang] was undoubtedly motivated by a desire to be impressive, which he might easily have tried to fulfill by recourse to the informal tradition of Fancy Talk. The same might be said of the Corpus Christi, Texas, Negro who, in the general context of a display of unconventional erudition (much of it said to be drawn from a *Book of Knowledges* which is otherwise unknown to me), proclaimed that, "Scientists now say the world ain't round; it kinda opaque."

It is perhaps in the area of malapropism that the value of the "quasi-foreign language" approach again becomes paramount. Amusing malapropisms abound in the area wherein Standard English is a quasi-foreign language, from the Spanglish *I cannot assist* ['attend'] *your class* to the "Tagarbage"

> . . . because I tend to say what I really mean in Tagalog and most often it is a contraception of Tagalog, Cebuano, and English.
>   (*Sociological Inquiry,* Spring, 1966, p. 250)

A native Tagalog speaker of my acquaintance used to amuse us by her mis-renditions of the clichés of popular entertainment, like "meanwhile, back at the ranch" as "meanwhile, behind the barn." This area, indeed, invites flippancy, yet it is precisely in this area that one of the greatest challenges is posed to educational researchers and to serious classroom educators, and in which some of the greatest pitfalls are to be found. Consider the findings of Arnold S. Carson and A. I. Rabin, in a category which they called

> Class 6. Error. The error response is totally
>   irrelevant to the stimulus word.
>   Response—"The dog 'wagons' his tail."

In this particular class 6, both Northern Negro and Southern Negro children scored a higher percentage of "error" than white children—a fact which, like many others, tends to document how a geographic approach is virtually useless in dealing with the problems of "culturally disadvantaged" Negroes.

In order to avoid the opposite extreme of slipping into racism, it is necessary to give serious study to the language and to the language-related traditions and institutions of the Negro in the United States. It is clearly not adequate on this ground—as it is also not adequate on other grounds—to content oneself with the tracing of Negro Non-Standard forms to obscure, scattered British dialect sources and to leave vital sociolinguistic facts and problems to a facile fiction like selective cultural differentiation.

Both kinds of elegance—sartorial and verbal—are too well attested from different places and times to be merely the chance results of observation of individual traits. William Ferguson, the pre-Civil War British traveler, was only one of many to observe that

> Some of the female costumes were very gaudy, and those of both sexes evidenced the characteristic love of showy dress.
>
> (*Across America by River and Rail*, 1856, p. 115)

An equally large number of observers reported the trait of verbal elegance.

Misunderstanding of Black traditions of eloquence may have contributed to one of the major tragedies of Reconstruction, the rejection of Black representation in the Southern legislatures. Bowers, in *The Tragic Era* (see Bibliography), documents how Negro members of the legislatures indulged themselves in oratorical flights which the Southern whites found pretentious and even ludicrous. (On p. 216 he quotes a North Carolina "delegate of color" who wished to "expatiate" to the convention and desired his words recorded "in the archives of gravity.") It seems quite probable that, lacking the formal training needed to master the highly ritualized language of legislative houses, the Blacks resorted to its nearest equivalent in their culture—the Fancy Talk tradition.

It has been difficult to achieve recognition for these behavior patterns as culture traits and not as evidence of inferiority by biased white observers; but there is no special virtue in the opposite flaw of pretending that they do not exist. To the cultural relativist, they are interesting and valuable proof of cultural continuity.

How the Ghetto Speaker Uses Language

As an occasional consultant at workshops on the education of the "disadvantaged," I have frequently had the experience of having fellow participants listen more or less patiently to an exposition of the grammatical differences between Black English and Standard English and then inquire, "But *what* do they say? That's what we're interested in—not *how* they say it." It is necessary to admit at this point that linguistics has little or nothing to offer about such a subject. Linguists are skeptical of any measures of "communicative potential" of a given language; those attempts which have been made to show that one speech variety is able to communicate certain ideas better than another have always been so defective in the basic aspects of linguistic methodology that it has been easy to conclude that the subject itself is just not capable of being investigated. Actually, it is closer to the truth that the methodology existing at the present isn't adequate to judge such a problem. It becomes a tenet of linguistics—although perhaps more an article of faith than the result of experimental demonstration—that any language or variety is adequate for any demand which the speech community can make upon it. Ultimately, then, all speakers would be equal in the number and complexity of "ideas" or "messages" which their language enables them to communicate—although we know perfectly well that the ideas and messages are themselves sometimes different. If this isn't true, any attempts to demonstrate its contrary have been so sadly lacking in linguistic sophistication and methodological skill that the proponents of the opposite idea have in effect strengthened the accumulated impressions of the linguists.

At about this time, the director of the workshop is likely to acquire an expression which says, "And I'm paying $150 a day for this."

In spite of the impatience of workshop directors and English teachers with the pedestrian facts of linguistic differences and their desire to press on to the ideational heights, they would probably do well to pay a little more attention to the groundwork. It might be just as well for them to adopt the linguist's skepticism about language systems' differences in "inherent communicative potential" or the like. Most of their favorite examples of the "poverty" of ghetto language are subject to the same strictures that linguists have always had against other attempts of the same type. Such attempts tend to participate in a near-universal folklore of language.

As one who has listened to hundreds of hours of recordings of ghetto children's spontaneous speech in planned activities (with signed releases from their parents to obviate any charges of invasion of privacy), I can say without doubt that those non-professional linguists who have called ghetto children "non-verbal" just don't know what they're talking about. To the linguist who is trying to separate out their words and sentences from a tape—with the very best of binaural recording and transcribing equipment—the little chatterboxes are *too* verbal. Of course, it can happen that a child from a poor home will be intimidated when he comes into, say, a psychologist's office with air-conditioning and fluorescent lighting and fancy furniture designed to impress the other members of the same project; the ghetto child, in such surroundings, may hang back and refuse to talk, whereas a middle-class child who knows more psychologists than day laborers will chatter away. The various researchers and plain conclusion-jumpers who have formulated analyses under conditions like that have obviously indulged in cultural bias of the worst sort.

At an equal level of absurdity is the fashionable statement that inner-city children have had their "sensibilities deadened" or "language drowned out" by loud television sets. I happen to be a television hater, not ever having owned a set; but I can see no evidence that ghetto children are any more tyrannized by television than anyone else. The children in the first block described in the first section of this chapter almost all had television sets in their poor apartments. But the streets were regularly packed by children—running, playing, arguing, fighting, interacting, TALKING—who could have been inside watching television if they had chosen to do so.

Equally absurd are statements as to the pathological effects of abnormal family structure. In the first place, like any other community, the Black community needs to be looked at in terms of its own characteristic family structure, which might be a great deal different from that of the middle class and which just might reflect even some African survivals. Even allowing, for the sake of argument only, that the family structure is pathological, it still does not follow that the children are lacking in language models. Like all other children, they learn language mostly from their peers, who are abundantly available. Whether the stereotype of the father who is absent or who refuses to talk to his children even when present is true or not, it has little relevance to the matter of language development. Dick Gregory seems to be a reasonably verbal type, yet his autobiography reveals many of the factors which are so often cited for their deadening effect.

Neither do the stories of the horrible environment make much sense in this respect. There have been printed recently many examples of the writings of ghetto children which show the effects of their environment. It is, of course, unfortunate that children have to live in an environment of junkies and criminals; there is, however, not the faintest shred of evidence that such an environment will reduce their verbal skills. There have been few more fashionable absurdities than that such children are "terrified out of their natural inquisitiveness." The only competitor in absurdity seems to be the stale saw about their "having few experiences." There is rare comedy in the maiden lady schoolteacher who

stands up and says that ghetto children are "lacking in experience." Many of them have more experience by the age of twelve
than that lady will ever have. And they're inquisitive about things
the existence of which she will never admit to herself.

The subject of experience brings up, of course, SEX; there is
the opposite notion of the emancipated ghetto dweller, freed
of the inhibitions that the middle class is subject to. It is a little
harder to go about debunking that one, but it seems to me to be
false. There is no denying the frequency of occurrence of [məvə
fəkə]; but, since obscenity, like anything else, is relative, such a
commonplace term can hardly be termed obscene in the dialect.
In the hundreds of hours of recordings which I listened to, there
just didn't seem to be much difference in the way the Negro
children talked about sex and the way white children of the same
age do. The imagined sophistication isn't there. Twelve- and
thirteen-year-old boys revealed the same type of half-funny, half-
pathetic misinformation about sex which practically all preteens
seem to have. Of the large population studied, one case of serious
perversion turned up (accidentally, of course—we were not looking into the sexual orientation of the subjects) and was given
help by a psychiatrist. The twelve- and thirteen-year-old boys
put to drawing (the best activity of all, it turned out, for getting
recordable conversation) drew . . . just what you'd expect any
boys their age to draw. In this case, they were interrupted by
the allegedly sophisticated (Black) block worker who had been
foisted off on us from another prestigious project, who wanted
them to "keep it decent." Needless to say, our project was not
interested in the drawings—decent or otherwise. (The drawings
were immediately destroyed, and students of psychology who
came looking for data were told firmly to look elsewhere.)

There are, of course, some characteristic topics, speech styles,
and modes of discourse. One of the more interesting is called
jonin' by the Washington community—*sounding* or *the dozens*
elsewhere. It is a quasi-ritualized game of verbal insult, with
recognized rules for excelling and status rewards. For an unsuccessful effort, the response is "weak" uttered on a quiet, low-
pitched syllable. At the time we made the recordings, there was

a fashionable verbal play about "What did James Brown say when . . . ?" with an answer expected in the shape of a title from one of the rock and roll star's songs. Some of the youngsters showed an amazing inventiveness within such frameworks.

From activities such as these it follows pretty naturally that the inner-city child's language models are not exclusively—perhaps not even primarily—those of middle-class, mainstream America. To some extent, they change their language in the direction of Standard English through age-grading; but it's not an uncomplicated process. And it shouldn't be assumed that the speaker of the most Standard English necessarily has the most attraction for ghetto imitators. They have their own models, which need to be studied seriously before any serious conclusions concerning their language practices can be drawn.

One of these is the storefront preacher, often as much an artist as a Calypso or blues singer. With a wide pitch range and impressive rhythmic sense, with the stylistic use of vocal rasp which is strongly reminiscent of Louis Armstrong, many a preacher of this type presents a better performance on Sunday than is ever to be seen on network television. With the intervention and cooperation of the congregation which Herskovits long ago likened to the West African call-and-response pattern, these preachers fill the radio air—even in Washington, Los Angeles, and New York—with their performances every Sunday. They are to some extent Fancy Talkers, like much-recorded (on Ethnic Folkways) Rich Amerson, who likened the bloody Doomsday condition of sun, moon, and stars to a "judgment hemmidge [hemorrhage]." Their sermons— or parts of them—are easily available on records like that of the Reverend J. W. Evans of Greater Mt. Carmel Baptist Church, Los Angeles (Léshun Records 601-B). Evans's congregation responds with "amen," "yeah," and even the supposedly unauthentic "sho nuff" to his effectively planned lead. His English is (perhaps intentionally) somewhat non-standard:

> if the king ax for me
> David and Jonathan was friends
> A true friend is one that we can confined in.

For less skilled preachers than Evans, the congregation's participation may have even a directive function. If the preacher slows or hesitates, one of the older women may pick up the tempo and propel the performance forward in a *vocalise* which is strikingly like the "breaks" utilized by New Orleans jazzmen. But a skilled speaker like Evans has control all the way. His use of rasp regularly signals an increase in the emotional pitch of the service. (This is undoubtedly what Zora Neale Hurston was referring to when she wrote of her father's "good straining voice" in *Dust Tracks on a Road*. It is a very accurate descriptive term, but I have no knowledge of its general use in the Black community.) The preacher probably plans very carefully his switch from speech to a quasi-singing of the words of a hymn at the peak of the sermon, but a listening outsider is not aware of the exact point of change. The congregation itself is propelled on to climactic (but perfectly ordered) emotional response, culminating in the possession ("coming through") of a few members.

The cultural unity of the Black community, in the light of participation in such institutions as the storefront church, is impressive. The younger militants, the Black Panthers, the Black Muslims are the *avant garde* and as such differ appreciably from the main body. There is even a certain amount of anti-clericalism among the younger activists.[19] There are the ones who fill the headlines and about whom American whites read, but the ghetto eighty percent is different in many respects. It participates in such activities as the storefront church to such a degree that the concept of "soul" as the unifying factor has a more than mystic significance for the coherence of the Black community. In spite of having accepted, formally, the standards of correctness of the advantaged white community (Evans says *whom* in his sermon, and uses *ain't* only when seeking a touch of intimacy), the Black community retains an impressive amount of cultural and linguistic solidarity. These are undoubtedly the reasons why Black English is the most homogeneous dialect of American English.

NOTES

[1] See Baratz (*Child Development,* 1969); Baratz, Shuy, and Wolfram; and Lambert and Tucker (in Bibliography).

[2] For a long period of time, "Negro," especially in the South, was more nearly a quasi-legal (essentially common law) than a racial term. It applied to anyone with even a trace of Negro "blood." Pauli Murray, *States' Laws on Race and Color* (1950) points up the haphazard nature of Southern statutory provisions concerning the matter. Cobb, *Inquiry into the Law of Slavery,* p. 67, ties the slavery relationship itself to the maternal line; yet post-slavery Southern attitudes made anyone with a trace of African "blood" a Negro.

The irony of such inconsistent classification has often been commented upon; it is, for example, the central theme of Sinclair Lewis's novel *Kingsblood Royal.* When the Supreme Court decision of 1954 removed any legal basis, the classification *Negro* became perhaps a social rather than a legal term. On the other hand, it has often been pointed out that there has been little *de facto* change, especially in the South, in the old classificatory system.

[3] See, for example, the poems of Victor Hernández Cruz (Bibliography). The writings of Labov (Bibliography) contain some promise but little performance insofar as the Puerto Rican use of Black English is concerned.

[4] See especially Chapter V.

[5] See Chapter IV.

[6] See Chapter III. The different cultures of the field hands and of the house servants, with the special privileges enjoyed by the latter, are a commonplace of historical sociology. Statements are easily found in LeRoi Jones, *Blues People,* p. 123, and in E. Franklin Frazier, *Black Bourgeoisie.* Both of these sources, like many others, point out the dialect differences between the two groups. A glaring example of failure to utilize this elementary sociological information can be seen in the writings of American dialect geographers (e.g., Lee A. Pederson, "Missouri Dialects: Marion County Phonemics," *American Speech* December 1967, p. 277, footnote 27).

[7] See Berreman (Bibliography).

[8] "Creole Slave Songs," *Century Magazine* XXXI (April, 1886).

[9] Age-grading, to some extent a universal feature of language, exists in such societies as that of England to some degree. M. V. O'Shea's *Linguistic Development and Education* (Bibliography), despite a great deal of old-

fashioned terminology and a certain amount of outright nonsense, makes that point fairly well. It appears likely, however, that Afro-American communities in general have more age-grading than white American communities. For Black American English, Labov, Cohen, Robins, and Lewis (Bibliography) give an excessively conservative account of age-grading. For more complete accounts, see Stewart's works (Bibliography).

[10] Although the importance of these factors has been reasonably well known for a long time in an informal sense, Stewart seems to have been the first to call the attention of the academic world to them ("Sociolinguistic Factors," Bibliography).

[11] See Shiro Hattori (Bibliography).

[12] In writing, a great deal of the ethnic flavor, despite the Standard English nature of the grammar, is kept in the writings of Robert Beck ("Iceberg Slim"—see Bibliography).

[13] The historical accuracy of Mezzrow's statement is doubtful.

[14] Quoted in Donald W. Hogg, "Statement of a Rastafari Leader," *Caribbean Studies* Vol. 6, No. 1 (April, 1966), pp. 37–39. For interesting and amusing examples of Fancy Talk from many parts of the world—most of them areas where Pidgin English has been in use—see Hunt (compiler), *Honoured Sir—from Babujee* (Bibliography).

[15] *Race*, 1969.

[16] *New York Times Magazine*, 25 December 1966.

[17] *New Republic* LXXXIV, No. 1083 (1935), reprinted in *The New World Negro*, ed. Frances S. Herskovits.

[18] Robert Deane Pharr's *The Book of Numbers* (1969) uses the phrase *fine talk* (p. 18) about the same type of language behavior but in a casual fashion which does not indicate that it is a widely used term. I have found no evidence that the Jamaican term *cutting English*, which designates the same phenomenon, was ever used in the United States. The analogy to musical styles—the freely improvisatory Afro-American style which stresses creativity even in lyrics as against the white style which places value on exactness of memory—is beautifully drawn in Alan Lomax's "Folk Song Style," *American Anthropologist* Vol. 61, No. 6 (December 1959), pp. 927–955.

VII

Black English and Education

T<small>HE</small> language differences of the English-speaking Blacks in the United States are nothing new, although they are forever being rediscovered and new solutions for the resultant problems are being sought. Around 1750, Quaker Anthony Benezet founded a wonderfully far-sighted but small-scale school for Negro children; in the 1960's, projects concerning the language of the "disadvantaged" (often a euphemism for the Negro) began to receive large grants from the Office of Education, the Ford Foundation, the Carnegie Corporation, and other foundations. None of these has been distinguished by any real perception of what the problem is. In the 1780's, Crèvecoeur and others most inappropriately characterized the Pidgin English or Plantation Creole stage as an "uncouth dialect" or a "crude jargon." In the 1960's, there has been a tendency to attribute the educational problems of the Negro to factors like linguistic and cognitive deprivation. There has been a great historical span, but no progress.

Different as the "inherent nature of the African" statements of the eighteenth and nineteenth centuries were from the false ecology of the twentieth ("the father is not at home to give the children practice in verbal interaction with adults"), they were not really much less accurate. All three centuries show the deep failure to perceive the realities of language and culture differences which have been hidden under a veneer of sameness imposed by the mainstream culture. There has been an incredible reluctance to realize that these differences can be explained by—indeed, are the inevitable result of—normal historical processes, especially insofar as language is concerned. Unfortunately, the information which historians of American English made available to serious students of the Negro in the United States was based on experience with language situations of a different and irrelevant type and was spectacularly inapplicable to the situation of the Black community. Linguists with relevant experience, especially in the West Indies, have been "intruders" upon the vested interests of the Establishment dialectologists. The misunderstanding has been tragic, but it is easily traced to its causes.

Anthony Benezet, who at least perceived the necessity of training his Black youngsters in what he conceived to be their "mother tongue" rather than in the classical languages,[1] got reactions from his teachers which closely parallel those from outspoken but linguistically naive whites in the twentieth century. More than one report[2] which has been widely consulted in the past ten years hints at about the same thing as this quotation:

> To find qualified teachers for the unhappy blacks was almost impossible. The Negro knew nothing and could learn nothing, so people said. In view of the universal prejudice, to teach Negro children was painfully humiliating, irksome, and monotonous, and one discouraged teacher succeeded another.
>
> (Brookes, *Friend Anthony Benezet,* p. 48)

We do not know what kind of success John Eliot—"The Apostle to the Indians" who taught Black and Indian children together in his home—had in seventeenth-century Massachusetts, but we can be sure that he did not begin a successful tradition.

It would be expecting too much to look, in the seventeenth and eighteenth centuries, for teachers anthropologically sophisticated enough to be able to see that cultural and linguistic differences did not constitute "inferiority"—that different learning patterns did not constitute "unteachability." Those teachers had little formal training. But in the twentieth century many of our teachers have had years of graduate school. Before they go into English teaching, they learn to be budding specialists in recondite subjects like the love life of Byron and the domestic affairs of Robert and Elizabeth Browning. Among all these, there surely could be a few whose training included some attention to linguistics and anthropology. One suspects that the discouraged teachers who still succeed one another in the ghetto continue to find their tasks "humiliating, irksome, and monotonous" because of the same lack of basic information about their students which incapacitated Benezet's teachers in the eighteenth century.

In the gulf between derogation of the Negro's brand of English and ignoring any difference because of some preconception, there is an island which is clearly the wrong one. A large number of speech correctionists and educators, along with a smattering of psychologists, have seen that there is some correlation between the Negro school dropout rate and the Negro's low grades in language arts and English classes, and have assumed that many Negroes suffered from the kind of disability which is subsumed under language pathology. One Negro speech correctionist-psychologist, dean at a large Negro university, went so far as to indulge in a little too-elementary learning theory: language, being a learned activity, can be learned badly. All of these people appear sadly wrong to the linguist—or to a linguistically sophisticated speech pathologist like Joan Baratz.[3] Recent linguistic theory has emphasized that the human infant comes into the world with a preparation for language learning of a type which makes it independent—insofar as the first language is concerned— of any teaching procedures. It is, of course, necessary that the first-language learner have a model upon which he can pattern his learning efforts; but, given that one advantage, he progresses at a pace which confounds pedagogical theory.[4] Some children, perhaps one-tenth of 1 percent of any population, have physical defects such as cleft palates or congenital deafness which inhibit their mastery of pronunciation. Insofar as the others are concerned, a judgment in favor of one child's speech ability in preference to another's is very likely a value judgment expressing an attitude which favors one child's culture over that of the other. The speech pathologist-correctionist, in the raw state, has singularly little to contribute to the problems of the "disadvantaged."

Recognition of the linguistic and cultural nature of the educational problems of the "disadvantaged" Negro began with the exposure of William A. Stewart to the young Negro population of Washington, D. C., in the early 1960's. Although he is no Quaker and might not be too happy to be compared to Benezet, Stewart shares many of the earlier man's attributes—not the least of which is a genuine concern for the education of the children. Benezet, in the years after 1750, set out to write grammar books for English classes which would be simple enough to be useful in the instruction of his students; Stewart, in the 1960's, began to show the educational world how the modern techniques which had been developed for teaching English as a Second Language (ESOL— or English as a Foreign Language, TOEFL) were the most useful for teaching in this "quasi-foreign language situation." A pamphlet which Stewart edited, published in 1964 and entitled *Non-Standard Speech and the Teaching of English*, contained Stewart's own essay "Foreign Language Teaching Methods in Quasi-Foreign Language Situations," which first brought this approach to the attention of the academic world and which launched the District of Columbia Urban Language Study. Stewart aimed his discussion primarily at the disadvantaged Negro group, but most of his ideas and arguments would have applied to other minority groups, including those discussed herein. Sadly, the academic world was not ready for Stewart's ideas, and an early research and materials development project was kicked about and not given a chance to realize its potential. But Stewart's ideas have made a lasting impression upon many who have heard his brilliant expositions, public and private.

Implicit in this approach is the understanding that abstract grammatical knowledge—the ability either to parse sentences or to write rules to generate them as do the more modern linguists—is of no practical value in the actual use of a language. The person who is to be educated through the medium of a language (or dialect) must have the rules of that language or dialect *internalized*, so that he uses them automatically. It is not enough to be able to quote the rule after some thought; in language, if you have to stop to think, it's too late. (Many of us have rueful experience of the truth of this, gleaned from our first attempts to converse in a language in which we made all A's in college!)

As developed especially by the Foreign Service Institute of the Department of State and at universities like the University of Michigan, with its huge Foreign Student Program, during World War II and somewhat thereafter, the technique consists of intensive practice to the point of overlearning, so that the student is virtually unable to use a non-English response to the stimulus of an English conversation situation—even if he wants to. There are influential teachers, like Ralph B. Long of the University of Puerto Rico, who have objected to this technique essentially on the grounds that students are bored. But in the proper teaching environment, even boredom is an advantage: the student who "goes to sleep" repeating in class will develop the ability to respond "in his sleep" in English. Much has been written during the past few years about teaching Standard English as a second dialect by TOEFL methods. Kenneth Johnson has actually completed a University of Southern California dissertation, *Teaching Grammatical Structures* (1968), which shows the experimental success of such a program in the Los Angeles school system.

The linguistically sophisticated approach to Standard English as a Second Dialect (ESD) does not condemn the learner's other language or languages as "impoverished" or "inadequate." Occasionally unsophisticated teachers in the Southwest have tended to treat Spanish as though there were something wrong with it as a language—banning its use on the schoolground and even in Spanish classes, which once were typically presented by *gringos* unable to speak, write, or read Spanish—but this malpractice seems to be vanishing. As adopted for the teaching of Standard

English as a second dialect, the ESOL technique would be the very opposite of the remedial technique. A student would not be asked to give up his home or peer-group dialect as something shameful; rather, he would be taught Standard English—in the dialect most advantageous to him—as a second, alternate system. This seems, also, somewhat more equitable: the school system would make the student able to use a second dialect *if he chose to do so.* If he preferred not to use it outside school, no teacher could find fault with him. And no student would have to go through the pathetic process of confessing that he spoke "bad" English and was basically inferior to middle-class students in such a fundamental activity as language.

It is very important to distinguish between the approach to second-dialect teaching advocated by Stewart and Johnson and the superficially similar approach sponsored by some of the deficit theorists. It must be remembered that the Black children have a fully viable language system and—insofar as anyone can measure it in any valid way—a fully viable conceptual system. Teaching them to say

If he can go there, I'll see him

rather than

Can he go there, I'll see him

involves teaching a grammatical structure only—NOT the "concept of conditionality." Unfortunately, some educators have thought that, for example, drills teaching negative transformations are the equivalent of instruction in the "concept" of negation. Obviously, the Black child who says

Dat ain' no cup

has the "concept" of negation as well as the white child who says

That is not a cup.

All the child learns by mastering the second is the manner of expressing negation in a new dialect. Surely no one would assert that Greek or Swahili lacks the "concept of negation" simply because neither language expresses it with *not*.

One of the neat tricks which Stewart has used—especially at Columbia—is to turn the tables, to put teachers who have been imposing their own system upon disadvantaged children into the place of students who have to learn the Standard English grammatical system. Thus, the linguist-teacher would give the cue sentence

He sick.

and demand "Negative!" The accurate response would be

He ain' sick.

To the cue sentence

He be sick.

the correct "negative" response is

He don't be sick.

Or he will demand the co-occurrent adverbial expression *all the time*; the only grammatical usage in the Non-Standard dialect is

He be sick all the time.

With *right now*, on the other hand, the grammar demands

He sick right now.

He sick all the time and *He be sick right now* are unacceptable; the asterisk denotes ungrammaticality in Black English, which has its own grammatical rules.

The aim of this kind of drill is to instill in the teacher not only respect for the language of the Black child but also the knowledge—internalized, not just intellectualized—that there is structure to the dialect, that one does not automatically produce Negro Non-Standard English by simply breaking the grammatical rules of Standard English. Even more important, it aims to convey to the teacher the feelings of a student who finds that he must use a language system superficially similar to but fundamentally different from the one he normally produces, so that his automatic responses may be subject to condemnation.

One of the more interesting pedagogical experiments which has been performed was done almost entirely by Stewart, with some help in the programming operation by others. A tape was made to give the teacher the experience of learning to use the pronunciation patterns of Black English. In this case, the teacher-learner was required to put the indefinite article *a* before every noun—not to vary it with *an* according to the automatic Standard English pronunciation rule, even if the following word began with a vowel. Thus, the learner would be required to say *a egg* and *a elephant* as well as *a table* and *a tiger*. Learning to omit a distinction is just as hard, often even harder, than learning to make one; Spanish-speaking learners of ESOL have that kind of problem when they have to learn to say *they* in English whether Spanish would have *ellos* or *ellas*. Virtually everyone assumes that it helps an ESOL teacher of Spanish-speaking students to know Spanish—the more the better. Why should not a teacher of Standard English to Non-Standard–speaking students feel the same necessity to learn the language of his students? It is of primary importance that such materials, like all TOEFL materials, take the student's native language (here, dialect) into full account. Failure to do so is the defect in all such materials prepared so far.

Unfortunately, the number of teachers willing to sacrifice cherished, if inadequate, techniques is very small indeed, so that a gigantic program of teacher training must precede any really large-scale use of such techniques. Many are the teachers who derive a kind of compensation for their limitations from the belief that they are superior to their students in their "better" grammar. Such teachers are frequently unwilling to entertain the idea that the grammar of their students is not worse but only different. Africans have undoubtedly suffered more linguistically than any other people, just as they have suffered more in other respects. In the French Cameroun, for example, a polyglot Camerounian is often handicapped educationally because his French is not that of a native, while a monolingual Frenchman is among the educationally and linguistically advantaged. The same thing frequently happens on the islands of the Caribbean. Where the teachers represent the consensus culture—and most especially where the teachers are themselves not completely secure in that culture—minority groups are almost certain to suffer from discrimination in language matters.

Well-meaning teachers, eager to impart the advantages of mainstream language and culture to their students, frequently cling to teaching techniques which are questionable if not worthless. In order to teach children that "sounds have meaning," language arts teachers frequently use gimmicks like toy whistles and rattles. These teachers seem unaware of the fact that the average two-year-old knows perfectly well what those sounds mean—for his own culture. In the sense that he uses sound to produce a desired result, every infant learns that "sound has meaning" within the first few hours after his birth. Instruction in such matters is comparable to swimming lessons for fish. A national magazine ran an article in 1966 in which teachers were encouraged to teach the disadvantaged that "things have names." Undoubtedly, the three-year-old is in reasonably good control of this kind of esoteric information; the fact may be, of course, that he has *different* naming patterns from those of the dominant culture. Here, as in so many cases, difference from the middle class is interpreted as lack.

Misunderstanding of the grammatical patterns of the disadvantaged Negro's speech frequently leads to the conclusion that he has no grammar, a completely untenable position from the point of view of any linguist. The child who says *Mary hat* and *he book* has a possessive grammatical category (possession by juxtaposition) just as surely as the one who says *Mary's hat* and *his book*. Yet a widely used teaching device is to draw a picture of the hat on Mary's head in order to "show" the child that it is Mary's hat. One virtuosa of this technique, at a national teachers' meeting, actually had a color wheel which changed the color of the hat, presumably to demonstrate that the color did not affect the vital fact of possession. Another was convinced, because the Black-English-speaking child has a different prepositional system from that of Standard English (e.g., *put the cat out the house* instead of *put the cat out of the house, I'm goin' over Grandma's* instead of *over to Grandma's, She teach Francis Pool* instead of *she teaches at Francis Pool*), that the children did not understand locational relationships! Her teaching device was that of the infamous ducky wucky: she carried about with her a little plastic duck and a little plastic red barn, and demonstrated by saying, "Look, the duck is *under* the red barn" as she picked up the barn and put the duck beneath it, etc.

To make such mistakes about the function of human language is, quite plainly, to give short change to human intelligence; and all of these children are human and have human intelligence. They are certainly not non-verbal although they may not talk about the topic that an interviewer wants them to talk about. And being in a fancy office may intimidate them at times. But if a teacher, or a researcher, naively assumes that his patterns are the only patterns, he may be misled into finding these children "deficient" in language or behavior patterns.

It is much too easy to jump to conclusions about these children, on the basis of one or two observations, especially if the observer has no knowledge about their cultural patterns. One example of this stands out in my memory: when the Washington project gave a picnic for the children who were our informants, one of our aims was to involve them in a softball game. The response to the appeals of the linguists was meager, and one of the more athletic linguists wound up batting fungoes to the other. One observer immediately commented that the group lacked organizational ability; "A middle-class group would have had a game going by now," he commented. What he overlooked was that the group had immediately found a floor surface in a building on the grounds which was ideal for dancing and had also somehow managed to procure a radio. Before the observer had made his comment, they had lined up in two rows and were performing very complicated dance patterns—patterns which none of the whites present had any idea of how to participate in. Again and again, it needs to be emphasized that the ghetto child "does his own thing"—and that, when he does it, he is as efficient as the comparably performing middle-class child. But our culture gives low status to some of the things which the ghetto child does. In the Caribbean too, children toddle to the dance halls with their parents in the evening and learn the intricate West Indian dances in the best way—without knowing that they're learning anything. Unfortunately, the stereotype can say nothing about these culture patterns other than "Negroes have natural rhythm."

Where verbal production is concerned, it is quite clear that the white middle-class and Negro cultures differ in emphasis. American mainstream education aims at "precision" in the use of words, a plain utilitarianism which not only does not encourage fanciness but which practically rules out its possibility. The Afro-American tradition, as indicated in Chapter VI, has as a definite informal educational tradition, especially among males, the production of Fancy Talk. To some degree, perhaps in other areas than language, the Afro-American tradition emphasizes elegance, with a tendency to let a bit of exactness go by the boards if necessary. We all recognize this in jazz and other improvisational music, like Calypso, and the more enlightened among us tend to receive it with enthusiasm. But the kind of verbal elegantizing which results even in the extemporizing of poetry by athletes (where is the white boxer or athlete who ever made up poetry?) usually works to the detriment of those who have inherited its verbal tradition. It is perhaps a part of general American cultural insecurity that a person guilty of a slight malapropism may be considered to be ruined intellectually; Puddinhead Wilson, in Mark Twain's novel, is not the only American to suffer because a mildly playful use of languages was misunderstood by his neighbors. This is another case in which it seems worthwhile to recognize the Afro-American tradition for what it is rather than try to change it. We should remember that there was once a feeling that jazz musicians just didn't know how to play Tin Pan Alley tunes "straight."

It is far too easy to resort to pseudo-ecological explanations of cultural differences—to explain, for example, the language of ghetto children in terms of the poverty in which they live. It is for this reason that I have paid so much attention to historical background, in order to show that Negro Non-Standard English has developed by orderly historical processes, just as any other language or dialect does. (Pidginization-creolization-decreolization is an orderly process, although not all languages or dialects develop by this process.) Poverty, within a certain culture, may be a correlate of certain language and behavior patterns; it is probably never a natural or necessary correlate—and certainly not a cause. Since people poorer than U. S. ghetto dwellers are polyglots in many parts of the world, it seems absurd to trace any kind of "language deprivation" to ghetto poverty.

Language handicaps in education may take many forms. A student of mine who taught anthropology at a Negro university once wrote a term paper in which she analyzed her students' language in comparison to their success in giving the right answers to the questions. She found—not surprisingly when all the implications are concerned—that those whose language was most nearly Standard English made the lowest grades. Those whose writing had few or no Non-Standard structures tended to put down very little real anthropological material on the three-hour written examination—sometimes no more than a page or two. The reason does not seem difficult to determine: the ones who let themselves go grammatically and concentrated on what they wanted to say managed to get in some anthropology, if not much "grammar" by the standards of the average English teacher. Those who struggled with the unfamiliar system of Standard English were unable to concentrate on anything else and thus succeeded in writing very little. (The possibility should not be overlooked that there was an occasional student who didn't know the answers and tried to compensate by making the little bit that he wrote notably standard in grammar.) The teacher/student had not given any instructions concerning the type of English to be used, but a general atmosphere of struggling to write Standard English prevailed on the campus.

There are many reasons why, in the education of disadvantaged Negroes, the educational system should come to terms with the English they now speak. It is quite true, as opponents of tampering with the "standards" of college English have frequently pointed out, that the internalizing of the second system of Standard English would be more easily done in the early grades, or even in pre-school. This would seem, on the surface, to be a convincing argument: prepare the generation now about to enter school so that it can go through college, perhaps through graduate school, and into the professions. It is true that some Negroes already in high school might remain laborers even though they have the ability to become members of professions if given an even chance; but the extremely talented are already finding their way to the top, without any special consideration.

The specious factor here seems to be that someone is considering that the first big generation of Black professionals is going to find it easy to enter upon professional functions which have never been exercised by Negroes before, or very seldom. It is probably a great handicap to be thought of as a *Negro* lawyer, or dentist, or accountant rather than just as a member of those professions. Talented Negro artists, for example, have drawn a great deal of attention to their resentment of the ethnic modifiers which always go with their professional designations. Not only will the present group which is trying to find its way into the low-to-middle professional groups suffer now, but the pre-school group trained in Standard English would suffer when, at graduation and job-seeking time, it arrived to face a situation in which a Negro architect or engineer is pointed out as an oddity.

English is, of course, only one of the obstacles to be overcome by any aspiring professional who tries to make college his path of entry. But the freshman English course is notoriously one of the great causes of dropouts at the freshman college level. In the vast numbers of tiny colleges, some now beginning to call themselves "universities," which the great majority of Negroes must attend instead of Harvard or Berkeley if they wish to get the education which will qualify them for the professions, the freshman English course is often the only really difficult one in the curriculum. And English faculties at such colleges have been known to boast that they will continue to do their part in "keeping up standards," which usually means that they will strive to keep the number of failures in the freshman class as high and the grade-point averages as low as those at the nearby large university.

Educational standards are great things, and I am not in favor of relaxing them by passing every last student or by eliminating justly renowned classics from the reading lists. Neither is there anything to be gained by giving degrees to students of basket weaving. But it is not necessary to lower standards—in fact, it would be possible to *raise* more important standards—in order to adjust to some of the realities of the students' culture and background. In the case of many such colleges, "maintaining standards" is simply the prevalent euphemism for passing on unchanged the same stale information which the professors themselves got in college twenty years ago. Obviously, it would not be lowering the standards of an anthropology department to accept a brilliant paper in Spanish by a South American student, nor would the level of English Department term papers go down if really good critical papers in foreign languages were produced— if they could be read by the professors. In the same manner, although most teachers would need to acquire some linguistic sophistication and some knowledge of Negro Non-Standard English before they would be capable of evaluating really good papers in that dialect, the use of the student's native dialect could easily result in an upgrading rather than a lowering of standards.

It has too long been the pattern in English Departments that a professor assigns a "research paper" and then confines his grading to the search for a misspelled word, a comma blunder, a sentence fragment, or the like. Often, the punishment for one of those mistakes has been an automatic failing grade. It is doubtful that such procedures serve any purpose, except that once he succeeds in finding one of those sudden-death "errors" the professor can be relieved of the work of reading the remainder of the paper. A really good paper on ghetto conditions, even in Non-Standard English, would be far better than what ever comes out of most college courses. Of course, the professor would have to learn to restrain himself from marking "sentence fragment" and an automatic "F" when he read *I writin a paper about my home turf.*

Still, the real tragedy of the educational system, far worse than the freshman dropout rate, is the young Negro child who just never does learn to read. There are many of them, as we have become well aware in recent years. The dropout rate in the public schools is seriously affected by the loss of confidence which any student must suffer when he cannot read well enough to do his assignments in geography or history. Discouragement of this sort is, of course, not by any means the only cause of dropouts; there is no way of determining, *a priori*, whether it is more or less important than the other factors. But it has great influence.

The young speaker of Negro Non-Standard English must, as a first step in the educational process, learn to master the reading process, which, in the usual analysis, consists of learning to turn those strange (to any six-year-old) marks on the printed page into the sounds of his language. There is the trouble—*his* language. The child who looks at a sentence like

Here are a cat and a dog

is all set if his grammar will generate that sentence. But suppose his own structure is

Higo (perhaps from *here go*) a cat and a dog.

In the very first word or two he finds a basic mismatch, one which may even keep him from perceiving the principle which more or less comes through to speakers of Standard English—

that, despite the bothersome irregularities, there is some relationship between what is written down there and what he says. For
the child whose purposive future is

> Ima eat (some candy)

the sentence

> I will eat some candy

or even

> I am going to eat some candy

is full of possible disruptions.

Learning to read is a difficult enough process for any youngster;
but the standard-dialect-speaker who tackles the task usually finds
that there is a direct relationship between his speech and the
squiggles on the piece of paper. It may all seem stilted to him—
he probably never actually says "Run, Dick, run"—but his grammar is capable of generating the sentences contained on the page
even if they are not part of his everyday language behavior. If he
says [bəyd] (like a Brooklynite) or [bəhd] (like a Deep Southerner) for *bird*, he nevertheless has a directly analogous expression in his own language for

> Here is a bird.

More complicated syntactic structures usually respond to the
same kind of treatment. There are, of course, higher reading
skills—comprehension of complex texts, critical reading, scan-
ning—which many a speaker of the standard dialect never
masters. It's hard to say how one person acquires the ability
to express critical judgment of a library whereas another never
gets beyond bare decoding of the racing form. But the user of
"higher" reading skills must obviously have success with the
"lower" skills first.

Young speakers of Negro Non-Standard have a great handicap
in acquiring those more basic skills because of the very great
difference between the syntactic structure of their own language
and that of the printed texts which the school calls upon them to

read. In Washington, D. C., in 1964, I watched a teacher of an
allegedly retarded group of reading students deal with a boy who
looked at printed

> his brother

and responded with

> he buvva.

It really seems far-fetched to call this a reading error at all. The
boy had done what a reader is supposed to do: he had looked at
a group of symbols in one kind of code (which, among other
things, indicated a grammatical category of "possession") and
had translated it into his own spoken code (which also included
possession, but which marked it only by juxtaposition). The
teacher—unfortunately, it seems to me—chose to regard it as a
visual problem: "Don't you see the final -*s*?" Of course, a reader
isn't expected to "see" the medial -*s*- in island!

"Silent letters"—signs in the spelling which do not represent
anything in pronunciation—undoubtedly plague any child who is
learning to read. Children who speak Standard English may react
to words like *island*, as did one little girl of my acquaintance, with
"That's a toughie!" For the Non-Standard-speaking child, the
"silent letter" problem is greatly compounded. The word *ball*, for
example, doesn't have an *l* in the dialect; *fairy* and *furry* do not
contrast in Washington basilect. (Before this leads to any facile
conclusions of "language deprivation," remember that *bowels* and
vowels don't contrast for Spanish speakers.) *Des'* (Standard *desk*)
and *was'* (Standard *wasp*) don't have final consonants; instructed
to add something, the basilect speaker often guesses wrong: *dest*
and *wast*. Final -*st*, -*sp*, and -*sk* of Standard English are all -*s* in
basilect, and learning which consonant to add is like a foreign-
language learning problem, without any intimation from the
school system that that's what it is.

In 1966 and 1967, a literacy researcher in a Washington, D. C.
project conducted a long series of tests in which disadvantaged
Negro children read a text in Standard English. He found that,

very frequently, the mismatch between Standard English and the children's dialect accounted for the "mistakes." Because tense is not an obligatory category in their grammar (see pp. 49–50, Chapter II), they read

swam	as	swim
began	"	begin
knew	"	know
held	"	hold
helped	"	help
delayed	"	delay

and so forth. Being aware that some kind of process of putting -ed endings on verbs sometimes pleased teachers, among whom they undoubtedly classed the literacy researcher, they committed the opposite "mistake"; they added -ed endings where the written texts had none:

stop	as	stopped
bump	"	bumped

In some cases, they added not one but *two* inflectional endings:

stop, or stopped	as	stopted
bump, or bumped	"	bumpted

Like the boy in the "retarded" class, they frequently imposed the dialect's possession by juxtaposition on the Standard English materials, reading

Mr. Jackson's car	as	Mr. Jackson car

As might be expected, dialect pronunciations like [æks] for *ask* were frequent; these pronunciation features are relatively unimportant for the reading process, although snobbish listeners might subject them to ridicule. In the same class is the addition of a second inflectional suffix for the past tense. It is somewhat more difficult, however, to account for the following misreadings:

almost	as	also
Idaho	"	Indiana
traveled	"	television
wheels	"	weeds

But the verdict of "simple misreading" is an oversimplified one. The syntax of one's native language (or dialect) is so familiar that the reader is able to predict a great deal of what is to come even before it is audible or visible. This is a function of what the linguist calls *redundancy*—a technical term which has none of the opprobrium attached to it by schoolteachers and which explains how we are able to understand sentences which we have not heard plainly or to read paragraphs in which a great deal of the print has been scrambled. With a different syntactic system, the speaker of Black English has a different kind of prediction pattern because of his own language's redundancy structure—a pattern which is "wrong" when the norm is Standard English.

This is not historically new. In the Civil War period, a writer from Port Royal described how "Uncle Sam," an older Negro,

> . . . read the first three chapters of Genesis, which he translated into his own lingo as he went along, calling the subtle serpent the most "amiable" of beasts, and ignoring gender, person, and number in an astonishing manner. He says "Lamb books of life," and calls the real old Southern aristocracy the gentiles.
>
> (Elizabeth Ware Pearson, ed., *Letters from Port Royal*, p. 158)

This description, which does not pretend to be professional, is a better characterization, *mutatis mutandis*, of the problems of Negro children trying to learn to read today than virtually anything done by reading specialists.

Thus, a great many of the Black English speakers who try to become literate in Standard English—from "Uncle Sam" to the children whom we tested on the Washington project—are "partial" readers. They are undoubtedly the ones that school principals are referring to when they talk of the average student in a certain school being a certain number of years "below the national average" in reading.

Learning to read in Black English would be much easier. Stewart's new organization, the Education Study Center in Washington, D. C., which has as its first project a program in teaching ghetto children to read, has produced three textbooks (*Ollie, Friends*, and *Old Tales*) in parallel Black English and Standard English versions. The near future should produce some experimental evidence as to the validity of the approach. In principle, once the beginning reader has learned the principle of correspondence between written letters and spoken language, transition to the reading of Standard English should be much easier. (Practically speaking, the main reason for the transition to Standard English is that there is little or nothing written in Black English.) It is obvious that a person who is literate in English does not have as far to go in learning to read French as does a person who not only does not speak French but does not know how to read his native English. The new project should produce evidence bearing on the proposition, violently opposed by some reading specialists, that the same principle can be applied to the Black English–Standard English situation.

The other possibility is to teach the child Standard English as a second system and then teach him to read—starting the instruction in Standard English and utilizing the same techniques that are used for middle-class youngsters. In the absolute sense, this is probably a weaker educational technique than the one advocated by Stewart and Baratz. On the other hand, it may be more acceptable to PTA's, school boards, etc., which are very likely to be afflicted with purist ideas and to resent the use—no matter how sensible—of Non-Standard English in the classroom. In order to be implemented with any effectiveness whatsoever, this technique needs to follow the teaching of Standard English according to ESOL techniques *in the preschool.* If the student must learn both Non-Standard and Standard English at the same time, he will certainly proceed at a slower rate than the student learning to read in his own language system.

If duckie-wuckies are bad language-teaching tools—and if plastic barns and color wheels are not much better—are there no special techniques for teaching Standard English to speakers of Black English beyond the ESOL drills referred to above? Suppose a school system has money for a laboratory—can it not find some practical use to which the machines could be put? Of course it can. But, especially if the students are very young, it had better take a close, hard look at the conditions under which children learn language. There seems to be evidence everywhere, particularly in the Black culture with its high degree of age-grading (see pp. 234–238), that children learn languages best at play with members of their peer group. Recordings of Standard English spoken by children the same age as the learners—or just a tiny bit older—would probably be ideal. Sex-grading has to be taken into account: will little boys be willing to learn seriously from records made by little girls, or by boys who impress them as being "sissies"? For a long time Ralph B. Long of the University of Puerto Rico has recommended closed-circuit television and movies of children at play for effective ESOL teaching on the island, and there seems to be good reason that they might prove effective in an ESD situation. But television shouldn't be considered some kind of miracle worker; the hoariest stereotype of them all is that ghetto children spend a vast amount of their time looking at television and still don't learn Standard English from it. (The actual time they spend may be exaggerated sometimes, but clearly many of them do spend a lot of time looking at it.) The activities must be of a type in which the children could really be engaged. The reason why children do not learn language from television is at least partly that they filter out the activities on the screen as not really relevant to them. When *Batman* was a big item on television, twelve- and thirteen-year-old boys in the Washington ghetto developed their own little chant with "Batman!" as a one-word refrain. It can't be quoted here, but it had nothing to do with the plot of the TV show!

One of the clear facts which emerges from a great deal of research in dialectology is that people are often exposed to dialects over long periods of time without learning them. The pedagogue's usual answer is "motivation"; the social dialectologist says "rules of behavior" (not necessarily *conscious* rules). One simple factor, either way you look at it, is that a child may or may not want to imitate the behavior of another person whose speech is held up to him as a model. Does it seem reasonable to conclude that poor Southern Negroes are going to be eager to imitate the pronunciation of well-off Southern whites? Well, recent studies indicate that Southern Negroes much prefer the consensus standard (herein called Network Standard, after Stewart) to the "educated" dialect of upper-crust local whites. The Negroes who did the evaluating in a project in Tougaloo, Mississippi,[5] reacted *indirectly* to a test of their language attitudes. Questioned directly about his language and his attitudes toward other language, the human being is much too subject to rationalizations to be depended upon to give valid answers. Like grammar, a certain part of language attitude is *out of awareness*. But, in a sophisticated experiment by psychologists Wallace Lambert and Richard Tucker, Mississippi Negro college freshmen showed a preference for Network Standard English on every one of the fifteen indices of the rating scale. Incidentally, white Northerners had an only slightly less striking preference for Network Standard, even in comparison to educated white Southern speech. The Negroes, as a matter of fact, rated the speech of educated Southern whites lowest among the varieties they were asked to choose from.

In many cases, the dialect held up to the integrating school child as the means of classroom integration is one to which he has an emotional aversion, since he may have good reason to hate some people who talk that way. Given a strong enough emotional impulse, a child in a multilingual household will sometimes even refuse to learn its mother's language. There are real reasons, much more relevant than the myths of "thick lips" or "isolation," that explain the Negro's not learning the dialect of Southern whites in slightly over a hundred years since the Civil War. "Motivation"—so often thrown around meaninglessly where language learning is concerned—takes on a new, objective significance in terms of such studies. Much care must be taken to match the target dialect to the dialect which the disadvantaged child is motivated to learn and therefore may reasonably be expected to learn.

According to Yeshiva University sociolinguist Joshua Fishman, the important basis for a nationwide speech community is symbolic identification with the nation. The community that identifies itself as speakers of Network Standard is of this sort. Participants in a national culture are likely to speak a national dialect; isolated groups with no hope of upward mobility are not likely to feel the need for such a national consensus dialect. In this sense, the preference of the Negro community for the regionally neutral dialect signals more hope for integration on a truly nationwide scale than might be expected in these days of Black Separatism. At least in their aspirations, this puts part of the Negro community among those who are inclined to meet together in urban centers, participate in education and technology, and in general indulge in the type of social mixing which goes with social mobility. Those people who have no interest at all in integration at the national level—or who have decided that they have no opportunity to participate at a national level in the culture of the United States—might be expected to retreat into a preference for a local or in-group dialect. The latter tendency shows up, as a matter of fact, in the preference of the Tougaloo community for both educated and uneducated Mississippi Negro dialect over local educated and uneducated white speech. But the fact that the Network Standard is strongly preferred to all the others seems to indicate, insofar as linguistic evidence may be interpreted in the matter, that the door to nationwide integration is still open. It should be obvious for many reasons that integration at the Mississippi level is becoming less of a possibility with the passage of every day.

Many are the well-intentioned people who are misguided in their attempts to devise something for the education of disadvantaged children. I know a Negro educator who, while fully convinced that language difference is a deterrent to the learning of reading, remains convinced that the disadvantaged children are also "deficient in concepts." He would delay the teaching of reading until the third grade, meanwhile giving the children instruction in Standard English and "concept building." Then, in the third grade, he would begin reading instruction—using Standard English.

While it is undobutedly true that any kind of realistic program aimed at teaching Standard English by some effective technique would improve the education of those children, it seems likely that the time devoted to "concept building" would simply be wasted. There is no evidence whatsoever, except the faulty evidence of culturally biased tests, that the disadvantaged child has fewer concepts than the middle-class child. (The decision as to whether the set of concepts possessed by one is superior to the set possessed by the other can be made only in terms of a value judgment. If, for example, a poor man has a concept called "poverty" and a rich man has a concept called "wealth," can we say that one or the other is a more complete master of his concept? Or that the concept accompanied by money is *ipso facto* better *as a concept*?) There is undoubtedly a certain strangeness for city ghetto children to read of ducklings and moo-cows in the first grade, but can we seriously maintain that ducklings and moo-cows are somehow "richer" concepts than subways and skyscrapers? There is something wildly absurd about certain "enrichment" programs which aim to acquaint the ghetto child with farm animals, and the children generally know it. Today, even a farm child is likely to be confused by the vocabulary of a sentence like

Oh, see the vixen.

Cultural conflict is an obstacle which is finally beginning to be appreciated at all levels of education, but the effect of the student's learning patterns on his "teachability" is still infrequently taken into account. In the small countries of Burundi and Rwanda, for example, teachers of ESOL using widely distributed (and generally well-designed) textbooks have found a major obstacle—the lessons treat of actions which the Africans do not like to discuss in public. In most parts of the world, food is more or less neutral culturally, and illustrations of the difference between count nouns and mass nouns (*a flower* but *some flour*) may be effectively presented and practiced in terms of meals (*The Smiths are having some eggs for breakfast; Do you ever have any cereal for breakfast?*) In the two countries in question, there is a revulsion against eating in public—and against talking about it. It probably does not help much that the elaborate meals described are beyond the reach of the Africans.

In this specific instance, there is an easily available solution to the cultural problem. These Africans think nothing of public drinking or of talking about alcoholic beverages. (It is interesting that this is virtually the exact reverse of the situation in the United States during Prohibition, when a radio comedian could produce laughter from his audience simply by saying the word "Beer.") A teacher can easily learn to take his examples from drink rather than from food (*some wine, some whiskey; Do you ever drink any cognac at a party?* etc.) Such quick, easy solutions are not always apparent in the case of cultural mismatch between reading materials and the Negro Non-Standard-speaker of the ghetto, but basic common sense could probably find some solutions. *John and Mary are dancing* is probably better than *John and Mary are riding in a fox hunt*. "Cultural enrichment" is hardly a compensating counter-argument. Can we seriously say that anyone suffers much from not having gone on a fox hunt, or that knowledge about fox hunting will enable the child to appreciate masterpieces of art or literature? On the other hand, the teacher probably should not let illusions of knowledge about the ghetto tempt him into using sentences like *John and Mary are smoking pot*.

In order for the teaching procedure, especially in the vital early years, to be fitted to the child's own cultural background, it is obviously quite important for the teacher to know something of that background. Now, no one seriously expects that graduate students seeking teaching certificates are going to allow themselves to be bitten by rats in order to understand the children who have been so bitten. (On the other hand, recent decentralization movements seem to suggest that ghetto parents are tired of having their children taught by people without those experiences.) At the very least, couldn't they read about such experiences? English majors, even those in programs especially designed for the disadvantaged, often find themselves furiously concentrating on the biography of Milton, or on Dryden textual criticism, in order to prepare to teach in the inner city. Why couldn't they read Richard Wright, James Baldwin, Ralph Ellison, Claude Brown, LeRoi Jones, Victor Hernandez Cruz, and many others from relevant backgrounds with relevant things to say? Are there no problems of textual criticism for any of these authors?

The vaunted standards of English departments would not be in the least endangered by the inclusion of some Negro authors. Charles W. Chesnutt, to take an obvious example, has written novels which are far superior to many of the things labeled Schoolboy Classics. A person could spend a lifetime reading Black authors and not come across anything as bad as the mawkishly sentimental works of O. Henry and Bret Harte which are a standard part of many high school curriculums.

And it is possible to find out a great deal about the American Negro and his background by choosing some white authors who are studied relatively infrequently. William Gilmore Simms, George Washington Cable, and Lafcadio Hearn have written, with varying degrees of perception but at their best with a great deal indeed, about the Negro in the United States in the last century. Why, instead of eternally reading about Benjamin Franklin walking down the streets of Philadelphia with a loaf of bread under each arm, don't our schoolboys learn how he and other early American leaders reacted to the slave trade? Why is reading about "Bonny Barbry Allen" a better approach to learning about folk song than reading—and hearing—"The Boll Weevil Song"? For that matter, why are the songs of the Wandering Scholars, though they are excellent and productive of a healthy new look at accepted standards, any better than blues lyrics, which show how a subculture reacts to its predicament in verse? And there's the added advantage that anyone with a little ingenuity or even a fair phonograph can come closer to a real perception of what the blues are about than the most renowned scholar could possibly come to the *Carmina Burana*.

Despite some recent changes, it is a rare graduate school that includes courses on Negro folk blues, Caribbean Calypso, and traditions such as the dozens, toasting procedures, rifting, the Caribbean Anansi ("Nancy") stories, and the related American trickster tales (told well by Joel Chandler Harris but also available from many other sources). The University of Puerto Rico, for example, proved to be more concerned that its English majors know about minor American authors than that they know about the oral literature of the islands which surround what is not quite a suburb of New York City. Some of the materials would be a bit strong for the squeamish who grew to understand the language—but so would Shakespeare's version of *Romeo and Juliet*, for that matter.

Why must most conferences on the teaching of disadvantaged children be conducted as though it were impossible for any teacher to enroll in an anthropology course? The concept of cultural relativity, upon which the concept of linguistic relativity must ultimately depend, is a very old one now. Why is it that it still seems shockingly new to almost the entire world of teachers? Many an English major can identify the author of "Thou shalt not commit a social science," but few of them seem to realize that they can acquire a nodding acquaintance with a field without "committing" it.

Traditional preparation in English language for teachers is no more praiseworthy, and can hardly be recommended. The teacher who takes a course in dialectology at most of our nation's institutions will come away with the impression that the only variations of any importance concern the variation between [s] and [z] in *greasy* and the use of *snake doctor, mosquito hawk,* and *dragon fly* for a spectacularly unimportant insect. Standard works on American dialects, particularly those put out by the National Council of Teachers of English, either ignore the matter of Negro Non-Standard English entirely or specifically deny that there is any such dialect. Recent publications purporting to treat "social dialects" are strongly biased against recognition of ethnic and other social variation in American English. Lack of study of dialects may be a positive virtue for the teacher, unless perhaps he has access to Stewart's courses at Columbia University.

A great deal has been done and is being done to bring linguistics to teachers, as though it were a panacea for pedagogical
troubles. I wish to suggest that the promise of such programs is
usually not fulfilled. The accurate study of linguistics is a highly
technical pursuit, and few are those who can impart anything to
the average teacher without distorting the content of the discipline beyond all recognition. Furthermore, the Linguistics for
Everybody approach at NDEA Institutes and other such fashionable summer activities virtually precludes any specially useful information being transmitted to any one group.

The teacher who learns Transformational-Generative analysis
or some other current grammatical practice at a summer institute
should beware of inflicting his new knowledge *directly* upon his
charges. Parsing sentences, by any method whatsoever, is of
doubtful utility in imparting practical language skills; one of the
noticeable features of ESOL courses is that, while the teachers
are expected to have analytical knowledge and even skill, the
students of the foreign language are not asked to do any analysis.
The learning of a language—or dialect—is distinct from learning
the grammatical terminology applied to that dialect; difficult as
it may sometimes be for the teacher to suppress his knowledge,
it is often advisable. It is only the insecure teacher who needs
to overwhelm his students with a display of his own erudition.

In dealing with speakers of Black English, it is, however, frequently useful to call attention to the students' language and to
point out its differences from Standard English. Surprisingly few
of the students who have been exposed to such practices have
shown any resentment, in our experience. (It is presupposed, of
course, that the teacher will not call Black English "bad" or
"incorrect," and that he will not attribute it to any physical or
genetic characteristics.) A healthy expression of interest on the
part of the teacher—supposing that the interest is genuine—is a
very good device for establishing rapport with the students and
for making them "language conscious."

In the final analysis, it seems impossible that anything of
pedagogical value can be accomplished without a recognition of
the differences (and of course the similarities) between Black

English and Standard English. In the case of newly integrated schools it sometimes seems a shame to separate white and Negro students, even for the brief period necessary to give special language drills to one group; but the period can be brief. Actual classroom experiments tend to show that five to ten minutes is ideal. In 1970, especially in a place like New York City with its emphasis on decentralization of the school system, it begins to seem that the Black community will no longer insist so strongly on integration—that it may actually seek its equality in a new kind of segregation. If autonomous local Black communities attain control of their own school systems, there seems to be no reason whatsoever to believe that they would object to special teaching procedures for Black-English-speaking children. The distinct possibility remains, however, that they may seek standardization of Black English instead of attempting to teach their children any current brand of Standard English.

As the Tougaloo experiment shows clearly, speakers of Black English are unlikely to want to identify linguistically with speakers of "regional" dialects, especially in the South. The alternative may be either a standardized Black English or a dialect of Standard English. The former alternative, although paralleled in a country like Norway, would involve more elaborate pedagogical changes than anything hinted at here and might be too much for the linguistically simple United States. For the less disruptive latter alternative, the Network Standard dialect, for which both white and Black speakers have shown marked preferences, is obviously the preferable target dialect. In New York City, as in Tougaloo, Blacks continue their preference for the Network Standard dialect and continue to react with special antipathy to forms which they identify with the Lower South.[6] Linguistic evidence shows that Blacks, unwilling to integrate to local patterns associated with long periods of snobbery, rejection, and worse, are more likely to be willing to integrate into some nationwide norm. This almost seems like the last alternative to Black Separatism in language and behavior—a pattern which is already widely advocated in the Black community but which could have regrettable consequences to the nation as a whole. Since Network

Standard dialect is the most neutral dialect we have—since learning it does not involve taking on identity with any white ethnic group—it seems to be the dialect which will continue to appeal to Negroes who are simply fed up with the notion that Black behavior patterns should give way to white ones.

There always remains the possibility, hinted at already, that the Black community, disenchanted with pretenses at desegregation and with the white man's attempts—futile and weak even on the part of liberals—to bring about social justice, may stop seeking to adjust itself to mainstream (white) culture. In that case, the teaching of Standard English to Black speakers may be rejected no matter what the method. And in that case a new use of Black English as a vehicle of education will become imperative. It seems inescapable that the Black community has the right to make its own choice, particularly in view of the white community's poor record of accomplishment in Negro education in the past decade. The consequences would be even more far-reaching: exact knowledge about Black English (which would be a more likely term than Negro Non-Standard in such an eventuality) would become, if possible, even more vital to the Negro community and to its educators. It might even come about, in some areas, that white children would need to learn Black English—by ESOL techniques of course—in order to be able to integrate themselves into Black-dominated school systems. And this new minority might just as well be prepared to hear statements like "The white knows nothing and can learn nothing."

NOTES

[1] See Brookes, *Friend Anthony Benezet* (Bibliography).

[2] See Section II of Bibliography for a list of research reports. The evaluations of Joan and Stephen Baratz are especially important for this problem.

[3] Dr. Joan C. Baratz is co-director (with William A. Stewart) of the Education Study Center in Washington, D. C. For her especially important writings in criticism of the "deficit" theory of Black English, see Section II of Bibliography.

[4] For natural rapidity of the child in native-language acquisition, see Noam Chomsky, *Language and Mind* (1969); Eric Lenneberg, *Biological Foundations of Language* (1967); and any other of the many recent treatments of language acquisition. The bibliography in the recent Berkeley *Field Manual for Cross-Cultural Study of the Acquisition of Communicative Competence* (1967) is excellent for references up to that date. For a glaring example of failure to understand this characteristic of native-language acquisition, see Hurst (Bibliography, Section II).

[5] Wallace E. Lambert and G. Richard Tucker, "White and Negro Listeners' Reactions to Various American-English Dialects" (Bibliography).

[6] William Labov et al., *A Study of the English of Negro and Puerto Rican Speakers in New York City*, I, pp. 21–22.

GLOSSARY

ACROLECT, a term coined by William A. Stewart, is used for the collection of linguistic features of most prestige among a given community of speakers. It is best understood with reference to its opposite, BASILECT (q.v.).

ATTESTATION means an occurrence of a language form in written sources. If a historical form, the existence of which is suspected on comparative grounds, is found in a reliable written source, it is said to be *attested*. If there are no such occurrences, it is hypothetical.

BASILECT, also coined by Stewart, is the term for the collection of linguistic features which has least prestige in a given community of speakers. The term, like ACROLECT (q.v.), is most useful in a situation like that of the Black-Standard English relationship in the United States, where the most "extreme" form of Black English can be called basilect. In some polyglot situations, the speech variety of least prestige is simply the language of the poorest group. In the American Black community, where prestige language still involves adaptation toward white norms, Black children are the principal speakers of basilect. A sentence like
  We don't suppose to go
is more nearly basilect than
  We ain't supposed to go
and is more characteristic of younger speakers, even though the second sentence would not be called Standard English by most Americans.

CHILD LANGUAGE is a term of convenience used to refer to what are really several stages in the acquisition of language. From the inception of speech, roughly at the age of two, until about five, the child is said to be in a stage of language acquisition and to speak child language. Although the community itself usually believes that child language is inaccurate imitation of adult speech, recent studies show that this is not literally true. Child language should be distinguished from "baby talk," which is what adults use to infants or to very young children (or in lovemaking, etc.), and which is not very much like the sounds made by a baby or by a child—except in the adult's imagination. This book does not deal with child language in this sense. This use of the term should be kept carefully distinct from the occasional use of the term "child Black English" (see Houston, Bibliography, Section III), which refers to what is called simply Black English herein.

CREOLE, in linguistic usage, refers to a language which was a PIDGIN (q.v.) at an earlier historical stage, but which became the only (or principal) language of a speech community. The best known creoles are Haitian (French) Creole and Sranan Tongo of Surinam. There are related creole languages in West Africa and in the Pacific.

CREOLIST refers to a linguist who specializes in the study of CREOLE (q.v.) languages.

DIALECT, as used in linguistics, has none of the opprobrium attached to the term in such popular phrases as *dialect comedy*, etc. It is a collection of IDIOLECTS (q.v.); that is, the speech pattern of a number of individuals whose language is similar in some significant way. (There have been few, if any, attempts to determine quantitatively the degree of similarity necessary.) In the usage of a restricted number of linguists, dialect refers to a set of features delimited geographically; *sociolect* to a socially distributed set. This terminology is avoided in this book, because of my belief that the geographic factor in language variation has been greatly overemphasized.

DIALECT LEVELING is the process of eliminating prominent, stereotypable features of difference between dialects. This process regularly takes place when speakers of different dialects come into some new phase of contact, such as in migration. (Speakers of different dialects may be in some stable contact situation, with well-defined social roles, for long periods without appreciable leveling.) The extreme case of dialect leveling is a KOINÉ (q.v.)

DIGLOSSIA means the use of different languages (or dialects) for different purposes. When a New York Puerto Rican discusses business in English—even with other Puerto Ricans—but uses Spanish for home affairs, he is engaging in diglossia. The term is thus more specialized than the better-known *bilingualism*.

DIGLOSSIC is the adjectival form of DIGLOSSIA (q.v.).

ENCLITIC, in this particular book, refers only to an added vowel which produces a consonant-vowel sequence (*house* becomes *housee* or *houso*). Other meanings, as in Classical Greek grammar, do not need to be considered here.

IDIOLECT is the characteristic speech pattern of an individual. It is customarily used to refer to the native language of a monolingual speaker. Under the most minute analysis, each speaker is to some degree unique in all aspects of his usage—syntactic and semantic as well as the "vocal fingerprinting," which has recently become such a familiar phonological example. There are, however, common features between idiolects; otherwise, no one would understand anyone else. Linguistics, which concerns itself with the social factor of communication, seeks out the common features of idiolects and ignores, to some degree, the differences. A collection of idiolects (in the strictest sense, any two or more) with sufficient common features is a DIALECT (q.v.).

INTERFERENCE is the influence of one language system on another —usually a subsequently learned system. Native speakers of Spanish, for example, tend to use *assist* in English for *attend* ("I assisted the concert last night") because of the meaning of *asistir* in Spanish.. Native speakers of German tend to use *already* when speaking English more than do native speakers of English, because its equivalent, *schon*, occurs more frequently in German.

ISOGLOSS, in a system of dialectology which I believe to be obsolescent, referred to an imaginary line which divided dialect features. If Southern speakers pronounce *greasy* with [z] and Northern speakers pronounce it with [s], then the isogloss runs roughly along the Mason-Dixon line. Of course, the factors of language variation are always more complicated than this. *Isogloss* seems to have developed by analogy with *isotherm*, etc., and to be thus an attempt to achieve a "scientific" character for the study of language variation by treating it as though it were something physical.

KOINÉ is the term for a "common" dialect which lacks the prominent features of the more conventional dialects of a language. It is the end résult of DIALECT LEVELING (q.v.). Impressively often, the koiné is characterized by the speakers of a language as "good" speech in that language. It tends to be required of actors (as in Stage German—*Bühnenaussprache*) or television announcers (Network Standard English in the United States). A koiné is often also a STANDARD (q.v.) dialect, but there is no necessary identity between the two.

LANGUAGE ACQUISITION or NATIVE LANGUAGE ACQUISITION refers to the process of learning to speak like the adults of a given community. Most studies of language acquisition assume that it occurs between the ages of two and five (sometimes six). Later developments, like age-grading, are not regarded as being part of language acquisition. It should be emphasized that every child (aside from pathological cases such as severely retarded or brain-damaged children) goes through this process. The rate of development, furthermore, seems to be more constant than is popularly believed. The acquisition of a second (or foreign) language is in many ways different from native language acquisition!

LINGUA FRANCA is a language used for purposes of wider communication, especially in a group when the native language of no member of the group will suffice. If a Puerto Rican, a German, an Israeli, and an Icelander speak to each other in English, then English is being used as a lingua franca. The Mediterranean *lingua franca* known as Sabir was an outstanding example of such a language. A *lingua franca* which has no native speakers (like Sabir, but unlike English) is a PIDGIN (q.v.).

PHONOLOGY is the systematic study of the sound patterns of language—either language in general in terms of "universal" phonology or of an individual language. Linguists would be furious at the following statement, but the average reader can probably substitute *pronunciation* for phonology without much distortion of anything in technical works on linguistics. There are many theories of phonology, and many phonologies of Standard English.

PHONOLOGICAL is the adjectival form of PHONOLOGY (q.v.).

PIDGIN refers to a language which has no native speakers. It thus exists only as LINGUA FRANCA (q.v.). When the pidgin becomes the only language of a speech community, it then becomes a CREOLE (q.v.). Pidgin languages are not necessarily used by inept speakers ("Me Tarzan; you Jane"), as anyone who has ever bargained with a West African trader knows. In a sense, a pidgin is to languages what a KOINÉ (q.v.) is to dialects—it dispenses with the unusual features which speakers from a great variety of languages would find strange or difficult to learn.

RELEXIFICATION is the replacement of a vocabulary item in a language with a word from another, without a change in the grammar. If I change the sentence

> I am very tired

to

> I am très tired

I have in a sense relexified the English sentence. A "Latin" sentence like

> ego amo tu

is of course simply a relexification of

> I love you

with Latin words.

A STANDARD language (or dialect) is one which has achieved official recognition in terms of having written grammatical descriptions (especially if they prescribe "correct" usage), dictionaries, and printed works with complete expositions (not just passages of dialogue) in the language. A speaker is not ashamed to use the forms of the standard dialect in public (as on the radio or on television), but he may feel subject to ridicule if he uses forms which are not recognized as standard. A standard dialect is often a KOINÉ (q.v.), although not necessarily.

STANDARDIZATION is the process of producing a STANDARD (q.v.) language or dialect. Note that it refers to social attitudes toward the language, and not to grammatical structure.

STYLE refers, as it is used by linguists, to variation in terms of formality, not to the literary sense of "excellence in expression" or the like. We can easily identify about four everyday stylistic levels in Standard English:

> Formal—I do not know
> Semi-formal—I don't know
> Casual—I dunno
> Intimate—a series of (unspellable) nasal sounds, usually accompanied by a shrugging of the shoulders and intelligible to the immediate family of the speaker

There are also rather unnatural, even stilted, styles:

> Indeed, I know not

as well as literary styles, which often tend to draw upon all five of these levels of formality.

VARIETY is a relatively neutral designation for something between a language and an IDIOLECT (q.v.). A DIALECT is, thus, a VARIETY; but a VARIETY is not necessarily a DIALECT. Those sociolinguists who continue to use DIALECT in a geographic sense sometimes use VARIETY in referring to social variation. (*Sociolect* and *genus* are also sometimes so used.)

APPENDIX

On the Pronunciation
of Black English

THERE are, of course, certain pronunciations characteristic of Black English at its various stages. The usual procedure is to deal with those characteristics first—and, indeed, to deal with them to the extent of omitting everything else (see, for example, Susan Houston, in Bibliography). The intention in this book has been to reverse that procedure—to slight pronunciation matters, if necessary, in order to insure that other aspects of Black English might be dealt with.

One of the disadvantages of dealing with phonology first has been that it has seemed to give some support to the "thick lips" fallacy; if phonology is the determining characteristic of the dialect, then it is only one brief misstep to the conclusion that physical characteristics of Blacks are the source of the dialect difference. Beyond that misplaced physiology, there is still the fallacy of a kind of racial "carelessness" in pronunciation—sometimes rationalized as being due to the apathy of lower-status human beings or to "not having been taught any better." Even some dedicated Black educators have fallen victim to that error. Finally, in the current state of analysis of Black English, we must perforce deal in differences from Standard English; the result is that, even involuntarily, we tend to deal in terms of what is "lost" from Standard English. It would take a much more complete phonological analysis than now exists to enable us to deal concretely with what has been "gained"—in other words, with what Black English has that other varieties of English do not have.

A thorough evaluation of phonological structures in Black English, according to current linguistic theory, can be undertaken only after more basic syntactic and morphological problems have been solved. A dissertation by Philip A. Luelsdorff (see Bibliography) has just appeared which is very strong in this theoretical sense. However, some spectrographic analysis—still too rudimentary to be reported here—has convinced me that there are differences which would not have been available to Luelsdorff's impressionistic transcription procedure, admirable as his accomplishment is in terms of such procedures.

Several features are often noted among Negro Non-Standard-speaking populations. It should be kept in mind that there is a great deal of phonological variation within those populations—much more than there is in syntax—and that these generalizations are perhaps not exclusively valid even for any one speaker.

(1) Vowels in General:

The low front vowel [a] (in addition to the low mid-to-front vowel [a] as in *father* in most American white dialects) is present in most versions of Black English. It also occurs in Southern white dialects, and may have spread to them from Black English. This vowel is between the [a] of *hot* and the [æ] of *cat*; even when lengthened, it sounds like the vowel of *cat* or *cap* to many speakers of Standard English. A New York teacher, for example, recently commented that she had "discovered" an unexpected "new homophone pair"—*island* and *Allen*—in Negro Non-Standard. Although the homophone set of Negro Non-Standard is different from (and almost certainly no greater than) that of Standard English, these two are not examples; [a·lən] contrasts with [ælən], but some speakers of Standard English can't hear the difference. Turner (*Africanisms in the Gullah Dialect,* p. 16) shows that this distribution is found in Gullah and in several West African languages.

The lengthened [a·] of *island* in Black English is, of course, [ay] ("long *i*") in Standard English. This "replacement" by Black English is shared with many Southern white dialects. Any theory of the direction of influence would require long and careful consideration. In some places (e.g., the Washington, D. C., Black community) there is less tendency to this phonological development before voiceless consonants [ptk] than before voiced consonants [bdg]; that is, the [a·] sound will occur in *ride* but the [ay] sound in *write*. The more extreme forms of Black English have the "substitution" everywhere. Black English vowels, like Southern white dialects, have a marked tendency to lengthen:

[pɪ·g] for [pɪg] *pig*

(2) The initial "th" of *the, then, that, those, though, there, this, these* is pronounced as [d]. (This feature is "shared" with certain Northern dialects, where any but the most incidental connection is extremely unlikely.)

(3) Final "-th" of *with, both, birth, mouth, truth,* etc., is sometimes pronounced as [f]. (This is an elegantizing pronunciation within Negro Non-Standard; the less elegant form is pronunciation with [t]. White dialects have the "substitution" of either [t] or [f], but not the stylistic relationship in which [t] is inelegant and [f] elegant. The pronunciation [θ], as in Standard English, is usually about equally elegant.)

(4) Medial "th" of *mother, other, brother* (always voiced [ð] in Standard English, not voiceless [θ], is pronounced as [v]. (This results in occasional dialect spellings such as *Move of God* in a store-front church name, where mainstream culture has *Mother.*) There is something of a stylistic alternation with [d], as in (3).

(5) Final [r] is "dropped," as in many other dialects of English; but, in the Black community, this persists in geographic areas which do not have the feature otherwise. Even in the South, it is more widespread among Negroes than in the white community—leading to amusing explanations about how the Negro imitated the whites "only more so." There has long been speculation about how Plantation Creole/Black English speech habits (although not called by those names) may have been the influencing factor in the Southern dialect, and not "r-dropping" British dialects; the more reasonable answer probably prefers a combination of the two, although it is absurd to speculate in Tower of Babel style about the "first" speaker who "lost" an [r]. Afro-American dialects of English, and even of French, have this same feature. The "r-dropping" is also common in certain North-eastern United States dialects—which, however, often have a differ-ence in the existence of "intrusive" [r] (*idear of it*).

In at least some versions of Black English, intervocalic [r] is "dropped," so that

mad	[mæd]
mired	[ma·d]
married	[mæ·id]

differ only in the vowel nuclei (which are so much alike, from the viewpoint of Standard English, that distinctions are not easily made). Farrison's dissertation (p. 259) records [æš] 'Irish.' Jamaican English also has this "r-loss" feature (Cassidy, *Jamaica Talk*, p. 59). *Harry* differs from *hay* mainly in the articulation of the first vowel. Cassidy cites the "local pronunciation of *Carolina*" (*Ca'lina* or /kælaynə/), apparently as proof that American white dialects do the same thing; however, the shwa vowel [ə] was very probably "lost" before the [r] in that local white pronunciation, making it a simple case of "r-dropping" before consonant [1]. There has yet to be advanced any convincing proof that the Southern English "dropping" of pre-consonantal [r] has anything to do with the U. S. situation. Of course, it is possible to treat this phenomenon in more detail than simple talk of "r-dropping" (there are various degrees of retroflexion of the tongue or of other structures which are more accurate designations than mere "loss"); these phenomena are subject to exact phonological study, but the studies have not so far been performed.

(6) The plural -es following a final -s (pronounced as a vowel plus [z] in Standard English), will have a plural which is a long [s]; [wɔs] 'wasp' will have the plural [wɔs·] (or [wɔss]). This is a feature of some white Southern dialects (including my own small-boy dialect). It is essentially grammatical, not automatically phonological, in scope; i.e., it does not occur with verbs like *races* but only with nouns like *races*.

(7) Stress patterns differ from those of Standard English. Thus,

> Joe sent mé

which in Standard English would mean 'me especially' or 'me and not someone else,' has no special emphasis on the object pronoun in Black English. The function of stress (prominence—even loudness—on given syllables) is different from that of Standard English, but has not been seriously investigated.

(8) The range of vocal pitch, excluding falsetto, is probably greater. No more has been done on this, so far, than the collection of a few impressionistic statements.

Several features often referred to pronunciation are really matters of lexicon rather than of phonology. Thus, the base forms of Black English are

> des'
> was'
> aks

(the apostrophes in the first two words are used only because the reader may not be used to seeing *des*, etc., in print) rather than

> desk
> wasp
> ask

Basilect speakers who are aware of the existence of an extra consonant in the first two words, in other varieties of English will often strive to add that consonant. Since it is not part of their underlying system, they produce

dest
wast

as often as they produce *desk* and *wasp*. (It is data like these which show us that the Black English forms are not merely casual style forms, like those of speakers of other varieties who produce *des'* and *was'* when speaking casually and *desk* and *wasp* when speaking more formally.)

In initial position [st-] and [sk-] have a slightly different articulation from that of Standard English. Code-switching, or some other process not so far examined, produces an occasional form like *skrong* for *strong*.

A phonological characteristic of Plantation Creole, found still in Gullah and sporadically in other forms of Black English, is the voiced bilabial fricative written [β] by phoneticians. This sound is very unusual to most English speakers (although they may have heard it between vowels in some varieties of Spanish), and it has caused endless difficulties to writers who have attempted to represent Black English in conventional orthography. Machine analysis reveals a more complicated sound, in some environments, which can be written [βbβ]. Dialect fiction writers traditionally varied in their rendering of Black pronunciations of a word like *heavy*: reacting to the fricative characteristics of the first and last of the three elements [β . . . β], they sometimes wrote *heawy*; perceiving the closure feature of the medial element [b], they sometimes wrote *heaby*; and sometimes they simply gave up and wrote it the Standard English way, *heavy*. (The fact that Black English speakers, in code-switching, sometimes pronounced the word in the Standard English way didn't make their tasks the least bit easier!) Many writers, over a period of something like two hundred years, have represented Black English pronunciations in this way, and many of the citations in this book show that practice. At times, it has caused confusion and has led to the conclusion that the writers were simply distorting Standard English. In the case of the minstrel show writers and a few other less responsible ones, this may very well be true. There is, however, a more respectable basis for the practice as systematically handled. Farrison's dissertation, *Phonology of the Illiterate Negro Dialect of Guilford County, North Carolina* (1936) shows such pronunciations as [βɛri] for *very*, [ouβa] for *over*, [ɛβə] for *ever*, [hɛβiweit] for *heavyweight*, [muβment] for *movement*, etc.

Pronunciation "problems" of Black children have motivated some
of the greatest pedagogical blunders of all. Speech correctionists, mis-
taking the pronunciation patterns of Negro Non-Standard for the
genuine deficiencies of the physiologically handicapped (cleft palate,
etc.) children with whom they are qualified to work, have extended
their own practices to areas in which they are not applicable. Black
children who already do so quite well are "taught" to make sounds like
"Oom" in weekly practice sessions. The Washington *Post* for December
22, 1968, pictured a little boy, six years old at the most, with his
cheeks puffed full of wind, enthusiastically participating in the weekly
session. It is to be hoped that the children derive some pleasure from
this activity, since it has no practical language value. There is no
phoneme of English which requires that the cheeks be puffed full of
wind, and it is unlikely that there is any other language which utilizes
such an articulation in its structure.

It is also to be observed that pronunciation, more obviously variable
than any other part of language except perhaps vocabulary, is less
consistent on a nationwide scale than the other features of Black
English. In New Orleans, for example, Black English speakers, like
lower-class white speakers, have "boid" [bɔyd] for *bird*; there is no
evidence I am aware of that Negro speakers in Brooklyn do the same
thing, but social relationships between Black and white are quite
different there. In many places, Black English pronunciation has
obviously been influenced by white non-standard dialects. Yet the
ethnic differences remain; one of my earliest memories of Negro dialect pronunciation is of a group of barbers in a small-town Texas shop
who loved to encourage the Negro shoeshine "boy" to talk about a
certain football game in order to ridicule his pronunciation *pena'ty*
(penalty). The poor fellow joined in happily with them, thinking
that they were laughing with him over the perfidy of referees.

BIBLIOGRAPHY

I. STUDIES OF BLACK ENGLISH

Bailey, Beryl Loftman. "A New Perspective on American Negro Dialec-
tology." *American Speech* XL, No. 3 (1965): 171–177.
————. "Some Aspects of the Impact of Linguistics on Language
Teaching in Disadvantaged Communities." *Elementary English*
45 (1968): 570–577.
Dalby, David. "The African Element in Black American English," in
Thomas Kochman (ed.), *Rappin' and Stylin' Out*, University of
Illinois Press, 1972.
————. *Black Through White: Patterns of Communication in Africa
and the New World*. Hans Wolff Memorial Lecture. Bloomington,
Ind.: 1969.
Dillard, J. L. "The Writings of Herskovits and the Study of New
World Negro Language." *Caribbean Studies* IV, No. 2 (1964):
35–42.
————. "The English Teacher and the Language of the Newly
Integrated Student." *Teachers College Record* 69:2 (1967):
115–120.
————. "Negro Children's Dialect in the Inner City." *Florida FL
Reporter* 5, No. 3 (1967).
————. "Negro Nonstandard Dialects: Convergence or Diver-
gence?" in *Afro-American Anthropology*, edited by Szwed and
Whitten. New York, 1970.
————. "The Creolist and the Study of Nonstandard Negro Dialect
in the United States." In *Pidginization and Creolization of Lan-
guages*, edited by Hymes. London, 1970.
————. Review of *Language Teaching, Linguistics, and the Teach-
ing of English in a Multilingual Society, Caribbean Studies* Vol. 8,
No. 1 (April 1968): 62–65.

——————. "Black English in New York." *The English Record* (Spring, 1971).

——————. "On the Beginnings of Black English in the New World." *Orbis* (1972).

Fickett, Joan G. *Aspects of Morphemics, Syntax, and Semology of an Inner-City Dialect, "Merican."* West Rush, New York, 1970.

——————. "Tense and Aspect in Black English." Unpublished.

Houston, Susan H. "A Sociolinguistic Consideration of the Black English of Children in Northern Florida," *Language* Vol. 45, No. 3 (September, 1969).

Labov, William. *A Study of the Non-Standard English of Negro and Puerto Rican Speakers in New York City*, Cooperative Research Project No. 3288, 2 vols. Mimeographed. 1968.

——————. "The Non-Standard Negro Vernacular: Some Practical Suggestions." In *Position Papers from Language Education for the Disadvantaged*, Report No. 3 of the NDEA National Institute for Advanced Study in Teaching Disadvantaged Youth, June 1968.

——————. "The Reading of the -ed Suffix." In *Basic Studies in Reading*, edited by H. Levin. 1970.

——————. "Rules for Ritual Insults." In *Language and Expressive Role Behavior in the Black Inner-City*, edited by T. Kochman. Chicago, 1970.

——————. "Contraction, Deletion and Inherent Variability of The English Copula." *Language* (December 1969).

——————. "Stages in Acquisition of Standard English." In *Social Dialects and Language Learning*, edited by Shuy. Champaign, Ill.: NCTE, 1965.

——————. "Some Sources of Reading Problems for Negro Speakers of Nonstandard English." In *New Directions in Elementary English*, edited by A. Frazier. Champaign, Ill.: NCTE, 1967.

——————. "Linguistic Research on the Non-Standard English of Negro Children." In *Problems and Practices in the New York City Schools*, edited by A. Dore. New York, 1965.

——————. "Reflections of Social Processes in Linguistic Structures." In *Readings in the Sociology of Language*, edited by Joshua A. Fishman. The Hague, 1968.

——————. *The Study of Non-Standard English*. Washington, D.C., 1969.

——————. "Variation in Language." In *The Learning of Language*, by Carroll Reed. Champaign, Ill.: NCTE, 1970.

—————— and Cohen, Paul. "Systematic Relations of Standard and

Non-Standard Rules in the Grammars of Negro Speakers." In *Project Literary Reports* No. 8, Ithaca, N. Y., 1967.

————, Cohen, Paul, Robins, Clarence, and Lewis, John. *A Preliminary Study of the Non-Standard English of Negro and Puerto Rican Speakers in New York City.* U. S. Office of Education Cooperative Research Project No. 3288, New York, 1965.

Loflin, Marvin D. "A Note on the Deep Structure of Nonstandard English in Washington, D.C." *Glossa*, 1, No. 1 (1967).

————. "On the Structure of the Verb in a Dialect of American Negro English." *Linguistics*, 1969. [A slightly different version of this paper was distributed as Technical Report No. 26, Center for Research in Social Behavior, University of Missouri, 1967.]

————. "On the Passive in Nonstandard Negro English." *Journal of English As a Second Language* 4 (1969): 19–24.

————. "Negro Nonstandard and Standard English: Same or Different Deep Structure?" *Orbis* XVIII (1969): 74–91.

————. "A Teaching Problem in Nonstandard Negro English." *English Journal* (December 1967): 1312–14.

Luelsdorff, Philip A. *A Segmental Phonology of Black English.* Ph.D. dissertation, Georgetown University, 1970.

Mitchell, Henry H. "Black English," in *Black Preaching.* Philadelphia and New York, 1970.

Mitchell-Kernan, Claudia. *Language Behavior in a Black Urban Community.* University of California, Berkeley, Language-Behavior Research Laboratory Working Paper No. 23, 1969.

Silverman, Stuart Harold. *The Effects of Peer Group Membership on Puerto Rican English.* Ferkauf Graduate School of Yeshiva University dissertation. 1971.

Stewart, William A. "Urban Negro Speech: Sociolinguistic Factors Affecting English Teaching." In *Social Dialects and Language Learning*, edited by Shuy. NCTE, 1964.

————. "Foreign Language Teaching Methods in Quasi-Foreign Language Situations." In *Non-Standard Speech and the Teaching of English*, edited by Stewart. Washington, D. C., 1965.

————. "Partial Non-Standard Verbal Paradigm." 1966. Mimeographed.

————. "Sociolinguistic Factors in the History of American Negro Dialects." *Florida Foreign Language Reporter* Vol. 5, No. 2 (1967), pp. 11–29.

————. "Continuity and Change in American Negro Dialects." *Florida Foreign Language Reporter* Vol. 6, No. 2 (1968), pp. 3–14.

————. "Non-Standard Speech Patterns." *Baltimore Bulletin* of *Education*, 43 (1967), pp.2–4, 52–65. [Epitome of transcripts from a series of lectures.]

————. *Language and Communication in Southern Appalachia.* Washington, D. C., 1967 (ERIC report No. ED 012 026).

————. "Sociopolitical Issues in the Linguistic Treatment of Negro Dialect." Report of the 20th Round Table, Georgetown University, 1970.

————. "Historical and Structural Bases for the Recognition of Negro Dialect." Report of the 20th Round Table, Georgetown University, 1970.

————. "Language Learning and Teaching in Appalachia." *Appalachia*, 4 (1971).

————. "Facts and Issues Concerning Black Dialect." *The English Record* (Spring, 1971).

Turner, Lorenzo Dow. *Africanisms in the Gullah Dialect.* Chicago, 1949.

————. "Notes on the Sounds and Vocabulary of Gullah." *Publications of The American Dialect Society* No. 3 (May 1945).

II. THE DEPRIVATION CONTROVERSY

Abrahams, Roger D. "Black Talk and Black Education." In *Linguistic-Cultural Differences and American Education*, edited by Aarons, Gordon, and Stewart. Miami, 1969.

Anastasi, Anne, and D'Angelo, Rita. "A Comparison of Negro and White Pre-School Children in Language Development and Goodenough Draw-a-man I.Q." *Journal of Genetic Psychology* 81 (1952), pp. 147–165.

———— and de Jesus, Cruz. "Language Development and Nonverbal I.Q. of Puerto Rican Children in New York City." *Journal of Abnormal Psychology*, 48, No. 3 (1953): 357–366.

Ausabel, David P. "How Reversible Are the Cognitive and Motivational Implications for Teaching the Culturally Deprived Child?" *Urban Education* I (1964), pp. 16–38.

Baratz, Joan C. "Who Should Do What to Whom . . . and Why?" In

Linguistic-Cultural Differences and American Education, edited by Aarons, Gordon, and Stewart. Miami, 1969.

————. "Language in the Economically Disadvantaged Child: A Perspective." *ASHA* 10 (1968), pp. 143–145.

————. "Language and Cognitive Assessment of Negro Children: Assumptions and Research Needs." *ASHA* 11 (1969), pp. 87–91.

————. "A Bidialectal Task for Determining Language Proficiency in Economically Disadvantaged Children." *Child Development* 40, No. 3 (September 1969), pp. 889–901.

————. *Language Abilities of Black Americans: Review of Research, 1966–1970.* Mimeographed. 1971.

————. "The Social Pathology Model: Historical Bases for Psychology's Denial of the Existence of Negro Culture." *APA,* 1969.

———— and Baratz, Stephen. "Early Childhood Intervention: The Social Science Base of Institutional Racism." *Harvard Educational Review,* 1970.

———— and Baratz, Stephen. "Urban Education: A Cultural Solution." *The Bulletin of the Minnesota Council for the Social Studies* (1968), pp. 1–4. [Reprinted as "Negro Ghetto Children and Urban Education: A Cultural Solution." In *Social Education* 33 (1969), pp. 401–405.]

Baratz, Stephen. "Social Science Strategies for Research on the Afro-American." In *Black Americans,* edited by J. Szwed. 1970.

————. "The Effects of Race of the Experimenter, Instructions, and Comparison Populations Upon the Level of Reported Anxiety in Negro Subjects." *Journal of Personality and Social Psychology* 7 (1967), pp. 194–198.

Barth, Ernest A.T. "The Language Behavior of Negroes and Whites." *Pacific Sociological Review* 4 (1961), pp. 69–72.

Bereiter, C. E. "Academic Instruction and Preschool Children." In *Language Programs for the Disadvantaged,* edited by Corbin and Crosby. *NCTE,* 1965.

Bernstein, Basil. "Elaborated and Restricted Codes. Their Social Origins and Some Consequences." In *The Ethnography of Communication,* edited by J. Gumperz and D. Hymes. 1964.

————. "Language and Social Class." *British Journal of Sociology* 11 (1960), p. 271.

————. "Linguistic Codes, Hesitation Phenomena, and Intelligence." *Language and Speech* 5 (1962), pp. 31–46.

————. "Social Class and Linguistic Development: A Theory of Social Learning." In *Economy, Education and Society,* edited by Halsey, Floud, and Anderson. New York, 1961.

Bing, Elizabeth. "Effect of Childrearing Practices on Development of Differential Cognitive Abilities." *Child Development* 34 (1963), pp. 631-648.

Brewer, John M. "Ghetto Children Know What They're Talking About." *New York Times Magazine* (December 25, 1966).

Bull, W. A. "The Use of Vernacular Languages in Fundamental Education." *International Journal of American Linguistics* 21 (1955), pp. 288–294.

Carson, Arnold S. and Rabin, A. J. "Verbal Comprehension and Communication in Negro and White Children." *Journal of Educational Psychology* 51 (April 1966), pp. 47–51.

Casler, Lawrence. "Material Deprivation: A Critical Review of the Literature." *Society for Research Child Development Monograph* 26 (2), 1961.

Cattell, R. B. "Are I.Q. Tests Intelligent?" *Psychology Today* 1 (1968), pp. 56-62.

Cazden, Courtney. *Environmental Assistance to the Child's Acquisition of Grammar*. Ph.D. Dissertation, Harvard University (unpublished), 1965.

Cohen, S. Alan. "Visual Perceptual Problems in Disadvantaged Children." In *Teach Them All to Read: Theory Methods and Materials for Teaching Disadvantaged Children*. New York, 1969.

——————. "Some Learning Disabilities of Socially Disadvantaged Puerto Rican and Negro Children." *Academic Therapy Quarterly* 2 (1966): 37–41.

Davis, Allison, and Havighurst, H. J. "Social Class and Color Differences in Child-rearing." *American Sociological Review* 11 (1946): 698–710.

Deutsch, M. "The Disadvantaged Child and the Learning Process." In *Education in Depressed Areas*, edited by A. H. Passow. New York, 1963.

——————. "The Role of Social Class in Language Development and Cognition." *American Journal of Orthopsychiatry* 25 (1965).

——————. "The Verbal Survey." *American Journal of Orthopsychiatry* 34 (1964): 213–214.

——————. "Minority Group and Class Status as Related to Social and Personality Factors in Scholastic Achievement." *Applied Anthropology Monograph* No. 2. Ithaca, N. Y., 1960.

—————— and Brown, B. "Social Influences on Negro-White Intelligence Differences." *Journal of Social Issues* 20 (1964): 24–35.

——————, Fishman, J., and Whitman, M. "Guidelines for Testing Minority Group Children." *Journal of Social Issues* 20 (1964): 129–145.

Dillard, J. L. Reveiw of Frederick Williams (ed.), *Language and Poverty. Language* (1972).

Dreger, Ralph M. "Hard-hitting Hereditarianism." *Contemporary Psychology* XII, No. 2 (February 1967).

Eells, K. W., et al. *Intelligence and Cultural Differences.* Chicago, 1951.

Higgins, C., and Silvers, Cathryne M. "A Comparison of the Stanford Binet and the Colored Raven Progressive Matrices I.Q. for Children with Low Socio-economic Status." *Journal of Consulting and Clinical Psychology* 22 (1968): 465–468.

Hunt, J. M. "The Psychological Basis for Using Pre-School Enrichment As an Antidote for Cultural Deprivation." *Merrill-Palmer Quarterly* 10 (1965): 209–248.

Hurst, Charles G., Jr. *Psychological Correlates in Dialectolalia.* Howard University Communication Sciences Research Center, 1965.

Iscoe, Ira, and Pierce-Jones, John. "Divergent Thinking, Age and Intelligence in White and Negro Children." *Child Development* 35 (1964): 785–797.

Jensen, Arthur R. "How Much Can We Boost IQ and Scholastic Achievement?" *Harvard Educational Review*, 1969.

————. "Social Class and Verbal Learning." In *Race, Social Class, and Psychological Development*, edited by Deutsch, Jensen, and Pettigrew. 1969.

———— and Rohwer, William D., Jr. "Syntactic Mediation of Serial and Paired-Associate Learning as a Function of Age." *Child Development* 36 (1965): 601–608.

John, Vera P. "The Intellectual Development of Slum Children." *American Journal of Orthopsychiatry* 33 (1963): 813–822.

————. "A Study of Sequential Speech in Young Children." *Project Literacy Reports* No. 2 (1964).

Johnson, Kenneth R. "The Influence of Nonstandard Negro Dialect on Reading Achievement." *The English Record* (Spring, 1971).

Jones, Arlynne Lake. *An Investigation of the Response Patterns Which Differentiate the Performances of Selected Negro and White Freshmen on SCAT.* Ph.D. dissertation, University of Colorado (unpublished), 1960.

Keller, Suzanne. "The Social World of the Urban Slum Child: Some Early Findings." *American Journal of Orthopsychiatry* 33 (1963): 823–831.

Kellmer, M. L. Pringle, and Tanner, Margaret. "The Effects of Early Deprivation on Speech Development." *Language and Speech* 1 (1958): 269–287.

Labov, William, and Robins, Clarence. "A Note on the Relation of

Reading Failure to Peer-Group Status in Urban Ghettos."
Teachers College Record 70 (1969): 395–405.

McQuown, Norman A. "Language-Learning from an Anthropological
Point of View." *Elementary School Journal* 54 (1954): 402–408.

Makita, K. "The Rarity of Reading Disability in Japanese Children."
American Journal of Orthopsychiatry 38 (1968): 599–614.

Newton, Eunice S. "The Culturally Disadvantaged Child in Our
Verbal Schools." *Journal of Negro Education* 31 (1962): 184–187.

————. "Planning for the Language Development of Disadvantaged
Children and Youth." *Journal of Negro Education* 33 (1964):
264–274.

Pasamanick, B. "Comparative Psychological Studies of Negroes and
Whites in the United States." *Psychological Bulletin* 59 (1962):
243–247.

————. "The Contribution of Some Organic Factors to School
Retardation in Negro Children." *Journal of Negro Education* 27
(1958): 4–9.

———— and Knobloch, Hilda. "Early Language Behavior in Negro
Children and the Testing of Intelligence." *Journal of Abnormal
Psychology* 50 (1955): 401–402.

Riesmann, Frank. "The Overlooked Positives of Disadvantaged
Groups." *Journal of Negro Education* 33 (1964): 225–231.

Sherwood, J., and Natapsky, M. "Predicting the Conclusions of Negro-
White Intelligence Research from Biographical Characteristics of
the Investigators." *Journal of Personal and Social Psychology* 8
(1968): 53–58.

Shuey, Audrey. *The Testing of Negro Intelligence.* 2nd ed. 1966.

Stewart, William A. "On the Use of Negro Dialect in the Teaching
of Reading." In *Teaching Black Children to Read,* edited by
Shuy and Baratz. Washington, D.C., 1969.

Stodolsky, S. S., and Lesser, G. "Learning Patterns in the Disadvantaged." *Harvard Educational Review* 37 (1967): 546–593.

Taba, Hilda. "Cultural Deprivation as a Factor in School Learning."
Merrill-Palmer Quarterly 10 (1964): 147–159.

Temple, Truman R. "A Program for Overcoming the Handicap of
Dialect." *The New Republic* (March 25, 1967): 11–12.

Templin, Mildred C. *Certain Language Skills in Children: Their
Development and Interrelationships.* Institute of Child Welfare
Monograph Series No. 26 (1957).

Wu, Jing-Jyi. "Black and White: Some Yellow Views." Forthcoming.

————. "Wanted: More Cross-Cultural Research in Education."
Educational Leadership 27 (1969): 165–171.

Zach, Lilian. "The IQ Test: Does It Make Black Children Unequal?" *School Review*, February 1970.

III. SOURCES AND GENERAL BACKGROUND

Aarons, Alfred C.; Gordon, Barbara Y.; and Stewart, William A., eds. *Linguistic-Cultural Differences and American Education*. Miami, 1969.

Abrahams, Roger D. *Deep Down in the Jungle*. Hatboro, Pennsylvania, 1964.

——. "Playing the Dozens." *Journal of American Folklore* XXV (1962): 209–220.

——. "Public Drama and Common Values in Two Caribbean Islands." *Trans-Action* (July–August 1968), pp. 62–71.

——. "The Shaping of Folklore Traditions in the British West Indies." *Journal of Inter-American Studies* (July 1967), pp. 456–480.

——. "Speech Mas' on Tobago." In *Tire Shrinker to Dragster*, Texas Folklore Society Publication XXIV, pp. 125–144.

——. "Traditions of Eloquence in Afro-American Communities." Forthcoming.

Adams, Edward C. L. *Congaree Sketches*. Chapel Hill, North Carolina, 1927.

——. *Nigger to Nigger*. New York, 1928.

Adams, Nehemia. *The Sable Cloud*. Boston, 1861.

Alegría, Ricardo. *La Fiesta de Santiago Apóstol en Loiza Aldea*. Madrid, 1954.

Allen, Virginia French. "Teaching Standard English as a Second Dialect." *Teachers College Record* LXVIII (February 1967): 355–70.

Allen, W. F., Ware, C. P., and Garrison, L. M. *Slave Songs of the United States*. New York, 1965.

Allsopp, S. R. R. *Expression of State and Action in the Dialect of English Used in the Georgetown Area of British Guiana*. Ph.D. dissertation, University of London (unpublished), 1962.

Andrews, Charles. *Colonial Folkways. A Chronicle of American Life in the Reign of the Georges*. New Haven, 1920.

Angell, Rose. *Osceola, A Great American*. Kissimmee, Florida, 1944.

Aptheker, Herbert. *American Negro Slave Revolts, 1526–1860*. New York, 1939.

Armstrong, Orlando Kay. *Old Massa's People*. Indianapolis, 1931.

Asbury, Herbert. *The Barbary Coast*. New York, 1933.

Ashe, Thomas. *Travels in America*. London, 1808.

Atkins, John. *A Voyage to Guinea, Brazil, and the West Indies*. London, 1732.

Atwood, E. Bagby. *A Survey of Verb Forms in the Eastern United States*. Ann Arbor, Michigan, 1953.

Bailey, Beryl L. *Creole Languages of the Caribbean*. Master's essay, Columbia University (unpublished), 1953.

————. *A Language Guide to Jamaica*. 1962.

————. *Jamaican Creole Syntax*. London, 1966.

Baker, G. Ray. *The Red Brother and Other Indian Stories*. Ann Arbor, Michigan, 1927.

Baldwin, James. *The Blues for Mr. Charlie*. New York, 1964.

Bancroft, Frederic. *Slave Trading in the Old South*. Baltimore, 1931.

Bank, Frank T. "Plantation Courtships." *Journal of American Folklore* VII (1894): 147–149.

Baratz, Joan C., and Shuy, R. W. *Teaching Black Children to Read*. Washington, D.C., 1969.

————, Shuy, Roger W., and Wolfram, Walter. *Sociolinguistic Factors in Speech Identification*. Final Report, NIMH Grant No. 15048. 1969.

Barbot, John. *Description of the Coast of North and South Guinea; and of Ethiopia Inferior, Vulgarly Angola*. London, 1732.

Barnes, James. *Doctor Snowball: A Negro Farce*. New York, 1897.

Barrow, David C. "A Georgia Corn-schucking." *Century Magazine* II (1822): 872–878.

Bartlett, John Russell. *Dictionary of Americanisms*. New York, 1848.

Bascom, William R. "Acculturation Among the Gullah Negroes." *American Anthropologist* (January–March 1941): 43–50.

Beach, L. *Jonathan Postfree*. New York, 1807.

Beck, Robert (pseudonym Iceberg Slim). *Pimp, The Story of My Life*. Los Angeles, 1967.

————. *Trick Baby*. Los Angeles, 1968.

————. *Mama Black Widow*. Los Angeles, 1969.

Bennett, Isidora. "Lang Syne's Miss, the Background of Julia Peterkin, Novelist of the Old South." *Bookman* 69 (1929): 357–366.

Bennett, John. "Gullah: A Negro Patois." *The South Atlantic Quarterly*. Part I, October, 1908; Part II, January, 1909.

Bernard, J. R. L-B. "On the Uniformity of Spoken Australian English." *Orbis* XVIII (1969): 62–73.

Berreman, Gerald D. "Caste in India and the United States." *American Journal of Sociology* Vol. 66 (1960–61): 120–127.

Bettelheim, Bruno. *The Children of the Dream*. New York, 1969.

"Black Watch of Texas." San Antonio *Express*, November 16, 1924.

Blair, Lewis H. *The Prosperity of the South Dependent Upon the Elevation of the Negro*. Richmond, Virginia, 1889.

Blok, S. P. "Annotations to Mr. L. D. Turner's *Africanisms in the Gullah Dialect*." *Lingua* VIII (1959): 306–321.

Bolingbroke, Henry. *A Voyage to the Demerary*. Philadelphia, 1813.

Botkin, B. A. *Lay My Burden Down: A Folk History of Slavery*. Chicago, 1945.

————. *A Treasury of Mississippi River Folklore*. New York, 1955.

————. *A Treasury of American Folklore*. New York, 1944.

————. *A Treasury of Southern Folklore*. New York, 1964.

Bowers, Claude G. *The Tragic Era*. New York, 1929.

Brackenridge, Hugh Henry. *Modern Chivalry*. Philadelphia, 1792.

Brackett, Jeffrey A. *The Negro in Maryland*. Baltimore, 1889.

Brawley, Benjamin G. *A Short History of the American Negro*. New York, 1921.

Brevard, Carolyn Mays. *History of Florida*. Delano, Florida, 1924.

Brewer, John Mason. *Negrito, Negro Dialect Poems of the Southwest*. San Antonio, Texas, 1933.

————. *American Negro Folklore*. Chicago, 1968.

————. "Afro-American Folklore." *Journal of American Folklore* 60 (1947): 377–383.

————. *Dog Ghosts and Other Texas Negro Folk Tales*. Austin, 1958.

Briggs, Dolores G. *Deviations from Standard English in Papers of Selected Alabama Negro High School Students*. Ph.D. dissertation, University of Alabama (unpublished), 1968.

Briggs, Olin Dewitt. *A Study of Deviations from Standard English in Papers of Negro Freshmen at an Alabama College*. Ph.D. dissertation, University of Alabama (unpublished), 1968.

Brookes, George S. *Friend Anthony Benezet*. Philadelphia, 1937.

Brookes, Stella Brewer. *Joel Chandler Harris, Folklorist*. Athens, Georgia, 1950.

Brooks, Cleanth. *The Relation of the Alabama-Georgia Dialect to the Provincial Dialects of Great Britain*. Baton Rouge, Louisiana, 1935.

Broom, Leonard, and Glenn, Norval O. *Transformation of the Negro American.* New York, 1965.

Brown, Claude. "The Language of Soul." *Esquire LXIX* (April 1968).

Bruce, Philip Alexander. *Economic History of Virginia in the Seventeenth Century.* New York, 1896.

Butcher, Margaret J. *The Negro in American Culture.* New York, 1956.

Butler, Melvin A. *Lexical Usage of Negroes in Northeast Louisiana.* Ph.D. dissertation, University of Michigan (unpublished), 1968.

Cable, George Washington. In *The Negro Question, A Selection of Writings on Civil Rights,* edited by Arlin Turner. Garden City, N. Y., 1958.

————. *Creoles and Cajuns.* Garden City, N.Y., 1959.

————. "Creole Slave Songs." *Creole Century Magazine* XXI (April 1886): 807–828.

————. "The Dance in the Place Congo." *Century Magazine,* February 1886.

Calkins, Frank W. *Tales of the West.* Chicago, 1893.

Carawan, Guy, and Carawan, Candie. *Ain't You Got a Right to the Tree of Life.* New York, 1967.

Carmer, Carl Lanson. *Stars Fell on Alabama.* New York, 1934.

Carmichael, Mrs. A. C. *Domestic Manners and Customs in the West Indies.* 2nd ed. London, 1834.

Cassidy, Frederic Gomes. *Jamaica Talk; Three Hundred Years of the English Language in Jamaica.* London, 1961.

————. "Toward the Recovery of Early English-African Pidgin." *Symposium on Multilingualism,* Brazzaville, 1962.

————. "Multiple Etymologies in Jamaican Creole." *American Speech* (October 1966): 211–215.

————. "Some New Light on Old Jamaicanisms." *American Speech* (October 1967).

————. "Iteration as a Word-Forming Device in Jamaican Folk Speech." *American Speech* XXXII (1957): 49–53.

———— and LePage, Robert B. *Dictionary of Jamaican English,* London, 1967.

Chamberlain, Alexander F. "Algonkian Words in American English: A Study in the Contact of the White Man and the Indian." *Journal of American Folklore* 15 (1902): 240–267.

Chesnutt, Charles W. *The Conjure Woman.* Boston, 1899.

————. *The Marrow of Tradition.* Boston, 1901.

Child, Mrs. Lydia M. "The Quadroon" and "Black Saxons." In *Fact and Fiction.* New York, 1867.

"Chinese Theatres." *Appleton's Journal of Popular Literature, Science, and Art* IV (24 September 1870): 373–374.

Christopherson, Paul. "Some Special West African Words." *English Studies* (1953).

————. "A Note on the Words DASH and JU-JU in West African English." *English Studies* (1959).

Clark, Lewis. *Narrative of the Sufferings of Lewis Clark, during a Captivity of More than Twenty-five Years, Among the Algerines of Kentucky, dictated by himself.* Boston, 1845.

Clemens, Samuel Langhorne. "Fenimore Cooper's Literary Offenses." *Works, Author's National Edition,* Vol. XXII.

————. *In Defense of Harriet Shelley and Other Essays.* New York, 1918.

Cohen, Inez Lopez. *Our Darktown Press.* New York, 1932.

Cohen, Octavus Roy. *Dark Days and Black Knights.* New York, 1923.

————. *Polished Ebony.* New York, 1919

————. *Florian Slappey Goes Abroad.* Boston, 1928.

Collymore, Frank C. *Notes for a Glossary of Words and Phrases of Barbadian Dialect.* Bridgetown, Barbados, 1957.

Combs, J. H. "A Word List from Georgia." *Dialect Notes* Vol. 5 (1922): 183–184.

Commonwealth History of Massachusetts. New York, The States History Cl., 1927–28.

Conrad, Earl. "The Philology of Negro Dialect." *Journal of Negro Education* XIII, No. 2 (Spring 1944).

Cooper, James Fenimore. *The Deerslayer.* Philadelphia, 1841.

————. *Redskins; or Indian and Injin.* New York, 1846.

————. *Satansoe; or the Littlepage Manuscripts.* New York, 1845.

————. *The Spy.* New York, 1821.

Courlander, Harold. *Negro Folk Music, U. S. A.* New York, 1963.

————, collector. *Negro Folk Music of Alabama.* Recorded in Alabama and Mississippi. Ethnic Folkways Library FE 4417–18, 4471–74.

Crane, Stephen. *The Monster and Other Stories.* New York, 1899.

Craven, Wesley Frank. *The Southern Colonies in the Seventeenth Century.* Baton Rouge, Louisiana, 1949.

Cremony, John C. *Life Among the Apaches.* San Francisco, 1868.

Crèvecoeur, Michel Guillaume Jean de. *Letters from an American Farmer.* London, 1782.

Criswell, Robert. *Uncle Tom's Cabin Contrasted with Buckingham Hall.* New York, 1852.

Cruikshank, J. Graham. *Black Talk; Being Notes on Negro Dialect in British Guiana.* Demarara, 1916.

Crum, Mason. *Gullah, Negro Life in the Carolina Sea Islands.* Durham, North Carolina, 1940.

Crume, Paul. "Big D," Dallas *Morning News,* July 13, 1967, Sec. 2, p. 1.

Curme, George O. *Parts of Speech and Accidence.* Boston, 1935.

Curtin, Philip D. *The Atlantic Slave Trade.* Madison, 1969.

Cushman, Dan. *Stay Away, Joe.* New York, 1953.

Dabney, Susan. *Memorials of a Southern Planter.* Baltimore, 1887.

Daughters of the Confederacy. *Report of a Joint Committee Appointed to Consider and Report on a Selection of New Words for "Dixie."* Opelika, Alabama, August 26, 1904.

D'Auvergne, Edmund B. *Human Livestock.* London, 1933.

Davidson, Basil. *Black Mother; the Years of the African Slave Trade.* Boston, 1961.

Davis, John. *Travels of Four Years and a Half in the United States of America During 1798, 1799, 1800, 1801 and 1802.* New York, 1909.

Day, Charles William. *Five Years Residence in the West Indies.* London, 1852.

DeCamp, David. "African Day-Names in Jamaica." *Language* 43 (1967): 139:147.

deCoy, Robert H. *The Nigger Bible.* Los Angeles, 1967.

Defoe, Daniel. *The History and Remarkable Life of the Truly Honourable Col. Jacque, commonly called Col. Jack.* London, 1722.

——————. *The Life and Surprising Adventures of Robinson Crusoe.* London, 1719.

——————. *The Family Instructor.* London, 1715.

Delaney, Martin R. *Blake: or, the Huts of America, in The Afro-American* I. January-July, 1859.

Demaret, Kent. "The Thoughts of Seven Killers as They Wait for the Electric Chair." Houston *Chronicle,* November 14, 1965, Sec. 2, p. 1.

Densmore, Frances. *Seminole Music.* Washington, D.C., 1956.

Dickens, Charles. *Martin Chuzzlewit.* London, 1844.

——————. Letter to Forster, April 15, 1842.

Dickinson, Jonathan. *Jonathan Dickinson's Journal; or, God's Protecting Providence, Being the Narrative of a Journey from Port Royal in Jamaica to Philadelphia between August 23, 1696 and April 1, 1697.* New Haven, 1944.

Dillard, J. L. "On the Grammar of Afro-American Naming Practices." *Names* Vol. 16, No. 3 (September 1968): 230–237.

————. *Afro-American and Other Vehicle Names*. Institute of Caribbean Studies Special Study No. 1. (March 1963).

————. "Beginning Formulas for Antillean Folk Tales, etc." *Caribbean Studies* Vol. 3, No. 3 (October 1963): 51–55.

————. "Some Variants in Concluding Tags in Antillean Folk Tales." *Caribbean Studies* Vol. 2, No. 3 (October 1962): 16–25.

————. "Names or Slogans:: Some Problems from the Cameroun, Burundi, the West Indies, and the United States." *Caribbean Studies*, 1970.

————. "How Not to Classify the Folk Tales of the Antilles." *Caribbean Studies* Vol. 3, No. 4 (January 1964): 30–34.

————. "Toward a Bibliography of Works Dealing with the Creole Languages of the Caribbean Area, Louisiana, and the Guianas." *Caribbean Studies* Vol. 3, No. 1 (April 1963: 84–95.

————. "Additional Notes on Stepping and Bending." *Caribbean Studies* Vol. 4, No. 4 (January 1965): 74–76.

————. "How to Tell the Bandits from the Good Guys, or What Dialect to Teach?" In *Linguistic-Cultural Differences and American Education*, edited by Aarons, Gordon, and Stewart. Miami, 1969.

————. Review of *Dictionary of Jamaican English*, by Cassidy and LePage. *Caribbean Studies*, 1970.

Diocèse de Nkongsamba. *Catéchisme*. Nkongsamba, Cameroun, 1959.

Dodge, Richard Irving. *Our Wild Indians; Thirty-three Years Personal Experience*. Hartford, Connecticut, 1889.

Dollard, John. *Class and Caste in a Southern Town*. New Haven, 1937.

Dorson, Richard. *Negro Folk Tales in Michigan*. Cambridge, Mass., 1956.

————. *Negro Folk Tales from Pine Bluff, Arkansas, and Calvin, Michigan*. Indiana University Folklore Series No. 23. Bloomington, 1958.

Douglass, Frederick. *My Bondage and Freedom*. New York, 1855.

Dove, Adrian. "Soul Story," *New York Times Magazine* (December 8, 1968).

Dow, George Francis. *Slave Ships and Slaving*. Salem, Mass., 1927.

Dowd, Jerome. *The Negro in American Life*. New York, 1926.

Doyle, Bertram Wilbur. *The Etiquette of Race Relations in the South*. 1937 (Kennikut Press reprint, 1968).

Drake, Francis. *Indian History for Young Folks*. New York, 1885.

Drake, Samuel G. *The Witchcraft Delusion in New England.* Roxbury,
    Massachusetts, 1866.
Dressler, Albert, ed. *California Chinese Chatter.* San Francisco, 1927.
*Drums and Shadows: Survival Studies Among the Georgia Coast
    Negroes,* University of Georgia Press, 1940.
Durrell, Gerald M. *The Bafut Beagles.* London, 1954.
————. *The Overloaded Ark.* New York, 1953.
————. *A Zoo in My Luggage.* New York, 1960.
Eastman, Mary H. *Aunt Phillis's Cabin; or, Southern Life As It Is.*
    Philadelphia, 1852.
Edmonds, Walter D. *Drums Along the Mohawk.* Boston, 1937.
Eliason, Norman. *Tarheel Talk.* Chapel Hill, North Carolina, 1956.
Elkins, Stanley M. *Slavery, A Problem in American Institutional and
    Intellectual Life.* University of Chicago Press, 1959.
Ellison, Ralph. *The Invisible Man.* New York, 1947.
Emmett, Daniel Decatur. "Dixie," New York, 1859.
Evans, The Reverend J. W. *Sermon and Songs.* Léshun Records,
    MR 601-A, N.D.
Fairbairn, Ann. *Five Smooth Stones.* New York, 1966.
Fanon, Frantz. *Peau Noire, Masques Blancs.* Paris, 1952.
Farrison, William Edward. *The Phonology of the Illiterate Negro
    Dialect of Guilford County, North Carolina,* Ph.D. dissertation,
    Ohio State University (unpublished), 1936.
Fauset, Arthur Huff. *Sojourner Truth—God's Faithful Pilgrim.* Chapel
    Hill, North Carolina, 1938.
————. "Negro Folk Tales from the South." *Journal of American
    Folklore* Vol. 4 (July-September), 1927.
Ferguson, Charles A. "Diglossia." *Word* 15 (1959): 325–340.
Ferguson, William. *Across America by River and Rail; or, Notes by
    the Way on the New World and its People.* London, 1856.
Fisher, Miles Mark. *Negro Slave Songs in the United States.* New
    York, 1963.
Fitchett, E. H. "Folklore from St. Helena, South Carolina." *Journal
    of American Folklore* 38 (1925): 217–238.
Fleming, Elizabeth McClellan. *William Gilmore Simms's Portrayal of
    the Negro.* Masters thesis, Duke University (unpublished), 1965.
"Folklore and Ethnology." *The Southern Workman* 24:8 (September
    1895) [reprinted in Jackson].
Forbes, Jack D. *Nevada Indians Speak.* Reno, Nevada, 1967.
Foster, Charles William. *The Representation of Negro Dialect in
    Charles W. Chesnutt's "The Conjure Woman."* Ph.D. dissertation,
    University of Alabama (unpublished), 1968.

Foster, Herbert. "A Pilot Study of the Cant of the Disadvantaged, Socially Maladjusted Secondary School Child." *Urban Education* II (1967): 99–114.

Foster, Lawrence. *Negro-Indian Relationships in the Southeast.* Ph.D. dissertation, University of Pennsylvania, 1935.

Franklin, Benjamin. "Information to Those Who Would Remove to America." In *Writings,* edited by Smythe, Vol. VIII, p. 606.

Franklin, John Hope. *From Slavery to Freedom, A History of American Negroes.* New York, 1956.

Frazier, E. Franklin. *Black Bourgeoisie: The Rise of a New Middle Class.* New York, 1957.

————. *The Negro Family in the United States.* Chicago, 1939.

Freeman, Richard Austin. *Travels and Life in Ashanti and Jamaica.* 1898.

Genovese, Eugene D. *The World the Slaveholders Made.* New York, 1969.

————. *The Political Economy of Slavery.* New York, 1967.

Giddings, Joshua Reed. *The Exiles of Florida.* Columbus, Ohio, 1858.

Gifford, John C. *Billy Bowlegs and the Seminole War.* Cocoanut Grove, Florida, 1925.

Gilbert, Olive. *Narrative of Sojourner Truth.* New York, 1853.

Gillespie, Elizabeth. *The Dialect of the Mississippi Negro in Literature.* Ph.D. dissertation, University of Mississippi (unpublished), 1939.

Gilman, Caroline. *Recollections of a Southern Matron.* New York, 1838.

Glasscock, C. B. *The Big Bonanza.* Indianapolis.

Gold, Robert S. *A Jazz Lexicon.* Ph.D. dissertation, New York University (unpublished), 1962.

Gonzales, Ambrose Elliott. *The Black Border.* Columbia, South Carolina, 1964.

————. *The Captain.* Columbia, South Carolina, 1924.

————. *Laguerre, A Gascon of the Black Border.* Columbia, South Carolina, 1924.

————. *With Aesop Along the Black Border.* Columbia, South Carolina, 1924.

————. *Two Gullah Tales: The Turkey Hunter and at the Cross Roads Store.* New York, 1926.

Goodman, Morris. *A Comparative Study of Creole French Dialects.* New York, 1964.

Gosden, Freeman and Correll, Charles. *Here They Are: Amos and Andy.* New York, 1931.

Grade, P. "Das Neger-Englisch in der Westküste von Afrika." *Anglia*, 1892.

Grainger, James. *The Sugar Cane*. London, 1764.

Graves, Richard L. *Language Differences Between Upper and Lower Class Negro and White Eighth Graders in East Central Alabama*. Ph.D. dissertation, Florida State University (unpublished), 1967.

Grayson, William John. *The Hireling and the Slave, Chicora, and Other Poems*. Charleston, South Carolina, 1855.

Greet, W. Cabell. "Southern Speech." In *Culture in the South*, edited by W. T. Couch. Chapel Hill, North Carolina, 1935.

Gregory, Dick. *Nigger, an Autobiography*. New York, 1964.

Grier, William H., and Cobbs, Price M. *Black Rage*. New York, 1968.

Griffin, John W. "Some Comments on the Seminole in 1818." *The Florida Anthropologist*, Vol. X, Nos. 3-4 (November, 1957).

Griffin, Mattie. *Autobiography of a Female Slave*. New York, 1857.

Grose, Francis A. *A Classical Dictionary of the Vulgar Tongue*. London, 1785.

Hall, Robert A., Jr. "The African Substratum in Negro English." *American Speech* 25 (1950): 51-54.

————. *Melanesian Pidgin English: Grammar, Texts, Vocabulary*. Baltimore, 1943.

————. Review of *Pidgin English*, by E. S. Sayer. *Language* 20, No. 3 (1944): 171-174.

————. "Notes on Australian Pidgin English." *Language* 19, No. 3 (1943): 263-267.

————. *Haitian Creole*. American Folklore Society. 1953.

————. *Pidgin and Creole Languages*. Ithaca, N. Y., 1966.

———— and Leechman, Douglas. "American Indian Pidgin English: Attestations and Grammatical Peculiarities." *American Speech* 30 (1955): 163-171.

Hancock, Ian F. "A Provisional Comparison of the English-based Atlantic Creoles." In *Pidginization and Creolization of Languages*, edited by Hymes. 1970.

————. "The Malacca Creoles and Their Language." *Afrasian* 3 (1969).

Hannerz, Ulf. "The Rhetoric of Soul: Identification in Negro Society." *Race* (1968): 457-465.

————. "Gossip Networks and Culture in a Black American Ghetto." *Ethnos* 32 (1967): 35-66.

————. *Soulside*. Columbia University Press, 1969.

Harris, Joel Chandler. "Plantation Music." *The Critic* III, No. 5 (December 15, 1883): 505-506 [reprinted in Jackson].

————. *Nights with Uncle Remus*. Boston, 1883.

————. *Uncle Remus, His Songs and His Sayings; The Folklore of the Old Plantation*. New York, 1881.

————. *Mingo, and Other Sketches in Black and White*. Boston, 1884.

————. *Free Joe, and Other Georgia Sketches*. New York, 1887.

Harrison, James A. "Negro English." *Anglia* VIII (1884): 232–279.

————. "Negro English." *Modern Language Notes* VII: 123.

Harte, Bret. *The Heathen Chinee*. Chicago, 1870.

Hattori, Shiro. "A Special Language of the Older Generations Among the Ainu," *Linguistics* 6 (1964).

Hayes, Jess G. *Apache Vengeance*. University of New Mexico Press, 1954.

Hearn, Lafcadio, *Children of the Levee*. University of Kentucky Press, 1885.

————. *Gombo Zhèbes*. New York, 1885.

————. *Youma: The Story of a West-Indian Slave*. New York, 1890.

Herskovits, Melville J. *The American Negro*. New York, 1919.

————. *The Myth of the Negro Past*. Boston, 1958.

————. *Suriname Folk Lore*. New York: Columbia University Press, 1936.

————. "What Has Africa Given America?" *New* Republic LXXIV, No. 1083 (1935). Reprinted in *The New World Negro*, edited by Frances S. Herskovits. Bloomington, Indiana, 1966.

Higginson, Thomas Wentworth. *Army Life in a Black Regiment*. Boston, 1870.

Hitchcock, Ethan Allan. *Fifty Years in Camp and Field*. New York, 1909.

————. *A Traveller in Indian Territory*. Cedar Rapids, Iowa, 1930.

Hoffman, Melvin J. "Bidialectalism Is Not the Linguistics of White Supremacy: Sense Versus Sensibilities." *The English Record* (Spring, 1971).

Hughes, Langston. *An African Treasury*. New York, 1960.

————. *Best of Simple*. New York, 1960.

————. *The Book of Negro Humor*. New York, 1966.

———— and Bontemps, Arno, eds. *The Book of Negro Folklore*. New York, 1961.

———— and Meltzner, Milton. *A Pictorial History of the Negro in America*. New York, 1963.

Hunt, Cecil. *Honoured Sir—from Babujee*. London, 1931.

Hurston, Zora Neale. "Cudjo's Own Story of the Last African Slaver."
    Journal of Negro History XII (1927): 648–663.
————. *Mules and Men.* Philadelphia, 1935.
————. "Hoodoo in America." *Journal of American Folklore* 44
    (1931): 317–417.
————. *Dust Tracks on a Road, An Autobiography.* Philadelphia,
    1942.
Hymes, Dell, ed. *Pidginization and Creolization of Languages.* Lon-
    don, 1970.
Ingraham, Joseph Holt. *The Southwest by a Yankee.* New York, 1835.
————. *The Sunny South.* Philadelphia, 1860.
An Interim Bibliography of Black English. University of Wisconsin
    Programs in English Linguistics Report No. 4, April 1970.
Irwin, Wallace. *Chinatown Ballads.* New York, 1906.
Ives, Sumner. "Dialect Differentiation in the Stories of Joel Chandler
    Harris." *American Literature,* 1955.
————. "A Theory of Literary Dialect." *Tulane Studies in English*
    I (1949–50): 137–182.
————. "The Phonology of the Uncle Remus Stories." *Publications
    of the American Dialect Society* No. 22 (November 1954).
Jackson, Bruce, ed. *The Negro and His Folklore in Nineteenth Cen-
    tury Periodicals.* Austin, Texas, 1967.
Jacob, Harriet. *Incidents in the Life of a Slave Girl.* Boston, 1861.
Janson, Charles William. *Stranger in America.* London, 1807.
Johnson, Charles Spurgeon. *The Negro in American Civilization.*
    New York, 1943.
————. *The Shadow of the Plantation.* Chicago, 1934.
Johnson, Guion G. *History of the Sea Islands with Special Reference
    to St. Helena Island, South Carolina.* Chapel Hill, N. C., 1930.
————. "Southern Paternalism Toward Negroes After the Civil
    War." *Journal of Southern History* XIII (1957): 499–500.
————. *Ante-Bellum North Carolina.* Chapel Hill, N. C., 1937.
Johnson, H. P. "Who Lost the Southern R?" *American Speech* III,
    No. 4 (April 1928): 377–383.
Johnson, Kenneth R. "Language Problems of Culturally Disadvantaged
    Negro Students." *California English Journal* 2 (Spring 1966):
    28–33.
————. "Improving Language Skills of Culturally Disadvantaged
    Pupils." *Teaching Culturally Disadvantaged Pupils.* Chicago,
    1966.
————. *Teaching Grammatical Structures.* Ph.D. dissertation, Uni-
    versity of Southern California, 1968.

————. "The Vocabulary of Race." In *Language and Expressive Behavior in the Black Inner City*, edited by Kochman. Champaign, Illinois, 1970.

————. "The Language of Black Children: Instructional Implications." In *Racial Crisis in American Education*, by Green. Chicago, 1970.

————. "The Culturally Disadvantaged—Slow Learners or Different Learners?" *Journal of Secondary Education* (January 1970), pp. 43–47.

————. "Pedagogical Problems of Using Second Language Techniques for Teaching Standard English to Speakers of Non-Standard Negro Dialect." In *Linguistic-Cultural Differences in American Education*, edited by Aarons, Gordon, and Stewart. Miami, 1969.

————. "When Should Standard English Be Taught to Speakers of Nonstandard Negro Dialect?" *Language Learning* (June 1970).

————. "A Strategy for Teaching Standard English to Disadvantaged Black Children Who Speak a Nonstandard Dialect." In *Teaching Language Arts to Culturally Different Children*, edited by Joyce, 1970.

———— and Hernandez, Luis F. "Teaching Standard Oral English to Mexican-American and Negro Students for Better Vocational Opportunities." *Journal of Secondary Education* 42 (Spring 1966): 151–155.

Jones, Charles Colcock. *The Religious Instruction of the Negroes*. Savannah, Georgia, 1832.

Jones, Charles Colcock, Jr. *Negro Myths from the Georgia Coast*. Boston, 1888.

Jones, Hugh. *The Present State of Virginia*. London, 1724.

Jones, James Apthearn. *Haverhill*. New York, 1831.

Jones, LeRoi. *Blues People*. New York, 1963.

————. "The Myth of a Negro Literature." In *Home: Social Essays*, London, 1968.

Jones, Peter. *History of the Ojibway Indians*. London, 1861.

Jordan, Winthrop D. *White Over Black: American Attitudes Toward the Negro, 1550–1812*. Williamsburg, Va., 1968.

Josselyn, John. *An Account of Two Voyages to New England*. London, 1674.

Kane, Elisha K. "The Negro Dialects Along the Savannah River." *Dialect Notes* V (1925): 354–367.

Kaplan, Arthur M. "A Master of Negro Dialect." *The Jewish Tribune*, New York (September 23, 1927), pp. 38, 61.

Keil, Charles. *The Urban Blues.* University of Chicago Press, 1966.

Kemble, Frances Anne. *A Journal of Residence on a Georgia Plantation in 1838–39.* New York, 1863.

Kennedy, John Pendleton. *Swallow Barn.* Philadelphia, 1860.

Kilham, Elizabeth. "Sketches in Color." *Putnam's Monthly* IV (March 1870): 304–311.

Kittredge, George Lyman. "Indian Talk." In *The Old Farmer and His Almanac,* 1920.

————. "Lost Works of Cotton Mather." *Proceedings of the Massachusetts Historical Society* XLV (1912): 431.

Kleeman, Richard P. "Washington Tries New Method to Teach Speech to Negroes." Minneapolis *Tribune,* 12 February 1967.

Klein, Herbert S. *Slavery in the Americas: A Comparative Study of Virginia and Cuba.* Chicago, 1967.

Knight, Sarah Kemble. *The Private Journal Kept on a Journey from Boston to New York in the Year 1704.* Boston, 1858.

Kochman, Thomas. "Rapping in the Black Ghetto." *Trans-Action,* 1969, pp. 26–34.

Krapp, George Philip. "The English of the Negro." *American Mercury* II, No. 5 (June 1924): 190–195.

————. *The English Language in America.* New York, 1925.

Kurath, Hans. "The Origin of Dialectal Differences in Spoken American English." *Modern Philology* XXV (May 1928).

Kurzgefasste Neger-Englische Grammatik. Bautzen, 1854.

Labov, William. *The Social Stratification of English in New York City.* Washington, D.C., 1965.

————. "Phonological Correlates of Social Stratification." *American Anthropologist* 66, Part 2, pp. 137–153.

Lady Nugent's Journal of Her Residence in Jamaica from 1801 to 1805. Kingston, Institute of Jamaica, 1966.

Lambert, Wallace E. "A Social Psychology of Bilingualism." *Journal of Social Issues* XXIII, No. 2 (April 1967): 91–109.

———— and Tucker, G. Richard. "White and Negro Listeners' Reactions to Various American-English Dialects." *Social Forces* 47, No. 4 (June 1969): 463–468.

Lanier, Sidney. Letter to *Scribner's Monthly, Works,* X, p. 156.

Leacock, John. *The Fall of British Tyranny.* Philadelphia, 1796.

Lee, George W. *Beale Street, Where the Blues Began.* New York, 1934.

Lee, Rose Hum. *The Chinese in the United States of America.* Hong Kong, 1960.

Lefler, Hugh Talmadge, and Newsome, Albert Ray. *North Carolina*, 1963 Revised Edition.

Leland, Charles G. *Pidgin English Sing Song*. London, 1900.

Leland, John. *The Virginia Chronicle*. Fredericksburg, Va., 1790.

Leopold, Werner F. "The Decline of German Dialects." *Word* 15 (1959): 134–153.

LePage, Robert B. "General Outlines of Creole English in the British Caribbean." *Orbis* VI (1957).

——————, ed. *Creole Studies II: Proceedings of the Conference on Creole Language Studies*. London, 1961.

—————— and David De Camp. *Creole Language Studies I: Jamaican Creole*. London, 1960.

Lindsley, A. B. *Love and Friendship*. New York, 1809.

Lloyd, John U. "The Language of the Kentucky Negro." *Dialect Notes* 2 (1901): 179–184.

Loban, Walter. *Problems in Oral English: Kindergarten through Grade Nine*. Champaign, Illinois, NCTE, 1967.

Loggins, Vernon. *The Negro Author*. Columbia University Press, 1931.

Loman, Bengt. *Conversations in a Negro American Dialect*. Washington, D.C., 1968.

Lomax, Alan. *Mister Jelly Roll*. New York, 1950.

——————. *The Rainbow Sign*. New York, 1959.

——————, collector. *Roots of the Blues*. Atlantic 1346.

——————. *The Blues Roll On*. Atlantic 1352.

——————. *Sounds of the South*. Atlantic 1346.

——————. *Negro Prison Songs*. Recorded in Mississippi. Tradition Records TLP 1020.

——————. *Blues in the Mississippi Night*. United Artists 4027.

——————, and Lomax, John A. and Ruby T., collectors. *Negro Prison Camp Worksongs*. Recorded in Texas. Ethnic Folkways FE 4475.

——————, and Lomax, John A. and Ruby T. *Afro-American Spirituals, Work Songs, and Ballads*. Recorded in the Southern states. Folkways Records FA 2650–59.

Lomax, Louis. *To Kill A Black Man*. Los Angeles, 1968.

Long, Ralph B. *The Sentence and Its Parts*. University of Chicago Press, 1961.

Low, Samuel. *Politician Outwitted*. New York, 1789.

Lyell, Sir Charles. *A Second Visit to the United States of North America*. London, 1849.

Lynch, Louis. *The Barbados Book*. London, 1964.

Mannix, Daniel Pratt, and Cowley, Malcolm. *Black Cargoes; A History of the Atlantic Slave Trade.* New York, 1962.

Marly; or, A Planter's Life in Jamaica. Glasgow, 1828.

Mason, Julian. "The Etymology of *Buckaroo.*" *American Speech* XXXV (February 1960): 51–55.

Mather, Cotton. *The Angel of Bethesda.* 1721.

Mathews, Mitford M., ed. *Dictionary of Americanisms.* University of Chicago Press, 1951.

————. *Some Sources of Southernisms.* University of Alabama Press, 1948.

————. *The Beginnings of American English.* Chicago, 1963.

McDavid, Raven Ior, Jr. *Communication Barriers to the Culturally Deprived.* Chicago, 1966.

————. "The Grunt of Negation." *American Speech* XXX, No. 1 (February 1955): 56.

————. Review of *Africanisms in the Gullah Dialect,* by Turner. *Language* 26 (1950): 323–333.

————. "American English Dialects." In *The Structure of American English,* edited by W. N. Francis. New York, 1958.

————. "American Social Dialects." *College English* 26, No. 4 (January 1965): 254–260.

————. "Historical, Regional, and Social Variation." *Journal of English Linguistics* 1, 1967.

————, with the assistance of David W. Maurer. *The American Language,* by H. L. Mencken [Abridged, edited, and considerably augmented; herein regarded as a separate work from that of Mencken, q.v.], New York, 1963.

———— and McDavid, Virginia. "The Relationship of the Speech of American Negroes to the Speech of Whites." *American Speech* XXVI (1951): 3–16.

————. "Plurals of Nouns of Measure in the United States." *Studies in Language and Linguistics in Honor of Charles C. Fries,* Ann Arbor, 1964.

McDowell, Tremaine. "Negro Dialect in the American Novel to 1821." *American Speech* V, No. 4 (April 1930): 291–296.

————. "The Use of Negro Dialect by Harriet Beecher Stowe." *American Speech* VI, No. 5 (June 1931): 322–326.

McIlwaine, Shields. *The Southern Poor White.* Norman, Oklahoma, 1939.

McKay, Claude. *Home to Harlem.* New York 1928.

McManus, Edgar J. *A History of Negro Slavery in New York.* Syracuse, 1966.

McReynolds, Edwin C. *The Seminoles*. Norman, Oklahoma, 1957.

Meier, August, and Rudwick, Elliott, eds. *The Making of Black America*. New York, 1969.

————. *From Plantation to Ghetto: An Interpretive History of American Negroes*. New York, 1966.

Mencken, H. L. *The American Language*. New York, 1919. Second Edition, 1921. Third Edition, 1923. Fourth Edition, 1936. Supplement One, 1945. Supplement Two, 1948.

Meredith, Mamie. "Longfellow's Excelsior Done Into Pidgin English." *American Speech* V, No. 2 (1929): 148–151.

————. " 'Tall Talk' In America Sixty Years Ago." *American Speech* IV, No. 3 (February 1929): 290–293.

Mezzrow, Mezz. *Really the Blues*. New York, 1946.

Miller, Mary Rita. "Attestations of American Indian Pidgin English in Fiction and Non-Fiction." *American Speech* (May 1967): 142–147.

Miller, Warren. *The Cool World*. Boston, 1959.

Mitchell, Margaret. *Gone With the Wind*. New York, 1936.

Montgomery, Albert James. *History of Alabama*. Charleston, S. C., 1851.

Moore, George H. *Notes on the History of Slavery in Massachusetts*. New York, 1866.

Moore-Willson, Minnie. *The Seminoles of Florida*. Kissimmee, Florida, 1928.

Morris, J. Allen. "Gullah in the Stories and Novels of William Gilmore Simms." *American Speech* XII (February 1947): 46–53.

Morton, Ferdinand. "Jelly Roll." *The Library of Congress Recordings*, edited by Alan Lomax. Vol. 1–12, Riverside RLP 1001–10012.

Murdoch, John. *The Triumphs of Love; or, Happy Reconciliation*. Philadelphia, 1795.

Murray, Pauli. *States' Laws on Race and Color*. Cincinnati, 1950.

————. *"All for Mr. Davis," The Story of Sharecropper Odell Walker*. New York, 1942.

————. *Proud Shoes*. New York, 1956.

Myrdal, Gunnar. *An American Dilemma*. New York, 1944.

Nathan, Hans. *Dan Emmett and the Rise of Negro Minstrelsy*. Norman, Oklahoma, 1962.

Nathanson, Y. S. "Negro Minstrelsy, Ancient and Modern." *Putnam's Monthly*, 1855 [reprinted in Jackson].

"Negro Cabin in Virginia." *The Family Magazine* I, No. 2 (February 1836): 42–49.

"Negro Patois and Its Humor." *Appleton's Journal of Popular Litera-ture, Science and Art II*, 5 February 1870, pp. 161–2.

Nelson, John Herbert. *The Negro Character in American Literature.* Lawrence, Kansas, 1926.

Neville, Lawrence. *Edith Allen.* Richmond, Virginia, 1856.

New England's First Fruits. London, 1643.

Newitt, M. D. D. "The Portuguese on the Zambesi from the Seven-teenth to the Nineteenth Centuries." *Race*, April, 1968.

Nichols, Thomas L. *Forty Years of American Life.* London, 1874.

Nonstandard Dialect. Board of Education of the City of New York, Champaign, Illinois, 1968.

Noreen, R. S. "Ghetto Worship: A Study of Chicago Store Front Churches." *Names* XIII (1965): 19–38.

North Carolina Folklore, Vol. I, *Games and Rhymes, Beliefs and Customs, Riddles, Proverbs, Speech, Tales and Legends.* Durham, N. C., 1952.

Norwood, Col. Henry. "A Voyage to Virginia." London, 1649. In *Force's Collection of Historical Tracts*, Vol. III, No. 10.

"Observations in Several Voyages and Travels in America." *The London Magazine*, 1745–6.

O'Donnell, E. P. O. "Canker." *Yale Review* 25 (1936): 784–809.

O'Keefe, John. *The Basket Maker.* London, 1789.

Olmsted, Frederic Law. *The Cotton Kingdom: A Traveler's Observa-tions on Cotton and Slavery in the American Southern States.* New York, 1861.

Opie, Iona Archibald, and Opie, Peter. *The Language and Lore of School Children.* Oxford, 1960.

O'Shea, M. V. *Linguistic Development and Education.* New York, 1907.

Osser, H., Wang, M., and Zaid, F. "The Young Child's Ability to Imitate and Comprehend Speech: A Comparison of Two Sub-cultural Groups." *Child Development* 4 (1969): 1063–1075.

Ottly, Roi, and Weatherby, William J. *The Negro in New York.* 1963.

Owen, Nicholas. *Journal of a Slave Dealer.* Edited by Eveline Martin, 1930.

Owens, William A. *Slave Mutiny.* London, 1953.

Page, J. W. *Uncle Robin in His Cabin and Tom Without One in Boston.* Richmond, Virginia, 1855.

Page, Thomas Nelson. *Social Life in Old Virginia Before the War.* New York, 1897.

————. *Marse Chan.* New York, 1892.

Parkman, Francis. *The Conspiracy of Pontiac*. Boston, 1870.

Paulding, James Kirke. *The Dutchman's Fireside*. New York, 1831.

Payne, L. W. "A Word List from East Alabama." *Dialect Notes* III (1903): 279–328, 343–391.

Pederson, Lee M. "Middleclass Negro Speech in Minneapolis." *Orbis*, 1968.

Peterkin, Julia. *Black April*. New York, 1927.

————. *Bright Skin*. Indianapolis, 1932.

————. *Roll, Jordan, Roll*. New York, 1933.

————. *Scarlet Sister Mary*. Indianapolis, 1928.

Pfaff, C. *Historical and Structural Aspects of Sociolinguistic Variation: The Copula in Black English*. Inglewood, California, 1971.

Pharr, Robert Deane. *The Book of Numbers*. Garden City, N. Y., 1969.

Pickford, Glenna Ruth. "American Linguistic Geography: A Sociological Appraisal." *Word* 12 (1956): 211–33.

"Pidgin English." *The Nation* No. 269, 25 August 1870, pp. 118–119.

The Plantation; or, Thirteen Years in the South, by "A Northern Man." Philadelphia, 1853.

Poe, Edgar Allan. *The Gold Bug*. Edited by Hervey Allen and Thomas Ollive Mabbott. New York, 1928.

"Poor Sarah." *The Religious Intelligencer*, 1821. Reprinted in *Interesting Anecdotes of Persons of Color*, compiled by A. Mott. New York, 1850.

Porter, Kenneth Wiggins. "Negro Guides and Interpreters in the Early Stages of the Seminole War." *The Journal of Negro History* Vol. XXXV, No. 2 (April 1950).

————. "Seminole Indian Scouts, 1870–1881." *The Southwestern Historical Quarterly*, 1952.

————. "The Seminole Negro-Indian Scouts." *The Quarterly of the Texas State Historical Association*, January, 1952.

————. "The Early Life of Luis Pacheco né Fatio." *The Negro History Bulletin* VII (1943): 52.

Pound, Louise. "The Dialect of Cooper's Leatherstocking." *American Speech* II, No. 12 (September 1927): 479–488.

Pratt, Theodore. *Seminole*. Gainesville, Florida, 1953.

Prince, J. Dyneley. "An Ancient New Jersey Indian Jargon." *American Anthropologist* 4 (1902): 508–524.

————. "A Modern Delaware Tale." *Proceedings of the American Philosophical Society* XLI (January 1902): 20–34.

———— and Speck, Frank G. "The Modern Pequots and their Language." *American Anthropologist* 5, No. 20 (April 1903): 193–212.

Puckett, N. N. "Names of American Negro Slaves." In *Studies in the Science of Society*, edited by George P. Murdoch. New Haven, 1937.

Purchas, Samuel. *Hakluytus Posthumus, or Purchas His Pilgrimes*. Vol. I–XX. Glasgow, 1905.

Putnam, George N., and O'Hern, Edna M. *The Status Significance of an Isolated Urban Dialect*. Baltimore, 1955.

Pyrnelle, Louise Clark. *Diddie, Dumps and Tot; or, Plantation Child Life*. New York, 1882.

Quinn, Arthur Hobson. *History of the American Drama*. New York, 1923.

Rampini, Charles. *Letters from Jamaica*. Edinburgh, 1873.

Ravenal, Henry William. "Recollections of Southern Plantation Life." *Yale Review* XXV (1936): 748–777.

Ray, Punya Sloka. *Language Standardization*. The Hague, 1963.

Read, Allen Walker. "The Speech of Negroes in Colonial America." *Journal of Negro History* XXIV, No. 3 (1939): 247–258.

————. "The English of the Indians." *American Speech*, Vol. 10 (February 1941): 72–74.

————. "British Recognition of American Speech in the Eighteenth Century." *Dialect Notes* VI, Part VI (1933): 313–334.

————. "The First Stage in the History of O.K." *American Speech* XXXVIII, No. 1 (February 1963): 5–27.

————. "The Second Stage in the History of O.K." *American Speech* XXXVIII, No. 2 (May 1963).

Recueil de Divers Voyages Fait en Afrique. Paris, 1674.

Redding, J. Saunders. *To Make A Black Poet*. College Park, Maryland, 1939.

Reid, T. Mayne. *Child Wife*. New York, 1869.

————. *The Headless Horseman, A Strange Tale of Texas*. London, 1866.

————. *Osceola the Seminole; or, the Red Fawn of the Flower Land*. New York, 1858.

————. *The Quadroon; or, Adventures in the Far West*.

————. *Ran Away to Sea*. London, 1859.

————. *Bruin*. London, 1861.

Reinecke, John. "Trade Jargons and Creole Dialects as Marginal Languages." *Social Forces* 17 (1938): 107–118.

————. "Pidgin English in Hawaii: A Local Study in the Sociology of Language." *American Journal of Sociology* 63 (1938): 778–789.

————. *A List of Loanwords from the Hawaiian Language in Use in the English Speech of the Hawaiian Islands*. Honolulu, 1938.

————. *Language and Dialect in Hawaii.* University of Hawaii Press, 1969.

————. *Marginal Languages: A Sociological Survey of the Creole Languages and Trade Jargons.* Ph.D. dissertation, Yale University (unpublished), 1937.

————, and Tokimasa, Aiko. "The English Dialect of Hawaii." *American Speech* 9 (1934): 45–58; 122–131.

Reisman, Karl. "Linguistic Values and Cultural Values in a West Indian Village." In *Pidginization and Creolization of Languages,* edited by Hymes. London, 1970.

Riddell, William Renwick. "The Slave in Early New York, The Dutch Period." *Journal of Negro History* VIII (1928).

Riessman, Frank. "Digging 'The Man's' Language." *Saturday Review,* 17 September 1966, pp. 80–81; 98.

Roberts, Margaret M. *The Pronunciation of Vowels in Negro Speech.* Ph.D. dissertation, Ohio State University (unpublished), 1966.

Rohrer, J. H., and Edmonson, M. *The Eighth Generation.* New York, 1960.

Rollins, Philip Ashton. *The Cowboy.* New York, 1922, 1936.

Rose, Dan. "Billy Brazelton, Highwayman." *Arizona in Literature,* edited by Mary G. Boyer. Glendale, California, 1934.

Rosenbaum, Peter S. "Prerequisites for Linguistic Studies on the Effects of Dialect Differences on Learning to Read." *Project Literacy Reports* No. 2, Ithaca, N. Y., 1964.

Ross, A. S., and Moverley, A. W. *The Pitcairnese Language.* London, 1964.

Royall, Anne. *Sketches of History, Life, and Manners in the United States.* New Haven, 1926.

————. *The Tennessean: A Novel, Founded on Facts.* New Haven, 1827.

Rush, Caroline E. *Way-Marks in the Life of a Wanderer.* Philadelphia, 1855 [?].

Rusling, James F. *Across America.* New York, 1875.

Russell, John H. *The Free Negro in Virginia.* Baltimore, 1913.

Sale, John B. *The Tree Named John.* Chapel Hill, N. C., 1929.

Saxon, Lyle. *Gumbo Ya-Ya, A Collection of Louisiana Folk Tales.* Boston, 1945.

Sayer, E. S. *Pidgin English.* Toronto, Canada, 1939 and 1943.

Schneider, Gilbert D. *Dey Don Klin; Rida Nomba Fo.* 1964. Mimeographed.

————. *First Steps in Wes-Kos.* Hartford, Conn., 1963.

————. *Wes-Kos Proverbs, Idioms, Names.* 1965. Mimeographed.

————. *West African Pidgin English*. Ph.D. dissertation, Hartford Seminary Foundation, 1966.

————. *West African Pidgin English: An Historical Overview*. 1967.

————. *Wes-Kos Glossary*. 1965. Mimeographed.

————. *Cameroons Creole Dictionary*. 1960. Mimeographed.

Schoolcraft, Mrs. Mary H. *The Black Gauntlet*. Philadelphia, 1860.

Schuchardt, Hugo. "Die Lingua Franca." *Zeitschrift für Romanische Philologie* XXXIII (1909).

————. *Die Sprache der Saramakkaneger in Surinam*. Amsterdam, 1914.

Sherif, Muzafer, and Cantrill, Hadley. "The Kingdom of Father Divine." *Journal of Abnormal and Social Psychology* 33 (1938): 147–167.

Sherwood, Adiel. *Gazeteer of the State of Georgia*. Charleston, S. C., 1827.

Shuy, Roger W., Baratz, Joan C., and Wolfram, Walter A. *Sociolinguistic Factors in Speech Identification*. NIMH Research Project No. MH 15048–01, Washington, D.C., 1969.

————, Wolfram, Walter A., and Riley, William K. *Field Techniques in an Urban Study*. Washington, D.C., 1968.

Simmons, William Hayne. *Notices of East Florida*. Charleston, S. C., 1822.

Simms, William Gilmore. *The Wigwam and the Cabin*. New York, 1845.

Sioui, Tak. *Huckleberry Finn: More Molecules*. Pecos, Texas, 1962.

Sledd, James. "Bi-Dialectalism: The Linguistics of White Supremacy." *English Journal* LVIII (December 1969).

Smith, Reed. *Gullah*. University of South Carolina Press, 1926.

Smith, William. *A New Voyage to Guinea*. London, 1744.

Smyth, J. F. D. *A Tour of the United States of America*. London, 1784.

Spencer, John, ed. *Language in Africa*. Papers of the Leverhulme Conference on Universities and the Language Problems of Africa, Cambridge University Press, 1963.

Spicer, Edward H. *Cycles of Conquest*. Tucson, Arizona, 1962.

Stampp, Kenneth M. *The Peculiar Institution*. New York, 1956.

Stanley, Oma. "Negro Speech of East Texas." *American Speech* XVI (February 1941): 3–16.

Stearns, Marshall W. *The Story of Jazz*. New York, 1956.

————. *Jazz Dance: The Story of American Vernacular Dance*. New York, 1968.

———— and Stearns, Jean. "Frontiers of Humor: American Vernacular Dance." *Southern Folklore Quarterly* XXX (1966): 227–235.

Steinbeck, John. *East of Eden.* New York, 1952.

Stewart, William A. "Creole Languages in the Caribbean." In *Study of the Role of Second Languages in Asia, Africa and Latin America,* edited by F. A. Rice. Washington, D.C., 1962.

————. "The Functional Distribution of Creole and French in Haiti." *Georgetown University Monograph Series on Languages and Linguistics* No. 15, 1962.

Stowe, Harriet Beecher. *Uncle Tom's Cabin.* Boston, 1852.

————. *A Key to Uncle Tom's Cabin.* New York, 1853.

————. "The Education of Freedmen." *The North American Review* CXXVIII (1879): 605–615.

————. "Sojourner Truth, The Libyan Sibyl." *Atlantic Monthly,* 1863, pp. 473–481.

Stribling, T. S. *Birthright.* New York, 1922.

Szwed, John F., and Whitten, Norman. *Afro-American Anthropology.* New York, 1970.

Taylor, Douglas MacRae. *The Black Carib of British Honduras.* New York, 1951.

————. "Language Shift or Changing Relationship?" *International Journal of American Linguistics* 26 (1960): 155–161.

————. "New Languages for Old in the West Indies." *Comparative Studies in Society and History* 3 (1961): 277–288.

Thompson, Robert W. "A Note on Some Possible Affinities Between the Creole Dialects of the Old World and Those of the New." In *Creole Language Studies* II, edited by R. B. LePage. London, 1961, pp. 107–113.

Thompson, W. T. *The Slave Holder Abroad.* Philadelphia, 1860.

Thomson, Peggy. "D. C.'s Second Language." The Washington *Post* (June 11, 1967).

Thoreau, Henry D. *The Maine Woods.* Boston, 1864.

Thornton, J. Randolph. *The Cabin and the Parlor; or, Slaves Without Masters.* Philadelphia, 1852.

Thorpe, Thomas Bangs (pseudonym Logan). *The Master's House; A Tale of Southern Life.* 1854.

"True African Wit." *New Hampshire and Vermont Journal,* 26 July 1796.

Tucker, George. *Valley of the Shenandoah.* New York, 1824.

Tucker, Nathaniel Beverly. *The Partisan Leader; A Tale of the Future.* Washington, 1836.

—————. *George Balcombe.* New York, 1836.

Turner, Lorenzo Dow. Review of *Some Sources of Southernisms,* by
M. M. Mathews. *Language* 26 (1950): 167–170.

—————. *Comments on Word Lists from the South.* American
Dialect Society Publication No. 3, Greensboro, North Carolina,
1945.

—————. "Problems Confronting the Investigator of Gullah." American Dialect Society Publication No. 9 (April 1948): 74–84.

—————. "Some Contacts of Brazilian Ex-Slaves with Nigeria, West
Africa." *Journal of Negro History* (1942).

—————. "Linguistic Research and African Survivals." American
Council of Learned Societies Bulletin No. 32 (1941): 68–69.

Twelve Years A Slave; Narrative of Solomon Northrup. Auburn, 1853.

Udell, Elizabeth. "[mʔm], ETC." *American Speech* XXIX, No. 3
(October 1964): 232.

Valkhoff, Marius. *Studies in Portuguese and Creole.* Johannesburg,
1966.

Van Doren, Carl Clinton. *Benjamin Franklin.* New York, 1938.

Van Hoffman, Nicholas. "The Acid Affair." The Washington *Post,*
(October 26, 1967), pp. E1–2.

"Varieties." *Appleton's Journal of Popular Literature, Science, and
Art* (September 10, 1870).

Voegelin, C. F., and Voegelin, F. M. "Languages of the World:
Ibero-Caucasian and Pidgin-Creole." *Anthropological Linguistics*
6, No. 8.

Voorhoeve, Jan. *Sranan Syntax.* Amsterdam, 1962.

—————. "The Verbal System of Sranan." *Lingua* VI (1957): 374–
396 (November 1964).

————— and Antoon Donicie. *Bibliographie du Nègre-Anglais du
Surinam.* 's-Gravenhage, 1963.

Walser, Richard. "Negro Dialect in Eighteenth Century Drama."
American Speech XXX (December 1955): 269–276.

Warren, E. W. *Nellie Norton.* Macon, Georgia, 1864.

Weinstein, Allen, and Gatell, Frank Otto. *American Negro Slavery,
A Modern Reader.* Oxford University Press, 1968.

Wenlandt, Oliver. *The Nigger Boarding House: A Screaming Farce
in One Act for Six Male Burnt-Cork Characters.* New York, 1898.

"Western Africa." *The Religious Intelligencer.* Vols. V & VI. New
Haven, 1820 & 1821 [same vols. *passim* under such headings as
"Intelligence from Sierra Leone"].

Whinnom, Keith. *Spanish Contact Vernaculars in the Philippine
Islands.* Hong Kong, 1956.

————. "The Origin of the European-based Creoles and Pidgins." *Orbis* (1968): 509–526.

White, Stewart Edward. *Blazed Trail.* New York, 1902.

Whitney, Anne Weston. "Negro American Dialects." *The Independent* LIII (August 22, 1901).

Wiley, Bell Irwin. *Southern Negroes 1861–1865.* New Haven, 1938.

Williamson, Juanita V. *A Phonological and Morphological Study of the Speech of the Negro of Memphis, Tennessee.* Ph.D. dissertation, University of Michigan (unpublished), 1961.

————. "A Look at Black English." *The Crisis* 78 (August 1971): 169–73, 185.

———— and Virginia M. Burke (eds.). *A Various Language: Perspectives on American Dialects.* New York, 1971.

Winks, Robin W. *The Blacks in Canada: A History.* McGill-Queens University Press, 1971.

Winslow, Ola Elizabeth. *John Eliot, Apostle to the Indians.* Boston, 1968.

Wise, Claude Merton. "Negro Dialect." *Quarterly Journal of Speech* XIX (1933): 522–528.

Wish, Harvey. *Slavery in the South.* New York, 1964.

Wissler, Clark. *Indian Cavalcade; or, Life on the Oldtime Indian Reservation.* New York, 1938.

Wittke, Carl. *Tambo and Bones: A History of the American Minstrel Stage.* Duke University Press, 1935.

Wolfram, Walter A. *A Sociolinguistic Description of Detroit Negro Speech.* Washington, D.C., 1970.

————, Shiels, Marie and Fasold, Ralph W. *Overlapping Influence in the English of Second Generation Puerto Rican Teenagers in Harlem.* Final Report. Office of Education Grant No. 3-70-0033(508). Washington, D.C., 1971.

———— and Clarke, H. (eds.). *Black-White Speech Relationships.* Washington, D.C., 1971.

Woodhull, John Frost. "The Seminole Scouts on the Border." *Frontier Times* (1937–38): 118–127.

Woodson, Carter G. *Miseducation of the Negro.* Washington, D.C., 1933.

Woordenlijst van het Sranan-Tongo, Glossary of the Surinam Vernacular. Paramaribo, 1961.

Zintz, M. *Education Across Cultures.* Dubuque, Iowa, 1963.

INDEX

ABOUT THE AUTHOR

J. L. DILLARD is a linguistics teacher, researcher and writer. He was born in Texas and received his B.A. and M.A. from Southern Methodist University, and his Ph.D. from the University of Texas.

He has taught in many universities in the United States and abroad, including Universidad Central in Ecuador; Inter-American University in Puerto Rico; the University of Puerto Rico's Institute of Caribbean Studies; Université Officelle de Bujumbura in Burundi; and the University of Southern California. He has also been associated with US AID in Yaoundé, Cameroun.

His articles have appeared in *Harvard Educational Review; Nueva Revista de la Filología Española; Afro-American Anthropology: Contemporary Perspectives; Language; Linguistics; Orbis; American Speech; The Florida FL Reporter; Names;* and *Caribbean Studies.*

Dr. Dillard is now at Ferkauf Graduate School, Yeshiva University.